SAN ANTONIO AND ITS MISSIONS

VISTAS

Sponsored by Texas A&M University–San Antonio

WILLIAM KISER, *General Editor*

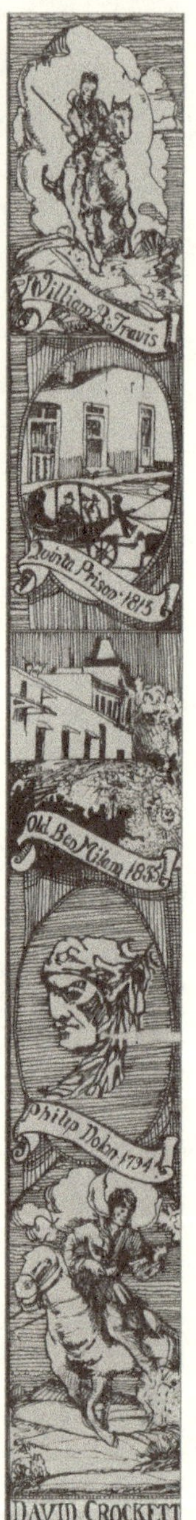

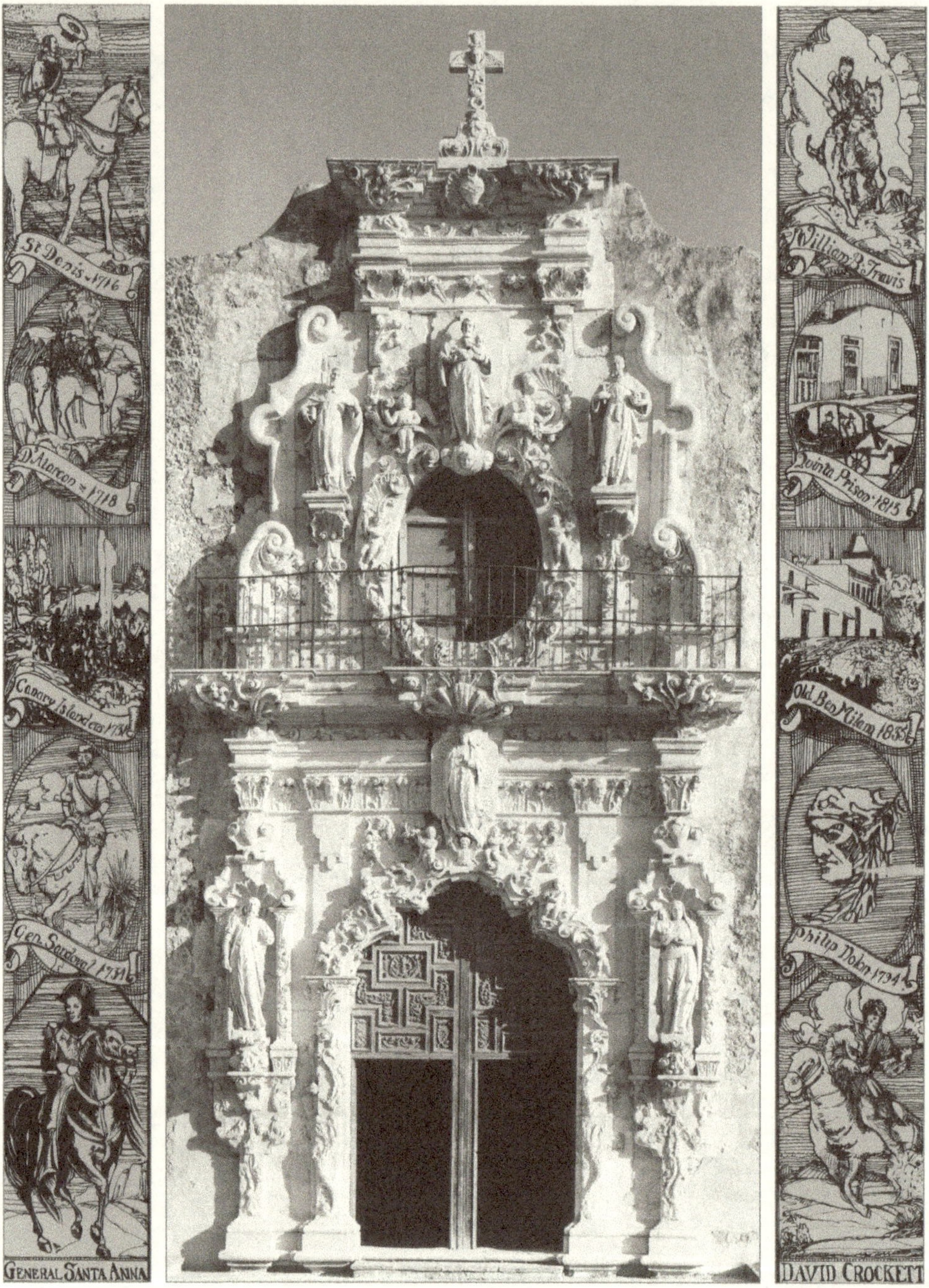
St Denis 1716
D. Alarcon 1718
Canary Islanders 1731
Gen. Sandoval 1731
General Santa Anna
William B. Travis
Quinta Prison 1815
Old Ben Milam 1835
Philip Dolan 1794
David Crockett

SAN ANTONIO AND ITS MISSIONS

THREE CENTURIES OF HISTORY, MEMORY, AND HERITAGE

JOEL DANIEL KITCHENS

TEXAS A&M UNIVERSITY PRESS
College Station

First edition

♾ This paper meets the requirements of ANSI/NISO Z39.48–1992 (Permanence of Paper).
Binding materials have been chosen for durability.

LIBRARY OF CONGRESS CATALOGING-IN-PUBLICATION DATA

Names: Kitchens, Joel D. author
Title: San Antonio and its missions: three centuries of history, memory, and heritage / Joel Daniel Kitchens.
Other titles: Vistas (Series: College Station, Tex.)
Description: First edition. | College Station: Texas A&M University Press, [2026] | Series: Vistas | Includes bibliographical references and index.
Identifiers: LCCN 2025031446 (print) | LCCN 2025031447 (ebook) | ISBN 9781648433405 cloth | ISBN 9781648433412 ebook
Subjects: LCSH: Catholic Church—Missions—Texas—San Antonio—History | Tourism —Texas—San Antonio—Religious aspects—Christianity | Spanish mission Buildings—Texas—San Antonio—History | Church architecture—Texas—San Antonio | Missions, Spanish—Texas—San Antonio—History | San Antonio (Tex.)—Buildings, Structures, etc. | San Antonio (Tex.)—Church history | San Antonio (Tex.)—History
Classification: LCC F394.S2118 A24 2026 (print) | LCC F394.S2118 A24 (ebook)
LC record available at https://lccn.loc.gov/2025031446
LC ebook record available at https://lccn.loc.gov/2025031447

For the people of the missions,
all of them, past, present, and future

Contents

Acknowledgments

One author's name will appear on the cataloging record metadata for this book. However, anyone who has written a book of this nature knows all too well it is not just through the efforts of a single person that books are created. Therefore, I will attempt to repay some of the significant intellectual and pedagogical debts to all the professors under whom I have studied and with whom I have worked: thank you one and all. I wish to call out for special thanks William Nicholas of Birmingham–Southern College for emphasizing the importance of primary sources and value of reading footnotes. I also thank Carolyn Conley of the University of Alabama at Birmingham, who taught the graduate historiography class that introduced me to the works of French historian Fernand Braudel, the *Annales* school, and the *longue durée.* Although I studied under Randall B. Woods of the University of Arkansas for only a short time, his advice to "cast your nets far and wide" when searching for sources is something I have taken to heart and have tried to pass along to students. In addition to Randall's sage advice was the invaluable instruction I received under Margaret F. Stieg Dalton (also a historian in her own right) of the University of Alabama's School of Library and Information Studies; my research methods are much stronger for her tutelage. I express my deepest gratitude to Cynthia Bouton from the History Department at Texas A&M University, who recommended the work of Pierre Nora to me as I was struggling to connect the missions to collective memory; Nora's concept of "sites of memory" turned out to be the linchpin of my argument. Additionally, I thank Angela Hudson, April Hatfield, and Brian Rouleau of Texas A&M

University's History Department, all of whom read individual chapters of this manuscript (some more than once) and offered excellent advice, critiques, and much-appreciated encouragement. Similar thanks go to Felipe Hinojosa, now at Baylor University. And at the University of Texas at Austin, Carlos Blanton deserves extra helpings of gratitude for directing my dissertation and patiently guiding a nontraditional doctoral student to the successful completion of the program. I also offer a special word of thanks to Anat Geva, Gabriela Campagnol, Kevin Glowacki, Nancy Klein, and Stephen Caffey of the Texas A&M University Department of Architecture and Clint Machan of Texas A&M University Department of English. And a big "thank you" goes to Patricia Limerick of the University of Colorado at Boulder for passing along one of her batons to me at a Western History Association meeting in San Antonio some years back.

I express my gratitude to my professional colleagues: librarians, archivists, and professional staff, who toil at preserving and making accessible the materials on which historians depend. I offer special thanks to the extraordinary people at my professional home for almost a quarter of a century: the Libraries of Texas A&M University (the Sterling C. Evans Library as well as the Cushing Memorial Library), but especially Bill Page for his keen insights and tenacity at finding newspaper and genealogy-related resources, as well as the whole team in interlibrary loan who managed to fill requests for which I held few hopes. I also thank the dedicated professionals and staff at the Dolph Briscoe Center for American History at the University of Texas at Austin; the Catholic Archives at San Antonio; the research library of the Daughters of the Republic of Texas; the library and archives of the San Antonio Conservation Society; the archives of the Texas General Land Office; the Catholic Archives of Texas in Austin; the DeGolyer Library at Southern Methodist University; the San Antonio Public Library; the Special Collections Library at the University of Incarnate Word in San Antonio; the research library for the Institute of Texan Cultures and the Special Collections Library of the University of Texas at San Antonio; the Center for Research Libraries in Chicago; and the John Carter Brown Library in Providence, Rhode Island. Without their hard work and diligence to collect, preserve, and make accessible the primary sources and other materials on which this work depends, it would not have been possible to write this book.

I would be remiss if I did not mention the efforts of Jay Dew and Thom Lemmons of the Texas A&M University Press and the dedicated staff who do all the "behind-the-scenes" work to bring this project to conclusion. I am also grateful for the two referees who read the manuscript and offered keen insight and valuable recommendations to make the finished product something of which we can all be proud.

Finally, I must pay respects to those who are no longer with us, but prior to their passing influenced and encouraged me at various stages of this project: my parents (Reverend Daniel Z. Kitchens and Emily Kitchens Keith), John W. Kitchens and Lynne B. Kitchens, Jerry Mosley, D. Gentry Steele, Father Balthazar Janacek, Rosalind Rock, Alston Thoms, and Candace Benefiel. As this project winds down, I only wish you all could see the finished product. And to Ginger (*Canis familiaris*), I hope you are getting all the smoked chicken a little Shih Tzu could possibly want on your side of the Rainbow Bridge.

This book has taken around twenty years from earliest conceptions to final printing. That is a long time. Throughout the process I have relied on the patience, generosity, encouragement, and support of my close family: Andy Keith, Glenda Mosley, and John D. Kitchens. It is only appropriate that this book is dedicated to them, but especially to my wife, Professor Emerita, fellow scholar and librarian, and Number One Best Editor, Pixey Anne Mosley, who, once again, read much more of this manuscript than either of us intended and offered much-needed admonishments against getting lost down rabbit holes. And while we have shared laughs about her having had less-than-inspiring history classes in public schools, her understanding of Texan culture from a native perspective was priceless for an outsider such as I. Equally priceless are her love, companionship, patience, and encouragement over the years.

SAN ANTONIO AND ITS MISSIONS

Introduction

WITH THE BEGINNING of the New Year in 2018, San Antonio, Texas, kicked off a year-long celebration marking the city's tricentennial. Some of the celebratory events included special exhibits at local art galleries and museums; lectures, oral history projects, and other educational presentations; concerts highlighting a variety of musical styles from classical to Tejano and pop; and community service opportunities. The week of May 1–6, 2018, was declared "Commemorative Week" in honor of the actual founding dates of Mission San Antonio de Valero and the Presidio San Antonio de Béxar.[1] Similarly, the January 2018 issue of *Texas Highways* magazine ran a feature article describing some of the planned celebrations with dates of major festivities listed. The article also mentioned that a number of the "Commemorative Week" celebrations would be accompanied by copious amounts of fireworks.[2]

From its humble beginnings on the outermost reaches of the Spanish Empire, the multicultural community that began in the eighteenth century endured and now in its third century is the seventh-largest city in the United States, as well as the numerically fastest-growing city in the nation.[3] Recognizing the city's significance for all Texans, journalist Jan Jarboe Russell proclaimed, "San Antonio is the Mother of Texas."[4] Additionally, the city retains such a significant part of its multicultural character that, despite attempts at repression, geographer Daniel Arreola called San Antonio the "Tejano Capital" of the State of Texas.[5] While these designations may read as so much hyperbole, they actually contain a keen level of insight. San Antonio is not the oldest city in Texas, but for so many (including Tejanos, Anglos, and many other racial and ethnic groups), Texas and Texan identity begins with San Antonio. Although the many various racial and ethnic groups arrived in the region at different times in the past and most Anglos (and their African American slaves) arrived after the city was already a century old, the city's central place in the state's creation myths cannot be underestimated. And as significant components of the community around which the city developed, the five missions have played an integral part of the history and identity for the city, the state, and beyond.

Landmark anniversaries such as San Antonio's tricentennial often invite a great deal of public nostalgia and celebrations of heritage but usually not so much in terms of critical historical reflection. As historian Michel-Rolph Trouillot cogently argues, commemorations "sanitize" lived history. Furthermore, these celebrations "contribute to the continuous myth-making process that" shapes history through which they "help to create, modify, or sanction the public meanings attached to historical events deemed worthy of mass celebration." As these rituals "package history for public consumption," the commemorations "create a past that seems both more real and more elementary."[6] Professional historians have a responsibility to provide a deeper and more authentic understanding of the context surrounding the events being celebrated, as well as to contribute critical historical reflections. This is accomplished through regularly reassessing and reinterpreting history based on the available sources. These reassessments must consistently be done as new sources are discovered or reevaluated and as each new generation searches for a usable past.

This story takes place in what earlier historians called a "frontier" and modern historians refer to as the "Borderlands." Earlier generations of historians imagined the frontier region that is now Texas as a vast, open space, where no "man" (understood at the time to be Anglo males) lived and the land was free to be exploited by those with the mettle to seize it.[7] But by imagining the frontier as an enormous and empty sector, these earlier historians missed the rich histories of Native Americans who had lived there for thousands of years. Modern historians tend to portray a more complicated, but more realistic, picture of the region as a contested area where different groups of Indigenous peoples, as well as various nationalities of European and African peoples met, clashed, traded, lived, loved, died, and otherwise interacted, with no single group able to establish complete hegemony over all others until decades after the initial contact.[8] Another way to conceptualize the "Borderlands" is as a "frontier" that scholars have explored from multiple sides as part of a more holistic examination. Again, if this more rounded examination results in a more complicated story, then it is likely to be a more accurate reflection of life as it really was. And despite the lack of cell phones, social media, advances in transportation and food production, and other conveniences (or distractions?) of modern life, existence in earlier times could be just as complex.

The missions of San Antonio reflect just those sorts of complexities that come from existing in the Borderlands across three centuries. The missions were and are different things to different people at different times in history; they are more than simply buildings and some surrounding curtain walls. Indeed, as historian Jesús F. de la Teja observes, "Although we tend to think of missions as places and buildings, in reality they were activities."[9] Early on, the missions were domiciles, education centers, community centers, farms and ranches, and sacred space for the Spanish friars and Native American groups who lived there.[10] And by playing these various roles, the missions became the nexuses and loci not only between the Spanish and Indigenous peoples but additionally between the sacred and the profane. After the missions were secularized in the early nineteenth century, they remained domiciles, community centers, and sacred spaces for the assimilated Indigenous and Spanish-then-Mexican mestizo populations who lived in the area. Even after Texan independence, people still lived on the mission grounds, farmed or ranched the former mission lands, and when a priest visited from the larger town, worshipped in the chapels or sacristies. Along the way the missions started to attract attention from visitors, travelers, and tourists who came to San Antonio for a variety of reasons. Besides sacred space and community centers, the missions became tourist attractions, and after the railroad connected San Antonio to the outside world in 1877, tourism increased exponentially. Different racial and ethnic groups, including Mexicans, Indigenous, Anglos, Germans, French, and Irish, interacted at the missions for a variety of reasons: to worship, to teach, to defend, or to gaze at the remnants. Through the years, these interactions among different cultural groups could be peaceful, contentious, or even violent. As historian Kenneth Hafertepe notes, "The story of different cultural groups is not simply one of adaptation and assimilation to an increasingly dominant 'mainstream' culture, but a dynamic interplay of cultural perspectives that has played out over many decades—and continues to be in play."[11] Resistance against each new group was constant as factions sought to protect their own places, traditions, and narratives. Nonetheless, for each group that came to the missions, a different understanding of the missions began to develop, sometimes accurate and sometimes less so. These understandings, or narratives, would be loosely based on traditions (religious or otherwise) and memories. The memories and their departure from history are primary among the interesting facets that define this book.

One important aspect of this book is the incorporation of the *longue durée,* which means exploring how the missions' roles, identities, and symbolism evolved over a long span of time. The primary advantage of looking at the missions across three hundred years is the ability to observe both stasis and change in various cultural institutions, as well as the ebbs and flows of interest in the conditions of the physical remnants of the buildings and their use. It is a very useful tool for contextualizing the missions. Many people know only of the Alamo and its role for Texas independence within the context of two weeks in 1836. They are unaware the Alamo had a different name, Mission San Antonio de Valero, and a very interesting history going back over one hundred years before that fateful morning. French historian Fernand Braudel would have considered stories like the Alamo battle to be *"l'histoire événementielle,"* or "a history of events." Braudel considered a lengthy approach more valuable for investigating historical myths, since "developing slowly, [these myths] correspond to structures of an extremely long duration."[12] Once the myths take root within societal memories, they prove exceedingly tenacious. Looking at the development, absence, and reappearance of certain myths about the Alamo and its defenders, as well as those related to the other missions, is another advantage of using a *longue durée* approach. Finally, simply considering the physical remains themselves, the construction, use, decay, and attempts at conservation and preservation across the centuries, lends itself to a long-term consideration as part of their future existence.

This is a book of history and memory. While these two concepts are related, they are not synonymous. History and memory have been linked since the ancient Greeks named Clio, one of the daughters of the goddess of memory, Mnemosyne, as the muse of history. Closer to our own time, historian Carl Becker recognized the intimate connection between memory and history when he distilled "history" into its most simple and basic terms as "the memory of things said and done."[13] Memory is integrally linked to both history and identity, and the missions provide something tangible on which the populations who claim them can build. Historians may cringe at references to philosopher George Santayana because his observation, "Those who cannot remember the past are condemned to repeat it," is so frequently trivialized as "history always repeats itself."[14] However, Santayana offered some additional thoughts on the complex relationship between memory, history, and society at large that lend valuable insights. He defined "memory" as "an internal rumor; and when to this hearsay within the mind we add the falsified echoes that reach us from others, we have but a shifting and unseizable basis to build upon. The picture we frame of the past changes continually and grows every day less similar to the original experience which it purports to describe." He continued, "While memory, then, is the basis for all historical knowledge, *it is not called history until it enters a field where it can be supported or corrected by evidence*."[15] His comments demonstrate the value professional historians bring to the table: to inquire, explore, locate, investigate, dissect, inspect, probe, and critically analyze as much of the existing evidence as can be found, which will then affirm and/or correct previous historians and, hopefully, adjust the collective memory.

What, then, is "collective memory"? French sociologist Maurice Halbwachs developed the concept prior to the Second World War. He recognized that individual memories of past events were dependent on the memories of others, but in order for others' memories to assist the individual, all of the memories must share an agreement of certain basic facts and assumptions.[16] This is the "collective" nature of societal memories. Halbwachs differentiated between the collective memory and academic history by stating that history is more detached, objective, and based on the available facts, whereas collective memory is not held to such high standards of evidence; thus, the historical accuracy of collective memories is, by nature, suspect.[17] In the same way, he observed that individuals frequently assume that their memories are much more accurate than they really are and tied to that person's present. Our memories of the past "remain under the influence of the present social milieu." Nevertheless, even with this corruption of memories, "society causes the mind to transfigure the past to the point of yearning for it."[18] Others have expounded upon Halbwachs and his ideas of societal (or public) memories. Historian John Bodnar suggests, "Public memory is a body of beliefs and ideas about the past that help a public or society understand both its past, present, and by implication, its future."[19]

Historian Michael Kammen directly connects societal memory to the idea of "heritage," which he defines as the "highly selective memory" in which societies tend to "remember what is attractive or flattering and to ignore all the rest. Heritage is comprised of those aspects of history that we cherish and affirm."[20] Kammen is not alone in warning against conflating "history" and "heritage." Museum specialist Frans F. J. Schouten cautions, "Heritage is history processed through mythology, ideology, nationalism, local pride, romantic ideas, or just plain marketing into a commodity."[21] Similarly, David Lowenthal, who has written extensively on heritage, memory, and history, cautions that heritage "borrows from and enlivens historical study, heritage is not an inquiry to the past, but a celebration of it, not an effort to know what actually happened but a profession of faith in a past tailored to present-day purposes." Furthermore, Lowenthal warns of divisive tendencies as "heritage builds collective pride and purpose, but in doing so stresses distinctions between good guys (us) and bad guys (them). Heritage faith, heritage commodities, and heritage rhetoric inflame enmity, notably when our unique legacy seems at risk."[22] These observations reinforce the connections between heritage as symbolized by the missions and the myths and narratives used to interpret, defend, and perpetuate actions by certain groups over others.

The fundamental idea for this book is that the missions are "sites of memory," based on French historian Pierre Nora's definition of "lieu de mémoire" as "any significant entity, whether material or non-material in nature, which by the dint of human will or the work of time has become a symbolic element of the memorial heritage of any community." Furthermore, Nora stated that these "sites of memory" exist in three interrelated forms: "material, symbolic, and functional."[23] Thus, the "memorial heritage" represented may be physical remnants but also cultural and less tangible (but no less important) in nature. San Antonio's missions meet Nora's criteria on multiple levels. At the most basic, the missions exist as physical remains that continue to function as sacred space. Even Mission San Antonio de Valero has been identified as a burial ground for numerous Indigenous people and thus is claimed as sacred space by those asserting to be descended from them. The Alamo will always remain a symbol for various segments of the state's population; whether for good or ill depends on to whom the question is put. Additionally, all of the missions were incorporated into travel narratives, tourist guidebooks, and promotional literature as visible symbols of a triumphant Texan/American Empire over an obsolete European past. Illustrations, silhouettes, or outlines of individual missions have been used to advertise San Antonio for many decades. Similar images or textual references to the missions have become tropes standing in for San Antonio's multicultural heritage. The Alamo has been used as a symbol of city, state, and national identity and heritage for well over a century, but it has also been weaponized to treat minorities as "Others." The missions are at once a "symbolic element" of the San Antonio community and symbols of that heritage.

In order to present a more nuanced and complex picture of the missions, this book undertakes an in-depth examination into many different sources from diverse disciplines. By taking advantage of a wide variety of primary materials, this book will give voice to some sources that have not been explored for many decades. Other sources come from equally disparate fields, including anthropology and archaeology, art and architectural history, memory studies, American studies, travel and tourism studies, women's studies, religious studies, and print culture. Formats used ranged from original archival documents, to those preserved on microfilm, to modern digitized renderings. In keeping with the *longue durée,* the book is primarily laid out chronologically as it explores the depictions of the missions from differing perspectives roughly between 1718 and 2015. However, there are occasional periods of overlap between chapters as the differing perspectives evolved at different rates. One particular thread readers should be aware of is the multiple identities the missions assume, mostly in the post-1836 period and especially after the arrival of the railroad in 1877. The multiple identities of sacred space (including the Alamo shrine), tourist attractions, community centers, and schools all shaped the collective memory of San Antonians, Texans, and Americans in what were sometimes competing ways.

Chapter 1 lays the foundation by exploring how the missions came to be, from their founding in colonial Spanish times through the secularization process. During this period, we see the genesis of some cherished myths held by people in our own modern times. This chapter investigates the origins, functions, and construction of the missions and surrounding community for their first century of existence. Additionally, this chapter takes advantage of recent, multifaceted scholarship to bring older historiography more in line with current trends, particularly those regarding the Native Americans for whom the missions were founded and whose labor helped build the structures seen today by millions of visitors. Chapter 2 covers the period between secularization through Texan independence, until shortly after the US Civil War. Many changes affecting the missions occurred during this time, including the 1836 siege and battle at the Alamo, through which it became an indelible part of American memory and identity. Chapter 3 begins with the arrival of the railroad that connected San Antonio to the rest of the United States. This connection caused an exponential increase in the number of tourists who came to visit the town. Railroad companies and local boosters presented the city as a romantic and exotic location for elites to spend the season in warm sunshine instead of the bitter snow and ice of the Northeast. Travel narratives and advertising brought textual and visual depictions of the missions to a wide national audience via expanding print culture, which inscribed the Alamo and other missions in the American memory.

Chapter 4 examines some of the initial attempts to protect and conserve the buildings after many visitors complained of vandalism and neglect in the early twentieth century. Some of the preservation efforts proved quite contentious, in one instance playing out on a national stage that served to reinforce the Alamo's place within the national collective memory. This chapter also explores the continuing appropriation of the missions, particularly the Alamo, as romanticized tourist attractions in the national literature to entice travelers to "See America First" instead of taking extended vacations abroad. The interpretation of the missions, especially the Alamo, within the context of the 1936 Texas Centennial celebration is also discussed here. Chapter 5 explores the publicity the missions received in the mid-twentieth century as tourist attractions and as the basis for major motion pictures, including midcentury classics by Walt Disney and John Wayne. After the Second World War, numerous Americans took advantage of newfound prosperity and vacation time to take pilgrimages to important places in the nation's history, which brought many to San Antonio. This chapter explores the increased tension and engagement around the various roles the missions occupied and increasing competition for influence and ownership in restoration efforts by differing parties. This chapter also sees some of the myths that originated earlier come to the forefront of the American collective memories and questions of identity in the post–Second World War and Cold War period.

Chapter 6 continues the exploration of mission-related myths and their impact on Texan and American identities. This chapter carries on the interrogation of narratives, advertisements, and other representations of travel to reveal how memories, heritage, identities, and historical evidence have interacted (and clashed) at the missions. There is also an interrogation into the debate regarding the exact nature of Davy Crockett's death and its meaning for Texan (and American) identities. In this concluding chapter, four of the missions are brought under the aegis of the US National Park Service; a resurgent Native American community renews its associations, memories, and identities to the missions; political conflicts over the stewardship of the Alamo challenge its place in local, state, and national memories; and the book concludes with the 2015 recognition of all five missions as a World Heritage Site by the United Nations. Despite the honors and advantages these changes brought, persons who felt their identities in relation to the missions were somehow threatened did not always recognize the changes as advantageous. Nonetheless, the missions' status as sites of memory is an enduring legacy that will always keep them in Texan and American identity.

1

Beginning of the Mission Age in San Antonio, 1718–1820

ON MAY 1, 1718, on the dusty plains near the San Antonio River, in the Spanish province of Tejas, a deputation commanded by newly commissioned Governor of Tejas Don Martín de Alarcón, and under the spiritual leadership of Fray (Fr.) Antonio de San Buenaventura y Olivares of the Franciscan missionary college in Querétaro, Mexico, established a mission, San Antonio de Valero. A few days later, Alarcón established the presidio and Villa de Béxar a short distance from the new mission between the river and San Pedro Creek.[1] Additional missions soon followed. Just two years after Valero's founding, Fr. Antonio Margil de Jesús established Mission San José y San Miguel de Aguayo (San José) just a few miles downstream for the Franciscan missionary college at Zacatecas.[2] By 1731, three missions located in East Texas were transferred to San Antonio: Mission Nuestra Señora de la Purísima Concepción (Concepción), Mission San Juan Capistrano (San Juan), and Mission San Francisco de la Espada (Espada). This chain of five extant missions represents the largest concentration of Spanish colonial sacred architecture in the United States and in July 2015 was awarded World Heritage Site status by the United Nations Educational, Scientific, and Cultural Organization (UNESCO).

In his March 13, 1720, report, Captain Juan Valdez described the founding ceremony and acts of possession for Mission San José, which had occurred the previous month. There is little reason to believe this ceremony differed significantly from those at the other missions. Captain Lorenzo García acted as translator for the Pampopas, Pastias, and Suliajames Indigenous recipients of the mission. Both Fr. Antonio de San Buenaventura y Olivares and Fr. Antonio Margil de Jesús represented the Holy Church for this solemn occasion. Valdez, acting under the authority of the governor, "grasped the hands of the said Indian chiefs" and led them around the site, granting possession of "land and water" to them. The chiefs "accepted it all quietly and peacefully" and, as the Spanish officials watched, went around the site and, as directed, "pulled up grass, threw rocks, cut off branches from the brush land and performed other acts of possession." The Spaniards understood these symbolic actions to mean the chiefs intended to live there with their people and improve the land. The Indigenous people declared themselves satisfied with the land and water and accepted the land on the Texas plain, "which the Governor in the name of the King had ordered us to grant."[3] There is more than a little irony as the Native American chiefs accepted the "grant" by a foreign monarch for land they and their ancestors had been living on for time immemorial. Yet, for the descendants of these Indigenous people who lived there and were eventually assimilated into the population of San Antonio, there are dynamics of ownership, belonging, and collective memory related to their forefathers being present at the creation of the missions. Evidence of such feelings reappears in the twentieth and twenty-first centuries, when peoples professing to be descended from these original inhabitants have made claims on the missions for the remains of their ancestors.

Rationale for Building Missions

Spain's imperial ambitions for North America drove the Spanish mission-building enterprise in Texas during the eighteenth century. As the Spanish Crown extended its territorial claims, it was obliged to defend its claims against other European powers with imperial ambitions of their own or against resistant Indigenous populations. When the Spanish encountered native peoples, they evangelized and converted as many as possible to Roman Catholicism, thus increasing the Catholic "Empire" in addition to its own. It was much less expensive to send small teams of missionaries and a handful of soldiers than to field an entire army to hold a given region. As the missionaries won converts, they believed they made allies who would assist the Spaniards against their European rivals.

The Spaniards advanced northward from central Mexico looking for both precious metals and souls to save. Although historians date Spain's earliest intrusions on what eventually became Texas soil to the early sixteenth century, organized expeditions to explore and colonize would not arrive until the late seventeenth and early eighteenth centuries.[4] The Spaniards came north seeking gold and silver as raw ores to be mined, and the trinkets decorating the bodies of the Indigenous peoples encountered suggested they were on the right path. Some of the reputed sources of these precious metals, such as Quivira or the Seven Cities of Cíbola, never existed except in tales offered to keep these strangers on weird beasts, and their dangerous weapons, moving away from the established native pueblos. Franciscans followed the expeditions with their own agenda to propagate the faith among the native populations. However, intrusions by French adventurers in 1685 and 1714 ultimately convinced Spanish officials that Texas needed more permanent colonization and inspired them to send missionaries to the Tejas and Caddo Indians. Mission San Francisco de los Tejas, founded in 1690, was the first of six missions established near the current Texas-Louisiana border.

Unfortunately, Spain's attempt to claim this area exceeded its logistical capabilities.[5] Because the Spaniards had no established harbor along the Texas coast, supplies had to come by oxcart via Mission San Juan Bautista, the nearest Spanish post. The trek from Bautista on the Rio Grande to East Texas entailed a perilous journey of around six hundred miles through hazardous terrain and resistant Native American groups. In 1691, Governor Domingo Terán de los Ríos, accompanied by Franciscan Fr. Damián Massanet, explored other potential routes to more efficiently supply the Tejas missions. During this expedition, they reconnoitered the area near present-day San Antonio, even holding Mass by the river.[6] Terán remarked on this region's potential to support missionary endeavors, describing the area as "fine country with broad plains, the most beautiful in New Spain." The Spaniards reached the area on the feast day of St. Anthony of Padua, June 13, 1691, which gave the region its name. Terán also noted the presence of the Native American group called Peyaye: "We observed their actions and I discovered that they were docile and affectionate, were naturally friendly, and were decidedly agreeable toward us. I saw the possibility of using them to form *reducciones*."[7] Terán believed the area that became San Antonio met the criteria for establishing a mission as a midpoint way station between the Rio Grande and the East Texas missions. His paternalistic comments seem particularly ironic and overly optimistic given Spanish dependence on Native American hospitality. Nonetheless, permanent European settlement of the area would not begin until 1718.

During the extended time between supply visits, the handful of Spanish friars and soldiers in what is now East Texas depended on their native hosts. While planting Spanish friars and soldiers in small numbers among Indigenous populations avoided much of the violence and financial costs associated with fielding a large, conquering army, it consequently put the Spaniards in a position of weakness vis-à-vis the Native Americans. Because of these small contingents, the Caddo peoples, including the Tejas and the Hasinai, never considered the Spaniards to be a dominant power.[8] The Caddo allowed the Franciscans to build their missions and listened to their entreaties but ultimately ignored the friars' pleas to dramatically change their way of life, particularly after smallpox began killing a disproportionate larger number of Caddo than Spaniards. The Caddo, as a nation of sedentary agriculturalists, had predictable sources of food and were militarily strong enough to repel enemy incursions. They saw no need for what the Spaniards offered, and after a few frustrating years, the Spaniards withdrew from East Texas.[9]

The French interloper Louis Juchereau de St. Denis entered from Louisiana in 1714 and trekked nearly six hundred miles to the Rio Grande before encountering any Spanish opposition, an embarrassing feat Spanish officials could not allow to be repeated.[10] Within two years an expedition headed by Captain Don Domingo Ramón and Fr. Antonio Margil de Jesús, the Franciscan's father-president and leader of the Texas missions, crossed the Rio Grande to reestablish the six missions in East Texas. While en route, the party stopped near the San Antonio River, which Terán and Massanet had visited in 1691. As part of their exploration of the region, they discovered and named San Pedro Springs, which pumped out what Ramón considered "sufficient water for a city of one-quarter league," as well as having ample fish, pastureland, and shade trees.[11] Unfortunately for the friars in East Texas, the expedition did not establish any new settlements along the long and arduous supply route. The Franciscans used gifts of food, clothing, and other material goods to reward Indian neophytes for learning the prayers, songs, and rituals of Catholicism. The friars thus depended on a steady supply of materials from Mexico and abroad, which explains their dependence on regular supply trains reaching them consistently. Just four months after refounding the missions, Margil wrote a rather pointed letter to the viceroy calling attention to the long distance and need for regular supply trains: "At a distance of more than 300 leagues from the nearest settlements, recourse cannot be had to our benefactors, nor is there reason to expect alms, nor can increased expenses and well known dangers from the natives be obviated. We are informing our superiors on this point so that they may make this especially plain to the paternal providence of Your Excellency from whom we await full relief."[12]

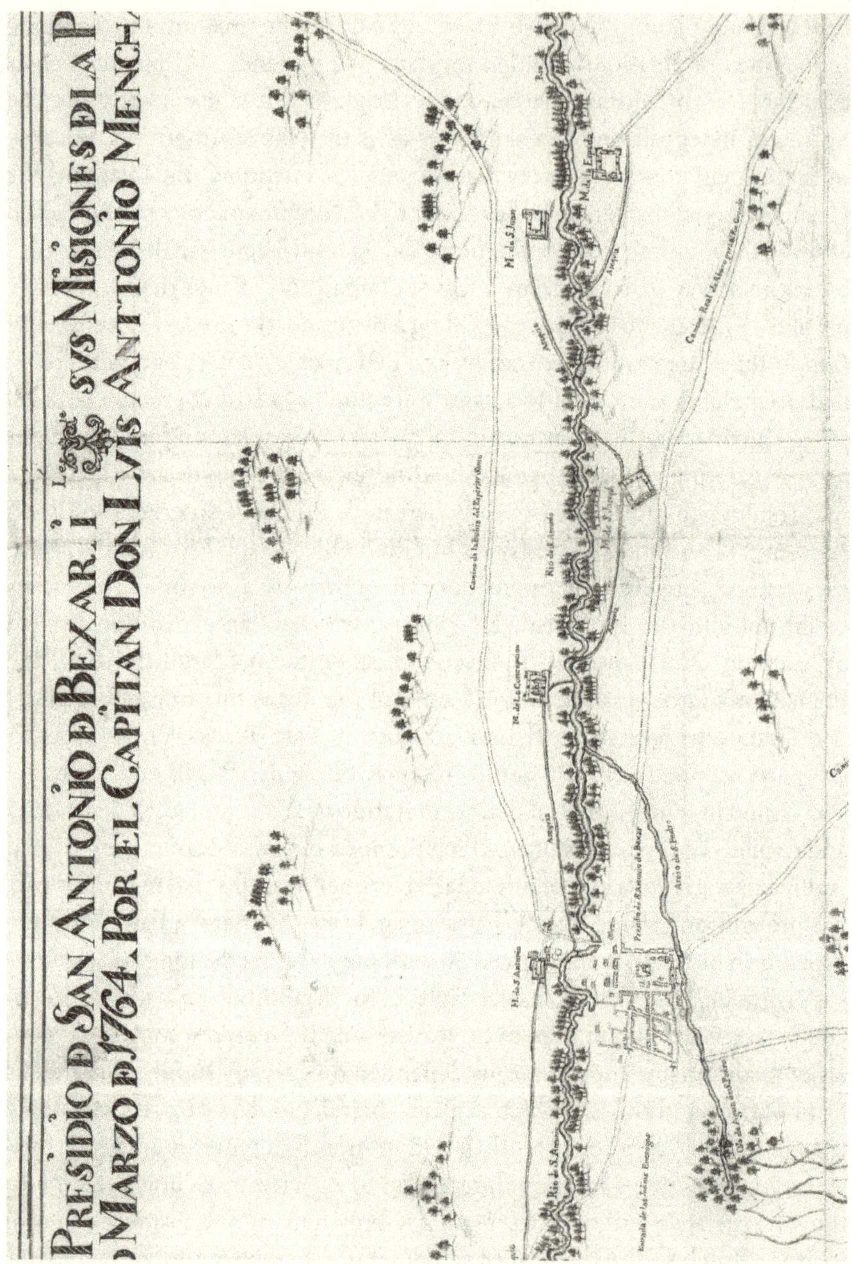

Map 1. Detail of a Spanish colonial map from 1764 of San Antonio de Béxar showing the presidio and each of the missions along the river. Courtesy of the John Carter Brown Library at Brown University.

Despite Margil's petitions, it took two years before the Spaniards planted the new mission and presidio settlement that is now San Antonio in 1718. In addition to its duties as a mission, this new settlement would act as a way station for supply trains traveling between the Rio Grande and the East Texas missions (map 1).[13]

Functions of the Missions

Despite some quibbles over semantics, the missions had four essential functions. First, the missionaries were to gather willing Native Americans into a frontier community. Second, the missionaries were to convert these Native Americans to Roman Catholicism. Third, the missionaries were to teach the new converts the essential vocational skills necessary to be a self-sufficient, civilized community on a remote frontier. Finally, the missionaries were to defend their neophytes, who by then were considered subjects of the Spanish Crown and expected to help defend their homes and fields against enemies, whether Apache or Comanche raiders or rival European forces. Another important feature of the missions was that they were supposed to be temporary. Theoretically, the steps from *indios barbaros* (uncivilized Indians) to *gente de razon* (people of reason) would only require ten to twenty years. At the end of this period the missionaries would turn the churches over to the diocese and all properties to the Christianized Indians to become a functional Spanish villa. The missionaries would then move farther into the frontier to begin the process anew. In theory this process had the benefit of continually expanding Spain's territorial claims.[14] Reality, however, would be very different.

The recruiting of nomadic Indigenous people and gathering them together to form a mission community was called *reducción* in Spanish, and the people living in South Texas who were invited to join the missions have been designated "Coahuiltecans." This was something of an umbrella term denoting several groups who shared a common linguistic stock.[15] Anthropologists have noted that because the Coahuiltecans lived in small nomadic bands eking out a meager subsistence, their reasons for joining the missions had much to do with self-preservation.[16] While numerous Coahuiltecans entered the missions in an attempt to preserve their lives and culture, many did not survive the transition. Mardith Schuetz, an anthropologist specializing in San Antonio's missions, explained that the precipitous decline in population occurred because of European diseases against which the Indians had no immunity, combined with the extreme cultural shock experienced by a previously nomadic hunter-gathering people who suddenly found themselves living in a strictly regimented and geographically constrained environ. Nonetheless, she asserted that these small, splintered bands were unable to compete with larger, more advanced tribal nations such as the Caddo. Unlike the Caddo, the Coahuiltecan hunter-gatherers were a "fragile" society. They lacked the ability to effectively defend themselves and their culture against external influences. By joining with the Spaniards at the missions, the Coahuiltecans exercised some agency to combat their own marginalization or even extinction within the larger Native American world. They just as easily could have chosen to assimilate with the Caddo or the Apache.[17] However, by accepting the Spanish offers of food and shelter at the missions, the surviving Coahuiltecans eventually developed from a people using "stone-age technology" to being Spanish subjects with access to a global trade network that brought both goods and techniques to facilitate survival on the eighteenth-century Texas frontier.[18]

Modern critics of the Spanish missionary enterprise described the drastic decline of Native American populations in the San Antonio missions as nothing short of a "demographic collapse."[19] Many Native Americans died shortly after they joined the missions, while others survived and their descendants became an integral part of San Antonio's multicultural heritage. Schuetz concluded that by the 1780s the Indian population in San Antonio appeared to be stabilizing and even rebounding with increasing numbers of births and a decline in childhood mortality.[20] Those who chose to associate with the Spaniards had their own reasons for doing so, and contemporary scholars are now beginning to take into consideration such examples as an indication of agency demonstrated by mission Indians.[21]

The second function of the Spanish missions is arguably the most controversial among scholars: to convert the indigenous peoples to Roman Catholicism. Historian David Weber claims that the "Franciscans had come to America with a militant vision that rivaled the more worldly dreams of the conquistadores." Armed with the Gospel and apocalyptic vision, the Franciscans marched northward from Mexico into New Mexico and eventually Texas, either with or just ahead of Spanish explorers.[22] However, for the past thirty years, historical scholarship concerning the motivations of the friars has been in a state of flux. While in the early 1990s historian Ramón Gutiérrez charged that many friars at the New Mexican missions seemed more interested in their own martyrdom than for their neophytes' well-being, historian David Rex Galindo recently countered that the eighteenth-century friars seeking to become missionaries actually had many motivations, but fundamentally they had the simple desire "to serve God."[23] Congregating the Native Americans into mission communities for religious indoctrination and cultural assimilation had been devised in part to correct the heinous abuses of the quasi-feudal *encomienda* system that originated among conquistadores of the fifteenth and sixteenth centuries. The Franciscans theoretically assumed the paternal role of instructing the Indians and molding them into tax-paying Spanish subjects, loyal to the Crown. Having the friars deliver religious-based instruction was considered a positive evolutionary step from a merely profit-driven, pecuniary system dependent on the naked and permanent exploitation of the Indian labor force. The Spanish Crown thus contributed financially to the missionary enterprise for religious reasons, in addition to defending the empire.[24]

As the friars labored to convert the Indigenous populations from precolonial religious beliefs to Catholicism, the Franciscans counted an individual Indian's baptism as a "conversion" in their record keeping. Although this practice had been established since the conquest of Mexico, it was not without controversy. A number of scholars have challenged the depth of commitment Indigenous populations in the Americas held for this new and foreign religion.[25] One of the Franciscans' primary concerns came from Indians' relapses into their previous lifestyle either through habit or as a means of protest. The punishments for apostasy could be severe; the friars, who looked on the neophytes as children, believed as many eighteenth-century parents did that the use of corporal punishment was justifiable.[26] As a result, some Native Americans merely added Jesus Christ, the Virgin Mary, the Holy Trinity, and the other saints to their existing pantheon and made nice for the friars but secretly kept a measure of their precolonial religion.[27] The reality was most likely dependent on each individual adapting what parts he or she found most useful.

In carrying out the third function—teaching their Native American wards the vocational and life skills they would need to function as an independent Spanish villa—the Franciscans found themselves facing a difficult conundrum. The friars were well trained in theology and homiletics before being accepted for missionary duty. However, not all friars were as knowledgeable in the skills of farming, livestock wrangling, weaving, blacksmithing, carpentry, and other vocational trades essential to building a frontier villa.[28] Former National Park Service archaeologist James Ivey concludes that the use of Indian labor in constructing the missions was absolutely essential for their acculturation into the Spanish lifeway. There were too few Spaniards to do all the work on the Texas frontier; therefore, they expected the Native Americans to take part in constructing their own churches and communities.[29] While some of the labor performed by the Coahuiltecans was undoubtedly coerced, for some it was part of the acculturation process and may have inculcated a sense of ownership and belonging within the newly established community.

The goal of the Franciscans was not to assimilate the Indigenous people into existing Spanish towns but rather to create a separate society of Christianized Indians loyal to the king of Spain. Nonetheless, the friars believed that the Indians had to first be living a "civilized" European lifestyle (including conforming to traditional European gender roles) in order to be successfully converted to Catholicism.[30] The rationale of keeping Indian mission communities separate from Spanish communities was partially based on the attempt to keep the Indians from picking up bad habits and vices from Spanish soldiers. Another reason centered on the friars' core belief that the success of the mission enterprise was absolutely dependent on their being recognized as priests in addition to religious educators for the mission communities, which gave them certain privileges regarding their flock.[31] This level of segregation proved impossible to maintain, especially in San Antonio, since the friars relied on the presidio soldiers to teach the Indians vocational skills, to defend the mission against attacks, and to assist in tracking down runaways.

In 1731, the community of San Antonio grew exponentially as the presidio and two existing missions (Valero and San José) welcomed the transfer of friars and their neophytes from three East Texas missions (renamed as Concepción, San Juan, and Espada) as well as the arrival of over fifty settlers from the Canary Islands sent by the Crown to the area.[32] The Canary Islanders (also known as *los Isleños*) proved to be a mixed blessing for the community, at least initially. While on the remote Texas frontier strength in numbers was generally advantageous as a defense against Apache raids, the new settlers unfortunately proved haughty, quarrelsome, and litigious for over a decade after their arrival to the point that one exasperated governor characterized them as being "more given to prejudice than progress."[33] Jealous of the missionaries' use of Indians as agricultural laborers and choice, irrigated farmland, the Islanders made numerous attempts to force the missionaries to relinquish the Indian neophytes to perform labor on their land. The missionaries, fearing the possibility of exploitation as well as corruption by the

Isleños, refused to allow the neophytes to work in Islanders' fields and insisted on being party to discussions regarding water rights and irrigation.[34] A bitter war of words wound its way up the Spanish colonial bureaucratic hierarchy in which calumny and misrepresentation were common tactics. Nonetheless, after several years of legal wrangling, neither the friars nor the Islanders could claim complete victory.[35]

Defending Imperial Spain's territorial claims was a significant role of the missions. Over the course of the eighteenth and nineteenth centuries the adversaries changed. Early rivals were European and the various bands of Native Americans that actively resisted missionary efforts. After 1720, the Lipan Apache began aggressively raiding San Antonio, taking horses, cattle, and people. As the mission compounds were constructed, the builders included defensive walls in the design, not just to keep the Indian neophytes in but also to provide a measure of protection against these hostile raiders. Starting in the mid-eighteenth century, the Comanche replaced all other rivals, European and Indigenous, as the main threat to Spain's North American empire.[36] The Spanish Crown viewed the missions as a means to expand and mark its extensive territorial claims with small villas with minimal outlay of funds. The missionaries themselves were aware of this important role early on, as Fr. Margil wrote in 1718 to the viceroy from East Texas: "By the founding of these two missions and the other three, any further progress on the part of the French has been blocked, and our captain has carried out the orders to establish missions until he should meet the French."[37]

Finally, the missions were originally intended to be temporary. Early Spanish laws required missionaries to complete their work and turn the chapels over to diocesan priests and the lands over to the Christianized and Europeanized Indigenous peoples after ten years. However, these laws had been established for the Indigenous peoples of what is now central Mexico and Peru, peoples already in more-advanced societies than the hunter-gatherers of the Texas plains. Working with the Coahuiltecans proved that ten years was insufficient to adequately inculcate in them the Spanish faith, culture, work ethic, and mores to the degree the friars believed necessary before leaving them for new missionary fields farther on the frontier.[38]

The primary reason the mission period in San Antonio lasted for nearly a century was the constant state of flux of the Native American population within the missions. In order to attract regional Indigenous people into the missions, the missionaries had to be able to offer stable food and shelter. However, the ability to offer food and shelter required a stable supply of labor to build shelters, make clothes, tend crops, and herd livestock. The missionaries were not expected to do all this labor by themselves; there were never enough. The missions' existence depended on the neophytes learning horticulture, animal husbandry, and construction techniques to build the mission communities, based on the instruction provided by the friars, their lay assistants, and soldiers. Serious labor shortages periodically arose when European diseases claimed large numbers of neophytes and sent others into flight in the attempt to avoid the contagions, leaving the friars to be continuously recruiting from the region's other Indigenous groups. This cycle of constantly bringing in new people to replace those who had died or fled left the missions with substantial populations who required remedial instruction.[39] Hence, the ten-year window developed for Spanish missionary endeavors in other parts of the empire proved impossible on the northern frontier.

Missions as Sacred Space

Intimately related to both the conversion and acculturation functions of the missions was the creation of the mission chapels as sacred space. A mission, as created on the eighteenth-century Borderlands, included living quarters for the friars and the neophyte Native Americans; storehouses for tools, supplies, materials, and produce; the surrounding farmlands and ranchlands for crops and cattle; and the mission churches. Over the intervening centuries, many of the protective walls, dwellings, and storage buildings deteriorated; some were restored or rebuilt, but others were not. The chapels and sacristies, however, partly as the largest structures in a given mission compound and partly reflecting the importance of their role as sacred space, were privileged over the other structures. This does not mean the chapels escaped the hands of vandals or were not allowed to deteriorate, but the chapels and sacristies have been repaired and restored to a greater degree of detail and function and, with the exception of the church at Valero, returned to being used for divine service. Because the chapels constitute so much of the remaining structures, these buildings are what many today identify as "the missions." While this is something of a misnomer, it does help in our understanding as we examine the missions' role as sacred space as a source of the collective memories associated with them.

Librarian and historian Adán Benavides astutely observed, "By commission, religious architecture is sacred, for it is the place for discourse with the divine."[40] While none of the San Antonio mission churches have been continuously used for divine service since the time they were built, they were originally consecrated as sacred spaces and have provided places for worshippers to engage in "discourse with the divine" across three centuries. As a house of worship, sacred space was, and is, the primary raison d'être for the chapels. Sociologist Maurice Halbwachs discussed the relationship between the sacred space of a church building and its community of believers, asserting that the "believer entering a church . . . knows he will recover a mental state he has experienced many times. Together with fellow believers he will re-establish, in addition to their visible community, a common thought and remembrance formed and maintained through the ages."[41] The mission churches were at the time of construction, and so remain today, houses of worship for those believers and the spiritual foundation for the communities that grew up around them. Their collective memories were but the first to take root, and while the faces of the congregations have changed over three centuries, the faith and memories remain.

One means of insight to understanding the central place the churches and chapels occupied during the mission period is to consider the decor and trappings used to encourage worshippers to enter into "discourse with the divine." The quantity and quality of materials and paraphernalia used for Holy Mass imported by the missionaries represented a considerable expense, not to mention difficulty in transport, given that the missions were located at remote borders of the Spanish Empire. The effort taken to perform the rites and rituals in a suitably dignified and exalted fashion suggests that sacred space was indeed a very high priority, even on the frontier. By 1762, the missions had found a relative level of stability. The quarrels of the 1730s with the *Isleños* had mostly ended by the mid-1740s, and the presidio, villa, and missions were growing closer to something resembling a single community as intermarriages and other obligatory relations bound various members of previously competing groups.[42] Although epidemics in the 1740s had taken dreadful tolls, Apache raids in this time were a greater threat to livestock than human life. Also, by the 1740s, the missions had reached a level of economic stability that allowed them to begin constructing permanent stone chapels. The beneficial effects of this stability began to bear fruit after a period of twenty years. In 1762, Fr. Mariano Francisco de los Dolores y Viana, then father-president for the missions administered by the College of Santa Cruz de Querétaro (e.g., Valero, Concepción, San Juan, and Espada), compiled a detailed report and inventory of their missions in which he described the materials used to conduct Holy Mass and religious instruction. He mentioned paintings on the altars, in addition to the monstrance, aspersorium, censer, and other ritual items crafted out of copper and silver. Dolores y Viana likewise remarked on the ornate liturgical vestments worn by those officiating at services being made of silk and decorated with velvet and damask.[43] Such opulence on the remote frontier reveals the priority the Franciscans placed on sacred space through conducting their rituals with proper dignity and reverence and honoring their God in an appropriate manner based on their comprehension at that point in history. The presence of these silks and other valuables not indigenous to the Americas also suggests the depth and complexity of trade routes throughout the Spanish Empire.

In addition to the food, shelter, and material goods the missionaries gave the neophytes, there were opportunities for creative, artistic outlets. The friars doubtlessly tried to maintain tight control over what was deemed acceptable in terms of expression. Nonetheless, besides contributing to the decor of the mission chapels through their labor, the neophytes made important contributions to the worship services and made and shared sacred space through playing musical instruments or singing in a choir. Music and singing made significant contributions in the conversion of the California Indians, and it was apparently of similar value in Texas.[44] On his 1767–68 inspection tour of the San Antonio missions, Fr. Gaspar José de Solís thought to comment on the musical ability of the neophytes at Mission San José: "Most of them play some musical instrument. . . . A choir of four voices, soprano, alto, tenor, and base [*sic*], with musical accompaniment, sings so beautifully that it is a delight to hear it."[45] At least some Coahuiltecans were willing to raise their voices to make a joyful noise, even when these were foreign hymns, in a strange tongue, to a new deity.

Across the centuries a multitude of struggles existed between the holy and the profane, between the Spanish friars and the Native Americans who joined the missions, and even into the present between ethnic or socioeconomic groups with competing memories, as well as between parishioners and tourists.[46] The tension between groups contesting the sacred space can be seen in examples of both resistance and assimilation, as there would be occasions when each side gave something, just as there would be times when each side gained something (even when the gains were not always equal).[47] Compared with that in other Spanish missions in the American Southwest, the level of resistance by the Coahuiltecan neophytes was rather mild, limited primarily to desertion and malingering. Desertions certainly exasperated the friars in San Antonio, who had to beg the assistance of the presidio commander for escorts to go out looking for the wayward members of their flock, just as they were also frustrated when the neophytes' resistance included faking illness.[48] At least one friar, in 1741, saw the desertions as a threat to the missionary enterprise in San Antonio because unless the neophytes were willing to live and work in the mission compounds, the religious conversion could not be successful.[49]

A more problematic and recurrent mode of resistance to the friars were the *mitotes*, dances the Indigenous people performed for a variety of reasons. Originally the dances were one of the methods used to communicate with the spirit world, to solicit aid in the form of rain, or to perform a fertility rite.[50] The friars found such expressions so offensive that when neophytes came for the sacraments of confession and penance, the officiating friar was specifically to inquire, "Has baylado mitote?"[51] This query was situated near questions of whether the penitent had eaten human flesh or fornicated with someone other than a spouse. Such attention to detail reflected the degree of severity the Franciscans placed on the dance, in addition to their attempts to quash any and all semblances of what they saw as paganism from their charges. The persistence of the *mitote* at the missions not only constituted a form of resistance to the friars' teaching but can also be read as a measure of its importance within Coahuiltecan culture.[52] Interestingly, this query regarding the *mitote* from a Catholic ritual manual, published both in Spanish and in one of the Coahuiltecan tongues, reveals one of the challenges the missions present to modern historians. On the one hand, the friars were reaching out and trying to meet the neophytes on their linguistic turf; on the other hand, it emphasized the friars' desire to root out and punish any pre-contact religious practices. However, nearly thirty years after this manual was published, an unknown Spanish friar writing to his successor in 1787 recommended keeping an open mind regarding the persistence of certain Indigenous practices:

> Regarding the lawfulness of the dance, called *mitote*, done by the Indians, (whatever one can say about it), this much is certain, that though some consider it evil, the missionary does make allowances. The claim is that the Indians cling to their superstitious practices and that for them this dance is like the *fandango* and *faraon* among the Spaniards. Therefore the missionary must be alert to prevent wrongdoing in the mission. Still, it is my conviction that when no superstition, no question of celebrating an enemy's death, nor any sinful motive are present, then the *mitote* is not unlawful when done

> for mere diversion, because among the Indians it is the same as the *fandango* among the Spaniards.[53]

This was but one example that questions the effective level of control exercised by the friars over their charges and confirms Mexican historian Silvio Zavala's observation that the friars "had to adjust to the conditions prevailing on the frontier."[54] Even if the friars sought to extirpate all pre-contact indigenous religious practices and replace them with their own, the very fact this advice was penned suggests the friars' recognition that the religious conquest was never complete.

Building San Antonio's Missions: Aesthetics and Style

Adán Benavides described some of the political travails of constructing a church building on the remote Texas frontier in the eighteenth century and opined, "In time, how they *became* is unimportant. The mundane matters of their construction are obscure and trite."[55] This book takes respectful, but adamant exception to his assertion that how certain buildings came to be is "unimportant," "obscure," or "trite." The design and execution, along with the resulting aesthetics, played significant roles in the embryonic formation of the collective memories based on the romantic and exotic appeal associated with these buildings. Architectural historian Louis P. Nelson notes, "As products of human agency, sacred spaces are inextricably linked to socio-political identity."[56] The buildings are what was and what currently are seen (physical manifestations), and a better understanding of the construction and decor makes the clashes between competing memories and historical fact stand out more clearly. There are few scholarly works that explicitly discuss the architecture and its meanings for San Antonio's missions in terms of form and sacred space.[57] These aspects are very important to a more complete understanding of the missions, what they meant then, and why they occupy such a place in our collective memory since through the built environment collective memory is made tangible.

In his history of the province, Fr. Juan Agustín Morfi marveled at the beauty of Mission San José: "No one could have imagined that there were such good artists in so desolate a place."[58] How indeed was such beauty created on the remote Texas frontier? San Antonio's mission churches and chapels appear small and plain compared to larger cathedrals in either Mexico or Europe; however, designing and constructing these churches on Spain's northeastern colonial frontier was no mean feat. Practical considerations as well as Spanish guild laws required the employment of specialists in stonecutting, carpentry, painting, and masonry. Having to hire this level of maestro meant that designing and constructing the permanent stone church buildings had to wait until the missions became wealthy enough to attract skilled tradesmen to the northern Spanish Borderlands. A few specialists had always been associated with the missions since the beginning, but they were primarily used as teachers for the Indian neophytes.[59] Hence the delays until there were two major construction "booms" in San Antonio: the first in the 1740s and the second in the 1760s and 1770s. The economic well-being of the missions as well as the rise and fall of Indian populations directly affected the pace at which construction progressed.[60]

Just as New Spain's northern frontier was a place where no one racial or ethnic group claimed undisputed dominion, the missions themselves were something of an architectural borderland where no single style reigned supreme. Construction drawn out over the course of several decades partly explains this. In European architectural history, it is possible to trace a building's construction timeline via the evolution of specific styles. An observer can reasonably see the evolutions from Romanesque to Gothic, from Gothic to Renaissance, and from Baroque to Rococo. However, in Mexico, specific architectural elements associated with the various popular European styles appeared out of order or otherwise "contemporaneous rather than successive."[61] In San Antonio the overall style of the mission churches is very much an amalgam, combining elements of Spanish Baroque and its even more ornate subset of Churrigueresque, as on the facade of San José, with other elements drawn from the Iberian Peninsula's rich history of Islamic, Visigothic, Romanesque, and Plateresque styles, as executed by Native American laborers.[62] Similarly, at San Antonio de Valero, the decor surrounding the chapel's main portal can be seen as a "classical triumphal arch," although it is questionable whether the Indigenous people would comprehend its colonialist meaning.[63] Perhaps the older styles of decor of the visible elements explains why some nineteenth- and early twentieth-century visitors described the missions as though they had been built during medieval times, while imagining Spanish soldiers in Texas wearing full suits of metal armor.

Also important for modern readers to understand is that none of the architects or master masons who began the construction stayed on the project long enough to see the work completed. The masons who finished the work had little to do with the original designs and planning of the buildings.

Many came, stayed a few years, then left, probably for more lucrative jobs in safer environs.[64] In terms of workforce and organization, the father-president of the missions generally acted as the patron and employer, whereas the buildings theoretically were designed and the construction monitored by the *maestro de albañil* (master mason). Additional specialists included carpenters, freemasons, smiths, stonecutters, and teamsters. Local Indigenous laborers made up the unskilled worker pool.[65] In 1736, the architects' guild in Mexico City prohibited non-Spaniards from becoming architects. The ordinance did allow *criollos* (persons born in the New World of Spanish parents) to qualify but specifically excluded Indians and mestizos.[66] However, while this ordinance may have rigidly controlled the racial and ethnic backgrounds of architects at the Mexican urban center, on the fringes of the northern frontier things tended to be less restrictive. If a building had "an arch, vault, or dome, a master mason built it"; however, the race or ethnicity of said master mason in frontier San Antonio might not have met the stringent guild requirements in more settled parts of the empire.[67] In her study on professional artisans in San Antonio, Mardith Schuetz included a chart plotting the names, race or ethnic identifier (if known), and rank (if known) of many of the artisans who worked in the villa during the eighteenth century. Of the ten specifically ranked as "master," she could identify only three as "Spaniard." The rest were listed as Indians of various tribes or mixed race.[68]

Antonio de Tello and the Scandal at Mission Valero

Multiple observers noted the difficulties of constructing monumental architecture on the Texas frontier in the eighteenth century, from Fr. Morfi's astonishment at the magnificence of Mission San José on the "desolate" frontier, to contemporary scholars who described the missionaries' difficulties in hiring a qualified maestro willing to move to the remote and still dangerous frontier, so that during San Antonio's early years, "no *maestros de albañil* lived in Texas."[69] Perhaps no account illustrates those difficulties better than the melodrama associated with the community's first mason, Antonio de Tello. Around the year 1740, the Franciscan friars of the College of Querétaro, Mexico, who operated the missions of Valero, Concepción, San Juan, and Espada, contracted with Spaniard Antonio de Tello, who claimed to be a master mason and sculptor from Zacatecas.[70] The twenty-seven-year-old Tello began an ambitious building program for four of the mission churches when he arrived on the Texas frontier. In addition to his work on the missions, Tello did some design work for the facade of the new parish church of Our Lady of Candelaria for the *Isleños*. In order to maintain a manageable workload, Tello began with the same basic template, a simple cruciform design, for the mission churches. However, each church had distinguishing features on the facade and other decorative elements, for example, the "main entrance doorways of Concepción, Valero, and Candelaria, and the unfinished *mixtilíneo* arched doorway at Espada are very much alike in the flat style called *plateresco*, more typical of the sixteenth century."[71] Sometime in 1741, Tello and his work crew began building Mission Concepción; three years later, after construction progressed sufficiently, Tello and his crew laid the cornerstone of Mission Valero on May 8, 1744.[72]

Unfortunately for the friars, Tello's personal life was not in alignment with his holy commission. On August 21, 1744, a gunshot shattered the peaceful evening. According to official testimony the victim, Matías Treviño, accused Tello, "mason of the mission of San Antonio," of shooting him at point-blank range. When pressed for a possible motive, the dying man admitted he had accused his wife and Tello of having an affair. When Don Alberto Lopez Aguado y Villa Fuerte, alcalde for the villa of San Fernando, interviewed Tello in the safety of Valero's sanctuary, he admitted to firing the fatal shot but claimed a case of mistaken identity; he thought the man he shot was an Apache about to attack him. The suspect also denied having illicit relations with Treviño's wife. Aguado, however, seemed incredulous that Tello could have shot a man at such close range to leave powder burns on the dead man's shirt and not recognize whom he had killed. As Aguado's investigation progressed, the evidence mounted against both the mason and the victim's wife, Rosa Guerra.[73] Three days after the shooting, Aguado and a company of soldiers from the presidio, with the permission of Fr. Dolores of Valero, went to arrest Tello, only to find the man had escaped. At this point, Tello disappears from history. With the primary suspect gone, charges against Guerra were not pursued.[74]

When Tello bolted from San Antonio in 1744, some of his building projects halted. Construction on the parish church as well as the chapel at Concepción stopped. As the church of Concepción was only half finished, the friars may have wanted to find another qualified maestro to complete the job. However, the friars and their neophytes continued to work on the Valero church and the Espada and San Juan granaries. Some of the laborers may have been journeymen masons and carpenters whom the friars believed to be qualified to carry on such modifications. Ivey claims they simplified Tello's plans by dropping the complex vaulted roofline in favor of a flat one, while an earlier archaeological study states the church's arched roof, dome, and bell tower were complete in the 1740s and early 1750s.[75] In his 1759 report, Fr. Dolores noted that the interior of the Valero mission church was complete and furnished with works of art, altars, and carved images.[76] The presence of these furnishings suggests a roof of some kind to protect them from the elements. Unfortunately, soon afterward this Valero church building collapsed. Even as late as 1762, Fr. Dolores, perhaps still stinging from the scandal, simply stated that the church collapsed "por la mala inteligencia del artifice." While this could be translated as "faulty structure," the Spanish term, *artifice* can also mean the builder, in other words, Tello. Whether Tello was too busy conducting his sexual affair to properly monitor construction at Valero, or whether Fr. Dolores was lamenting Tello's poor moral choices, which ultimately caused him to flee, leaving the community with no qualified builder, Tello's "mala inteligencia" cost the friars deeply.[77] After the Tello scandal, future maestro contracts included provisions for moving wives and families to San Antonio as part of their compensation.[78]

New Architects, New Directions

Of the masons that followed Tello to San Antonio, maestro Joseph Palafox from Saltillo was perhaps the most talented artisan to work on the San Antonio missions given his multiple specializations. Mission account ledgers referred to Palafox as a master mason, stonecutter, and foreman.[79] Between his arrival in 1761 and departure in 1765, Palafox made several major contributions to the missions that modern tourists see today. He designed the church for San José that stands today, although he inexplicably left before construction actually began. Approximately two years after Palafox left, Fr. Gaspar Solís participated in the ceremony to begin construction at San José with Governor Hugo O'Conor. Solís described the planned church as a large stone structure 150 feet long and 30 feet wide. At the ceremony, he "blessed the foundations and the first stones. . . . Don Hugo O'Conor laid one of the stones and I laid the other."[80]

One of Palafox's more interesting influences on the missions involves the door of Mission Espada. The permanent church for Espada had been designed nearly two decades before by Antonio Tello but never completed. This design included ornamentation for the main door. However, the chapel seen and used today was intended to be the sacristy of a larger church building. In its current state, the arch over the door appears broken (fig. 1.1). The twentieth-century

Fig. 1.1. Portal showing the "broken" Mudéjar arch. Mission Espada. Photograph by the author.

architect and preservation specialist W. Eugene George argued that Espada's doorway arch is "one of the few Mudejar arches known to exist in the region." However, the voussoirs were "incorrectly placed during the initial construction period."[81] George believed that the stones had been precut and left for later installation by a designer who ultimately was not present to answer any questions the laborers might have. Had these stones been installed correctly, a much more harmonious arch would result, giving the overall appearance of some of the horseshoe arches used in the Great Mosque of Córdoba, Spain. He concluded that the directions regarding the stones "might not have been fully comprehended. Having never seen an arch with elements that first spring outward from an opening prior to curving inward, the work crew must have been baffled."[82]

James Ivey, on the other hand, disputed any notion that the stones were installed incorrectly. He contended that the Espada chapel seen today was not designed to be the mission's permanent church but as the sacristy for a larger sanctuary that was never built. Therefore, the arched portal was never intended to be placed where it is. When a decision was made to forgo construction of the larger church and make the sacristy into the chapel, Palafox repurposed the stones Tello had left for the main portal. Unfortunately, Tello designed the main church to be larger than the sacristy, and the arched doorway would not fit the front of the smaller edifice. Therefore, Palafox altered the design and rearranged the stones. This change made the design both narrower and lower by two feet "to match the smaller scale of the sacristy/church and to avoid having to disturb the choir loft." Palafox made these alterations to save time and money, both of which may have been in short supply, rather than create a new design from scratch.[83]

The next *maestro de albañil* after Palafox to have a significant impact on the missions was Antonio Salazar, who was listed as a mulatto on the 1779 roster and an Indian (no tribal affiliation given) on the 1792 census. He was born in Zacatecas and arrived in San Antonio with his family sometime after 1768.[84] There is some dispute over the degree to which Salazar contributed to Mission San José. Mardith Schuetz claimed, "It is now possible to identify the genius behind the magnificent baroque church with a reasonable chance of being correct" and credited Salazar as the designer and builder of the ornate mission chapel.[85] Ivey, however, asserted that Palafox designed the church and Salazar only modified the design.[86] Both conclusions rely on a fair amount of speculation, as the records for San José before 1779 have yet to be found. Schuetz believed it was no coincidence that Salazar was from

Zacatecas and friars from the apostolic college in that city had founded Mission San José.[87] Even if Salazar did not design the entire church, Ivey noted that he "had a strong influence on this era of mission architecture in the San Antonio area. . . . His contributions may be found at all the missions." At Valero, Salazar built supporting ribs for the vaulted ceiling as well as those to support the planned dome and groined vaulting. He also worked on the granary at San José. And at both San Juan and Espada, Salazar added similar *espadañas* (raised walls or gables cut for bells to be mounted) that distinguish the outline of these two small chapels into the present day.[88]

In late December 1777 and early January 1778, the inspection tour of Teodoro de Croix, commandant general of the Provincias Internas, lodged in San Antonio. While Croix offered little regarding church designs, his chaplain, Fr. Juan Agustín Morfi, kept a diary and in his later history of the province provided his own assessment on the ecclesiastical environment. Morfi's diary remarked that in January 1778, the chapel at San José was not yet completed, although even in its unfinished state was strikingly beautiful. He noted the vaulting over the nave and a dome. He also described how the white stone used on the facade was easily worked into the fantastic shapes by the carvers. The mission chapel was so lovely that by comparison the church of the villa did not fare nearly as well.[89] Later in his history of Texas, Morfi expanded his admiration for Mission San José. He considered San José "in truth, the first mission in America, not in point of time, but in point of beauty, plan, and strength."[90] If he found fault at all, it was in the excess of ornamentation on the interior and facade of the church. Perhaps Morfi had developed more cosmopolitan tastes in Mexico City, where the elaborate ornamentation of the Churrigueresque was being supplanted by a more restrained Neoclassicism.[91] Nonetheless, Morfi thought the chapel at San José was of such beauty as to "grace a large city as a parish church."[92]

Pedro Huizar, the Supreme Artiste of San José

Just as previous master masons worked with fellow, skilled artisans, Antonio Salazar had assistance while he worked on the mission churches. While Salazar was apparently a master mason, he was not a master fine carver or sculptor. At San José in the 1770s, that person was the legendary Pedro Huizar. Depending on which version of the legend one finds, Huizar appears as a young Spaniard arriving on the frontier to begin plying his trade, or alternatively, he is already a master sculptor, sent personally by the king of Spain to San Antonio to decorate this specific church because he is a direct descendant of the artist who created the Alhambra. Waiting for him across the wide ocean is the love of his life, Rosa. Again, depending on the version, Rosa ships passage to the New World to marry Pedro but is lost at sea; or Rosa remains in Spain but tires of waiting for Pedro and marries another man. Heartbroken, poor Pedro pours out his devotion and anguish into the intricate carvings that embellish the south-facing window of San José's sacristy, known as the "Rose Window" or "Rosa's Window," and by some tales, dies a very lonely man shortly after completing the decorations.[93]

According to the historical record, however, Pedro Huizar was not a Spaniard but either a mulatto or a mestizo from Aguas Calientes.[94] Huizar appeared on a 1779 roster of the presidio and villa as a thirty-nine-year-old mulatto with a wife, two children, and a servant. His occupation is listed as *escultur*, or "sculptor."[95] Besides decorating Mission San José, he later did considerable work surveying mission lands in preparation for closing and secularizing the missions in the 1790s. The 1792 census of families living at Mission Concepción listed "Huisar" as a mestizo carpenter, having a wife and five children between the ages of four and fourteen. Antonio Salazar acted as godfather to several of Huizar's children. Huizar's sons later served as local officials for mission communities in the early 1800s. Schuetz considered Salazar to be the mastermind behind the elaborate decoration of Mission San José's facade and sacristy window and in a 1983 article dismissed Huizar as a talented man, but "there is no evidence that he ever worked as a sculptor." However, she likely did not know about the 1779 roster that unequivocally listed him as such. Conversely, Ivey claimed there was no reason not to believe that Huizar was, indeed, the brilliant artist responsible.[96] The 1779 roster listing Huizar as a sculptor should be more than sufficient to credit Pedro Huizar (or a team directed by him) with creating the ornate sculpting that decorates the sacristy window and facade of San José (fig. 1.2).

If we briefly interrogate the legends of the "Spanish" Pedro Huizar, several questions related to race and ethnicity on the Texas frontier appear. The first question is whether he was deliberately "whitened." Did the legends' proponents believe that a mixed-race individual was incapable of executing such a large-scale and magnificent oeuvre, to the degree that they had to make the artist of European stock? Some of the earliest legends to appear in print were published in the 1870s, a time when San Antonio's Spanish heritage was being romanticized for popular consumption.[97] If we examine another side of the legend, if Huizar was supposedly descended from the artist who decorated

Fig. 1.2. Rose Window, Mission San José. Photograph by the author.

the Alhambra, he becomes Moorish, or by the eighteenth century, Mudéjar. In this case, Huizar is not "whitened" but instead "Orientalized," although being sent with European royal blessing may render his talents more acceptable to Anglos in the late nineteenth century. The tragic love story element is pure romantic fiction since census records clearly show Huizar was married

Fig. 1.3. Facade decoration, "Tree of Jesse," Mission San José. Photograph by the author.

with a family. Those responsible for the legends may have had only the man's name and little additional information regarding Huizar's ethnicity. As happens so often, the entertainment value becomes more important than historical reality, and the tale grows with the telling. The consequence is the increasing divergence between collective memory and historical fact.

Maudlin romance aside, the sacristy window and the facade are superb examples of Baroque flourishes and sculpture. Whether Pedro Huizar designed and carved the tracings, scallop motifs, figures of saints, cherubs, and flowers by himself or whether he directed a team of stonecutters and assemblers in the work, the result is nothing short of impressive. When the work was completed, the friars could use the sculpting around the main portal as a teaching tool for converting the Coahuiltecan Indians to Catholicism. Unlike the much flatter reliefs surrounding the main door of Concepción, where the imagery highlighted specific examples of Franciscan symbolism, the facade of San José shows in graphic detail the biblical "Tree of Jesse," or a genealogy of Jesus Christ. On the first level at either side of the elaborately carved wooden doors are niche-pilasters with statues set out from insets in the wall behind (a common decorative technique for this era). The figures represent Saint Joachim and Saint Anne, traditionally held as the parents of the Virgin Mary, mother of Jesus. Centered just above the door on the arch keystone is the Virgin Mary as Our Lady of Guadalupe, patroness of New Spain.[98] On the second level of the design above an oval window is a statue of Saint Joseph (in Spanish, "San José," titular saint of this mission) holding the Christ child. He is flanked on either side by statues representing Saint Francis of Assisi and Saint Dominic (founders of the mendicant orders). At the top of the facade is the icon of the Sacred Heart (a heart wrapped in thorns) representing Christ and his outpouring of love for the world. As Schuetz marveled, this "visual representation must have been awesome to the Indian neophytes" (fig. 1.3).[99]

Secularization and Its Discontents

As the eighteenth century began to wane, changes across the entire Spanish frontier profoundly affected San Antonio's missions. While these changes were largely beyond the missionaries' control, some modern critics of the missionary efforts point to these as indicators of the missions' failures. All of the missions' functions transformed as the frontier became more settled and larger numbers of Hispanic settlers were able to reside at the missions.[100] Some of the adjustments were merely administrative; in 1767, the king of

Spain expelled the Jesuit order from the empire. The Franciscans from the apostolic College of Querétaro moved to administer the former Jesuit holdings in modern-day California and Arizona, which necessitated some reshuffling of responsibilities elsewhere on the Spanish frontier. In 1773, the Querétarans relinquished control of their San Antonio missions (Valero, Concepción, San Juan, and Espada) to their brethren from the apostolic college in Zacatecas and moved westward.[101]

Other changes having a more direct impact on the missions coincided with shifting Spanish strategies in dealing with the Apache and Comanche, European power struggles, and fiscal issues. Historian Pekka Hämäläinen observes that the vast North American empire of Spain was merely "a fiction that existed only in Spanish minds and on European maps." Indeed, during the latter part of Spanish rule, Texas had become "a money-draining, often tributary defensive province" and siphon by which Spanish treasure fueled the Comanche empire.[102] In an attempt to get a handle on the provincial finances, in early 1778, Commandant General Teodoro de Croix declared all unbranded livestock to be Crown property and fixed a tax on killing or selling livestock outside of the province. Croix set a four-month grace period before this edict went into effect for the missions and ranches to round up and brand what they might from area herds. Unfortunately, the missions, whose populations had already been declining for a variety of reasons, could not field or contribute enough wranglers for these roundups and thus lost most of their potential wealth.[103] In his 1785 report to his superiors in Zacatecas, Fr. José Francisco López, father-president of the San Antonio missions, laid the blame for the missions' struggling circumstances primarily on Croix and his parsimonious policies. López indicated the resident Indian populations had been severely reduced by a recent plague of "buboes," and the missions were struggling to adequately feed the populations that remained. These hardships prevented the missions from participating in the roundups of cattle in the limited time Croix allowed. On the other hand, López described the chapels of Valero, Concepción, and San José as being made of cut or wrought stone with carved gates and good locks. He also remarked on the beautiful decorative touches, such as the facade of Valero and Concepción's twin bell towers and "cupola" (dome), and he judged that San José's church and sacristy, based on "their architecture, are the most beautiful structures to be seen anywhere this side of Saltillo." López estimated the fine furnishings necessary to conduct religious services valued at a combined twenty-two thousand pesos but noted the combined population of the three missions amounted to only 261 (of whom only 32 were neophytes; the rest of the "Indians" had been Christianized).[104] This suggests that the missions' physical plant was well built and of fine workmanship but badly underpopulated, which made carrying out the mundane tasks of feeding and caring for the neophytes all the more difficult.

After 1780, the Franciscans began preparing the missions for secularization. Part of those measures included wrapping up as many building projects as possible. Churches not yet finished were completed as soon as possible; or, if unable to be completed, other stone buildings such as granaries and sacristies were converted to be used as the permanent churches, as was the case at San Juan and Espada.[105] It is paradoxical that just as the mission communities were completing the permanent stone churches, their function to their community changed so dramatically. Nonetheless, part of the original plan was that the missions be temporary. In preparation for the transition to secular life, the Franciscans reduced the amount of time spent in basic evangelism and, with the assistance of local villagers who moved into the mission communities, began instructing the Indians in the civic duties expected of all royal subjects.[106]

In a follow-up report in 1792, Fr. López argued that the time had come to convert the San Antonio missions into secular holdings and send the missionaries farther afield to begin the process anew. López reported that the Indians at Valero were "so instructed in the Christian dogmas and gospel teaching . . . that they are not now, nor can they be called neophytes, or even Indians." López observed that since most were the children of mixed marriages, it could "therefore be inferred that this mission cannot be called a mission of Indians but a gathering of white people."[107] His statement, by which he so facilely raised mixed-race children to the level of European white people, even if delivered off-the-cuff, gives modern historians pause to wonder what manner of statement he might have been trying to make (if any) regarding caste. Given that he sent this report to his Franciscan superiors in Zacatecas and was recommending beginning the secularization process with Valero, describing the people living there as "white" strengthens his argument to that end. Furthermore, López claimed that there were no Indians remaining in a sixty-league area around Béxar. Within that boundary, all Indians had been converted; outside that boundary, the Indians could not "be taken out of their land without violence to their nature, without offending the laws of humanity," or against other royal and pontifical edicts relating to evangelizing among indigenous peoples. Hence the missionaries must move outward farther into the frontier.[108] These comments are at minimum prima facie evidence that the missionaries had succeeded in establishing the Catholic faith in a region previously unchurched by Christians, as well as successfully establishing a Spanish community, which in combination with the villa and presidio held the area for the Crown until the nineteenth century and the end of the Spanish Empire.

To accomplish his plan, López recommended reorganizing the mission structure in San Antonio. He began by secularizing Valero, retaining missionaries at Concepción and San José, and converting San Juan and Espada into "settlements of visitation [mission stations]" of the previous two. He intended for the missionaries at Concepción and San José to also be responsible for regularly visiting the two smaller, outlying missions to conduct services and minister to the needs of the populations, and the missionaries at those missions would be released to establish new missions. The plan was accepted and executed in 1794, but not quite as López had suggested. Valero was fully secularized in 1793. Missionaries were retained at San José and Espada, while Concepción became a mission station to San José, and San Juan a mission station to Espada, a more logical plan from a geographical perspective.[109] All of the San Antonio missions were fully secularized by 1824.

The 1805 census for the Mission Concepción community listed 22 persons identified as "Indians," 15 "Spaniards," and 4 of unidentified ethnicity. The mayor of the community was Don Antonio Huizar, and a ninety-year-old Indian, José Manuel Cueves, was listed as governor of the "pueblo."[110] Interestingly, Don Antonio, son of the mixed-race Pedro, was identified as "Spaniard" in this census, which listed only two racial categories. On the colonial Spanish frontier racial categories could actually be quite fluid. A person's racial status on the census was malleable depending on the person's social status within the community.[111] Four years later, the number of Indians decreased by one, to 21, while the number of Spaniards increased to 32. Don Antonio Huizar was still mayor and lived with his wife, María Teodora Guerra, and three of his siblings. Two of Pedro Huizar's sons were farmers, another a musician, and one a carpenter. All members of the Huizar clan were listed as "Spaniards" even though their father had been considered of mixed race on an earlier census. José Antonio Huizar commented that the Indians who were "citizens of this Mission" all had houses within the walls and one *suerte* of farmland. However, Huizar also noted that while the land had been distributed by Governor Don Manuel Muñoz, the Indians were still waiting for titles to their holdings.[112]

A few years later, the Mission Espada census revealed an even greater disparity between Spaniards and Indians. In February 1815, enumerators recorded 16 Indians but 101 Spaniards. Similar to the Concepción records, no additional ethnic breakdown was given. The record listed a Spanish mayor, José Antonio Bustillos, a native of Béxar, married with two children, and an Indian governor, Emeterio Espinosa, a fifty-eight-year-old farmer, with no additional family.[113] In 1819, census takers combined the returns for the Mission Espada community with that of Mission San Juan. Additionally, a more detailed racial breakdown of the populations was given. At San Juan there were 16 Spaniards, 13 mestizos, 7 mulattos, 6 lobos, and 3 Indians. Meanwhile, at Espada there were 14 Spaniards, 62 mestizos, 13 mulattos, and 27 Indians.[114] The secularization process for the Spanish missions was quite complex and not always followed consistently, although the common assumption that all the Indians immediately lost their lands to Spaniards is probably overstated. Some lands thought to be lost by Indian families may have actually been passed down to later generations via inheritance through second marriages.[115] Historian Félix Almaráz Jr. reached a similar conclusion and suggested that by tracing landowning widows, whether using their maiden name or if remarried, a second husband's name would clarify how parcels of land came to have different names attached yet remain the possession of the original families.[116] This is not to say that none of the mission Indians were cheated out of their property by unscrupulous agents. However, here is another layer to the complex equation of trying to trace land possession among mission Indians who were given Christian names upon baptism or married into Spanish families, and even if not fully Christianized, the layers of assimilation conceal their Indian heritage from modern historians.

While some Indians remained living at the Concepción and Espada communities, such was not always the case at each mission during the secularization process, which lasted three decades. American explorer Zebulon Pike traveled through San Antonio in 1807 as he was being escorted out of Spanish territory. The town's missions created such a striking impression on him that he made a special note in his journal: "Those buildings for solidity, accommodation, and even majesty, were surpassed by few that I saw in New Spain."[117] Pike also described meeting a local priest, loved by all, who treated him with "the greatest hospitality" and with whom he had an interesting exchange regarding the Native Americans. When Pike asked what had become of the natives at the missions, this respected clergyman replied that "it appeared to him that [the Indians] could not exist under the shadow of the whites." Pike believed the priest "had formed an idea that God never intended them to form one people, but that they should always remain distinct and separate."[118] Perhaps the priest's comments reflected more his own frustration than divining the will of God or Pike's own racial outlook. Still, Pike's experience indicated the secularization process was complex and inequities and prejudice existed. Subsequent publication of Pike's exploits spread word of San Antonio's missions to the American reading public. His published journals proved popular with other travel writers, including Josiah Conder, who in 1830 repeated Pike's commentary on the missions.[119]

Not every visitor to San Antonio was sufficiently inspired by the missions to remark on them at the time. Frenchman Pierre Marie François Pagès visited the town between 1767 and 1771. While he recorded some critical observations about the Franciscans and relations with their Indigenous charges, he did not mention the architecture at all.[120] Similarly, German explorer Alexander von Humboldt included a brief mention of San Antonio in his explorations but reserved more detailed descriptions for the Spanish missionary endeavors in California.[121] Should the lack of visitor descriptions of San Antonio's missions in a few travelogues invalidate those that do include a description (particularly if the descriptions were embellished and romanticized out of proportion)? No, although true that these early notices were unlikely to anchor San Antonio's missions in the cultural memories of the American public in the early nineteenth century, the fact that some visitors found them sufficiently noteworthy to include in published descriptions is interpreted in this book that the missions could and were garnering attention during this time.

Secularizing the missions was a lengthy process that began with Mission Valero in 1793 and was not completed for the other four missions until 1824. As part of the secularization process, the church buildings of the missions were intended to be used as parish churches for the new Indian villas, except at Valero. When the missionary activities at Valero ceased, the priest from San Fernando parish picked up the spiritual responsibilities, but only for a few years. A new parish at Valero was founded in 1801, which lasted until 1825.[122] The flying company of cavalry, the Compañía Volante del Alamo de San Carlos de Parras, arrived in 1802 and was posted at the mission site. The company's chaplain used the sacristy for Mass, as the chapel itself had never been completely rebuilt. In 1810, after the old mission's friary had been established as the hospital, a proposal was drawn up to roof the church, not for divine service but as an artillery storehouse.[123] Although earlier construction efforts on the church had left some supports still in place, by this time those were no longer safe, and in the end the roof project proved too expensive and was never carried out. The church would have to wait until the late 1840s and the US Army before it was once again closed to the elements, but in the meantime, it had acquired a new identity, "the Alamo."[124]

By 1824, San Antonio's missions ceased to exist as missions. Félix Almaráz has asserted that either because of, or in spite of, a "cumbersome" process to divide and distribute the secularized mission lands to both resident mission Indians and other qualified recipients, "a rampage of malfeasance and destruction" was prevented.[125] With the mission lands in private hands, what became of the buildings? For their fate we must depend on the observations and descriptions of tourists who left recorded commentaries. From these descriptions we can construct images of the mission churches and their decay and gain insight into the curiosity they inspired over time.

One such visitor was the French naturalist Jean Louis Berlandier, who accompanied Mexican General Manuel de Mier y Terán on his 1828 inspection tour of the borderland between Mexico and the United States. Terán left no description of San Antonio or its missions, but his keen-eyed traveling companion was sufficiently fascinated with what he saw of the missions and the town of San Antonio to record his impressions. Berlandier was most charmed by the remnants of the Alamo chapel (née Mission San Antonio de Valero), opining it "could pass for one of the loveliest monuments of the area, even if its architecture is overloaded with ornamentation like all the other ecclesiastical buildings of the Spanish colonies." Although somewhat critical of the dated Baroque style, Berlandier did not dismiss what he observed. He additionally noted of the other four missions, "Although in ruins, these edifices still bear the traces of a former splendor."[126] Despite the deteriorating condition, the buildings retained enough beauty to catch a European eye.

It is tempting to end the stories of the missions here; after all, the missionary functions to the area's indigenous people ceased with secularization. However, the mission church buildings persisted as relics, as ruins, as curiosities, as dwellings, and indeed as sacred space. This persistence continues into the next chapter and begins to have a curious effect on Anglo-Americans, particularly those with an imagination fired by romantic hero tales and an eye for the sublime. The mission churches' ornate decor, the statuary, and the symbols that were important to Catholic belief would be looked on as curious relics of a foreign past. The mission age in San Antonio sets the stage for the physical remnants on the frontier from which numerous legends and collective memories would be constructed, but the story of the missions does not end here; indeed, the end of the mission period is merely the prologue in the creation of a mythical and romanticized Spanish past and a diverse collection of identities.

2

Changing Times at the Missions, 1821–1877

AS MARY A. MAVERICK reminisced, it was a cool, sunny day in November 1839 when she joined a sightseeing party from Houston (which included a cabinet member of the Republic of Texas) who were visiting San Antonio. Mary was the wife of early Texas land speculator and politician Samuel A. Maverick, and she became the matriarch of a family intimately involved in San Antonio politics and life for much of its history. The tourists first rode up the western side of the San Antonio River to its head, north of town. From there, Maverick remarked, they could see "three of the missions including San Juan Capistrano" in the distance. The group returned down the eastern side of the river. Because of the potential of attack by Comanche Indians, all members of the party, including the women, were "armed with pistols and bowie knives." Maverick noted everyone very much enjoyed their excursion, despite the group feeling they were under constant surveillance from the Comanche, who still represented a significant threat to Anglo expansion in the region.[1]

The mission churches no longer served strictly Native American congregations and very quickly began suffering from neglect (and in one particular instance, the violence of warfare). Nevertheless, they were never completely forgotten by the church, locals, or visitors interested in exotic ruins. As this and subsequent chapters show, residents and visitors both were sufficiently interested in the edifices to include descriptions (of varying degrees of accuracy) in correspondence and reports. Historian Raúl Ramos observes after the cessation of their responsibilities to the Native Americans in 1824, "the missions of San Antonio de Béxar retained symbolic value, helping to define the image and history of the town."[2] However, Ramos does not explore further how the "symbolic value" of the missions created this defining image, whereas this book seeks to elucidate how that symbolic value was created during this period.

Dramatic changes swept through San Antonio during the period between Mexican independence in 1821 and the arrival of the railroad in 1877. Between 1820 and 1850, the town changed from a remote outpost on the Spanish frontier, to an outpost on the Mexican frontier, to a major town within the new Republic of Texas, to a remote outpost once again, this time on the American frontier. Also during this period, Mission San Antonio de Valero became the Alamo and was elevated to new heights of romantic embellishment. Some of the hyperbole came in the form of booster tracts, written to highlight advantages Texas held for farmers and businessmen alike. The missions were appealing enough to be mentioned in these publications. Travel narratives written by visitors from the more urbane sections of the United States began appearing in popular magazines and exhibited colonialist attitudes toward the South and Southwest. These narratives contributed to Anglo collective memories as they romanticized the region's Spanish past. The authors began a process that culminated in the construction of a dominant American identity that consigned the missions to antique relics of a dead past, particularly through references to San Antonio as an "ancient" villa, giving an air of authenticity to the ruins and a mysterious and exotic aura the (mostly urbane and elite) tourists found so attractive. References to "Moorish" design features effectively "Orientalized" the missions. Although seen as part of a foreign past, the missions became an important symbolic part of San Antonio's history as it was incorporated into the Anglo-American nation.

The significant political changes and violence that accompanied Mexican independence from Spain created a spiritual power vacuum, as many in the Catholic hierarchy sided with Spanish royalists and were chased out. Any new Catholic leadership organization depended on Rome, and negotiations with the new government in Mexico City prevented an efficient transfer of power and property. The cumulative effects that the protracted struggles for Mexican and Texan independence had on the Catholic Church, particularly regarding San Antonio's missions, were calamitous.[3] During this period there were not enough diocesan priests in the area to attend to the spiritual needs of all of San Antonio's parishes. As a result, a few of the Franciscans continued at the missions to care for the remaining population until final secularization was complete.[4]

As the populations surrounding the missions shifted, many people (particularly from the missions closest to the town) began attending Mass at San Fernando Cathedral. Two goals of the new government in Mexico City were "the end of the mission system and the privatization of the mission lands mostly into the hands of Tejanos."[5] As mentioned earlier, considering the level of racial mixing among the Indians and local populations, using the term "Tejano" raises questions about exactly who gained land and who lost. Through assimilation and intermarriage, many Indigenous people used Spanish names, challenging attempts to identify who benefited from the land distribution. Nonetheless, the Mexican legislative body facilitated the ability of Tejanos to purchase former mission lands along with the all-important irrigation rights from the mission Indians. Consequently, as secularization was completed, speculators found little in the way of legal protections to impede them in separating many mission Indians from their land.[6]

The Missions and Texas's Quest for Independence

One of the missions' original functions was defense, protecting the inhabitants from attacks by outside forces. Nineteenth-century French observer Jean Louis Berlandier noted the "enormous battlement" at the Alamo that spoke of this necessity.[7] During the lengthy struggle for Mexican independence from Spain, the violence and chaos that followed each successive government culminating in the Texian revolt, San Antonio and its missions witnessed their share of turmoil. As early as 1813, the Mexican revolutionary José Bernardo Gutiérrez briefly established a headquarters outside San Antonio at Mission Concepción before capturing the city in April of that year.[8] However, it would be the Texas Revolution that brought armed forces again to Concepción and would change the identity of Mission Valero in a clash that would be forever burned into Texas and American public memory.

Texian revolutionary violence came to not one but two of San Antonio's missions. On October 27, 1835, advance forces under the overall command of Stephen F. Austin drew the attention of Mexican forces protecting San Antonio under General Martín Perfecto de Cos. The Texians had advanced from positions near Espada and taken up a position near Concepción. Early the next day, Mexican infantry supported by two cannons moved out of the town and engaged the Texians, commanded by James Bowie. The Texians held the better defensive positions and repelled multiple charges before staging their own, which drove the Mexicans back into the town. Fortunately for the mission building itself, the fighting took place some distance from the church. Austin then laid siege to San Antonio until early December, when an assault was mounted. After several days of close fighting, Cos surrendered.[9]

The Texians held San Antonio from December 1835 to early March 1836. Had Texian General Sam Houston received permission from Governor Henry Smith, he planned to order Colonel James C. Neill to destroy the Alamo and move eastward with all munitions and supplies intact, thus denying its use as a fortress for Mexican forces.[10] If this had occurred, the famous Battle of the Alamo never would have taken place. However, Smith did not authorize the destruction of the Alamo, and the familiar story of its siege and capture played itself out. Colonels James Bowie and James Neill began fortifying the city against the anticipated Mexican offensive. William Barrett Travis and a small party of men arrived shortly afterward followed by former Tennessee Congressman and raconteur Davy Crockett with several companions. In early February, Colonel Neill took a leave of absence to deal with a family illness and left Travis in command. Although the Texians knew a substantial Mexican army was moving north toward their position, they did not do an effective job of monitoring its progress and were surprised on February 24 to find a very large army commanded by none other than General Antonio López de Santa Anna at their gates.[11] Though the siege lasted thirteen days, the outcome was never in question. A few Texian rebels broke through the Mexican lines to take their place among the Alamo defenders but not enough to alter the course of the battle. In the predawn darkness of March 6, 1836, Santa Anna unleashed his forces and in less than two hours overwhelmed the Alamo defenders, putting the entire garrison to the sword.[12]

From a military perspective, an extended siege and bloody battle to take the fortress was of questionable value. Indeed, a Mexican officer in Santa Anna's army, Lieutenant Colonel José Enrique de la Peña, rhetorically asked his diary, "To whom was this sacrifice useful?"[13] As if to answer de la Peña's question, Texian General Sam Houston rallied his troops only a few weeks later at the Battle of San Jacinto with the battle cry, "Remember the Alamo!" The ragtag Texian army won a stunning victory, catching the numerically superior Mexican forces unprepared.[14] From a symbolic perspective, the massacre at the Alamo very quickly took on a life of its own, and the battered mission was transformed into what French historian Pierre Nora calls a "lieu de mémoire," or "site of memory," which he defines as "any significant entity . . . which by the dint of human will or the work of time has become a symbolic element of the memorial heritage of any community."[15] However, for buildings within the Alamo compound, glory in battle did not immediately translate into protected status. Differing versions of Alamo myths emerged within days of the 1836 battle, and those myths took the Alamo on a very different trajectory in collective memory from that of the other four missions. Nevertheless, its physical location in San Antonio was not regarded as "sacrosanct until the very end of the nineteenth century."[16] An 1841 newspaper article mentions that a stonecutter named Nangle had moved to San Antonio from Philadelphia around 1839 and was making a living using limestone taken from the Alamo that had been "consecrated by the blood of the bravest of the brave" to make a variety of quotidian objects, such as "seals, paper weights, pipe bowls, little vessels."[17]

Racial Context in San Antonio After 1836

While the events of 1836 brought about a dramatic reordering of the racial power structure in San Antonio, it did not materialize overnight, nor was it complete. Anglos had been arriving before Texas independence; however, once the break from Mexico was achieved, many more came pouring in. The established Tejano families, who initially acted as "cultural brokers" for the Anglos, eventually found themselves outnumbered and supplanted as the primary socioeconomic citizens in town.[18] Yet this convoluted web of familial and other relationships connected the Anglos, Tejanos, and Indians, which, combined with fluid racial definitions, complicate this tale of historical memories. Historian David Montejano notes that the Anglo-Americans represented a "new class" that grafted onto, but "did not completely transform," the existing Mexican socioeconomic structures. The newcomers intermarried with the established families to the benefit of both while "the class structure of the Mexican settlements" remained as the society's foundation.[19] Even so, historian Arnoldo de León opines that the Tejanos' world post-1836 was not "catastrophic." Despite the new Anglo group of interlopers inserting themselves into the existing community power structure, Tejanos "retained their 'Mexicanness,' identified with old traditions and beliefs, and carried on Hispanic practices while rejecting certain Anglo-American ones." And, similar to other colonialized populations, they developed means that gave them a modicum of agency within their lives.[20] Finally, Andrés Reséndez describes the malleability of identities as being somewhat relative: "A person was not a mission Indian *or* a Mexican, a black slave in Mexico *or* an American, a foreign-born colonist *or* a Texan, but could be either depending on who was asking."[21] In considering these historians' positions on how complicated San Antonio's power structure became, it is little wonder that all groups struggled early on to make their place in the emerging local culture.

Mary Maverick chronicled in her memoirs some of the early interactions between her Anglo family and their Tejano neighbors in the years following Texan independence. She recorded that in December 1840, her family was invited to participate in the celebrations and dances for the feast day of Nuestra Señora de Guadalupe, "the patroness saint of Mexico, and whom the priests had identified with the Virgin Mary." Maverick, a Protestant, described the processions, decorations, and devotions as "all quite a novel and interesting scene to me." Part of the remainder of the day she spent "exchanging calls" with other elite families, including the Navarros, Seguins, and Veramendis.[22] The "novelty" Maverick mentioned could be seen as paternalistic, exoticizing the Tejano Other, but it also reads as innocent curiosity about a different culture as well.

Maverick's participation in the Guadalupan celebrations deserves additional consideration. How much significance should be attributed to the Tejanos inviting their Anglo neighbors (and the significance of the Anglos accepting the invitations) to fiestas honoring the patroness of Mexico? Religion is "a crucial component of ethnic identity" that goes beyond mere "denominational affiliation" to also include "public ritual practices."[23] Tejano inclusion of Anglos in such an important religious festival denoted a significant degree of acceptance of the new arrivals. Even though Mary Maverick acknowledged that the Tejano families with whom they associated represented the upper crust of San Antonio society, historian Timothy Matovina argues, "Anglo-American participation in the Guadalupan feast showed the strength of local traditions at San Antonio and the Tejano desire to incorporate newcomers into those traditions."[24] So the town's Tejano elite appeared to offer a measure of hospitality and inclusion, or even reverse assimilation for the new Anglos. Conversely, other scholars look at religion and its expression as one means of resistance by a marginalized group to a dominant one.[25] While Anglos at Guadalupan feasts revealed an early degree of peaceful coexistence with their Tejano neighbors, at least among elites, Anglos would eventually usurp the leading Tejano families and relegate the majority of Tejanos to more servile positions and menial labor, although this outcome may not have been clear in 1840. Despite the eventual political usurpation, Tejano religious expression served as a means of preserving their Mexican Catholicism in the face of the growing Protestant Anglo majority. Although not in continual use for divine service during this time, the Catholic Church consecrated the missions as sacred space, and as such for many Tejanos, the missions were a spiritual home where they could express their religiosity in their preferred manner. By retaining this sacred function, the missions maintained their status as sites of memory for many local Tejanos, allowing them to retain a sense of their identity.

During this evolutionary time, instances of the Tejano sacrifices on behalf of the Texas republic began to disappear from published sources such as newspapers. Eventually, a more effective suppression of Tejano participation at the 1836 Alamo battle began to take effect late in the nineteenth century when the Anglos, as the dominant racial and ethnic power, "silenced" contributions by Tejanos.[26] By deliberately erasing or unconsciously ignoring Tejano participation at the Alamo and in the Texas republic more generally, Anglos exercised control over the construction of the collective memories regarding the Alamo. Control over the collective memories included their uses and interpretations, which could be altered as needed to cement Anglo societal, economic, and political control in San Antonio.[27]

Early Romantic Depictions of the Alamo

The coupling of the Romantic movement and the San Antonio missions comes from the rhetorical devices and the purple prose commonly used during this period. Orators and editors inflated the sacrifices of the Alamo martyrs to biblical proportions. Alamo commanders William Barrett Travis, James Bowie, and Davy Crockett became something akin to a "Holy Trinity" in the creation myth of Texas.[28] One of the phrases that became quite popular and often repeated, however, conflated Travis and the Alamo garrison to a nineteenth-century version of King Leonidas and his doomed Spartan warriors. Within weeks of the Alamo's fall, Texas politician Thomas Jefferson Green coined a phrase that quickly entered into the Alamo lexicon, "Thermopylae had her messenger of defeat—the Alamo had none."[29] And while Green's phrase became an indelible part of the collective memory related to the Alamo, it completely ignored historical reality. The Alamo did indeed have messengers of defeat. Unlike those from Thermopylae, the messengers from the Alamo were not combatants and, due to their race, gender, and age, were considered of lowly status: Susanna W. Dickinson and her infant daughter, Angelina (sometimes referred to as "the babe of the Alamo"); Joe, a slave of Travis; as well as six Tejano women: Concepción Charlé Gortari Losoya, Andrea Castañon de Villanueva, Juana

Navarro Pérez Alsbury, Gertrudis Navarro, Juana Francisca Losoya Melton, and Ana Salazar Castro Esparza, plus their children, including eight-year-old Enrique Esparza, all of whom were related to Alamo defenders or other Texian revolutionaries.[30] Santa Anna sent Susanna Dickinson and her child, along with Joe and another slave, as messengers of defeat from San Antonio to General Sam Houston and the Texians in rebellion. The Thermopylae trope lives on as part of the Alamo myth and accentuates further the divergence between history and collective memory.

The speakers and authors creating tributes to the Alamo dead during the nineteenth century "thought, wrote, and spoke the language of the romantic age," and the flowery rhetoric was not limited to Texan or even American writers.[31] In 1841, Arthur Ikin, British consul to Texas in London, wrote a book that included the mawkish poem titled "Hymn to the Alamo," in which Travis and his band embraced the "Spartan's death" at "this new Thermopylæ," for "Freedom's breath of life."[32] Ikin's intended audience was potential British immigrants, and he evidently believed including an ode dedicated to the Alamo martyrs would help them acclimate to the new culture. Two years later a Houston artist created and exhibited a monument in memory of the Alamo dead created from materials directly taken from the mission walls. One local newspaper hailed it as the "most beautiful and impressive piece of sculpture ever completed in the Republic." The journalist lamented his inability to adequately describe the monument but gushed that the sculpture was a "relic hallowed by the blood of martyrs."[33] In keeping with the spirit of the times, the sculptor's use of stones taken from the site where the heroes died made the monument even more sacred to the intended audience.

Tales of doomed forces making last stands, as well as total massacres being transformed into victories by the glorious sacrifice of martyrs, holds a romantic appeal and remains popular across time and cultures. And historian Paul Hutton observes, no matter what the culture, "the heroes are always vastly outnumbered by a vicious enemy from a culturally inferior nation bent on the utter destruction of the heroic band's people."[34] Analogous self-sacrifices during this period and similarly sensationalized by Romantic-era rhetoric include poet Lord Byron's death of a fever while fighting for Greek independence (1824), the "Charge of the Light Brigade" (1854), and General George A. Custer's last stand at Little Bighorn (1876).[35] Meanwhile, Anglo-Americans as well as Anglo-Texans condemned Santa Anna and his Mexicans to the position of the "culturally inferior" Other determined to destroy the Anglos' self-proclaimed liberties. Consequently, San Antonio's

Tejano population found themselves swept into this "Other" category by association, and their important contributions to Texan independence were quickly silenced and dropped from Anglo memories.

Bishop Odin and the Missions as Sacred Space

Early visitors to San Antonio's missions observed Mass occasionally being held at San José. For the Catholic Church, the period of Mexican and then Texan independence, US annexation, and subsequent war with Mexico was a chaotic one, challenging efforts to reestablish a significant Catholic presence in San Antonio. During these first decades of the early nineteenth century, church activities drifted. This changed when Father Jean Marie Odin of France arrived in Texas. Odin was an energetic man, charged with rebuilding a Catholic presence in what had been Spanish Catholic territory. He eventually became the first bishop in Texas when he took over as bishop of the Galveston Diocese.

In 1840, Odin arrived in Texas as the vice prefect apostolic, tasked with inspecting Catholic operations in Texas and tending to whatever their needs might be. What he found appalled him. One of his first actions was to sack both Father Refugio de la Garza of San Fernando and Father José Antonio Valdez from Mission La Bahía del Espíritu Santo in Goliad. The justifications for taking such drastic action against the two aging priests who had grown up in the community were for dereliction of their duties to their congregations and for living in sin with women.[36] In addition to repairing the clergy in San Antonio, Odin began earnestly repairing the church's physical facilities. Leaks in the roof of San Fernando were first on Odin's agenda, but he was also "struck by the beauty of the abandoned church and convent of San José." He believed that San José, with its surviving buildings and large campus, could "easily be converted into a college or a seminary" or even a school for boys.[37] Odin expressed hope to an American Catholic magazine that Missions Concepción and San José might be repaired and returned to service until more prosperous times brought the means to build new facilities.[38] Although it took years to come to fruition, Odin actively recruited Catholic groups such as the Society of Mary and the Benedictines to use the facilities at both missions. Odin also purchased or recommended that other religious members purchase land around the missions. For ten years beginning in 1859, brothers of the Society of Mary lived at Concepción, and the lands surrounding the mission were leased for farming.[39]

Odin contacted Benedictine Abbot Boniface Wimmer in 1859 about bringing several members of that house to live at San José and minister to the German Catholic community in the region. A local newspaper editor celebrated the commitment Odin (now bishop of Texas) was making toward the missions by "resuscitating and re-constructing the relics of the different Missions. . . . We devoutly bid him God speed, protestant though we be, we cherish the relics of these antique Missions and hallow their memories, as much as the Athenians do that of the Parthenon."[40] Despite theological preferences, the quotation reveals the significant value an important community voice placed on the missions and his appreciation of Odin's efforts on their behalf. Before the Benedictines began their religious work, they carried out an extensive rebuilding project at San José led by Father Alto Hoermann and four associates. Former National Park Service archaeologist James Ivey states that much of the remodeling work was done to the *convento* in 1860, and during this project Gothic (sometimes called "lancet") arched windows were installed on the second floor.[41] These windows clash with the earlier, more rounded, Roman arches and are easily identified today by the use of red brick instead of original limestone on their outline. Unfortunately, before much progress could be made, Odin was assigned to be archbishop of New Orleans, and the outbreak of the Civil War prevented the Benedictines from taking up residence. Although Odin's attempts to return the mission chapels to regular use for services were not as successful as he hoped, it nonetheless indicates an official recognition of the importance these churches held for the local populations who looked on them as sacred spaces and sites of memory.

Early Texas Boosters' Discovery of the Missions

Early descriptions of Texas in the first half of the nineteenth century were considered "histories" by some and promotional literature by others. Indeed, as one historian remarked, "They liberally mixed the genres of travel narrative and advertising with the historical exercise to create a kind of boosterism in historical disguise."[42] This genre bending was reflected in many of the print sources used for this and subsequent chapters. Anglo-American interest in Texas for potential settlement and seemingly limitless exploitable land, as well as the possibility for annexation to the United States, began appearing just a few years after Mexico won its independence from Spain. Boosters did their best to stir up interest in new territory. The booster of the period was essentially a pitchman who stressed the land's potential to the point of exaggeration while ignoring or slighting perceived liabilities. When written in Romantic-era prose, they produced extremely florid (even fanciful) depictions of Texas and its potential.[43]

In 1832, the Richmond *Enquirer* reprinted an article from the Nashville *Banner*, lamenting that Texas was not already "annexed to our Federal Union, but is under a government little suited to our taste, habits, and sympathies." The author mused how it was yet "possible, that a territory inhabited by our citizens, and bordering on our western, frontier, should permanently continue a province of the Mexican Empire." In advocating annexation, the author noted that Texas, "from geographical position, seems naturally to belong to us and to be required to round off and complete the symmetry of our south-western border, should by contract and mutual consent, be made to constitute a part—and a most delightful part it will certainly be—of this great nation."[44] In the same year Texas won independence from Mexico, Joseph Emerson Field published a small booklet extolling the benefits available in Texas for commercial or agricultural pursuits. In his opening paragraph, however, he paid homage to the architectural ornamentation and splendor of San Antonio's missions, observing that the buildings "have suffered but little . . . by the hand of time. . . . The front, or most imposing parts of these churches are adorned with sculptured representations of angels."[45] Field must have considered the missions' aesthetic qualities as one of the cultural attractions that would bring people to San Antonio.

British diplomat and consul to Texas William Kennedy published a massive, two-volume description of Texas after his 1839 visit that was intended to guide British citizens and immigrants in Texas. Kennedy included a general history of Spanish colonization in North America, where his caustic anti-Spanish, anti-Catholic observations regarding the administration of the missions reflected long-held British prejudices.[46] For much of the book, Kennedy, in true booster fashion, waxed prodigiously on Texas's natural advantages in climate, soil, inexpensive labor, minerals, game, and transportation. However, Kennedy also included descriptions of San Antonio's missions and their grand ornamentation, including large bells and paintings. Similarly, he called readers' attention to San José as "no mean specimen of architecture," complementing Spanish aesthetics, which significantly contrasted with his comments reprising the "Black Legend" of the priests savagely and violently indoctrinating their Indigenous charges into Catholicism.[47]

Other boosters lionized the Alamo martyrs. Richard Hunt and Jesse Randel, land agents in Houston and New York, offered their services to potential immigrants through a slim volume that gave a brief outline of Texas history from 1821, the various empresarios, and important Mexican and Texas land laws and regulations. Additionally, Hunt and Randel included brief descriptions of rivers, counties, and towns. In their description of San Antonio de Béxar, they noted it was "one of the most ancient towns in North America," with a population of around fifteen hundred. But their picture of San Antonio was not complete without also referencing "the ruins of the Alamo . . . styled the Thermopylae of Texas, in commemoration of the heroic defence of Travis and his brave comrades."[48]

While many boosters targeted English speakers in Great Britain and the United States, some pursued a different demographic. Ferdinand Roemer of Germany took advantage of the interest in Texas shown by his countrymen and published one of the earliest books for potential immigrants written in the German language. Roemer's book straddles the line between travelogue and booster tract. By comparison, his descriptions are detailed and factual with less the flood of superlatives so prevalent in others. Roemer balanced for his readers the advantages of warm climate and rich soils for longer and more productive growing seasons, with disadvantages including disease, incomplete transportation and communication networks, and the slave system, which socially and competitively disadvantaged small landowners and those committed to free labor.[49] Besides his descriptions related to agriculture and geography, Roemer included some observations regarding the missions. His initial impression of the Alamo was to contrast its foreign appearance with the prevailing American population. Like so many others, he repeated the comparison of the 1836 Alamo battle to Thermopylae. He documented the missions' irrigation system and Mission Concepción's dome. More interesting was the "strange impression" that he, as a cultured and worldly European, felt while contemplating such a stately building, "no doubt erected with considerable expenditure of effort," in its "forsaken and wild" location.[50] Later, when his party reached San José, Roemer noted that the exterior wall was still partially intact and "several Mexican families live in miserable huts built out of the ruins of the building," and there was a corn crop growing on the grounds. He called particular attention to the "west side" (the main entry) that was "still decorated carefully and tastefully with sculptures which, as traces still indicate, were painted in gaudy colors." He compared the stone used for the cupolas and arched ceilings of the mission churches with similar "limestone or travertine" material in the Leiner Valley near Göttingen. In visiting Mission San Juan, which also had poverty-stricken Mexican families living on the grounds, he noted, "Their presence rather increases than diminishes the impression of desolation and decay which the general view presents."[51] His observation and impression of poor families using the missions as an abode seemed to amplify stark feelings of loneliness and privation and may have struck chords of tragic romance that inspired readers to visit the missions.

Early Tourism, Romantics, and the Missions

One facet of the Romantic period's influence at the San Antonio missions relates to the nascent tourism industry in the United States. Besides being a money-making enterprise, tourism influenced the creation of the American national narrative. Historian John Sears observed, "Tourism played a powerful role in America's invention of itself as a culture" and connected the influence exerted by the Romantic movement on early American tourism. Additionally, Americans were similar to their British relations who, under the influence of Romantics such as William Wordsworth, Sir Walter Scott, and Lord Byron, self-identified with the landscape they inhabited.[52] Such identification with the physical territory tied manifest destiny and Anglo-America's presumed right to the entire continent together and described it using the sentimental language often employed by Romantic travel writers in a rapidly increasing number of printed outlets, including newspapers, popular magazines, and books. In the years between Texas independence and the arrival of the railroad in San Antonio, most tourists in the United States came from the genteel elite. These travelers went on the road seeking the "sublime or picturesque," based on European traditions, which would have encouraged them to find some sort of moral lessons for themselves or to "cultivate their aesthetic sensibilities."[53] Because many found the missions so "picturesque" and charming, their heavily romanticized travelogues linked these buildings on a remote frontier to the larger movements regarding the construction of a national identity going on in the core metropolitan regions of the United States.[54] In this manner, the missions represented an archaic and foreign past, which the authors of these travel narratives believed gave the young nation a degree of credibility on the world cultural stage. Many writers assumed the missions' foreign past was, or would soon be, overtaken by a modern, Anglo-dominated future.

Many of the visitors to San Antonio in this time could be considered "travelers" who actively pursued previously unknown or little-known places off the beaten track, where the journey itself was part of the adventure. Late in this period, and certainly after the railroad arrived in San Antonio and made the journey much more pleasurable, the "tourists" followed, having purchased the experience as a consumer commodity. Although there is a distinction between "tourist" and "traveler," this book treats them nearly synonymously, being more interested in their published descriptions of San Antonio and the missions and less concerned with how modern scholars might categorize the nature of their journey. Whereas the tourists used more clichéd terms and phrases and travelers used more clinical and scientific language, San Antonio's missions intrigued both groups sufficiently to be mentioned in their published descriptions.[55]

George Wilkins Kendall, a survivor of the 1841 Texas–Santa Fe fiasco, was a keen observer and included his impressions of the missions in his book on the expedition. He asserted, "By far the greatest curiosities in the neighborhood of San Antonio are the *missions*." Like William Kennedy, Kendall had few compliments for the Spanish missionaries, although he did suggest that select Indigenous rituals were permitted to coexist with the Catholic ones. However flawed Kendall believed their theology may have been, he credited the friars with constructing beautiful sacred spaces on the frontier. He also lauded the strength of construction and elaborate ornamentation. Mission Concepción was described as a "very large stone building, with a fine cupola, and though plain, magnificent in its dimensions and the durability of its construction." At Mission San José, Kendall observed several Mexican families living on the grounds within the walls. Although he considered the church's interior "plain," he remarked that the main western entrance was "surrounded with the most elaborate stone carving of flowers, angels, and apostles." He claimed that despite the length of time Texan troops were quartered at the mission, "the stone carvings have not been injured." Interestingly, Kendall also noted that San José had "been repaired, and Divine service is performed in it."[56] This would have been as an extension or visitation of the San Fernando Church, where the priest or his assistant came to San José on a regular (if not weekly) basis to minister to the people living there. Hence, the mission still served its religious function as sacred space.

Englishman William Bollaert arrived in Texas in 1842 and spent two years exploring the country with a mind to possibly make it his permanent home, carefully recording his impressions. As a foreigner, he was shown where Crockett, Travis, and Bowie allegedly fell and a clump of peach trees near the Alamo where the ashes of the Texan dead were said to have been buried. He remarked with some curiosity that stones from the Alamo were being used for a monument to the heroes as well as pipes for smoking tobacco, an early form of kitschy Alamo souvenirs. He tried his hand at making sketches of the Alamo ruins and believed that the Alamo chapel at one time had beautiful scrollwork on the facade. While making his sketches, an elderly Mexican woman who claimed to have known the defenders happened by. Looking at his drawings, she lamented, "Had you but seen the Alamo on a Feast Day, as I have seen it, not like it is now, in ruins, you would have been delighted. . . . I am glad you love the Alamo; I'll give you a crucifix made from the stone."[57]

The next day Bollaert and his party passed by Missions Concepción, San José, and Espada. He was sufficiently impressed to later note in his diary, "It is reviving to the European, to behold in the far West of the New World, edifices partaking the character of the sacred buildings he has left behind him; and we cannot withhold our praise from the Spanish ecclesiastics who designed and reared with the assistance of the Indians the churches." He described the architecture as a mix of Italian and Spanish and considered the ornamentation, statues and figures, and especially the scrollwork to be of "superior character." These impressions, recognizing the value of Indigenous laborers and beautiful Spanish Baroque, should not be casually dismissed because coming from an Englishman. In early October, Bollaert accompanied a party on a second excursion to the missions, but then he was able to look with a more critical eye. At Concepción, he complained about the odor of bat guano inside the church. San José also had a bat infestation, but Bollaert observed that "mass is occasionally said to some 8 or 10 Mexican families who live within the walls." He refined his earlier assessment of the style, mistakenly considering the churches "half Gothic." After visiting San Juan and Espada, the party retired to the sacristy of San José, where they enjoyed a convivial evening of wine and song.[58]

Upon his return to England, Bollaert published selected stories from his diary in British periodicals, often anonymously. In one example, he mentioned that members of his party smoked their souvenir "Alamo pipes" carved out of the soft rock from the Alamo. Bollaert described San Antonio as the "Thermopylae of Texas" and briefly explained the Alamo massacre to his British audience. He also described "descending into its romantic and picturesque valley" where the traveler would see Missions Concepción and San José. Bollaert informed his readers, "The turrets of these missions rise in solitary grandeur amid the forests of the west, forming an interesting feature in the scenery of that wild country."[59] The mission churches do not have "turrets" as might be found on a medieval English castle. Bollaert was probably aggrandizing and taking a bit of artistic license with the drums and domes of Concepción, San José, and possibly even San Fernando Cathedral in downtown San Antonio to embellish his narrative.

Peripatetic merchant Josiah Gregg spent several years traveling between Missouri and Mexico on business, but in 1846, as part of the Arkansas Volunteers, he arrived in San Antonio and recorded his opinions of the missions. The town of San Antonio de Béxar did not make a good first impression on Gregg. While he allowed that he had not expected much in the way of charm or culture in a frontier town, by the same token, "I did not expect to see so poor and wretched a looking place." He complained that the streets were "dirty, crooked, and narrow" and the houses were no better, being thatched roof *jacales* or "shabby looking" adobe. The missions, conversely, fared much better under his eye and through his pen. He noted the Alamo dimensions and that it retained some architectural detail in the facade. He also recorded "the roof rested upon an arch" but had since fallen in. At Concepción, the accumulation of bat guano prevented his exploration of the interior, but he did describe some of the exterior stonework and ornamentation. San José, on the other hand, utterly charmed him, and he observed that it was "the best piece of ancient architecture in this country." He waxed lyrical over the "sculptural elegance" of the facade with the "handsomely carved" figures (which he lamented had been horribly damaged by target practice). Gregg also estimated between 60 and 70 poor Mexicans living on the mission grounds. The chapels at San Juan and Espada were in ruins, but he estimated a total of 140 poverty-stricken Mexican residents living in the surrounding communities.[60] Even in a neglected state, the missions piqued the interest of tourists, as well as provided a home and community for the Mexican Americans living there.

The Missions and the Mexican War

Josiah Gregg was but one soldier on whom, on his way to the Mexican War, the missions made an indelible impression as he passed through San Antonio. As more US soldiers and the journalists following them marched through San Antonio on their way to invade Mexico, some recorded and published travelogues containing their impressions of the town and its attractions. Being a staging area for US troops heading south brought a level of stability, prosperity, and more important, curious attention to San Antonio. After the war that curiosity led to an increased number of visitors as well as immigrants as Anglo-Americans came to sightsee and to settle the newly gained territory.

One unnamed soldier-correspondent traveling with the First and Second Regiments of the Illinois Volunteers sent a series of reports to the popular *Niles National Register* magazine. He reported that his regiment had arrived in the San Antonio region in late August 1846. After a few days of camp life, the soldier described some of the sights encountered on their maneuvers, "and among these, I know of none more striking than the vestiges which now remain of the early Spanish settlements." He informed readers that while the missions were, at the time of his visit, "moss covered ruins," he emphasized that these had been the "only outposts of Christianity in the wilderness of savages." His stated reason for calling these buildings to readers' attention was that as he found them interesting, he believed "being now within the undisputed limits of our own country might prove worthy of the attention of tourists and travelers in general." While marching through the area, he encountered the "stupendous mission" of San José. After measuring the dimensions of the San José compound and buildings, he enthusiastically described the facade as "adorned with a richness of architecture and statuary so far superior to anything of its class among the religious edifices of our country that it strikes an American with awe and admiration." The sculptural elegance and aesthetic details on the exterior and interior of the chapel inspired this reporter to encourage fellow Americans to visit San Antonio in order to appreciate it for themselves.[61]

Although the Battle of the Alamo was widely reported in multiple newspapers shortly after it occurred in 1836, American troops again fighting Mexican foes ten years later gave some newspapers and magazines the excuse to revisit the massacre. One US Army officer in San Antonio claimed the "most interesting object however in the vicinity is the Alamo." He then launched into a lurid and highly embellished retelling of the Alamo siege in which Crockett, as last survivor, falls, making his last stand at the door of the Alamo chapel.[62] In printing dispatches received from Texas and Mexico, a New Hampshire newspaper printed a very abbreviated version claiming the town of San Antonio had been "defended to the last by Crocket [*sic*], Bowie, and about 200 other Texans, for three [*sic*] days, against Santa Anna's invading force. In the Alamo, the principal fortress, they sold their lives the dearest." And as an offhand comment for potential tourists or immigrants, "The climate is said to be delightful."[63] Poetry, no matter how maudlin and racist, could also find a home in some newspapers, such as the Georgia newspaper that published "Song of the Texan Ranger," which described all manner of graphic violence directed at the "Mexican herd" with the refrain, "The 'Alamo!' the 'Alamo!'—remember the word."[64] Reducing the enemies of the Alamo heroes (and Anglos in general) to a "herd" effectively dehumanized Mexican soldiers under Santa Anna in 1836, as well as in 1846. Unfortunately, the damaging effects of these racist sentiments affected interracial relations between Tejanos and Anglos for generations afterward. Nonetheless, some of the results of this short war with Mexico were the exposure to a wider, American audience of the interesting sights in San Antonio and the alteration of the Alamo facade to its current appearance.

How the Alamo Got Its "Hump" (with Apologies to Kipling)

Whether one considers it the "humped facade," a "gabled parapet," a "bell-shaped parapet," or the top of the quatrefoil motif seen at the other missions, the front facade of the Alamo chapel is arguably its most recognizable feature and has been prominently displayed in advertising San Antonio tourism up to the present day. However, the facade is also representative of the contentious relationship between collective memory and historical fact because at the time of the 1836 battle, the building's facade looked quite different. How the Alamo chapel acquired its unique facade is one of the more interesting but lesser-known tales of the missions that is often overlooked in the American imagination.

San Antonio made a convenient staging area for the US military as it prepared for its invasion of Mexico. Edward Everett, a sergeant and clerk for his unit, the First Regiment, Illinois Volunteers, arrived in San Antonio in August 1846 and made camp near the Alamo.[65] He described the Alamo as being "highly picturesque . . . and having an Oriental style, which might perhaps be traced to its derivation from the Moors of old Spain."[66] In a letter to his brother, Everett observed "the men making pipes out of the stone" taken from the Alamo ruins.[67] The regimental colonel assigned Everett and four others to collect information about the history and customs of the areas through which they traveled. Everett's drafting talents had been recognized, and he was specifically tasked with executing the drawings. He made sketches of the Alamo, but San José really captured his attention (fig. 2.1).

This mission, he noted, "was remarkable for its façade, which was elaborately carved in stone, scroll work, supporting statues of the Virgin and Saints, surrounding the entrance and central window. The workmanship was

Fig. 2.1. Mission San José. Drawn by Edward Everett, lithographed by C. B. Graham. Edward Everett Collection. Image and scan courtesy of the Cushing Memorial Library, Texas A&M University.

excellent, and the design unique and rich." He opined that the bell tower was a "rough Moresque style." Plants were growing on the walls and roof, "and though occupied as a church, it showed neglect of ordinary care" (fig. 2.2).[68]

On the night of September 11, 1846, Everett, as sergeant of the evening guard, was shot just above the knee during an altercation and crippled.[69] The injury prevented Everett from marching south with his unit. After a month in the hospital, Everett was reassigned to help the newly appointed assistant quartermaster, Captain J. H. Ralston. By early 1847, Ralston concluded that his current building was insufficient for their needs and began looking for something to better protect the various stores of materials. He considered the Alamo compound and charged Everett with making drawings, plans, and working up estimates to convert the Alamo chapel and nearby remaining buildings into a usable facility (fig. 2.3).

Despite his injury, Everett was able to make satisfactory recommendations to Ralston, who forwarded them up the military chain of command. Meanwhile, Ralston's immediate superior officer, Major Charles Thomas, quartermaster, contacted Bishop Jean Marie Odin in Galveston and secured his permission to remodel the buildings, as there was some question about

Fig. 2.2. Mission Concepción. Drawn by Edward Everett, lithographed by C. B. Graham. Edward Everett Collection. Image and scan courtesy of the Cushing Memorial Library, Texas A&M University.

whether the Catholic Church still owned the property. However, the army bureaucracy moved at a near-glacial pace, and Ralston had to proceed with some of the repairs and renovations without approval from Washington, DC, in order to protect some of the stores and material from the elements as well as thieves.[70]

When hostilities in Mexico ended in 1848, Everett, Ralston, and many other soldiers returned home. The army, however, maintained a presence in San Antonio and at the Alamo. A new quartermaster, Major Edwin Burr Babbitt, arrived in March 1849. Shortly thereafter, he sent a proposal to Quartermaster General Thomas Jessup in Washington, declaring the existing Alamo site inadequate for his needs. Babbitt recommended either razing the existing Alamo or acquiring other city property, but in either case, he planned to spend over $51,000 to construct the facilities he believed were needed. Jessup balked at the notion, ordering Babbitt to make repairs to the existing facilities since it was not clear how much land beyond the church belonged to the Catholic Church.[71] The work was delayed until 1850 because Babbitt and former San Antonio Mayor Bryan Callahan spent several months wrangling over the rent to be paid to the City of San Antonio (fig. 2.4).[72]

Fig. 2.3. Ruins of the Alamo, exterior. Drawn by Edward Everett, lithographed by C. B. Graham. Edward Everett Collection. Image and scan courtesy of the Cushing Memorial Library, Texas A&M University.

Fig. 2.4. Ruins of the Alamo, interior. Drawn by Edward Everett, lithographed by C. B. Graham. Edward Everett Collection. Image and scan courtesy of the Cushing Memorial Library, Texas A&M University.

Babbitt wanted a large arched roof built over the Alamo chapel to better protect the supplies and materials stored within. However, the existing facade wall was too short to provide the necessary support, so the quartermaster turned to architect John M. Fries, a recent immigrant from Germany, to design the structure.[73] There is some debate on the source of the inspiration for the "hump," or gabled parapet. Historian Kevin Young suggests Babbitt made the design recommendations when he specified the arched roof. Babbitt also added two second-floor windows to the front of the Alamo chapel at the same time.[74] Art historians Thomas Smith as well as Susan P. Schoelwer and Tom W. Gläser give more design credit to the architect Fries and his stonemason, David Russi.[75] Schoelwer and Gläser suggest that while Fries was familiar "with formal architectural styles, the sources of the design for the Alamo gable remain a puzzle. This simple arched gable, no doubt intended to at least echo the original façade design, actually seems more reminiscent of urban Dutch architecture than of Spanish Baroque ecclesiastical buildings." This speculation makes more sense given that Fries recently emigrated from Germany, where he probably had little opportunity to make a careful study of Spanish churches. Conversely, Smith argues that Fries may have copied the "hump" motif from the sacristy and *convento* walls at Mission San José.[76] Architectural historian Marshall S. McLennan, however, declares this shape is far from unique and offers numerous examples of how "the baroque parapet with a curvilinear or stepped gable devolved from the high-style rococo-baroque cathedrals" in Spain to the much more "simplified, minimal vernacular baroque parapets" seen throughout the American Southwest from the nineteenth century onward.[77] However, Smith's explanation that the "hump" or arch most resembles the top leaf of a quatrefoil, which is a frequently used design motif in the exterior sculpting, frescoes, and painted surfaces of San José, is most attractive. Although Babbitt may have wanted an arched roof, an archaeological report suggests what he got was a basic "frame gable roof" that was replaced in 1920.[78]

Edward Everett, back in civilian life, was not impressed with the changes and recorded as much in his journal: "There were no pretentions to ornamental architecture except in the façade of the church and portions of the interior." The surrounding buildings were removed or altered according to the army's needs "without remorse," but "the Church we respected as an historical relic and as such its characteristics were not marred by us." Despite this deference Everett and his crew gave the chapel, "I regret to see by a late engraving of this ruin that tasteless hands have evened off the rough walls as they were left after the siege, surrounding them with a ridiculous scroll, giving the building the appearance of the headboard of a bedstead." Nonetheless, Everett recognized that the alterations continued the functionality of the building and preserved it from destruction: "The care thus showed however questionable the taste of its exterior is highly commendable, when compared with the wanton destruction with which other curious buildings in the vicinity have been visited by relic hunters or other Vandals and iconoclasts."[79]

Everett was one of the more talented artists to make images of San Antonio's missions during this period. He later made watercolors, lithographs of which were included in a government report on the army's activities in San Antonio.[80] Art historian Richard Ahlborn commends Everett's watercolors on three levels: aesthetics, historical value, and "individual experience." During the mid-nineteenth century artists working in the American West ran the gamut in talent from exceptional to amateurish. He places Everett's ability to capture the buildings, as well as a feel for their settings, on the better end of the spectrum. Ahlborn suggests skilled and professional artists, including Everett, Seth Eastman, and Theodore Gentilz, who also created images of the San Antonio missions, actually helped preserve the missions by capturing their appearance at a given moment in time: "These artists not only preserved a contemporary record, but their depictions of the missions popularized and stimulated interest to the point that preservation of the original structures could begin." Finally, he suggests that Everett's "individual experience" was his scrupulous approach and demand for accuracy, as illustrated by his displeasure at the alterations Babbitt and Fries made to the Alamo chapel. Ahlborn concludes that Everett's legacy was to capture sensitive and "selective portrayals of historic buildings" that reflect foreign origins as the country rapidly expanded across the continent and consumed non-Anglo cultures.[81]

Additionally, Ahlborn asserts that Everett's images appeared in the popular journal *Gleason's Pictorial Drawing-Room* in 1854. However, this claim is problematic. The drawings in that journal were not credited to Everett or his lithographer Graham. Furthermore, the *Gleason's* images bear only a passing resemblance to Everett's lithographed images. The most glaring error is in the buildings' scale; the missions would be several stories tall based on the size of the people standing nearby, although perhaps this is a comment by the artist on the missions' importance (see fig. 2.5 and contrast with fig. 2.3). It is entirely plausible that the *Gleason's* image was merely a poor attempt at copying Everett's drawing, which the plagiarist attempted to conceal by adding the

104 GLEASON'S PICTORIAL DRAWING-ROOM COMPANION.

MISSION OF CONCEPCION, VALLEY OF THE BEXAR.

RUINS OF THE CHURCH OF EL ALAMO.

Fig. 2.5. "Bexar and Its Antiquities," *Gleason's Pictorial Drawing-Room Companion*, February 18, 1854, 104. Page image and scan courtesy of the Cushing Memorial Library, Texas A&M University.

carriage and people. Everett did not include people in his illustrations and, on the whole, demonstrates a much better comprehension of scale; Ahlborn had earlier remarked on his fidelity to the original. Otherwise, Ahlborn's assessment is absolutely correct: "The romance of the mission age had begun."[82]

While the debates over the source of inspiration for the curvilinear arch atop the facade of a ruined church building on the frontier may seem frivolous, the Alamo and its facade, as it currently appears, is nothing short of an icon. As Schoelwer and Gläser conclude, "Despite the parapet's artistic and historic anachronism, it was quickly and irrevocably assimilated into the authentic fabric of both the Alamo site and symbol . . . [illustrating] both the pervasiveness of mid-nineteenth century romanticism and the nascent influence of the Alamo legend."[83] The Alamo by Babbitt and Fries became "the Alamo" for the American collective memory.

The Missions Between the Wars

After the war, Mexico and the United States created a commission with representatives from both countries to explore, survey, and document what would eventually become the political boundary separating the two nations. Citizens of northern Mexico found themselves living on American soil and under American laws with no more effort than the stroke of a pen. Just as San Antonio had been a convenient staging area for the military moving south and west, it reprised that role for the Boundary Commission, headed by John Russell Bartlett. Furthermore, with Texas now firmly part of the United States, tourists and other explorers, spurred on by the concept of manifest destiny, arrived to see the newly won territory for themselves.

Who were these tourists and explorers? They came from a variety of walks of life. There were the famous, the not-so-famous, and even those-who-were-not-yet-famous, although most were drawn from the middle and upper classes.[84] In addition to the politician Bartlett, Frederick Law Olmsted, who would become a renowned landscape architect, ventured into Texas to proselytize on the virtues of free labor. Future US President Rutherford B. Hayes also visited the town in 1849. While at the Alamo he seemed rather disillusioned to find a "party of California emigrants cooking in the room where Crockett fell." He also described San Antonio's missions as "ruined castles with statuary, carved work, and painting, built for worship and defence in the most magnificent style; now in heaps of ruins affording shelter to bats, Mexicans, and venomous and filthy reptiles."[85]

Journalists attempting to describe San Antonio occasionally offered conflicting views within the same commentary. The Pittsfield, Massachusetts, newspaper reprinted an article from the New York *Journal of Commerce* describing a visit to San Antonio. Initially, the correspondent was far from captivated: "A week here gives me few pleasant impressions. The 'Americans,' perhaps one tenth of the population, are, as always, kind and hospitable, but all else is so strange, so purely Mexican and half barbarian." Yet after touring the missions, the author seemed on the verge of ecstasy: "I have visited the Old Missions. They are wonderful—almost too much for human credulity—these vast piles erected when the country was wilderness." Concepción, although "fast going to decay," still exhibited "traces of great beauty." But the grandeur of San José left the author awe-struck: "I have never seen a piece of architecture so astonishing." He described the facade as "embellished with the richest carvings from solid rock with countless figures, heavily gilded with silver, gold, and bronze. The doors are solid oak, with costly finish." The sanctuary suggested "tens of thousands of dollars having been expended in its embellishment," with carvings and paintings all of the highest quality and "exquisite workmanship." He even claimed the roof was strong enough to support cannon. Despite the mission's dilapidated state and bat infestation, the correspondent queried, "Who is not lost in wonder that these magnificent structures, which would do credit to any age and any people were built in a wilderness, inhabited by the most relentless savage, far away from civilization."[86] Was the correspondent so impressed with the missions that he lavished such adoration on them? Or did he decide the missions, as sole highlight, deserved the lion's share of praise to balance out his earlier negative experiences?

According to historian Patricia Nelson Limerick, John Russell Bartlett, appointed head of the US–Mexican Boundary Commission, was unfortunately a dilettante, a "bookseller, amateur scholar, and lay politician from Rhode Island" who was hardly up to the task of leading such an important and contentious group. His strengths lay in close observation and accurate rendition of flora and fauna, not in navigating the treacherous waters of human relations, team building, and international politics.[87] Despite his shortcomings, Bartlett was an optimist, and his published journals offered his observations and opinions regarding the territory newly incorporated into the United States.

As Bartlett and his party approached San Antonio, his first impressions were that it was a place of exotic beauty: "The place seems to be embowered in trees above which the dome of the church swells with an air quite Oriental." But this congenial view did not last as they made their way through "the filthy buildings of the Mexican suburbs to the plaza, or public square. The town is a strange mixture of massive old Spanish buildings and recent American structures." Nevertheless, Bartlett considered the town "delightfully situated" with plenty of fresh water and the capacity for hydraulic power if more mills could be built.[88] He believed the town had good potential, blessed with fertile land surrounding it, except for the Mexican population whom he callously wrote off as indolent. He perpetuated the generally held stereotypes of American energy overtaking Mexican slothfulness for economic and agricultural production. The fact that San Antonio had no railroad connection and depended on Mexican freighters was a serious drawback for future economic development in his estimation.[89]

While in San Antonio, Bartlett paid visits to the missions, beginning with the Alamo, considered "one of the principal objects of interest to the stranger in [town]." He remarked that the building had been remodeled for use as a storehouse by the US Army quartermaster and "retains little of its former appearance." However, he claimed that "the principal doorway, ornamented in the Moorish style, remains tolerably perfect."[90] He also recorded that "near the town and upon the banks of the San Antonio River are the remains of extensive mission establishments." Bartlett managed to visit San José, Concepción, and San Juan before leaving on his appointed commission. He opined that San José had been the "largest and wealthiest mission; and its buildings were constructed with greater display of art, and still remain in better preservation, than the others." The main entrance to the church itself "is surrounded by elaborate carving, which extends the whole length of the front, and includes numerous figures, among which San José, the patron of the church, and the Virgin and Child are conspicuous." He erroneously declared that the material used for the carvings was a type of "stucco." Bartlett lamented the vandalism from the various military forces over the years who found the ornamentation and statues convenient targets for firearms practice, which proved "their contempt for the Mexican belief." Bartlett additionally recorded the existence of remnant tracings and decorations in red and blue on the flat surfaces of the building. The pinnacle, however, was Rosa's Window: "The most perfect portion of the church is an oval window in the sacristy, which is surrounded with scrolls and wreathwork of exceeding grace and beauty." Unlike previous visitors who indicated the church was regularly used for Mass, Bartlett observed that San José was "seldom used for religious purposes; as the Mexicans of the neighborhood are poor and cannot often afford the fifty dollars charged by the San Antonio priests for officiating." Bartlett was disappointed in the other missions, indicating very little remained of San Juan to explore, and the day was fading quickly when he arrived at Concepción. He was disgusted at finding the sacred building being used as a barn for cattle, and between the accumulated filth and a noisy bat infestation, "we found nothing of interest to repay us for encountering their disagreeable presence."[91]

On the heels of Bartlett, another New England native, a young agriculturalist, fervent abolitionist, roving journalist, and future landscape architect named Frederick Law Olmsted made his way into Texas from New York. Keeping copious notes of his experiences, he later published accounts of his wanderings. As he journeyed south and west, Olmsted's writings revealed a typical amount of Northern chauvinism. Many travelers from the northern states described the South as "backward" and even potentially "dangerous," especially when contrasted against the North as the nation's "dominant cultural, political, and economic region."[92] Before Olmsted reached the German community of New Braunfels, Texas, he marveled "in the whole journey through Eastern Texas, we did not see one of the inhabitants look into a newspaper or a book, although we spent days in houses where men were lounging about the fire without occupation," and otherwise denigrated the victims of the soul-crushing poverty endemic to the population regardless of race. Conversely, once in New Braunfels, Olmsted believed himself in Germany and so much closer to Paradise than he had experienced after weeks on the road. The lodgings, food, and level of intellectual stimulation all met with his unqualified approval.[93] Olmsted believed that the Texas German population with its free labor and industry would be the state's saving grace and the example that all Texans should emulate. However much he might have been tempted to remain, the road called him farther south to San Antonio.[94]

Olmsted's initial impressions of San Antonio bear some semblance to a travel agent's description, hoping to inspire others to follow and share his experiences:

> We have no city, except, perhaps New Orleans, that can vie, in point of the picturesque interest that attaches to odd and antiquated foreignness, with San Antonio. Its jumble of races, costumes, languages and buildings; its religious ruins, holding to an antiquity, for us, indistinct enough to breed an unaccustomed solemnity; its remote, isolated, outposted situation, and the vague conviction that it is the

> first of a new class of conquered cities into whose decaying streets our rattling life is to be infused, combine with the heroic touches in its history to enliven and satisfy your traveler's curiosity.[95]

Finding the "picturesque" was a highly desired commodity for the nineteenth-century traveler, and giving San Antonio this designation would certainly boost tourists' interest. Similarly, the "jumble of races" Olmsted described reinforces the modern construct of the Borderlands region as a meeting ground for multiple cultures.[96] However, Olmsted's encounters and descriptions of the Tejano population as "brown idlers" reinforced widely held Anglo stereotypes as a foreign and exotic element and cast them as racial Others.[97]

Given that Olmsted is most famous for his landscape architecture and civic parks, his reaction to the missions is surprisingly reserved. His description of the missions did not drip with the saccharine superlatives of others, but instead Olmsted employed incisive understatement to great effect. He introduced them as "celebrated religious establishments," similar to those elsewhere in the American Southwest. He revealed an unexpected and overt sympathy for the Catholic friars whose "patient courage" eventually won over the Indigenous "cruel brutes" who lived there. As part of this conversion effort, they constructed these "ponderous but rudely splendid edifices." Olmsted noted that the Alamo was "a mere wreck of its former grandeur." But because of its role in 1836 and Texan independence, he insightfully described it as a "monument, not so much to faith as to courage." Olmsted noted, "They are in different stages of decay, but all are real ruins, beyond any connection with the present—weird remains out of a silent past." His comments at once confirm the authenticity of the missions that was important for travelers to find and distinguish the dead foreign past from the living Anglo present. Although he considered the missions "of various magnificence," contrasting to other visitors who rhapsodized over detailed sculptures, he expressed contempt at the "rude heads of saints" and lack of "grace" in the "mouldings." Nevertheless, Olmsted concluded, "Many is the picturesque sketch offered to the pencil by such intrusion upon falling dome, tower, and cloister."[98]

Like William Bollaert, Olmsted published selections from his journals in other popular media of the day. One of the reasons for Olmsted's journey south was for a series of letters to be published in the *New York Daily Times*.[99] The articles appeared between March 6 and June 7, 1854. However, the letters dedicated more space to debates of free labor versus slavery in Texas.[100] Conversely, some of Olmsted's adventures in San Antonio were published in

May 1857 in the journal *Friends' Review*, probably to help publicize his book about his trip to Texas.[101] While the extra publications may have generated additional revenue for the authors, there was also the added benefit of placing vivid descriptions of San Antonio as an exotic location with its picturesque architecture in front of more potential travelers.

Romantics at the Missions and Expansions of Print Technology

Despite the national convulsions leading to the Civil War, American tourists continued to find their way to San Antonio. Indeed, one author of the times suggested it was part of the national character: "We are a nation of travelers.... It is natural for an American to travel."[102] A local newspaper pleaded that the town really needed a top-quality hotel of "magnificent character." The journalist argued that no traveler can consider his trip to Texas complete without visiting San Antonio, claiming, "He wishes to see [the Alamo] before he dies," as well as the other missions. Because of the need to accommodate an anticipated increasing number of tourists, the author continued, San Antonio needed a hotel of sufficient status with which to link its identity. Just as New Orleans had its Saint Charles Hotel and New York had its Astor House, "San Antonio should have its 'Alamo House.'"[103] The town boosters understood that in linking tourist attractions and identity to enhance the attractiveness of the package, romance was the key. Whether describing having a pleasant picnic on the mission grounds or genuflecting at the room where Davy Crockett allegedly died, many visitors wrote about visiting the missions with ostentatious prose.

In addition to textual descriptions of the missions, nineteenth-century printing technology had sufficiently advanced to make it more cost-effective to include images printed from woodblocks engraved from sketches. These pictorial images were frequently no more accurate than written descriptions but did show the ruined state, the Baroque design, or both to the reading public. Changes in engraving techniques increased cost-effectiveness for printing images in weekly magazines, which in turn dramatically increased popularity and demand. The 1850s marked the time when illustrated periodicals began increasing in popularity in the United States, only to explode during the Civil War period with titles such as *Frank Leslie's Illustrated Newspaper* and *Harper's Weekly* leading the way.[104]

Although printed images supplemented text, flowery, Romantic prose still painted the most vivid images of the missions in the mid-nineteenth century.

A US Army officer reconnoitered San Antonio, perhaps as he made his way home from the Mexican War or as part of Bartlett's Boundary Commission, and described his encounters for *Graham's American Monthly Magazine.* Just below the article's title sat a dark, Gothic-looking image claimed to be the Alamo, "where the lamented Crocket [*sic*] fell." The author visited the Alamo and though mistaking the church for a "cathedral," claimed the surviving sculpting of column and saint "would do credit to some of the best European sculptors." Similar accolades were given to the facade of San José. Finally, overcome with his own inadequacy at describing the picturesque scene, the author invoked the Romantic hero poets and authors: "It was then we wished for the genius, the fire, and the conception of a Byron, a Scott, or a Stephens, that we might give vent to our feelings, and portray the beautiful prospect that surrounded us."[105]

After the Civil War's hostilities formally ended, Eastern journalists returned to the city. As one correspondent for *The New York Times* observed, San Antonio was "the largest and most delightful, as well as the most interesting city in Texas." He pointed out that "among the attractions of this city are the Convent, which is one of the most complete and thorough institutions of the kind in the country" (perhaps a reference to Mission San José). Similarly, he noted many of the buildings were constructed "in the Mexican style of architecture." Additionally, he described the Alamo: "Formerly an old Spanish convent, where in 1836, Santa Anna, after a successful siege butchered 188 Americans, including Davy Crockett." He said that at the Alamo there lived a "camp of Indians, who subsist by hunting, fishing, etc., and who dress fantastically and use the bow and arrow," whereas for the Mexican part of the city, he described "fandangos and other Mexican amusements."[106] Although the depictions of San Antonio were somewhat restrained when compared to other travel narratives describing the city and its attractions, the printed article reveals an interest in the city that survived the Civil War.

Celebrated Southern writer and poet Sidney Lanier journeyed west into Texas "as valet to his right lung," seeking relief from the tuberculosis he contracted in a Civil War prison camp.[107] Lanier arrived in San Antonio in February 1873 and wrote a lengthy essay that appeared in *Southern Magazine* that summer. His essay included a history of the town from its founding as a Spanish colony, through the turmoil of Mexican, then Texan independence, and wrapped up with current events as Lanier observed them. He was so taken with the picturesque nature of the city that he began his narration, "If peculiarities were quills, San Antonio de Bexar would be a rare porcupine."

The Romantic history (especially the 1836 Battle of the Alamo), the ethnic and cultural diversity, and varied climate all riveted his attention and provided ample fodder for his pen.[108] His comments on the city's diversity described "the queerest juxtaposition of civilizations, white, yellow (Mexican), red (Indian), black (negro), and all possible permutations of these significant colors," and he remarked that "religious services are regularly conducted in four languages, German, Spanish, English, and Polish." Like some earlier visitors, Lanier mentioned the Moorish influence on the sacred architecture in the town, which he discovered at the missions, "notable places about the town which the stranger must visit." He explored Concepción's roof before moving on to San José, which he stated was more ornate and lovely. Lanier concluded with a blissful and bucolic scene for his audience: "Religious services are regularly conducted here; and one can do worse things than to steal out here from town on some wonderfully calm Sunday morning, and hear a mass, and dream back the century and a half of strange, lonesome, devout, hymn-haunted and Indian-haunted years that have trailed past these walls."[109]

Following Lanier was a journalist for *Scribner's Monthly*, Edward King. Similar to Frederick Law Olmsted, King recorded sights and scenes as he traveled throughout the Southern states. He published excerpts in the widely read magazine *Scribner's Monthly*, as well as compiling his narrative into a monograph, *The Great South*.[110] King's descriptions of San Antonio and Texans was an attempt by certain Northern factions to extend the olive branch to Southern elites after the horrors of war and disappointments of Reconstruction. His narrative takes the reader by stagecoach from Austin down to San Antonio. Like Lanier, he captured the colorful dialect of the stagecoach driver and others, adding spice and interest to the tale. The thirty-two illustrations included Concepción, the ornate facade of San José (incorrectly identified as San Juan), the sacristy window of San José (Rosa's Window), and the Alamo. Also similar to Lanier, King included a detailed but heavily romanticized history of San Antonio from colonial times to the time of his visit. He described the "old San Antonio road" as "the most romantic route upon the western continent" for over a century and a half.[111]

King described the missions with much more detail than Olmsted did. Like other visitors, he remarked on the "Moorish spirit" behind Concepción's decor, perpetuating the exotic and Orientalist vision of the region.[112] At San José he lamented, "Mute, mighty, passing beautiful,—it is rapidly decaying; and the government should not willingly let it crumble into dust. The Catholic Church in Texas, to whom the missions and the mission lands now belong, is too poor to attempt the restoration of this superb edifice." King also asserted, "One of the most famous of Parisian architects, in a recent tour through this country, pronounced the mission the finest piece of architecture in the United States." He did not identify or suggest who this famous architect might have been, leaving many future authors to simply repeat the assertion and perpetuate the mystery. In a similarly questionable assertion, King claimed that the reigning monarch of Spain "sent an architect of rare knowledge and genius to superintend its erection. This architect, Huizar, finally settled in Texas, where his descendants still live."[113] James Ivey claims that this mention of Huizar as having been sent directly by the king of Spain is one of the earliest published instances of the romanticized Huizar legend.[114] Other variants on the legend would follow shortly afterward. King named the Alamo "the shrine to which every pilgrim to this strange corner of America must do utmost reverence. As mission-church and fortress, it is venerable, and has been so baptized in blood that it is world famous." He criticized the army's repurposing of the Alamo as a depot for materials: "The government, which would use Washington's tomb for a store-house, rather than build a proper one, if Mount Vernon were a military depot, has cumbered it with boxes and barrels."[115] King was probably not alone in the sentiment that trying to look beyond the army's mundane stores detracted from the reverence due a proper memorial to the martyrs of this American Thermopylae.

King's penchant for emphasizing the abundant natural resources in Texas begging to be exploited by capitalists is reminiscent of the booster literature of the 1840s. Just as earlier depictions of Texas as a new "Garden of Eden" included Romantic descriptions of the missions, King also included romanticized textual images at the same time he encouraged capitalistic exploitation of bountiful resources. King's call for new, energetic, and well-funded people to come and exploit Nature's bounty much more resembled the earlier booster materials. King's and Lanier's "local-color" writing style, interjecting conversations and quaint sayings in unusual dialects, is certainly more enjoyable to read than Kennedy or Kendall, whose style, despite the layer of superlatives, was often a dry recitation of facts, climatic data, and estimated population numbers. King and Lanier should therefore be credited with bringing more literary appeal if not grace to booster literature in the second half of the nineteenth century. Nonetheless, the effect is still that of the booster, to bring people (and their money) to Texas.

Many of the travel narratives and booster publications from this time period described the mission buildings as crumbling or in dilapidated shape.

In December 1868, part of the north wall of the chapel of San José collapsed, severely weakening the remaining portions. Church services were then moved from the main sanctuary to the sacristy. However, during Christmas Eve Midnight Mass in 1874, most of the remaining roof, dome, and vault came crashing down.[116] These validate James Ivey's observation: "The late nineteenth century has been traditionally viewed as the 'period of neglect' or the 'era of decline,' and the missions popularly thought of as deserted ruins."[117] The missions were indeed in dire shape, but they had not been completely abandoned, nor were they ever completely forgotten. Although no longer serving only the original Native American populations for which they were founded, the mission churches remained as shelter and sacred space for the local Tejano population (which was largely made up of assimilated mission Indians and their Mexican neighbors). Unlike the Alamo, the church buildings survived two Mexican invasions and the Mexican-American War and were fortunate that no hostilities occurred on the grounds. The US Army, with the assistance of Edward Everett, Major Edwin Babbitt, and John Fries, had converted the Alamo into a serviceable warehouse whose romantic history completely eclipsed its mundane function. Local Bishop Odin's plans for the missions as sacred space hinged on recruiting either the Society of Mary or the Benedictines to move in so he could reclaim the buildings for educational purposes. And that Mass was being sung at San José as late as 1874, when the roof collapsed, attests that the facilities were still used as sacred space.

As Ivey presciently states, "The romantic view of the abandoned mission in the wilderness, prevalent in the late nineteenth century, would apparently have been diminished by such an observation [of people actually living in close proximity to or regularly using the missions for religious services]."[118] Nonetheless, the Tejano population of San Antonio was being colonialized by these narratives; their contributions at the 1836 Battle of the Alamo were silenced, and their poor living conditions turned them into tourists' spectacle. These colonialist mentalities not only persisted but were also exploited to market San Antonio and the missions to tourists well into the next century. Indeed, it is precisely these romanticized views and depictions of the missions during this period that would soon be most effective in advertising the railroad and promoting travel to San Antonio as an attractive destination. It is this image of the lonely, ruined mission, then, that was passed down to the tourists.

Travel narratives, including those written by Frederick Law Olmsted, Edward King, and others from the more urbane sections of the United States, appeared in popular magazines such as *Harper's* and *Scribner's* and sometimes exhibited colonialist attitudes toward the South and Southwest. Flush with the purple prose of the Romantic movement, these narratives contributed to Anglo collective memories as they created a mythological Spanish past, an imagined Franciscan "errand into the wilderness." The authors of these narratives began a process that eventually culminated in the construction of a dominant American identity that looked on the missions as ancient relics of a dead past. Numerous references to "Moorish" or "Oriental" design features "Orientalized" the missions in the collective memories, particularly those of (mostly urbane and elite) tourists. Likewise, there were numerous references in travel narratives to San Antonio as an "ancient" villa, which lent an air of authenticity to the ruins and compounded the mysterious and exotic aura tourists found so attractive. Although seen as a foreign past, as sites of memory the missions became an important symbolic part of San Antonio's history as it transitioned into the Anglo-American nation. After 1877, when the railroad finally arrived in San Antonio, these exotic interpretations of the missions would be a very successful formula for travel writing and marketing.

3

Arrival of the Iron Horse in San Antonio, 1877–1890s

ON FEBRUARY 6, 1877, the *San Antonio Daily Express* crowed, "Achieved at Last—San Antonio a Railroad City," as the Galveston, Harrisburg, and San Antonio (GHSA) rail line reached town.[1] A local journalist invited "the world to our city," which he dubbed an "Elysium Field" destined for greatness.[2] Two weeks later when regular passenger service opened, the celebration lasted several days as the town was flooded with important railroad officers in addition to civic leaders from the state and municipalities along the line. The Menger Hotel, considered the finest in town, was decorated appropriately for the occasion and played host to the main celebrations. Another local reporter observed that "even the dark and frowning old Alamo brightened up and seemed to come out of the gloom of its ancient tragedies and partake of the cheerful influence of" the festivities going on in the town.[3] During the celebrations, a number of the visitors, eager to see the notable sights of San Antonio, made their way to the missions. A local newspaper reported that some of these tourists "inscribed their names upon the old grey walls." Given the festive spirit of the time, however, the writer seemed willing to overlook the vandalism, suggesting that their progeny might return and point with pride to the proof their ancestors had been present for such a momentous occasion.[4] This chapter explores the impact of the dramatic influx of tourists in the late nineteenth century and their ongoing national and international reframing of the stories of the San Antonio missions, particularly as the stories appeared in the expanding print culture. Readers of the illustrated press consumed a narrative that defined American identity as Anglo, Protestant, and male from the middle to upper classes. Understanding how this narrative was constructed requires a close and critical reading of the travel narratives and descriptions of San Antonio, the missions, and the city's multicultural population. The descriptions, images, and cultural references within the expanding print culture take on an added level of importance as these both illustrated and contributed to the creation of collective memories relating to American identity.

The relative ease with which travelers of the day could hop a train in the cultured centers of the Northeast and just a few days later be deposited on San Antonio's dusty streets brought more wide-eyed tourists to the American Southwest. Railroads and local boosters promoted travel to the region through advertisements, brochures, and guidebooks, hoping to sell land to westward-bound immigrants in addition to tourists' fares. People from the urbane Northeast consumed these materials published as tourist guidebooks and travel narratives in popular periodicals and newspapers of the day. Based on the frequency with which San Antonio's missions appeared in these published travel narratives, they obviously remained popular tourist attractions. Visitations and subsequent publications describing the missions provided ample opportunity for the proliferation of collective memories within the American imagination. Through the expansion of both print culture and tourism, collective memories related to the missions acquired an increasing role in shaping the larger narratives related to the creation of an American national identity.[5] In these collective memories, the missions represented a romantic and exotic past that Anglo-Americans exploited as they constructed a national identity during pivotal decades while the country lurched to a more urbanized and industrialized economy. Within this narrative, Anglo tourists frequently marginalized the local Tejano population, depicting them as a benighted "Other."[6]

The expansion of the railroad to San Antonio brought new opportunities and wealth to some but discomforts to others, including San Antonio's Tejano population. Many of the local Tejano businessmen began selling the choice commercial lots around San Antonio's main plazas near the time of the railroad's arrival because "they had fallen into debt or because they thought it best to move."[7] Three years before the railroad's arrival, a correspondent for *The New York Times* accused the "older Mexican families" of the city, upon hearing a rail line would be built to the town, of predicting disasters, including "epidemics, fevers and all manner" of similar evils. The correspondent reproached them for retreating to their bucolic estates to remain as the world passed by rather than embracing the new opportunities.[8] Historian David Montejano notes that many Mexican American businessmen removed their operations to west of San Pedro Creek to avoid the "new business methods and banks" that enforced strict time limits on mortgages and other Americanized business practices.[9] Such retreats also had the unfortunate effect of reinforcing Anglo stereotypes of Tejanos as a backward people uninterested in commerce.

The New York correspondent who accused the Tejanos of superstition and backwardness at the same time issued a direct appeal for special care and preservation of the Alamo and the other missions. He clearly recognized the value of these picturesque and romantic old buildings. The approaching rail lines promised to bring tourists who would delight in visiting "one of the most celebrated of the shrines of American liberty" and introduce "some of the most noted bits of architecture on the continent, and the finest in the United States." The journalist implored, "If San Antonio must be transformed from a dreamy and charmingly antique town into a bustling fashion and health resort, . . . let the Missions, whatever happens to other remnants of the past, be saved." This writer warned that while it was pleasant to dream that in remote parts of the United States, some "ghost of a dead romantic past lingered, never to be frightened away" by the inexorable advance of modernity, the attractions the mission buildings held for tourists would exist only as long as the physical remains did.[10]

The Alamo's status as a site of memory rested primarily on the 1836 battle that occurred there.[11] The other San Antonio missions became sites of memory based on something that would become a hallmark of the American Southwest, a notion derided by California journalist Carey McWilliams as a "fantasy heritage." In this mythical interpretation of history Anglo-Americans were the true heirs of a bounteous land where most aboriginal inhabitants had conveniently died off or assimilated as peons into the relatively more advanced Spanish society as a result of the efforts of saintly mission friars. The other Spaniards were dons, who lived as idle rich in the comfort of their extensive haciendas, staying out of the way of the Anglos. The intervening Mexican period was conveniently overlooked. Although McWilliams did not coin the phrase until the mid-twentieth century, adding the trope of saintly friars bringing the blessings of European civilization to peaceful Native Americans at the Spanish missions (either in McWilliams's California or in San Antonio), the concept already had taken a firm hold on the American imagination in this period.[12]

Travel Narratives, Print Culture, and Constructing an American Identity

"Travel narratives" are synonymous with "representations of travel" and include guidebooks, published travelers' accounts, and travelogues appearing in popular magazines and newspapers of the day.[13] Landscape historian Herbert Gottfried endorsed the scholarly value of travel narratives, noting that "guide books and viewbooks are material manifestations of American culture." Many travel narratives consulted for this chapter also include historic-based articles and historic fiction (often romantic and embellished). Gottfried notes these "historical references remind tourists that American places have a past, and those local historic persons, places, things and events have the capacity to add indications of authenticity to a location."[14] Another vitally important function of the guidebook was to mediate the sights for the viewers, "to instruct" tourists in "what to see and how to see it."[15] Despite the advances in transportation technology that railroads represented, cross-country travel primarily for leisure continued to be limited to middle- and upper-class white tourists. Nevertheless, aided by increasingly illustrated travel narratives published in popular magazines, newspapers, and guidebooks, others could still enjoy the touristic experience vicariously through armchair travel and similarly construct their own imagined identity.[16] Indeed, some women of this age participated in travel clubs by which they engaged in fictional (comparable to "armchair" or "vicarious") travels. The clubs studied specific places and cultures around the world through extensive bibliographies, guest lectures, and visual media, as if preparing for an actual physical journey. Whether physical or purely vicarious, "travel became a way to escape the tedium of everyday life, projecting oneself into an exotic milieu."[17] Certainly, vicarious travel through the consumption of travelogues became but one manner in which those without money and time for leisure travel could indulge in exotic travel fantasies. Nonetheless, where the information disseminated in these guidebooks was faulty or overly embellished for dramatic effect, it resulted in some memories being constructed on false and unreliable foundations.

Many of the travel narratives recommending the missions as interesting San Antonio tourist attractions appeared in popular magazines and major newspapers published in the urban Northeast. These periodicals, including *Scribner's Monthly* (retitled *Century Illustrated* shortly after it began publication), *Harper's Weekly* (and *Harper's New Monthly*), and *Frank Leslie's Illustrated News*, brought news, opinion, fiction, and adventure to increasing numbers of readers as advances in technology of printing, illustrating, and papermaking allowed print culture to expand exponentially.[18] Through magazines such as *Century* and *Harper's* Northeastern elites attempted to "guide and improve the taste, manners, and behavior of America's middle, and sometimes, lower classes." Unlike some of their competitors, the editors of *Scribner's/Century* intentionally set out "to create a diverse yet unified image of America" through fostering native writers. However, this "unified image" remained decidedly white, "middle- and upper-middle-class readers who shared the editors' views and values." Even with such a limited audience, this magazine alone easily circulated to nearly one million people.[19] Sociologist Matthew Schneirov emphasized the importance of these periodicals, which were read by "educated middle-class Americans" and "helped shape the thinking and tastes of a generation of readers" between 1865 and 1900. The effects of this expansion of print culture cannot be underestimated, as "popular magazines, more than any other medium, seemed to represent 'America' itself."[20]

Readers of the illustrated press consumed a particular narrative that the magazines and newspapers offered. The significance of the elite audience consuming these magazines is reflected in the narratives, identities, and collective memories attached to the Alamo and other missions. Because of the potential for bias, historian Alan Trachtenberg's observation regarding the usefulness of these kinds of resources becomes all the more important: "Figures of speech, tropes, images, metaphors . . . are vehicles of self-knowledge of the concepts upon which people act."[21] Employing Trachtenberg's method to study San Antonio's missions requires a close and critical reading of the travel narratives and descriptions of San Antonio, the missions, and the city's multicultural population. The descriptions, images, and cultural references within the expanding print culture take on an added level of importance as these both illustrated and contributed to the creation of collective memories as they related to American identity.

The reactions of early railroad tourists and dignitaries such as Oscar Wilde to the missions illustrate the continued appeal of using overly sentimental prose in these travel narratives. Between the boosters' boasting and syrupy romance that characterized this genre of literature, accuracy frequently took second priority to superlatives and hyperbole. Some of the tales about the missions printed within this environment became integral parts of current mission legends. Through examining these "representations of travel," we are better able to appreciate how "writers and artists" from the Eastern United states engaged with and comprehended the Southwest.[22] Travel and identity fed each other, as "the process of modern nation-building must incorporate the exploration of the areas within the borders and the creation of a hegemonic national culture."[23] Because the Southwestern Borderlands contained significant populations deemed "foreign" to begin with, the establishment of a dominant society in that region of the country was not accomplished quite so easily; but because foreign "Others" existed within the boundary of the nation, it became even more vital for Anglos to incorporate this region into the national narrative in a palatable manner.

Tourism, whether in the form of the nascent tourist industry of hoteliers, railroads, or steamboats or in the form of actual travelers and armchair tourists, was an important connection between San Antonio's missions and the creation of memories and identities. Historian Marguerite Shaffer warns us not to underestimate the importance of this connection:

> As the tourist infrastructure expanded, public and private tourists' advocates worked together to develop a canon of American tourist attractions that manifested a distinct national identity. They encouraged white, native-born, middle- and upper-class Americans to reaffirm their American-ness by following the footsteps of American history and tradition across the American landscape, defining an organic nationalism that linked national identity to a shared territory and history.[24]

Some writers and promoters of the time already considered the Alamo part of this American canon, but this period cemented its position as an important site of memory within the wider Anglo-American narrative, a narrative Shaffer argues was "part of a larger dialog about personal and public memory as well as individual and national identity."[25]

Historians describe the closing of the nineteenth century and the opening of the twentieth as a chaotic period of great societal and economic unease. One of the sources of this unease was the manner in which democracy extended into the lower ranks, particularly through "the rise of the big city machines" that were sustained by the purportedly ignorant immigrant labor class and shook the elites' power structure.[26] On the other hand, these elites took some comfort in the travel narratives published in the pages of illustrated periodicals or through their own active tourism. As Shaffer observes, in these travel articles, minorities and lower classes were characterized as "Others" who became part and parcel of the tourists' "spectacle," which "further allowed tourists to define and distinguish their social status."[27] If socioeconomic changes in the North and East were part of the source of elite discontent at this time, where might solace be found? The West. Trachtenberg points out the attraction of the mythic West in dime novels, which "served as an image of contrast to Eastern society."[28] Even though the elites might not have been the primary readers of these dime novels, historian John Sears also points out that the American West of the closing decades of the nineteenth century "was a place of wonders and curiosities in which fact and fiction, history and theater, actual and staged events were blurred together. It was a tourist's West."[29] And because most tourists were elites, tourist sites catered to that particular demographic and their sensibilities.

Romantics at the Missions (Again)

Once the railroad arrived, its web of iron and steel bound San Antonio to the rest of the nation, bringing curious travelers and tourists in its cars. Although the Romantic movement was waning, this early period of rail travel to San Antonio brought plenty of people still under its influence. They rhapsodized about the picturesque city, its foreign atmosphere, and the quaint ruins of the missions. Melodramatic tales of the Alamo massacre still held wide appeal despite an attempt by R. M. Potter in 1878 to publish a more accurate account. Even then, he felt compelled to preface his article with the disclaimer, "When horror is intensified by mystery, the sure product is romance."[30]

The October 1877 issue of *Harper's New Monthly Magazine* introduced San Antonio, its new railroad, and its missions to the magazine's national audience. The article contained eighteen high-quality illustrations, many of which were of the missions. The luxurious prose described the romantic passage along the GHSA's "Sunset Route" from Houston to San Antonio as a journey through endless fields of innumerable flowers. The author assured readers that although still within the North American continent, "San Antonio is, in fact, a Spanish town today, and the only one where any considerable remnant of Spanish life exists in the United States," where "land is still measured here by the vara" and "Spain is at the foundation of the whole of it."[31] The town, its population, and the missions were thus wrapped up in sentimental prose and presented to readers as some foreign and exotic place. Similarly, the writer emphasized San Antonio's romantic "Spanish-ness" throughout the article rather than permit it to be inhabited by Mexican Americans.

The author Orientalized all the missions through extravagant prose suggesting Moorish origins and design. Missions Concepción and San José were described in the most detail since more of those structures remained visible. Missions San Juan and Espada, by this time, were mostly in ruins, "a melancholy haunt of poetry and dreams." The two dark towers and domed roof of Concepción contrasted with the "luminous" sky, and "its existence is a romance, its condition a mystery, and a vague pathos haunts its broken arches."[32] San José was considered even more beautiful and intriguing, although the author erroneously claimed the building's style originated with the Jesuits culminating in Louis "Quatorze" (Louis XIV). The author lamented that the ornate facade was intricately designed with a plethora of scrolls, cherubs, and flowers but ruined by vandals over time. The walls still retained traces of what originally had been brightly colored frescoes of blue and vermillion. Divine service was held weekly in the sacristy since the sanctuary was in ruinous condition. The mention of weekly Mass reinforces that local parishioners still valued the missions during this period as sacred space. Neither was the Alamo exempt from the embellishments. Although the *Harper's* author incorrectly identified it as the last mission built, and despite its lowly status as a storehouse for the US Army, the writer insisted that "the Texan visits it as a shrine, and thrills with pride in a history that is more to him than all the Monmouths and Lexingtons and Cowpens and Yorktowns of the Revolution." The correspondent's rhetoric elevated the tragedy of the Alamo martyrs and the glory of Sam Houston and his brave Texians at San Jacinto to that of a Homeric epic.[33]

The correspondent for *Harper's* painted a glowing and romantic picture of the missions but also emphasized the importance of the missions for the Anglo-American culture beyond mere aesthetics:

> These missions have an interest for us quite apart from their beauty, for they stand up in their solitude and decay, still giving silent testimony to the immense debt that we, as a people, owe today to the old conquistadores of Spain. They are a part of the visible romance of our country too. . . . The monks of these missions, moreover, were those who opened to the world the resources of this great empire of the West; with their patience and labor . . . they cleared the way for a new power among the peoples of the earth.[34]

Although the author acknowledged the Spanish contributions to the new American Empire, her understanding and her descriptions were nonetheless filtered through this lens of a mythological Spanish past. And she expected her audience to construct their identities as the "new power among the peoples of the earth" accordingly.

Five years later, the Southern Pacific Company reproduced this *Harper's* piece almost in its entirety in a booklet describing the sights and scenes to thrill tourists traveling its Star and Crescent and its Sunset lines from New Orleans to California.[35] These melodramatic descriptions retained enough appeal that Southern Pacific was willing to negotiate with *Harper's* for permission to reproduce it in their own marketing literature. Texas, as historian Richard Orsi noted, was "portrayed as an incipient paradise where civilization was replacing the fading frontier."[36] Twenty-first-century readers may sneer at this purple prose or dismiss its overt sentimentality, but for this time period, such embellishment was the mode of the day. Were this *Harper's* article the only discussion of San Antonio's missions that treated them to such romanticized descriptions, it might be possible to write it off as one author's flight of fancy. However, many of the descriptions found for this book tend to be variations along similar themes, suggesting through a preponderance of evidence that the romanticized image of the missions would dominate in readers' collective memories.

Although Irish celebrity and dandy Oscar Wilde had a complicated relationship with the Romantic movement in literature and the arts, his visit to San Antonio inspired comments that could easily fall into a "Romantic" category. Wilde's flamboyant personality and outspoken advocacy for aesthetics embodied some of the cultural dissonance associated with this period. Wilde arrived in San Antonio in June 1882 as part of a lecture tour through the United States. Interviewed by the *New Orleans Daily Picayune* shortly after his Texas adventures, he gushed over how much he enjoyed San Antonio. In the city he "found more to please [him] in the beautiful ruins of the old Spanish mission churches and convents, and in the relics of Spanish manners and customs impressed upon the people and the architecture of the city."[37] The archaic mission ruins struck him as being in such contrast to a youthful American national character. He exclaimed, "Those old Spanish churches with their picturesque remains of tower and dome, and their handsome carved stonework, standing amid the verdure and sunshine of a Texas prairie, gave me a thrill of strange pleasure."[38] Although Wilde endured constant criticism throughout his American tour, his celebrity status and his comments regarding the beauty of the Spanish missions corresponded with the sentiments expressed by many Romantics who came before and followed him.[39]

During the 1880s and 1890s, people continued to come to San Antonio and continued publishing sentimentalized descriptions and images of the missions. In its July 1883 issue, *Frank Leslie's Popular Monthly* author, Mrs. V. T. Polk, proclaimed, "To those interested in antiquities and art, perhaps there is no field in our country which presents greater attraction than the historic city of San Antonio and vicinity." Although Polk's historical sketch of the missions contained some embellishments, her inclusion of names of known Spanish officials along with names of Indian tribes that joined the missions gave her article a more authentic air than earlier depictions, most of which mentioned Indigenous peoples and Spaniards only in the abstract. She described the overall aesthetic of the missions as "Spanish Moresque" and referenced San José's ornate facade (lamenting the damage wrought by vandals) as being "one of the most beautiful pieces of ornamental stonework to be seen anywhere." Polk contributed to the mythology of the missions by repeating a church legend claiming the stone intended for the facade of San José had been "transported overland from some distant port, probably Vera Cruz, on the shoulders of the faithful Indians, who vied with each other in claiming the privilege of transporting material for the erection of a temple to the Almighty God."[40] Polk was particularly impressed with the acoustic qualities of the large dome of Mission Concepción and claimed that "a whisper can be heard in almost any part of the room." She also noted that there were "quite a number" of Mexican families living on the grounds and that services were still conducted on an occasional basis.[41] The instances of Mexican Americans living on mission grounds were frequently mentioned as casual observations by many of these nineteenth-century sources, which reveals a measure of how the missions' physical remains continued to serve not only as a house of worship but also as a community center for those families living in the immediate vicinity.

Popular magazines such as *Harper's* and *Frank Leslie's* were not the only periodicals to print travel narratives describing the missions. Newspapers also printed similar stories. Occasionally visitors who happened to be traveling to, or through, San Antonio would pen a description for their local newspaper. The Romantic rhetoric came through even if these ersatz journalists were not intentionally embellishing their story for greater appeal. Such was the case of a Baptist missionary from Georgia who described San Antonio's verdant beauty and foreign character. The city was "a Spanish town yet, and the only one in the United States where any considerable remnant of Spanish life exists."[42] The correspondent described the missions, emphasizing their defensive roles, which led to a recounting of the 1836 Battle of the Alamo.

In this particular rendition of the battle, Travis and his compatriots of fewer than 150 men inflicted the astounding casualty rate of over 25 percent on Santa Anna's army of 4,000 just in the siege alone, even before the final storming of the fortress. The seemingly obligatory comparison to Thermopylae was repeated, and the author noted the State of Texas had recently purchased the Alamo building to preserve it from relic hunters (which included a member of the author's own party).[43]

Major newspapers, including *The New York Times*, also printed articles from travelers, but whether they commissioned the travel narratives or simply received them from tourists is rarely discernible, as in the case of an 1887 visit. Despite some glaring inaccuracies, an appearance in the *Times* nevertheless had the effect of bringing San Antonio and the missions to the attention of arguably the nation's largest and most important cultural center. The Alamo's aesthetics originally made a negative impression in that the "building attracts by its ugliness." But the supreme sacrifice by the defenders made up for its lack of beauty, even if the author mistakenly asserted that the 1836 "fight of extinction ended on the roof." Later, when describing San José, the writer claimed, "In some of the arches is found a red brick and the curious feature about it is that such brick is not made to-day, as it is not known where the clay is to be found. . . . They are a constant source of wonder to Texans."[44]

Travelers from Europe, the correspondent opined, had frequently looked down their noses at the youthful American nation and its lack of "ruins." However, this journalist argued that San Antonio's mission ruins gave Americans more credibility and a greater sense of history to throw back in the faces of pompous Old World visitors. "A more complete set of ruins than the old Mexican missions of San Antonio it would be difficult to find in the most debilitated state in Europe," the journalist boasted, although at the same time admitting that the missions had not originally been built within US boundaries but in territory later captured through military conquest. Nonetheless, the missions, particularly as ruins, appeared much older than they were, as the writer observed: "If [Concepción] stood on the banks of the Rhine the guide book might quote its age as 500 or 1000 years and be believed." Similarly appealing was the ornate facade of San José with its "carvings and paintings." Finally, the correspondent assured readers that "the ruins are worth seeing, and visitors often spend days in examining them."[45] This allure of "missions as ruins" reinforced theories put forward by both archaeologist James Ivey and historian Phoebe Kropp, who posits, "The more anachronistic the missions appeared, the more precious was their romance, and thus the more popular they became. This kind of tourism exoticized the past by casting missions as products of a distant age and a foreign people."[46] Although Kropp was writing about the California missions, her concept is equally valid for those in San Antonio.

Travel narratives also appeared in newspapers published outside the Northeast metropolis, such as Atlanta and Philadelphia. A journalist for the *Atlanta Constitution* traveled to San Antonio in 1891. His illustrated article referenced the Alamo's identity as "Thermopylae of the Texans," as well as the Spanish Crown's role in building the missions, which included sending "the celebrated artist Huica [*sic*]," who "devoted several years to carving its various ornamentation."[47] Two years later, another Atlanta correspondent described visiting "quaint old Santone . . . one of the quaintest towns on the continent." This journalist, perhaps reflecting a streak of chauvinism, was put off by the cosmopolitan and multicultural population encountered and made disparaging remarks on the observed lack of personal and public morals. But, the journalist claimed, the Alamo was the "first resort of every stranger" who visited the city.[48] The Alamo's claim as a tourist attraction of national interest remained strong. A Philadelphia journalist concurred as he traveled on Southern Pacific's line from New Orleans to San Francisco: "San Antonio is the city of the Alamo, and the visitor is not allowed to forget it during his stay. . . . Alamo stores, Alamo saloons, Alamo relics and Alamo gimmicks meet him at every turn."[49] Local merchants had obviously learned to take advantage of associations with the town's most famous landmark, but this journalist suggested they had taken it too far into the realm of kitsch.

Author Margaret Kennedy visited San Antonio for *Peterson's Magazine* and began her travel narrative by assuring her readers that "no city in the United States is so quaint and picturesque as San Antonio, Texas." As proof of its venerable condition, she claimed that the missions were erected in 1718, "fourteen years before the birth of Washington." Even as she referenced US Founder George Washington, she emphasized San Antonio's foreign and exotic nature. Flores Street conjured thoughts of Venice, and on all streets, tourists could observe "queer Mexican customs" and habits of dress. "But the object of most general interest in San Antonio," Kennedy states, "is the Alamo, fitly called 'The Thermopylae of Modern Times.'" Her altering the original "Thermopylae of Texas" away from its status as a regional icon to one of more general interest reflected the broadening appeal of the Alamo heroes among Anglo-Americans and brought this frontier outpost firmly under US control. Her graphic imagery of the "wholesale butchery" that accompanied the fall, including seven survivors, was another "bloody shirt" justifying Anglo conquest. Although with little justification, she assured readers the battle damage had been repaired and "the carvings on the façade are still beautiful."[50]

Kennedy opined, "No one should leave the 'Alamo City' without visiting Concepción and San José Missions." She described Concepción's architectural design as "Christianized Moorish" and said that this mission had been built on a "far more magnificent scale than the Alamo," to the point of being considered "'one of the noblest churches ever erected in America.'"[51] She noted that services were again being conducted in the church, which reflected its continued importance to the diocese and local parishioners as sacred space. Kennedy was so enraptured by Concepción that "words cannot describe the beauty of a lofty dome. . . . Although severely plain, such is its grace and majesty that one stands enchanted and can scarcely leave it!" Nevertheless, she did manage to tear herself away from Concepción and found San José, which inspired another torrent of purple prose. This mission, she informed her readers, had been proclaimed "the finest of all these edifices. . . . One of the most famous Parisian architects, visiting this mission, pronounced it the finest piece of architecture in the United States."[52] Kennedy also asserted that the king of Spain had sent "a genius named Huizar to superintend its construction. He spent several years in carving the various ornamentations of the building."[53] Sparing no superlative on San José, she exclaimed, "Nothing can exceed the loveliness of the fruit and flower and arabesque—nothing more seraphic can be imagined than the many angel faces, and the Virgin Mary just above the door." Tourists visiting San Antonio with its beauty, architecture, and history, would retain these as the "loveliest pictures in memory's gallery."[54] Some of Kennedy's rhetoric may be explained as her own enchantment with the beauty of the missions; or, perhaps more cynically, she may also have been paid by the word. Then again, she may have been trying to give those armchair travelers who would never set foot on San Antonio's dusty streets a vivid description in order to better construct their own imagined journeys to San Antonio and the missions. Historian T. J. Jackson Lears contextualizes Kennedy's (and others') ecstatic and rapturous prose during this fin-de-siècle period by showing their co-opting Catholic aesthetics and "mysticism" to promote an "intense" and "authentic experience" as they sought to offset discontent wrought by society's rapid modernization.[55]

In addition to the travel narratives published in magazines, Herbert Durand published a guidebook, *The City of Missions*, in 1894, one of the earliest publications found bestowing that particular description on San Antonio.

His subtitle, *Its Romantic and Patriotic History*, was accurate in describing the content of the book, although numerous inaccuracies littered the text. Readers were (erroneously) informed that in 1718 Franciscans arrived at an already existing presidio where they founded Mission San Antonio de Valero; construction of Mission San José was completed in 1731, when work began on the other mission churches; and in 1744, the cornerstone of the Alamo church was laid. Finally, Durand claimed that despite the Franciscan efforts to "convert the numerous and hostile savages," the Spanish population kept decreasing, to the point that both Missions Valero and Adaes in East Texas were abandoned and the population transferred to the presidio of San Antonio, which now gave its name to the town.[56] In addition to histories of each of the mission churches and cathedral, the book included a maudlin poem by R. M. Potter to the martyrs of the Battle of the Alamo. An accompanying drawing showed Crockett, identified by his characteristic hat, standing tall with a few fellows in front of the main doorway of the Alamo chapel. Closing in on these heroes were the uniformed Mexican regular forces armed with rifles, followed by Mexican peons dressed in white shirts and sombreros and armed with daggers. Supplementing the regular forces with stereotypical, knife-wielding Mexican peasants did little to improve the prevailing view in the minds of most Anglos that the Mexicans were a cowardly and dangerous Other, but as historian James Crisp suggests, it was de rigueur for the time.[57]

Romantic Fiction and the Missions

Helen Hunt Jackson published her 1885 novel, *Ramona*, to call attention to the plight of various Indigenous tribes living in and around California's old Spanish missions. She hoped the novel would raise awareness among white readers, just as Harriet Beecher Stowe's *Uncle Tom's Cabin* had done for Southern slaves. Unfortunately, her efforts failed to have the desired effect, as readers became so caught up in the tragic romance of the story, they completely lost sight of the dire problems California's mission Indian populations were facing. Instead, readers began blurring the lines between fact and fiction through hunting down the places mentioned in the novel, making pilgrimages to special locales, even planning their weddings at the exact mission chapel where Ramona and her beloved Alessandro exchanged their vows. A cottage industry formed to meet the expectations of this "Ramona craze," which lasted into the 1920s. Although no available evidence indicates whether the pilgrimages to Ramona shrines created a similar surge of interest among tourists to San Antonio's missions, there are examples of fiction created expressly to inform tourists about the Texas missions. Within these fictional works are striking similarities in the rhetoric used by travel narratives describing both the California and the San Antonio missions, particularly the Alamo, which had been subject to high melodrama ever since the 1836 battle.[58]

Most materials published by Southern Pacific carried purely basic demographic, climatological, and economic data about the major stops along the way. Other publications took a different approach, even going as far as creating a fictional group of tourists and using dialogue between characters to convey the same type of encyclopedic data. Author Ben Truman had previously published titles highlighting the golden bounty that awaited tourists and immigrants to California. For Southern Pacific, he concocted a fictional narrative about an upper-class family of five, who along with a family friend, traveled the company's premier line, the Sunset Route, from New Orleans to California to spend the winter months. The party dedicated a forty-eight-hour layover to explore San Antonio and "enjoy the exquisite sunshine and lovely surroundings of this highly-romantic place—so long an outpost of Western civilization." Along the list of attractions San Antonio had to offer were quality hotels, churches, libraries, clubs, gardens, theater, and even a casino.[59] However, Truman proclaimed the "greatest of all attractions" were the missions, second only to the warm climate. Some of the historical highlights mentioned were the arrival of the Canary Islanders in the mid-eighteenth century and the work of the Franciscans to "induce the milder Indians to cultivate rich lands, improve their own condition, and enlarge the revenues of the Church, without any doubt performing a great work of civilization." The Alamo was the first mission the fictional traveling party visited and "Col. King," the most experienced traveler of the group, read an account of the 1836 battle from an earlier guidebook titled *Eden* (published just four years earlier by the GHSA railroad). The description of the battle was typical melodrama of the time, pandering to the patriotism of the party members (and more important, to readers).[60] This type of narrative fiction introduced and contextualized the West both for an Eastern public with means to travel and those who were limited to armchair travel.

Almost ten years later in 1895, Southern Pacific's Passenger Department put out another example of romantic travel fiction, *Through Storyland to Sunset Seas*, written by H. S. Kneedler. It was essentially a guidebook with basic factual information, climatological data, economic statistics, and points of interest. However, this information was delivered in the form of a fictional, romantic travel narrative of four characters, again traveling from New Orleans to California along the Sunset Route. Printed on high-quality paper with over two hundred pages and many photographs, it was much more substantial than many other pamphlets and travel guides, including the earlier publication from 1886. The book added interest in the form of a love story between two of the characters: Jack (the primary narrator), who by the end of the book had become engaged to fellow traveler, "the Girl" (the only female character, who remained unnamed). The other two characters were worldly travelers and primarily served to dispense encyclopedic facts relating to places and sights along the route: the Colonel (father of the Girl) and the Growler (a rather pessimistic and cynical male contemporary of the Colonel who acted as foil).[61] The narrative reflected typical prejudices of the time regarding gender and racial and ethnic minorities.

The chapter describing the party's stopover in San Antonio emphasized the missions and the Alamo as primary tourist interests. By the time they were shown their hotel rooms, the Colonel had already hired a carriage and organized a tour of the missions as their first priority. As the four explored Mission Concepción, the Growler pointed out existing traces of "gaudy yellow frescoes . . . ornamented with red and blue quarterfoil [*sic*] crosses." While the Colonel described the richly carved decor of San José, he curiously made no mention of the legendary artist Huizar and gave an erroneous date for the completion of the San José church seen today. The party made their way to each of the missions south of town, briefly visiting San Juan and finishing their tour with Mission Espada. The narrative mentioned the tireless and effective work of local priest Fr. Francis Bouchu (a real person) in repairing and restoring Espada back to useful service. Upon the party's return to town, they visited the Alamo, about which the Colonel proclaimed, "If deeds of daring sanctify the soil that witnesses them that should be to every American one of the sacred places of the land" and recounted for the book's readers the story of the 1836 battle and glory heaped upon the Alamo martyrs. Later that evening, "we did what all tourists do—made a trip through the Mexican quarter of town." There they cast their elitist tourists' gaze on the poverty and squalor of the Tejano population "in characteristic attitudes of idleness" as "picturesque" sights to be enjoyed as part of the overall experience. They also partook of the popular Tex-Mex cuisine in Milam Plaza, so their consumption of San Antonio was complete.[62]

Interest in this guidebook lies both in the quality of its printing, including the photographs, and the inclusion of a fictional romance story. Although far from being high literature, and the fact the romance is somewhat subordinate to the descriptions of points of interest and exotic sights to be experienced along the route, a review of this publication in the "Literary Notes" column of the *Chicago Daily Tribune* described the book in glowing terms. The reviewer opined that this book had set a high bar as "one of the best books of the kind ever issued."[63] A similar complimentary review appeared in the *Austin Daily Statesman*, and one advertisement for the book described it as "printed on fine enameled paper," saying it was the "story of the romance of the country traversed by the Southern Pacific."[64]

Including a romance as part of the story reveals a marked degree of insight on the part of Southern Pacific's publishing arm by recognizing in that era, while most travel decisions would be made by men in their traditional head-of-household role, women could and did influence travel plans. The romance was included as an appeal to women readers who would influence their husbands to take them on a similar journey. Southern Pacific perhaps assumed men would prefer the drier rendering of population and economic statistics, climatic data, and daring stories of military action, whereas the "lady of the house" would prefer following a young couple falling in love during an extended adventure. Because *Through Storyland to Sunset Seas* was published as a book, members of the lower classes who could not afford lengthy trips to "spend the season" away from jobs and responsibilities could still enjoy the vicarious travel experience through Kneedler's romance. However, in the closing decades of the nineteenth century, railroad fares were dropping, thus enabling more people from the middle classes to travel physically to the exotic Southwest of which they had read.[65]

Local Guidebooks and the San Antonio Missions

Guidebooks penned by locals were not necessarily more accurate or any less sentimental, but they did lend a sense of being more authentic. Journalist and secretary of the San Antonio Merchants' Exchange Stephen Gould published *The Alamo City Guide* in 1882, while eight years later San Antonio bookseller and civic booster William Corner published his own.[66] Both guidebooks were part local history and part city directory with important information on hotels, local transportation, restaurants, and other facts travelers and tourists needed. Gould and Corner also included detailed information about the city's business climate, opportunities for investment, agriculture and commodities markets, and economic development. Much of this information was delivered with no shortage of superlatives that characterized booster propaganda of the day. While Gould's book came first and had more details, Corner's book offered maps, interviews with local celebrities, and more images to highlight its many interesting sights and scenes, particularly the missions. Additionally, just as Southern Pacific reprinted Harriet Spofford's *Harper's* article in its own promotional travel literature, Corner incorporated Sidney Lanier's 1870 history of the city practically verbatim. By reproducing his historical sketch for a new audience, Lanier's florid prose (as well as historical inaccuracies) was perpetuated for a new generation of tourists.[67] These two books, appearing relatively early after the railroad reached the city and being written by locals, offer interesting insights into how San Antonio and its missions were attached to national memories.

Despite the similarities, there are some significant differences between Gould and Corner. Gould spent more time describing San Antonio's history from precolonial times to his own, concentrating on violence and conquest. He claimed, "Every street and plaza" within the thirty-six square miles of city territory "marks the grave of a hero, friend or foe." Gould took pride in this brutal past with "almost every stone baptized in human blood shed in the defence of liberty" and "the thoughts of visitors naturally turn to the romance of the past." His description of the 1836 Alamo battle was equally blood-spattered and overly romantic, even including a day-by-day description of the siege. Gould did state that multiple accounts existed regarding the fates of Bowie, Travis, and Crockett but suggested the latter two survived the onslaught, were taken alive to Santa Anna, and executed on his command. Another difference between Gould and Corner is that Gould relegated his recommendations for tourists' sightseeing to nearly the end of the book. He offered tourists a three-day itinerary where a trip to see the missions comprised only the afternoon of the first day (although he did not miss the opportunity to remind readers as they crossed Alamo Plaza that they walked on sacred ground, baptized with the blood of heroes).[68]

In an earlier chapter on San Antonio's religious institutions, Gould described the missions' art and architecture in detail. The Alamo, he admonished, as the "Mecca of Texas tourists," was "worthy of a more honourable fate than being converted into a grocery warehouse." He claimed that architecture of the first mission (Concepción) "might not be inaptly named Christianized Moorish." Fading examples of paintings and frescoes depicting religious scenes and figures remained visible in several rooms. Finally, Gould argued that the sanctuary dome was "less massive, but far more beautiful in its proportions than that of the Capitol at Washington." The second mission (San José) was "the most elegant and beautiful of all the Texas missions." Part of the beauty came from the work of "celebrated artist Huica [*sic*]," who was "sent from Spain at the time of the founding of this mission, and spent several years in carving the various ornamentations of the building." Even as a ruin, it would "well repay a visit." Gould considered the final two missions almost too dilapidated to merit attention, although he observed that the priest at San Juan was "possessed of a rich fund of information regarding its early history, which he delights to tell appreciative visitors." The architecture of San Juan and Espada did garner a few compliments, including a reference to Espada's "sword shaped tower."[69]

By contrast, Corner's guidebook offered new arrivals directions from the rail depot where they arrived to the best hotels, boardinghouses, and restaurants via streetcars and horse-drawn carriages in the first few pages. Under the heading "What There Is to See and How to See It," he recommended, "The Alamo of course leads the list, that is a shrine before which every pilgrim to San Antonio bows. . . . All four Missions have different points of interest and will repay a thousand times in pleasure any difficulty in getting to them." An additional experience worthy of tourists' attention included "the curious custom of the all-night outdoor Supper on the Plazas. The stranger should certainly take a Mexican supper. The Mexican quarter and its denizens, trans-San Pedro Creek, should be done."[70] Corner's narrative reinforced San Antonio's Mexican American citizens as exotic "Other," facilely turning San Antonio's poverty-stricken Tejano population into a tourist attraction, and assured his readers the tourists' experience would not be complete without its consumption.

Unlike descriptions in Gould and so many other guidebooks and travel narratives, Corner's description of the Alamo did not wallow in the gory details of the 1836 siege and subsequent massacre beyond directing attention to the "sublime recklessness" the Alamo defenders showed in choosing to remain until the end. Although Corner mentioned some of the subsequent repairs and restoration work performed on the Alamo chapel, including Major E. B. Babbitt's 1849 work, his frustratingly stingy details left little to modern scholars regarding the gabled parapet and the building's now familiar facade. Corner also reported the sale of the chapel in 1883 to the State of Texas for $20,000 as "the right and proper thing to do" to recognize the heroism of the Alamo defenders of 1836 and attempt to prevent future harm to the structure.[71]

Corner began his chapter on the other missions by excoriating the rampant vandalism tourists (and perhaps locals as well) inflicted on the missions' walls. He observed that travelers to San Antonio make "anxious" inquiries regarding directions to the missions, and he admonished visitors that just seeing one did not equate to seeing all. Similarly, he warned that unless one was an experienced horseman, visitors would enjoy the trip more by carriage. Corner provided readers with excellent maps of the mission compounds, as well as descriptions of the decor of the chapels. Like so many other chroniclers, he seemed convinced that all domed ceilings such as Concepción's chapel and San José's sacristy were necessarily of Moorish origins and the detailed carved facade at San José was Renaissance (instead of the more accurate Baroque). Corner also explained the incongruous Gothic arches at San José as having been rebuilt in the late 1850s by a group of Benedictines from Pennsylvania, recruited to reoccupy the mission.[72] Archaeologist James Ivey asserts that instead of being rebuilt at this time as Corner claimed, this was actually the point at which the Gothic arches were initially installed.[73] At San Juan, Corner noted the existence of numerous frescoes despite decades of neglect. He quoted the resident priest, Fr. Francis Bouchu, who speculated that the frescoes were created well after the chapel had been completed, probably "to satisfy the Indian nature's love of color."[74] While earlier narratives had briefly mentioned remnants of these frescoes at the missions, Corner's descriptions are the most detailed found to date.

Unlike Gould, Corner did not mention Pedro Huizar or credit anyone else as the master sculptor at San José. A photograph of "Rosa's Window" is simply identified as the "South Window of Baptistry, Mission San José," with no mention of the doomed romance between Huizar and the fictitious Rosa. Corner also informed his readers not to expect too much in the way of information regarding Concepción from the family that lived on the premises: "To them the past of the Mission is as a sealed book and it has no romance for them." If Corner found the residents unimaginative, he suggested it need not be so for readers, who were encouraged to indulge in fantasies of an imagined past. He also concurred with Gould, repeating the local tradition that Mission San Francisco de la Espada ("St. Francis of the Sword") was so named because the bell tower was supposedly shaped like the hilt of a sword.[75] However, Ivey has challenged this bit of local lore, noting that the church had been named "of the Sword" well before the stone building had even been constructed. Similarly, Ivey describes Espada's "bell-tower," or more correctly an *espadaña*, as being nearly the same as the one at Mission San Juan, both having been built by maestro Salazar in 1790.[76]

Father Francis Bouchu: Renaissance Man and Savior of Espada

Corner recognized Fr. Francis Bouchu as being a true Renaissance man, "priest, lawyer, bricklayer, stone mason, photographer, historian, printer," and asserted that Mission Espada would have been lost without his tireless efforts.[77] Born in Sainte-Colombe, France, in 1829, he landed in Galveston, Texas, in December 1854. Just three months later, Bishop Jean Marie Odin ordained him. By April 1855, Bouchu had arrived in San Antonio and was assigned to assist Fr. Claude Marie Dubuis at the San Fernando church. Bouchu and a fellow assistant priest were sent out to the missions for several weeks at a time to minister to those who lived away from the city. Around 1867, Bouchu was appointed as priest to Mission Espada (fig. 3.1). According to his obituary in a Texas Catholic newspaper, he lived very simply and frugally, echoing the poverty of his parishioners. The paper noted that "when asked why he did not seek a more lucrative" position that his years of experience might secure, he replied that "if he did not remain and attend to his poor Mexican people, no one else would be likely or able to do so."[78] Bouchu was devoted to his profession and his flock, and despite harboring some paternalistic opinions about them, he was their spiritual "father," leading them in the faith. In a letter to his uncle in France, he noted, "Our poor Mexicans . . . have nothing of their own . . . wretched as dogs and soft as cats . . . impossible to trust, although to see them they seem okay."[79] He also created and printed a Spanish-language catechism that became the official catechism for Spanish-speaking Catholics in San Antonio.[80] Bouchu lived simply, and what money he saved, he put back into Espada. In his last will and testament, Bouchu bequeathed to the parish church of Mission Espada the three bells in the *espadaña,* along with the sacred vessels, vestments, and accoutrements for divine service, which he had purchased, "the church having nothing of its own." Additionally, he forgave a debt of $825 the parish owed to him for his work in "rebuilding, repairing and adorning" the church building.[81]

It is no exaggeration to suggest that without Bouchu's efforts and talents, Mission Espada as seen today might have been lost. According to Ivey, Bouchu began much of the restoration at Espada in 1884. He paid for the materials by purchasing church-owned properties and, after selling them, turned the profits back into the restoration work. As Bouchu rebuilt the Espada chapel, Ivey asserts that Bouchu added transepts to the original design.[82] Without critical sources directly attributable to Bouchu, historians can only surmise his motivations, but clearly his long tenure of service and devotion to his flock suggest he recognized that Espada was important to the parishioners and those

Fig. 3.1. Fr. Francis Bouchu. Image and scan courtesy of the University of Texas–San Antonio Libraries, Special Collections, 083-0198.

living nearby, both as sacred space and center for the local community.[83] In this respect, Mission Espada was a vital site of memory for those residing in its immediate vicinity.

"Madame" Candelaria's Tales and Alamo Myths

In addition to Fr. Bouchu, Corner interviewed local celebrity Señora Candelaria before she passed away in 1899. Who this lady was, and why her passing warranted mention in newspapers across the nation, only adds to the national-level infatuation with all things Alamo-related. Señora Candelaria purported to having been an eyewitness to that formative event in Texas history, even supposedly receiving a cut on the chin by a Mexican bayonet as she cradled the dying James Bowie in her arms.[84]

According to Corner, Andrea Castañon was born at Laredo in November 1785. She was twice married, and her second husband was Candelario Villanueva, through whom she became known as "Señora Candelaria" to many locals. She asserted that she was inside the Alamo chapel during the final Mexican assault on the compound; she was giving Bowie, whom she believed was dying of typhoid fever, a drink of water when Mexican soldiers burst in and bayonetted the bed-ridden commander. Additionally, Candelaria recalled that Crockett died early in the final assault as he ran to his post, in a manner similar to Travis, rather than toward the end of the battle. Corner's guide printed 166 names of Anglos who died at the Alamo that were inscribed on a monument in Austin, but he amended this list to include four Mexican names Señora Candelaria gave him. Corner asked about other specific individuals associated with San Antonio during Texas's war for independence, including Ben Milam and fellow Alamo survivor Susanna Dickinson. Milam's name did not evoke any association, but she remembered with "an expression of considerable repugnance" the name Dickinson, who, according to the elderly Tejana, "hated Mexicans" (fig. 3.2).[85]

Corner was not the only correspondent to interview Señora Candelaria. By the late 1890s, she made a small subsistence recounting the glorious sacrifices of the Alamo martyrs and her own harrowing escape. In 1891, she petitioned the Texas legislature for a pension, which they granted.[86] Other journalists found their way to her humble abode, and through one of Candelaria's English-speaking relatives, she recounted her tales. However, perhaps because of her advanced age and failing health or for some other reason, her stories were not consistent. While she generally confirmed the legend of Travis drawing the line in the sand, she told Corner and another journalist that Crockett died early in the final assault, while at other times she claimed he died toward the end. Similarly, Corner reported that Bowie died from Mexican bayonets as he lay in Candelaria's arms, but in at least one telling she asserted that a fever had killed Bowie hours before the final assault. In yet another tale, she danced with a young and dashing cadet Antonio López de Santa Anna, who came to San Antonio in 1813 to quell a rebellion.[87]

Several of those who interviewed Candelaria, or reprinted earlier interviews, remarked on her talent as a raconteur and printed the tales with little or no critique. Why then, should modern historians consider her, given concerns about the inconsistencies and embellishments? In their respective books on memory, myth, and the Alamo, anthropologists Richard Flores and Holly Beachley Brear inexplicably make no substantial mention of Señora Candelaria and her reminiscences.[88] Historians Randy Roberts and James S. Olson only briefly mention her claims and express their own doubts regarding her veracity.[89] Whether she was or was not present at the Alamo that fateful

Fig. 3.2. Portrait of Andrea Castañon Villanueva, Ernst Raba Collection, San Antonio Conservation Society Foundation, date unknown. See also Portal to Texas History, https://texashistory.unt.edu/ark:/67531/metapth460044/m1/1/?q=raba%20AND%20candelaria (accessed May 22, 2025).

morning will likely never be known for certain and is ultimately irrelevant for this book. The real significance is how far and wide beyond San Antonio's city limits her tales traveled. Through the magazine articles and newspaper obituaries people in Chicago, Baltimore, St. Louis, and elsewhere read of this poor, elderly Mexican woman remembered for having given succor to the patriots and martyrs for the nascent nation of Texas. Such widespread coverage confirms the American reading public's significant degree of fascination with the Alamo that went far beyond Texas's borders. There is also the inconvenient issue of her ethnicity. In a time when Tejanos were often seen as traitors and blamed for the Alamo massacre, Señora Candelaria was celebrated as a battlefield angel for her service and pensioned by the state. Conversely, perhaps the Anglos in local and state governments did not see such an elderly woman as a threat to the existing power structure. Her ethnicity may challenge certain contemporary and monolithic interpretations of race and ethnic relations; nonetheless, modern scholars should not ignore her contributions to the collective memories regarding the Alamo.

Southern Pacific's "Propaganda Machine"

Between the late 1880s and 1890s, land sales became significantly smaller parts of the Southern Pacific railroad's overall business. The Passenger Department was then given the task of promoting California (home of Southern Pacific) as well as the other regions throughout the Southwest where the rail line operated. Rail travel was improving with the introduction of Pullman sleeper cars and greatly lowered fares, as the Southern Pacific competed against the Santa Fe line to bring tourists through the American Southwest.[90] With tourists responsible for increasing company revenue, the Passenger Department became the main publishing arm for promotional materials. This increased role of the Passenger Department resulted in an exponential expansion in the number and types of publications "aimed at tourists, as well as those seeking new homes and farms." Little wonder historian Richard Orsi describes the Passenger Department as the rail company's "propaganda machine."[91]

Over a three-year period in the early 1900s, Southern Pacific published "heroic quantities of pamphlets and other materials advertising opportunities for travel" and immigration to the American Southwest, approaching some ten million pieces.[92] Besides the romance by Kneedler, Southern Pacific printed more traditional types of books offering basic factual data on the cities and towns along the Sunset Route. In the opening decades of the twentieth century, Southern Pacific's Passenger Department issued several editions of the book *Wayside Notes on the Sunset Route.* This profusely illustrated guidebook offered brief descriptions of cities, towns, and interesting geographical features that could be seen along the route. The 1908 edition listed San Antonio as having a population of 105,000 and being the economic hub for livestock, cotton, and farm produce. Visitors would find "a most salubrious climate" and a hotel featuring a hot sulfur spring and spa "with hundreds of cures to its credit." However, the booklet stressed that "San Antonio cannot be so engrossed in its present glories as to forget that it holds the Alamo. Historic and patriotic interest largely centers in its immortal Alamo," and it included the usual paean to Travis, Bowie, Crockett, and the rest of their fellow martyrs.[93]

One more turn-of-the-century publication type from Southern Pacific's Passenger Department worthy of note strictly focused on the missions of the Texas and Juárez, Mexico, region. This view book is distinctive for its early multicolored photographic prints of Texas missions. Another feature of this view book is that two other missions are included besides those in San Antonio: La Bahía near Goliad and Mission Iglesia Guadalupe in Ciudad Juárez, Mexico. The text described the missions as being "speaking monuments" that tell of the faith and persistence of the Spanish "priests and monks" who came to proselytize "among the savage tribes." However, despite the noble cause for which the missions toiled, with the decline and fall of the Spanish Empire, the crumbling walls are all that remain to tell "the long, long story of a dead past." The description of the Alamo begins with the claim that it was the story "of the bravest of the brave." As is so often the case with these tourist guidebooks, some of the facts presented were erroneous, highlighting the differences between historical facts and memories. The description of Mission San José was similarly problematic. The text credited the Spanish sculptor "Huica [*sic*]," who came "across the seas for the purpose" of carving the ornate facade and oaken doors. It also claimed that the work was completed within eight years of the founding date of the mission. Finally, the description missed most of the names of the various saints adorning the facade. Conversely, the description mentioned that Oscar Wilde had proclaimed the sculptural ornamentation as "unsurpassed by anything in the old monasteries of Europe."[94] Minor errors these might seem, but the cumulative effects are seen in the clashes between history and memory.

Southern Pacific's "propaganda machine" was tasked with churning out high-quality printed materials promoting travel on the company's trains between New Orleans and California. These materials took a variety of formats from romance stories to more mundane brochures with basic facts. San Antonio's missions drew frequent mention as "must-see" attractions for passengers riding the rails. More important was the rhetoric used to create the impression within Eastern *mentalité* that they were traveling to an exotic locale peopled by unusual (but inferior) Others. The historic sights they would see were relics of a dead past being swept aside in the name of Anglo-American progress, to which they were the beneficiaries. But the "dead past" would not go quietly, for there were those who believed that certain relics of the past needed to be appreciated and preserved for future generations.

Early Visitors' Calls for Preservation of the Missions

In the closing decades of the nineteenth century, tourists continued to come to San Antonio. Some found the romantic sights they sought; others seemed dismayed at what they found. Indeed, the latter sometimes took San Antonio's city fathers to task for allowing such a revered building as the Alamo to fall into such a state of decay. These complaints highlight some of the tensions within San Antonio between those who wanted to present the city as a modern city open for business and investment and those who wanted to portray the town as remaining a tangible part of the American Western frontier with visible remnants of a romantic and exotic past. Both groups found material to reinforce their position in travel narratives written by outside observers that appeared in a variety of media outlets, carrying the stories of San Antonio's romantic missions to a wide audience.

During this period, the prose style of the narratives themselves underwent a significant change. There was less of the florid, romantic hyperbole of the previous decades; nevertheless, the descriptions of the missions still pandered to readers' emotional sympathies. While some of that change may have reflected changing tastes on the part of the reading public, it also reflected that the West itself was changing. This was the time in which historian Frederick Jackson Turner made his famous observation that the frontier, conceived as the open range of the West and long considered an endless commodity, had closed.[95] With the closing of the frontier, the taming of the Wild West began; although Southern Pacific's promotional literature promised travelers both the Wild West and a domesticated Mild West, both open for business.[96]

In 1892, Richard Harding Davis, journalist and managing editor of *Harper's Weekly* magazine, published a series, "The West from a Car Window," narrating his three-month journey via rail through Texas, Oklahoma, and Colorado. The people and landscapes Davis encountered both confirmed and challenged his preconceived notions about the American West.[97] That same year, Walter B. Stevens traveled across Texas for the *St. Louis Globe-Democrat*. His narratives were then collected and published by the Passenger Department of the Missouri Pacific Railway. Prior to the turn of the century, famed novelist and journalist Stephen Crane found San Antonio and the West similarly difficult to explain, as did another *Harper's Weekly* correspondent, Kirk Munroe. One common facet that struck all four of these men was the recognition of the appeal of San Antonio's Spanish missions and the need to protect and preserve them against further decay.

As his train rolled across South Texas, Davis, an Eastern dandy, described with palpable apprehension one of his fellow passengers nonchalantly opening a window and firing his pistol at the passing telegraph poles. A train official calmed passengers' fears by identifying the shooter as a local deputy sheriff and his actions as nothing more than an impromptu target practice session.[98] Davis's anecdote reflected the contradictory nature about the West where reality and legends frequently clashed. This incongruity led him to scold San Antonio's citizenry who "do not, as a rule, appreciate the historical values of their city." He believed that San Antonio "possesses historical and picturesque showplaces which in any other country but our own would be visited by innumerable American tourists prepared to fall down and worship." But to Davis's chagrin, the San Antonio city officials seemed to place more value on the newest and largest buildings, the new Post Office, and City Hall, and riding the new cable car system, which they believed to be indicators of Gilded Age economic progress. Progress was all well and good for Davis, and he suggested that the town just lacked a first-rate hotel. But even more so, he argued, it needed a proper appreciation of its past. He rebuked city authorities: "But the missions which lie just outside of the city are what will bring the Eastern man or woman to San Antonio, and not the new waterworks." He also admitted that it was "impossible to write comprehensively about southwest Texas . . . and say nothing of the Alamo." Davis compared the old mission chapel to "what Independence Hall is to the United States, and Bunker Hill to the East." More important, however, he claimed that "the pride of [the Alamo] belongs to every American, whether he lives in Texas or in Maine." The Alamo as a national site of memory was once again reinforced by an elite tourist and journalist visiting from the East. Davis closed his visit to Texas by noting that one tended to forget the minor inconveniences, discomforts, and isolation from traveling along the frontier and "remembers only the Alamo."[99] For as Davis emphasized to his readers, the Alamo and the missions were truly the primary attractions to see in San Antonio.

Similar to Davis, Walter B. Stevens, a special correspondent for the *St. Louis Globe-Democrat,* visited the state and published a series of letters describing his adventures. In San Antonio he interviewed Señora Candelaria regarding her role at the Battle of the Alamo, as well as Tom Rife, the acting custodian of the Alamo building, who challenged the accuracy of the elderly Tejana's recollections. Stevens observed that the State of Texas had recently come around to the notion that the Alamo deserved some sort of protection, although he broke from the usual "saintly missionaries" rhetoric of so many other contemporary travel narratives and accused the "priests" of forced conversions and enslavement of the Native Americans. Stevens also noted that at Concepción, "the chapel has been used in recent years for a service by a bishop who venerates the past." As did so many of his fellow travel writers, Stevens mistook Concepción's dome to be Moorish, an observation that not only reflects a limited understanding of architectural history but also characterizes the mission builders as Orientalized Other.[100]

Stevens speculated there was some competition in decorating Mission Concepción and Mission San José. He described Concepción as having been ornamented with frescoes that could still be seen in his time. San José, on the other hand, had been decorated with skilled hands, hammer, and chisel "in the most wonderful manner." Stevens credited "Huica [*sic*]" as the Spanish artist who traveled such a great distance to "do the finest of chiseling on the San Jose portal and windows," which took several years to complete.[101] As he traveled the mission trails, Stevens described San Juan as a complete ruin with little to see since the Spanish gave up on the mission system before the main church could be completed. Mission Espada, on the other hand, had been restored to such a fine degree that "it has lost its interest as a ruin," an observation reinforcing the notion that the missions' touristic value depended on being between total ruin and functionally restored.[102] Ultimately, Stevens concluded that the Alamo and other missions were "the wonder of all strangers who visit San Antonio."[103]

In 1897, another *Harper's Weekly* correspondent, Kirk Munroe, made his way to Texas and described San Antonio as "a very Mecca of American pilgrims who visit [the city] not for its present, but for its past. They go to be thrilled by the story of its Alamo." Munroe, like Davis earlier, chastised the "apathetic neglect" of the Alamo and declared "the battle-scarred structure should have been sacredly preserved as an enduring monument." He later compared it to Independence Hall, Mount Vernon, and Sutter's Fort, reminders of "the glorious past, to be reverently cared for by an association of native sons and daughters." Munroe was particularly offended by the "atrocious wooden building, used as a grocery [that] at once hides and degrades [the Alamo]." Despite the architectural horror committed upon the church, "defaced, shorn of its once stately proportions, and degraded by its environment, [the Alamo] is of such remarkable character... [that it] commands [visitors'] attention to the exclusion of all surrounding objects."[104] And while the Alamo was the city's "chief attraction to the visiting pilgrim," there were others. The other four missions "present examples of ancient ecclesiastical architecture unexcelled for beauty and design and exquisite detail" in the United States. Particularly noteworthy was the "carved ornamentation of which the artist Huica [*sic*], sent out from Spain for the purpose, devoted many years of his life. The west portal of the chapel affords ample proof of his genius while one window on the south side of the baptistery has been named the finest thing of its kind in America."[105] Munroe's narrative was accompanied by five illustrations, four of which depicted the Alamo, the facade and south sacristy window of San José, and the twin towers of Concepción. And five years after Davis called for one, Munroe concurred, the city still needed a "first-class tourist hotel."[106]

Novelist and correspondent Stephen Crane also visited San Antonio prior to the turn of the century and published his take on the city. Concurring with earlier journalists, he recommended the city do more to preserve its historical heritage. His astute observations regarding the appeal of the Alamo, as well as San Antonio, are instructive for modern historians. Crane asserted that before his arrival in San Antonio, all that he heard about the place suggested the city symbolized "the poetry of life in Texas," possibly referring to earlier wild, frontier times. Crane's expectations seemed to rely on some "eloquent description of the city which makes it consist of three old ruins and a row of Mexicans sitting in the sun." However, once he arrived in San Antonio, he was "astonished" by the "totally modern aspect" of the city. Instead of a sleepy little frontier cow town, he found that "principal streets are lanes between rows of handsome business blocks" and the local populace engaged more in commerce and were Eastern fashion slaves to such a degree that "the victorious derby hat of the North spreads its wings in the holy place of legends." He effectively captured the conflict between the progressive economic forces characterized by the Anglo population in fashionable bowler hats and the earlier, slower, preindustrial time of the Spanish missions.[107]

Crane noted that despite the construction of business blocks and telegraph wires strung into a web over the streets, there remain "little old buildings, yellow with age, solemn and severe in outline, that have escaped by a miracle or by importance, the whirl of the modern life." However, he cautioned, these old buildings faced a new and serious danger, for "trolley cars are merciless animals. They gorge themselves with relics. They make really coherent history look like an omelet." And while trolleys threatened historic sites in town, the missions south of town were "besieged" by mesquite. "Relic hunters with their singular rapacity have dragged down little saints from their niches and pulled important stones from their arches. They have performed offices of destruction of which the wind and rain of the innumerable years was not capable." Even though he acknowledged the admonitions from Corner's guidebook against damaging the old buildings, he mused that it would take a supernatural army of all the ghosts of Spanish friars and soldiers to scare off the vandals and prevent further damage.[108]

Crane's observations and descriptions reflect a changing nature of writing styles about the Alamo and San Antonio's missions. While he acknowledged the piety and dedication of the Spanish friars who founded the missions, he also implied that the same friars were resorting to violence, "cudgeling their Indians in and out of the church," and when more souls for conversion were needed, sending out the soldiers to drag more into the mission. Some of his observations took on a sardonic tone, suggesting that "literary aspirants of the locality as soon as they finish writing about Her Eyes, begin on the Alamo. Statistics show that 69,710 writers of the state of Texas have begun at the Alamo." Nonetheless, Crane asserted that "the Alamo remains the greatest memorial to courage which civilization has allowed to stand." Crane did not wallow in the gory details of the 1836 siege and battle as had earlier writers. He nevertheless described how the building "maintains a dignity amid the taller modern structures" as "the tomb of the fiery emotions of Texans. . . . Whether the swirl of life, the crowd upon the streets, pause to look or not, the spirit that lives in this building, its air of contemplative silence, is as eloquent as an old battle flag."[109] Unlike some of his literary predecessors, Crane did not pour buckets of purple prose into his essay but, perhaps reflecting changing tastes, tempered his observations more with acerbic wit. Crane's essay appeared in newspapers across the nation in cities such as Pittsburgh; St. Louis; Washington, DC; and Salt Lake City.[110] His shrewd observations, coupled with his celebrity status, lent a certain credibility and interest to his admonitions to preserve the missions of San Antonio.

The turn of the twentieth century was a stressful time of significant change not just in San Antonio but for the Southwest and nation as a whole. As the national economy lurched from an agricultural to an industrial economy through concomitant economic crises, the population continued to shift from the farms to the towns and cities, where they often met increasing numbers of immigrants. With the drastic changes in the nation, people looked for something tangible to preserve their sense of identity. One effective method by which elites could reinforce their sense of identity was through travel, exploration, and the consumption of the nation. Those who benefited from the Gilded Age economic shifts traveled the railroad over its ever-increasing steel web that connected major urban centers to the remote frontiers. Once in San Antonio, these travelers made pilgrimages to the Alamo as a shrine of heroism and an icon of an expanding Anglo empire. Even those without means could take advantage of revolutions in print technology that allowed them to follow along vicariously through printed guidebooks and travel narratives, often with accompanying illustrations, giving readers a graphic idea of what the scenery looked like. The creators of these representations of travel were actually mediating the meanings of the sights and ordering how tourists should experience them based on their own elite bias. The result was a shared sense of collective identity among the consumers based on "a sense of difference."[111] In the case of the missions, this included the construction of the trope of a fantasy Spanish heritage. In this manner, the authors and publishers of the guidebooks and travel narratives continued the formula that characterized San Antonio as an exotic tourist destination and its Mexican American population as foreign Other. However, sometimes the narratives and illustrations were not accurate, as authors and engravers embellished scenes, taking artistic license or relying on local folklore for source material. These inaccuracies and other legendary tales simply became part and parcel of the collective memories that grew around San Antonio's missions.

4

Preserving the Missions and Marketing the Myths, 1870s–1936

"SAN ANTONIO: A foreign tour on American soil!" an advertisement proclaimed, and to underscore the foreign and exotic nature of the attractions, an image of the Spanish Baroque bell tower of Mission San José y San Miguel de Aguayo appeared alongside the text. "Even Continental Europe cannot show you more interesting ruins and relics of medieval times than are here."[1] Using both text and illustration to good effect, the advertisement's creator hoped to capitalize on interests in the historical, the quaint, and the picturesque, in addition to the mild winter climate, to bring Northern tourists to this Borderland city.[2] By the time this advertisement appeared, San Antonio's five eighteenth-century missions were dilapidated and needed repairs. However, for tourists under the influence of romanticized guidebooks and with little sense of chronology, the buildings probably resembled "medieval" relics more than functional churches.

This was a very important period for the missions, as various entities used illustrations and textual descriptions of the missions in multiple media formats to market a romanticized and exoticized portrait of the city. Some emphasized romance and nostalgia, while others appealed more to heroic and patriotic sympathies. A wide variety of sources demonstrate the important role of early preservation projects at San Antonio's missions in the construction of collective memories, which take their cues from a variety of sources, but architecture and visual images are vital as tangible remains. In San Antonio, the efforts of elite women to preserve the Alamo and other missions provided the mortar joining historic preservation, collective memories, and tourism.[3] Images of the missions reinforced the notions of a mythological Spanish past that became ingrained in the collective memories of many Anglo-Americans. Travelogues and advertising descriptions of San Antonio's missions informed the Mission Revival movement, which became the defining architectural style in the Southwest for much of the twentieth century. Likewise, in the opening years of the twentieth century, "See America First!" became the mantra of the nascent tourist and transportation industries. Sun, fun, and romantic history have been San Antonio's stock-in-trade for decades, and pictures of the missions helped lure travelers south and their money into city coffers. During this time period, advertisements promoting tourism, guidebooks, and postcards frequently contained illustrations of the missions along with textual descriptions. These various sources sometimes included legends associated with the missions but occasionally failed to distinguish the myths from history, further enhancing an exoticized image of the missions as a fundamental part of the city's romanticized Spanish past.

Changing Times and Ethnicities in San Antonio

San Antonio's racial climate, which had always been complex, remained so during this first third of the twentieth century. Though not without racial tensions, when compared to other parts of Texas, the city appeared relatively progressive. In Texas, the local political situation had greater impact on the racial landscape than the rigid, binary system that ruled the Jim Crow South. In urban areas such as San Antonio, relations between Mexicans and Anglos were "more relaxed" than in rural regions where Anglos held firm economic control.[4] A significant demographic shift between 1900 and 1940 further complicated the situation. The Mexican population of San Antonio grew from 13,722 (25.7 percent) to 103,000 (46.3 percent). During this same period, the Anglo population increased from 32,000 (60 percent) to 131,221 (46.7 percent), a loss in percentage despite a sizable numerical increase.[5] Part of the increase in the Mexican population resulted from an influx of refugees fleeing the political violence in Mexico.[6] Despite Mexicans being an established group and community, San Antonio elites boosting their city as well as outside observers typically described the local Tejano population as little more than benighted Others.

Women and Preservation in the Progressive Era

In the spring of 1886, American operatic soprano Clara Louise Kellogg visited San Antonio, gushing to a local journalist her delight in visiting this, the most "quaint" city on her travels. Like it did for so many other tourists, part of her itinerary included visiting the missions, "the most interesting ruins I have ever seen." Nonetheless, she was horrified "to see how neglected they are and the vandalism exhibited by that wretched creature, the tourist, whose rude hands have damaged in minutes that which took years to perfect." She informed her interviewer of her intention to speak with Governor John Ireland on her next trip through Austin "to exhort him to protect these fine ruins from further destruction." The journalist noted that other Northern visitors had echoed similar sentiments and hoped the State would take care of the missions.[7] However, it would be many years before the State of Texas made significant efforts toward caring for the missions. Despite purchasing the Alamo's church building from San Antonio's Catholic Diocese in 1883, the State did little in the way of preserving or protecting the structure. The City of San Antonio had been tasked with the upkeep and to that end hired a series of caretakers who acted as tour guide and custodian, but nothing was done to restore the old building.[8]

From the mid-nineteenth century well into the twentieth, elite women frequently spearheaded preservation efforts, and many found their public voices through their work on such projects. One reason for women's leadership in the historic preservation movement harkens to what historian Barbara J. Howe calls a "cult of domesticity," which elite women used to define their sphere of influence in community improvement.[9] Historian James Lindgren adds that in earlier periods of American history the "ideal of republican motherhood encouraged women to learn history for their children's education, as well as their own edification." By the Progressive Era, women had seized on historical preservation as a means to counter the "excessive materialism" and impersonal commercial interests that dominated the male world.[10] Additionally, during this period white, middle-class Anglos traced their ancestors in an attempt to burnish their American credentials and distinguish themselves from the large numbers of immigrants then arriving from Eastern Europe. Membership in hereditary patriotic organizations including the Daughters of the Republic of Texas (DRT) and the Daughters of the American Revolution (DAR) gave these women a platform through historic preservation to stake their claim.[11] Preservation historians Max Page and Randall Mason note, "Preservation in the United States has always been driven by patriotism—not just national patriotism but also a more local 'civic patriotism' that has been closely allied with boosterism."[12] Historian Judy Mattivi Morley asserts that these ideals "gave women the moral authority to preserve the nation's heritage."[13] Similarly, historian W. Fitzhugh Brundage concurs that "many white middle-class and elite women found in history an instrument for self-definition and empowerment." The women's general modus operandi included asserting "a cultural authority over virtually all representations of the region's past."[14] Memory and historical accuracy (or "authenticity") are frequently at odds, and the attempts of these Texas women at preservation reflected more of their own vision of an imagined past than an authentic one.[15]

In 1900, the *San Antonio Express* reported that the Lorenzo De Zavala Chapter of the DRT had begun efforts to preserve the missions. The author commended this "most laudable enterprise and [it] should have the encouragement and substantial aid of everybody. Neglect and vandalism have pretty much destroyed one of the old missions and without such attention as is proposed to be given there would soon be nothing left of it."[16] Two years later, Adina De Zavala and the DRT were still soliciting money to preserve San Antonio's missions, and as another *San Antonio Express* reporter observed, the money was still sorely needed: "Strangers visiting the Alamo City have frequently expressed surprise that more care has not been taken to preserve the ancient missions which stand as decaying memorials of" early attempts to Christianize area Native Americans. The *Express* journalist offered the example of Helen Gould, socialite, philanthropist, and eldest daughter of rail baron and financier Jay Gould, who contributed fifty dollars toward the DRT's preservation efforts of the missions. The journalist thanked Gould, an outsider, and appealed to locals' sense of "patriotic citizenship" to assist De Zavala and the DRT in its efforts.[17] Outside Texas, the *St. Louis Post-Dispatch* took an interest in the preservation work and published stories highlighting De Zavala's efforts. One story included photographs of four of the missions and one of Adina De Zavala. In return, De Zavala expressed her gratitude to the St. Louis correspondent for publicizing their labors to a much wider audience. She commented that they had received letters of encouragement from across the country, including an endorsement from the Federation of Women's Clubs.[18]

The federation's willingness to adopt this cause may also have been influenced by the impassioned appeal Adele B. Looscan of Houston and historian for the DRT gave at the federation's meeting the week before. In her address, Looscan specified the missions as a "sacred heritage of Texas" that excited "the interest of every intelligent traveler" who visited the state. She also reminded the women that preserving this sacred heritage fell within their bailiwick and recalled the efforts of Mary Hemenway of Boston and Ann Pamela Cunningham of Virginia, both of whom organized preservation projects within their respective localities.[19] Looscan claimed that preservation was a women's prerogative and challenged her audience to work diligently on the missions "to show to the appreciative tourist or offer for the study of the historian and archaeologist." She exclaimed, "We have still within our borders the finest examples of old Spanish architecture in the United States, if not the continent. The missions of Texas are unique both in the manner and material of their construction." Comparing the loss of one of the missions from neglect to "the destruction of a sole surviving member of a race," she reminded the listeners of the Spanish artist "Hincar [*sic*], who came from Spain to execute the carvings on the Mission San José and with the difficulties encompassing their erection in the midst of a wilderness inhabited by the most savage of Indians." Looscan proselytized the missions' value as tourist attractions and for scholarly inquiry as she strove to inspire fellow clubwomen to join her in preserving the heroic and romantic version of Texas history.[20]

Looscan, De Zavala, and the DRT were pleading for the missions generally, not just the Alamo. Despite the Alamo's direct role in Texan independence, the women recognized that all these buildings from the earlier Spanish period had value as tourist attractions. In 1903, Looscan and De Zavala rode out to Mission Espada and visited F. Francis Bouchu to learn about his work in restoring the mission's chapel. The two women declined his offer to share his meager noontime repast of fried onions, cream cheese, and bread, but once he finished his meal, he took them on a tour of the surviving structures around the compound. Some of the remaining fortifications were used as a school. The women also noted that at Mission San Juan, bells once again rang from the mission's *espadaña*. A *San Antonio Express* article described the visit and mentioned Looscan's claim that the wife of the Alamo's custodian was a direct descendant of the Spanish artist "Huicar [*sic*]" sent specifically to carve Mission San José's ornamentation. She continued to emphasize the value that the Alamo and missions held for San Antonio as tourist attractions.[21]

The DRT and the "Second Battle of the Alamo"

The "Second Battle of the Alamo" pitted two factions of the DRT against each other with the consequence of affecting what subsequent generations of visitors would see at the Alamo. The conflict has been discussed elsewhere but warrants describing here because the feud demonstrated women having a direct influence on how certain collective memories related to the Alamo were constructed in the era prior to women having a meaningful political voice.[22] At the same time, this clash garnered interest from outside Texas, as the internal quarrels between two blocs of a Texas women's heritage organization played out in the national press. Anthropologist Holly Beachley Brear asserts that the DRT's claims on the Alamo (and other historic preservation projects within San Antonio) stem from a charge issued by an early president of the organization, Mrs. Anson Jones. Jones exhorted her sisters in the organization to stake their claim as guardians of the state's "holy past" and pass the reverence for it down through the generations. Brear opines that based on societal norms of the time, the appropriate domain of women was to protect and preserve the sites of memory created by men.[23] For modern readers, the quarrel reiterates the clash between historical memory and commerce.

The leaders of the opposing factions were Adina De Zavala and Clara Driscoll. De Zavala, granddaughter of Republic of Texas's first vice president, Lorenzo De Zavala, founded the De Zavala Chapter of the DRT in San Antonio in 1893, just two years after the DRT itself began. Her life's passion centered on preserving historical sites celebrating the history of the state of Texas in glorious fashion. Driscoll was the daughter of Robert Driscoll and spent her early childhood on a large ranch near Corpus Christi. Despite being something of a tomboy, she attended private schools in San Antonio and received additional education in New York and France. As a New York socialite, Driscoll wrote short stories, novels, and musical plays and later married H. H. Sevier, a newspaper publisher and Texas legislator.[24] What brought the two women together and ultimately drove them apart was the dilapidated condition of the Alamo *convento*. Driscoll and her supporters came to represent the idea that the Alamo church, the building with the strongest walls, had been the logical "last stand" of the Alamo heroes and as such was sacred ground; all other remnants were of secondary importance and expendable.[25] In early 1905, Driscoll claimed that the DRT had no intention of restoring the *convento* and that "the chapel . . . is the main feature of the Alamo," indicating the marked difference in interpretation between her and De Zavala.[26] Conversely, De Zavala and her followers believed the worst fighting and heaviest Texan casualties occurred in and around the *convento*, now known as the "Long Barracks," but their definition of "Alamo" included the original compound in its entirety.

Complicating the issue was that between the 1836 battle and the beginning of the twentieth century, the Alamo compound changed hands several times among the Catholic Church, the State of Texas, and private individuals. Amid these real estate transactions, the church building became separated from other parts of the compound, including the nearby *convento*.[27] The church building, with its anachronistic facade and roof courtesy of the US Army, had been owned by the State of Texas since 1883. Meanwhile, a local grocery wholesaler firm incorporated the walls of the Long Barracks into a warehouse. Other mission walls had been destroyed to build streets and other buildings needed at the time. When the DRT turned their attentions to the Alamo compound, they "devoted themselves to its preservation, not with an eye to accuracy or archaeological authenticity, but to the re-creation of a dreamlike 'national' shrine, imbued with the idyllic."[28] De Zavala negotiated a purchase option with the firm of Hugo & Schmeltzer, then owners of the building, including the Long Barracks. But when the grocery firm received an offer in 1903 to buy the building, De Zavala could not match the asking price. In what became a Faustian bargain, De Zavala connected up with Driscoll, and the wealthy heiress fronted the money for the DRT to acquire the Long Barracks and adjoining plots.[29]

In faraway Olympia, Washington, a news headline read, "Historic Alamo: Texas Ladies Save It from Destruction." Adelaide E. Byrd's article claimed the threat to the Alamo was very real until De Zavala and the DRT bought the buildings. Byrd's article was decidedly in favor of De Zavala, with no mention of Driscoll having put up the money to buy the property. She admonished Texans for neglecting the Alamo "until the women of the state took up its cause." Byrd claimed, "With its old Spanish missions and forts," Texas was "more of a link between today and four centuries ago than almost any other state." She implored "rich Americans" nationwide to "'Remember the Alamo' financially and aid the patriotic ladies," but she especially challenged "all the women of the United States" to support the DRT. Byrd mentioned that De Zavala had presented a paper to a meeting of the state Federation of Women's Clubs reiterating her stance that the Long Barracks was the location of the Texans' last stand, thus deserving preservation along with the church.[30] Byrd's impassioned article denotes that interest in the Alamo heroes had expanded beyond Texas and blossomed in collective memories there. Moreover, by challenging all American women to support the DRT, Byrd reiterated earlier claims by Jones and Looscan regarding historical preservation being a proper platform for their gender.

The *St. Louis Post-Dispatch* followed this power struggle with curious interest. In late November 1905, it described how custody of the Alamo property had been given to Driscoll, only to be usurped by De Zavala. The correspondent stated that both De Zavala and Driscoll shared many important qualities necessary for leading the fight to save the Alamo but complimented Driscoll, who was being "feted" both within and outside Texas for having put up hard cash, while portraying De Zavala as more jealous and bitter that her earlier toils had gone mostly unrecognized.[31] There may also have been financial interests motivating this outside coverage. A St. Louis hotel group had a commercial stake in property directly behind the old *convento*, then in dilapidated condition and projecting into the recently modernized Alamo Plaza. The hotel company proposed clearing away what they considered an eyesore at their cost and replacing it with a park, preserving the site's sacred status, which they also proposed to the head of San Antonio's Business Men's Club.[32]

Early in 1907, the *Post-Dispatch* reported that the proposal by the St. Louis hotel group to tear down buildings to construct a "beautiful park" next to the church along with their hotel "has aroused the fighting spirit" of the DRT. De Zavala's reply was predictable: "Tear down the Alamo! Why even the school children know better and would rise to the defense of the Alamo against the would-be perpetrators of such a sacrilegious act!"[33] De Zavala invoked Texan patriotism and the "sublime sacrifice" of the Alamo martyrs and emphasized that despite being hidden by the Hugo & Schmeltzer building, the Long Barracks remained part of the Alamo. But, she proclaimed, "these sacred buildings and grounds were not purchased for the purpose of making a park." The DRT, De Zavala declared, had been charged by the State of Texas to maintain the site "as a sacred memorial to the heroes who immolated themselves upon that hallowed ground" and would continue that work "for the advancement and interest and glory of Texas, her children and citizens."[34]

A week prior to De Zavala's tirade, the *Dallas Morning News* briefly mentioned that a group of businessmen were petitioning the Texas legislature to "tear down the walls of the Mission San Antonio de Valero, adjoining the Alamo." The correspondent observed that the petition "has raised a storm" in the DRT, who questioned whether the men signing the petition also owned property near the Alamo. The DRT repeated their claims that the walls of Mission Valero under threat were indeed part of the Alamo. The journalist predicted a vigorous fight, with De Zavala leading the charge.[35] An editorial describing the controversy in greater detail appeared a week later, giving De Zavala much-needed public support. The author stated that despite the Alamo being located in the City of San Antonio, "it is the treasured property of the people of all Texas" and predicted forceful resistance to "any scheme to commercialize any part of it." The editorial warned both the DRT and "the people of Texas" not to fall for the "insidious song that is being sung to them by 'St. Louis capitalists' who preach about parks and monuments." The *News* included much of De Zavala's reply to the St. Louis paper and closed the issue, stating, "There is really no room for argument in a case in which commercialism is thus arrayed against the patriotic sentiment and purpose of a great people."[36] The Dallas newspaper applauded the Progressive Era women's blistering critique invoking patriotism as the moral high ground against men's excessive material interests.[37] The next month, the *Dallas Morning News* reported Driscoll's advocating the removal of the Long Barracks on the basis it obscured the view of the chapel and was never really part of the Alamo proper. However, the *News* appeared to side with De Zavala, stating that "the proposition to remove the walls of the old mission originated with St. Louis parties who purchased a lot in the rear on which to build a hotel and who desired to face on Alamo Plaza."[38]

In April, De Zavala received encouragement from California Spanish missions expert George Wharton James. He excoriated the hoteliers for wanting to destroy any portion of the Alamo compound for mere commercial interests. While the hotel might be attractive, James declared the loss of a single Alamo stone was too great a price, for "every stone of the Alamo is sacred property, consecrated by the blood of heroes," not just for Texas but beyond. He placed the Alamo in a similar category as Westminster Abbey, Notre Dame, and St. Peter's in Rome, "sacred to the heart of the world."[39] By equating a humble mission in the Texas-Mexican Borderlands to some of the most majestic and renowned examples of sacred architecture in Western Christianity, James reinforced the power that the romantic and sublime story of sacrifice and courage held in the hearts and minds of De Zavala and her associates, further invigorating their crusade to preserve as much of the original buildings as possible.

In her defense of the Alamo against the St. Louis hotel interests, De Zavala appealed directly to Texan pride and nativism. She claimed the blood of the Alamo martyrs had anointed the very bricks and saturated the soil, thereby consecrating them as holy ground. De Zavala's public rhetoric invoked a "civil religion" of Texas nativism and the glorious memory of the ultimate sacrifice paid by Travis, Crockett, Bowie, and the rest of their comrades. Religious scholars David Chidester and Edward Linenthal opine, "Sacred space is often, if not inevitably, entangled in politics. Since the nineteenth century, the most potent mythic orientations have linked sacred space with nationalism, celebrating the 'sacred nation' as the most encompassing spatial symbol of inclusion (and exclusion) in the world."[40] For the DRT and their sympathizers, this heroic interpretation became the dominant, Anglo, narrative of the Alamo, passed down through collective memories for decades. Gregg Cantrell and Elizabeth Hayes Turner observe, "Texas women used gender power to gain authority over the symbolic representation of white collective memory."[41] Chidester and Linenthal also note, "Sacred places are always highly charged sites for contested negotiations over the ownership of the symbolic capital (or symbolic real estate) that signifies power relations."[42] De Zavala and Driscoll's feud aside, the Second Battle of the Alamo illustrated Progressive Era women holding sacred memories against males' pecuniary interests.

By the end of their annual meeting in April 1907, the DRT was in a great schism, as the De Zavala faction and the Driscoll faction each claimed to be the legitimate DRT and hurled excommunications at the other. A St. Louis correspondent urged the Texas legislature to take back control of the Alamo property from the DRT and give it to a state-appointed commission (this eventually happened more than one hundred years later on July 10, 2015). However, the correspondent recognized that the governor and legislators embarked on such a drastic action at their peril, because "to get some of the leading women of Texas against one of them would come near meaning political defeat in the future."[43] Ultimately, the Driscoll faction resorted to the courts, who decided in their favor and legally recognized them as the governing body of the DRT.[44]

With legal recognition, Driscoll's party gained clearer title to the Alamo property and the right to take over daily operations as caretakers. De Zavala had not given up and stole a march on her rivals, seizing the building on February 8, 1908. By barricading herself in the building against civil authority (the local sheriff had tried to execute a legal injunction against her) and being a petite female, De Zavala gained nationwide attention. The story made banner headlines across the country: "Fair Texas Girl Holding Alamo Against Odds" (*Atlanta Constitution*); "Alamo in Siege Again; Defended by Lone Woman" (*St. Louis Post-Dispatch*); "Another Siege at Historic Alamo" (*Courier-Journal* [Louisville]); and "Defending the Alamo" (*New York Times*).[45] For three days De Zavala refused to allow the sheriff or his deputies to serve the injunction or take control of the building. Conversely, the sheriff and his deputies refused to allow her friends to supply her with food and drink.[46] She responded to a telegram sent from the *St. Louis Post-Dispatch*, addressed to the "Women of St. Louis," and showed despite the chill and lack of nourishment, her indomitable will remained. She invoked her renowned ancestors, "who suffered every privation to defend the freedom of Texas. I, like them, am willing to die for what I believe is right." De Zavala's battle was for more than just possession of the building but for the "immortal principle of liberty and right," and she believed women would stand with her.[47] The attention from various newspapers guaranteed that readers across the United States would remember the Alamo and the theatrics of one woman in particular.

After three days of negotiations, De Zavala struck her flag, but as the *Atlanta Constitution* headline stated, "She'll March from Fort with Her Colors Flying."[48] According to the agreed terms, De Zavala turned the Alamo over to W. C. Day, state superintendent of buildings, sent by Governor Thomas M. Campbell to defuse the situation. *The New York Times* reported that De Zavala left the building nearly too weak to stand, although she was cheered by friends and supporters. A second article described her actions more as a source of amusement to tourists. The journalist noted that De Zavala had "been heroically reviving memories of the bloody incident that gave the fort its name" but questioned whether such a strong reaction was warranted, being skeptical the State of Texas would permit the complete destruction of the Alamo.[49] De Zavala, Driscoll, and the DRT needed the Alamo as part of their Texan identity and collective memories; their disagreement centered on which parts were the authentic Alamo. Their actions confirm geographer Yi-Fu Tuan's observation: "The passion for preservation arises out of the need for tangible objects that can support a sense of identity."[50] Even today the physical remains of the Alamo are the foundation on which many Texans build their identity.

Although De Zavala may have won the battle of popular opinion, she lost the war. Several more years of court battles went against her, and she lost her control of the DRT in addition to custody of the Alamo. Ultimately, she even lost the Long Barracks. In late December 1911, Governor Oscar B. Colquitt led a meeting between the warring factions during which he offered to return the Alamo to its appearance just after the 1836 battle (which could have demolished the now familiar facade). However, nothing substantive came from this meeting.[51] Two years later the state legislature gave Colquitt $5,000 for repairs to the structure. At the time, the governor remained adamant that the Alamo should be restored to its appearance in 1836 and under no circumstances would he approve a park built on State property.[52] De Zavala believed Colquitt would not permit the State to dismantle the Long Barracks. However, while Colquitt was out of state, local city authorities, with the acquiescence of the lieutenant governor, took down the second-story walls of the Long Barracks in 1913.[53] Driscoll and her supporters within the DRT then lobbied the legislature and the courts to prevent any additional funding for work done on Alamo property.[54]

De Zavala did not take defeat lightly and marshaled allies, including Colquitt, Adele Looscan, and Charles Hueurmann, a former employee of Hugo & Schmeltzer. Hueurmann corresponded with both Colquitt and De Zavala, encouraging their efforts, noting in one letter that each stone of the original Alamo was a greater, "more sacred" monument to Texas than any made of "marble or granite."[55] In early 1913, Hueurmann tried to win over Texas State Representative Julius Real for De Zavala. However, Real responded that despite having several letters advocating De Zavala's position, he also had "telegrams and letters from several hundred people in my district," with a disparity of "a hundred to one" favoring the Driscoll faction.[56] De Zavala tried to sound encouraging, expecting a win in the Senate and "making converts every day."[57] Supporter Julius H. Erkner of San Antonio wrote to Adele Looscan, advocating for continuing the fight. He accused the Driscoll DRT faction of being "saturated with masculine notions." Erkner based his arguments on observing American tourists in Europe flock to castles, cathedrals, and Stonehenge, although "none have a history anything like the Alamo." He claimed, "These European ruins are not venerated for their religion or intrinsic value, but for monetary value." Erkner then turned his ire to the local press, accusing them of playing political games: "Their selfish motive is disgusting and I hope our brave Governor will soon complete and forever settle this question of trying to make money out of a sacred monument."[58]

Colquitt tried to defend himself in an editorial written to the *New York World*, claiming he had not authorized the dismantling of the second floor of the Long Barracks and threatened "criminal prosecution" against those responsible. The governor insisted he had tried to secure funding for preservation but was stymied by a cowardly legislature. The editor of the *World* was not sympathetic, charging that the motives driving the removal of the Long Barracks were "material and sordid" and openly wondered how long before it was decided that the church itself was expendable. The editor then scolded, "Texans boast of the bigness of their State, but if they permit the Alamo to be destroyed, America will conclude that, however big the State is, it is inhabited by a mighty small people."[59] Cantrell argues that Colquitt represented the male side of progressivism, being less affected by appeals to nostalgia and more driven to take control of the "Alamo away from the female amateurs of the DRT and place its fate in the hands of modern, professionally trained, male archaeologists, architects, and historians."[60] However, given that the DRT retained possession of the Alamo and the accompanying narrative for the next 102 years indicates that Colquitt was not successful in giving professional males control over the former mission. As a result of this Second Battle of the Alamo, the Alamo chapel with its distinctive facade remains the dominant feature of the compound to this day.

Adina De Zavala's Preservation of San Antonio's Spanish Past

Although Adina De Zavala lost control of the DRT and the Alamo, her efforts on behalf of San Antonio's other historic buildings and the missions had never waned, even during her struggles with the DRT. One individual interested in preserving San Antonio's old missions wrote to De Zavala recommending she "restore them to their original form and protect and preserve them for all future time, as sacred relics of a most interesting and pathetic period of our early settlement."[61] Besides research and writing, she continued efforts to preserve local landmarks, including the (misnamed) Spanish Governor's Palace. Indeed, along with architect Harvey P. Smith and (after 1924) the San Antonio Conservation Society (SACS), De Zavala's efforts "changed the course of [historic] preservation in Texas . . . opening the way for the restoration of the Spanish missions." But her efforts commanded a dreadfully heavy price to be paid, "the fabrication of history."[62] In 1917, she published her book, *History and Legends of the Alamo and Other Missions in and Around San Antonio*, which was part guidebook, part history, and much folklore. Herbert Gottfried observes that guidebooks in general "remind tourists that American places have a past, and those local historic persons, places, things and events have the capacity to add indications of authenticity to a location."[63] Her book, and particularly its ability to add the sense of authenticity Gottfried described, was a paean to the Alamo and the other missions as sites of memory.[64] While she did her research well for the time and employed a number of primary sources (including some colonial Spanish materials), her narrative was predictably hagiographic in terms of the Franciscan friars and the Alamo martyrs. Her work was indeed a product of its time but also of her own strong personality and her complex relationship with Tejanos, Anglos, and Texas history.[65]

Anthropologist Richard Flores critically examines Adina De Zavala and her motivations, concluding that she was, consciously or not, suppressing her Mexican heritage in favor of a larger "American" identity, which claimed that the heroic Anglo-Texan Alamo martyrs sacrificed their lives to transition Texas from the Spanish-Mexican past to a glorious American future. Flores argues that by including several examples of Spanish-Mexican folklore related to the Alamo and the missions in her book, she was acknowledging, even celebrating, her own Mexican heritage but at the same time sublimated it to Texan heroism and American progress.[66] De Zavala's backstory and Flores's critique give modern readers insight regarding the convoluted relationships she had with her subjects, beyond merely looking at it as the worshipping of the Anglo heroes at the Alamo.

Despite her defeat in the Second Battle of the Alamo, De Zavala was more historically correct than Driscoll. While the mystery remains whether the Long Barracks was indeed the site of the heaviest fighting and casualties, as the *convento* of Mission San Antonio de Valero, De Zavala's position that the Long Barracks was part of the original Alamo becomes much more defensible.[67] With this in mind, modern readers can see her righteous indignation showing up in the text of the book. De Zavala's descriptions of the mission compounds included maps showing exterior walls and related buildings, not solely the churches (a swipe at Driscoll's interpretation). Another jab at Driscoll appeared in the legend of the map of the Alamo and surrounding area where De Zavala pointedly reminded readers: "C. Front of the Main Building of the old Alamo Fort [to which we now refer as the Long Barracks]. The Alamo proper, where the heroes died, which together with the Church (1) is all that is left of the original Alamo."[68] The *San Antonio Express* applauded her book for having "supplied a long felt want" that was both "authentic" and portable for tourists visiting the missions.[69] Three days later came a more extensive description recommending the book to the larger-than-usual body of soldiers stationed at Fort Sam Houston (in preparation for the US entry into the First World War), in addition to interested readers nationwide. The reviewer concluded that there was "a wealth of romance and history and folklore" within the book and a reader would "not rest content until he or she has come to the spots bathed in the blood of heroes or golden with the chronicles of adventure and romance."[70]

Early travel narratives and guidebooks often included one or two abbreviated mission legends but generally did little to differentiate myth from documented history. De Zavala at least inserted a degree of separation between the two in her work. Of the twenty-nine chapters, eighteen are either poetry (typically maudlin) or legends. The legends are "real" in the sense that they are not fabrications of De Zavala's own imagination. She recorded but did not create these legends, but they are folklore and not necessarily supported by historical facts. Having her fact-based history coupled with the legends gave tourists more information that imbued a greater sense of authenticity to what they saw, what they told their friends back home, and the construction of collective memories about the Alamo and the missions.[71]

Marketing San Antonio's Missions in Southern Pacific's *Sunset* Magazine

Southern Pacific's *Sunset* magazine, launched in 1898, became the company's premier lifestyle and promotional publication. Although Southern California was the primary field of interest for *Sunset*, nationwide readers learned about the Spanish origins and mission period of the American Southwest. Some early articles introduced San Antonio and its missions to *Sunset* readers in general through nearly encyclopedic language or as reminiscence.[72] One *Sunset* correspondent, H. M. Mayo, claimed as early as 1899 that San Antonio had the sobriquet of "City of Missions" for "the many Spanish churches in the city and vicinity"; however, the name goes back a little further.[73] Similarly, G. C. Collingwood's 1906 essay read much like the booster tracts of earlier times, boasting of plentiful natural resources and a business-friendly atmosphere. But promises of "romance," "thrills," and "beauty" were just as prominent if not more so. Collingwood additionally complimented "strong, warm-hearted women," including Adina De Zavala and Clara Driscoll, for having "rescued" the old Alamo "from the despoiler."[74] However, journalist Alice Keatinge used more descriptive and colorful language to describe the city and its missions to *Sunset*'s readers. San Antonio owned "an inheritance greater than any other in the United States in her richly carved and sculptured old missions." She observed that local officials had constructed a streetcar line to "take you within a block of this mission [Concepción]," suggesting the city recognized the appeal of the missions to tourists. She also described that Concepción's "twin towers and Moorish dome rising out of the brush and small timber in the vicinity fill one with a mixture of wonder akin to the mystery of fairies, with a delight of the picturesque." Keatinge built the sense of mystery by asserting that local tales of underground passages connecting all of the missions were true. She also rhapsodized over the Moorish domes at San José and reported a conversation with Fr. Francis Bouchu, priest at Mission Espada. While she lamented the dilapidated condition of the missions, the elderly priest offered a different perspective, suggesting the $25,000 needed to restore the buildings would go much further to feeding and caring for his local Mexican parishioners who subsisted in crushing poverty.[75]

In a series of articles published in 1913, Agnes Laut rhetorically asked her *Sunset* readers, "Why go abroad?" Her articles romantically described different points of interest in the Southwest. Through colorful and florid descriptions, she invited readers to imagine visiting a distant land, comparable in exotic charms to the Holy Land, Persia, and the Alhambra of Spain, and even characterized the people living there as "Orientals" (despite the fact she was writing about Mission San Xavier del Bac and the Papago Indians just outside Tucson, Arizona).[76] Similarly, her reference to San Antonio as "America's Egypt" did not reflect much progression of style. She dubbed the town "the gateway city to the land of play and mystery." She remarked on the clashes between the old and the modern styles as both "Spanish-Moorish ruins" and "sky-scraper hotels that are the last word in modernity" flanked the "Spanish plazas."[77] Her articles were well illustrated with photographs of the Alamo and Concepción and drawings of the bell tower at San José.

Despite the examples of modernity all around it, Laut implored visitors to the Alamo to approach in solitude and silent reverence: "Let the mysticism and wonder and mystery of it sink in your soul! Soak yourself in the traditions of the past! Let the dead hand of the past reach forward and touch you! You will live over again the heroism of the Alamo; the heroism that preceded the Alamo—that of the Franciscans who tramped 300 leagues across the desert of Old Mexico to establish these missions."[78] Her pathos-fueled rhetoric drew readers deep into a romanticized version of history. Historian T. J. Jackson Lears argues that references such as Laut's that invoked the mystical and supernatural appealed to a middle class disenchanted with the dramatic social and economic changes wrought during this period in history. He suggests that those disillusioned with modern and industrial America sought refuge in "more intense forms of physical or spiritual experience supposedly embodied in medieval or Oriental cultures." Through these experiences, they believed they might gain "an ability to cultivate fantastic or dreamlike states of awareness, an intense otherworldly asceticism."[79] The missions had been considered medieval by more than one travel writer, and Laut's fantastic rhetoric encouraged readers to wrap themselves in the thick layer of just this kind of mystique to further enhance their tourist experience.

Several years later, Paul Ewing similarly described a "Thrilling Trip—to Borderland Missions This Time—for Western Autoists [*sic*] and Visitors to the West" that meandered from Texas, through New Mexico, to Arizona. The first page of the article featured a large photograph of Mission San José of San Antonio. Ewing's interesting observations began with the Alamo, which "symbolizes to Texas everything that's glorious in her history," and as a public shrine was "cherished by all Texas quite as reverently as Virginians cherish the home of Washington." Ewing characterized San Antonio as "the place 'where the Southwest begins.'" He opined that travelers from the Northeast might expect to find the arid climate, "the heavy proportion of Spanish-speaking people, . . . the old missions and the irrigation works built by the Spanish priests and still in use" much farther west than San Antonio. Nonetheless, Ewing insisted the stories of the missions in Texas, New Mexico, and Arizona were no less "colorful," the missionaries no less courageous, and "the churches no less influential in shaping the course of later events" than Fr. Junipero Serra and the California missions. Besides the Alamo, Ewing described San José as the most popular of the Texas missions, "largely because of its famous window" (Rosa's Window).[80] His article is noteworthy for being addressed to both motorists and railroad passengers, recognizing that the halcyon days of rail travel were numbered. Additionally, he raised the missions of San Antonio to a level on par with the missions in California, which usually received more publicity.

San Antonio and Mission Revival Architecture

Preserving works of historic architecture benefits not just tourists but also architects and designers who draw on the preserved works for inspiration. As sources of inspiration for design, articles (some illustrated) describing the missions of the Southwest appeared in professional architectural and building trade journals and magazines nationwide. These articles often perpetuated romanticized images of the missions to an important audience who frequently incorporated motifs and themes from the missions into the designs for their clientele, thereby reinforcing the fantasy Spanish heritage that inspired future preservation efforts. Historian Richard Orsi observes, "*Sunset* also helped to popularize the Spanish colonial revival, a movement after the 1890s to romanticize the mission period and to create a distinctive regional architectural and artistic style for the California and Southwest borderlands."[81] *Sunset* magazine was not the only publication touting the missions as architectural muse. In Texas, this style was often called "Alamo Revival" for the recurrent uses of the familiar gabled parapet motif from the Alamo's facade, particularly on railroad stations.[82] Train stations, government buildings, and even private residences designed and constructed in the Southwest after 1890 frequently incorporated stylistic motifs and features originally seen on a mission chapel. And whether the missions were in California or Texas, being mentioned in professional journals or lifestyle magazines effectively romanticized and commodified them into common design motifs. Thus, Southern Pacific advertisements and other promotional literature during this period frequently illustrated San Antonio's missions, thereby contributing to readers' collective memories.

Even before *Sunset* began glamorizing the mission period, architects and builders had begun looking at the San Antonio missions. In 1897, journalist Arthur Howard Noll described the Texas missions for the premier architectural journal *American Architect and Building News* and included some comparisons to those in California. Noll deemed the Alamo to be the only San Antonio mission worth preserving, although he considered San José worthy of note as "one of the finest examples of mission architecture on the continent" for its Churrigueresque facade expertly carved by the famous Spanish artist "Huica [*sic*]" sent from Spain for that sole purpose. Noll declared, "This elaborately sculptured façade is one of the marks differentiating the style of this building from that of the missions of the Pacific coast, though all the Texas missions are more distinctly Mooresque [*sic*] than those of California."[83] Noll's assertion that the Texas missions exhibited greater Moorish influence helped Orientalize both the missions and the eighteenth-century builders. It also reinforced the foreign and exotic attraction of mission architecture to American architects, builders, and their clients.[84]

Noll was neither the first nor the last architect to make the connection between Moorish influences on mission art and architecture. In 1903, architectural historian Olaf Cervin proclaimed, "The Christians in Spain showed repeatedly that they had learned a lesson in architecture from the Moors. In fact they learned it so well they never quite forgot it" and applied these stylistic influences all across the new world.[85] Like it had so many visitors earlier, the extensive decoration surrounding Rosa's Window enamored Cervin, but he erroneously speculated that the work was first carved in Spain and then transported and reassembled in San Antonio, although he credited "Huicar [*sic*]" as the artist.[86] In 1904, *Builder* magazine correspondent William S. Rice suggested San Antonio's "wonderful" missions were a "rare treat" for artists and architects alike. Despite a lurid recounting of the 1836 Alamo massacre, he observed that Missions Concepción, San José, and Espada still hosted religious services. Rice also praised the "gorgeous frescoes" and "graceful and daintily carved scrolls" on San José's "grand façade." He lamented the missions' ruinous condition because they were something "in point of architectural beauty many Americans would cross the Atlantic to see" and challenged his fellows in the construction industry to take inspiration from the many exotic and picturesque sights found within the United States rather than travel abroad.[87]

Architect Harvey Partridge Smith arrived in San Antonio in 1915 and was quickly captivated by the romanticized interpretation of the city's past. Nonetheless, he recollected being appalled that the early Chamber of Commerce booklets promoting San Antonio did not mention the history of the missions.[88] In 1918, he wrote his own version, *Romantic San Antonio*.[89] His descriptions of the city and the missions overflowed with superlatives, and his description of the 1836 Alamo siege and battle bordered on the fantastic (his authoritative description of Crockett's actions and final moments strains credulity). In the original version of his book, Santa Anna's troops are derided as "greasers," but by the 1936 edition, Smith omitted the racial slurs for more neutral "Mexicans" or "soldiers."[90] His depiction of Mission San José also changed from being the "Pearl of all the missions in New Spain."[91] By 1936, Smith proclaimed with little apparent modesty, "What is now the finest and grandest Spanish Mission in the United States once more takes on the appearance of its more glorious and prosperous days when San José was known as the 'Queen of all the Missions in New Spain'!"[92] Smith cited no authority for elevating San José from simply "Pearl" to royal "Queen."[93] Nonetheless, the mission retains the nickname "Queen of the Missions" into the twenty-first century as an indelible part of its mystique and aura.

Rexford Newcomb, a young professor of architecture, opined that visitors would find that "nothing holds more fascination for lovers of history and romance than the old Franciscan missions in and about the city." He limited his study to only the intricately carved facade of the Alamo, which he put on par with "Rosa's Window" of San José and even the California missions. He considered the column capitals, despite the ravages of time and battle damage, as "half Spanish, half Moorish in style, with perhaps even a touch of Indian," the Indigenous influence evidently being something unique in his experience with mission architecture. Newcomb was so fascinated with the building's facade that he ignored the Alamo's distinctive roofline (or perhaps this was his tacit recognition that it was not original). He surmised that the church was never completed and included a drawing of what he speculated the original designer was trying to achieve.[94] Newcomb's commentary reveals an early level of scholarly interest in the Texas missions, suggesting a closer relationship between popular and academic publications.

Atlee B. Ayers, one of San Antonio's most prominent architects, published one of the more comprehensive descriptions of the San Antonio missions in the journal *American Architect and the Architectural Review*. Unfortunately, while Ayers's descriptions were indeed comprehensive, they were not the most accurate. His reliance on earlier works resulted in perpetuating such earlier inaccuracies as assigning Spanish ethnicity to "Huicar [*sic*]" and crediting him with designing all five San Antonio missions. Ayers's writing style suggests he was more a local booster with a vested interest in keeping some of the myths alive for potential clients who might be interested in the then-popular Mission Revival style. Conversely, his essay carried the authority of a practicing architect from San Antonio. He opined that San Antonio's five missions were the "most beautiful survivals of Spanish American architecture on this continent." For Ayers, these buildings represented American manifest destiny. As "eloquent memorials of the opening battle of the great conquest of the American wilderness, they remind us of a heroism and religious devotion now little remembered." Ayers emphasized that the missions were built in a "quaint and peculiar style" with their "Moorish" qualities that highlighted their exotic nature, which might appeal to potential clients and fellow architects. He claimed that "connoisseurs" considered San José's intricate facade ornamentation "to be the finest gem of architectural ornamentation existing in America." Additionally, Ayers averred that unnamed experts adjudged the decoration adorning the renowned south sacristy window "as perfect in form and workmanship as anything found in the cathedrals of the Old World," reminding readers that exotic sights could be found on this side of the Atlantic Ocean.[95]

The next year, F. S. Laurence toured the American Southwest and named San Antonio as one of two locales where visitors could be enchanted by an "atmosphere of an ancient past." He limited his commentary to the missions' aesthetics. His rhetoric resembled Laut's as he indulged his imagination, conjuring a romantic scene that invited readers to "see the white robed monks of the old orders who ventured into this one time savage wilderness," addressing an assembly of "their aboriginal wards garbed in all the brilliant coloring of their" blankets and headdresses, as a "Spanish sentry in mediaeval breastplate and helmet with his glittering halberd" stands watch: "Truly a subject for the palette of a Titian!" Readers with equally vivid imaginations and less sense of anachronism could easily be drawn into his construction of a mythological

Spanish past at the missions. Laurence opined that San Antonio's missions were a hidden gem and that not enough of the American populace and particularly too few professional architects were aware of their existence. He thought that the missions could "be the pride of any country and the source of superb inspiration for an architectural style" that was both native to the soil and well suited to the climatic conditions of the southern tier of the country. Laurence concluded by challenging architects working in the Southwest or using the Mission Revival style that San Antonio's missions were just as inspirational as those in California and perhaps, he mused, even more so.[96]

Laurence, Ayers, Newcomb, Smith, Rice, Cervin, and Noll expounded on the exotic appeal held by Mission Revival style and its extensive influence in buildings across the Southwest. These attractions may have seemed innocuous at the time, but it also exemplified the endemic Orientalism and cultural appropriation of this period.[97] Conversely, these architectural experts asserted that Mission Revival was a native style, created within the boundaries of the United States, and thus an important part of America's stylistic heritage.[98] Nonetheless, by the second decade of the 1900s, the Mission style, along with its Spanish, Moorish, and Mexican influences, helped fuel what historian Helen Delpar described as an "enormous vogue of things Mexican."[99] Since Ayers and Smith were locals, their descriptions of the missions full of booster-style hyperbole should come as no surprise. That other professionals in the arts and architectural fields added their own superlatives indicates the importance San Antonio's missions held. What these numerous appearances in architecture-related publications infers is that while the missions were indeed neglected, they were never completely forgotten, at least by architecture scholars and professionals whose attentions justified efforts at preservation.

Advertising "Romantic San Antonio" and Enticing Tourists to "See America First"

From the closing decades of the nineteenth century throughout much of the twentieth, drawings, pictures, photographs, and textual descriptions of the missions were used for commercial purposes. The images most frequently appeared in advertisements in newspapers and magazines, pamphlets, and guidebooks, which in turn, offer insights on motivations and expectations of the traveling public.[100] These images sold travel and tourism to San Antonio and the American Southwest; they additionally sold the particular modes of travel besides the specific companies specializing in the modes. As the public consumed these images, the advertisements encouraged the formation of an American identity based on the construct of a mythological Spanish past. About this time, many of the same companies that created these advertisements pushed the idea that Americans should "see America first" rather than take their vacations (and money) across the ocean to Europe. The goal of these "see America first" advocates was to inculcate among Americans a sense of "virtuous consumption," and that by touring (and thus consuming) the nation, they would make themselves better Americans with a stronger sense of national identity.[101] Those involved in the nascent tourist advertising industry colluded with boosters in producing guidebooks and advertisements that favorably compared American attractions to those in Europe.

Historian Michael Zega offers some useful observations on the advances in advertising during this time period, especially the ad campaign used by the Atchison, Topeka and Santa Fe Railway (better known as the Santa Fe). He notes that from the beginning, the "printed page" was the centerpiece. Advertisements placed in the mass media of the day (newspapers and magazines), supplemented by tens of thousands of printed booklets, constituted the campaign's "driving force." He also claims the Santa Fe was unique in linking "a mythic West" to marketing Southern California. However, the Santa Fe was not "unique"; the Southern Pacific Railroad was using a similar strategy of illustrated advertisements in mass media supplemented by booklets selling an equally romantic and exotic vision of a different part of the American Southwest that included Texas. Despite the "strikingly beautiful" view of the Southwest in the advertising images, Zega argues that the effectiveness of the images stems "from a pervasive climate of thoughtless cultural appropriation that characterized the era" and calls modern viewers' attention to the "exploitative attitude" that created them.[102] In this aspect, other companies were using similar strategies and were just as culpable.

Because the Southern Pacific's premier line, the Sunset Route, ran farther south than the Santa Fe, the images used in the advertising frequently emphasized the Spanish and Mexican character of the land rather than images of Plains or Pueblo Indians that made up the bulk of ads created for the Santa Fe. The graphic advertisements and booklets created to promote the Sunset Route could be just as exploitive of San Antonio's Mexican American population and just as easily portrayed San Antonio as a romantic and exotic playground for American elites from the sophisticated Northeast. In 1911, Charles S. Fee, Southern Pacific's passenger traffic manager, described for *The Graphic Arts* trade magazine some of the various methods used to get the company's message to consumers. From 1910 to 1911, thirty-one booklets with "artistic covers, beautiful photographs, and interestingly accurate information" had been issued with a combined print run of 1,358,000 copies. Fee asserted that these booklets were available worldwide and were used in conjunction with "postcards, sky-signs, photographs, lantern slides, and motion pictures." Although these were advertisements, Fee described them as "the highest examples of photographic art."[103] Southern Pacific enjoyed considerable marketing success from the power and value of advertising. The Passenger Department was responsible for the bulk of advertisements, whether they appeared in the mass media or as printed booklets, and between 1888 and 1911, Southern Pacific's advertising and printing budget ballooned from $150,000 to $1.8 million.[104] Women's travel clubs of the era were just some of those who would use these materials as they prepared for actual or, more likely, vicarious journeys to San Antonio's missions.[105]

Large transcontinental railroads such as the Southern Pacific and Santa Fe had their own advertising and printing department to churn out advertisements, guidebooks, and other print materials by the thousands. Although smaller railroad companies did not always have those advantages, collaborating with San Antonio's Chamber of Commerce provided useful information to highlight the romantic and exotic attractions potential travelers would find by visiting the city. These smaller rail lines included the Missouri, Kansas, and Texas (better known as MKT, or "The Katy"), and the Iron Mountain (also known as the St. Louis, Iron Mountain, and Southern railroad, which was affiliated with the Texas & Pacific line). The advertisements resembled those by Southern Pacific in emphasizing romance and the exotic adventures that awaited tourists who ventured to San Antonio. Generally, the ad featured an illustration (often of one of San Antonio's missions) with text highlighting the various attractions visitors would find, including golf, hunting, fishing, polo, balls, and banquets, all in a hospitable climate. Then would be text describing the railroad, train amenities, and sometimes schedules. There would also be a name and address for San Antonio's Chamber of Commerce, whom potential visitors were encouraged to contact for additional information.[106]

Advertisements such as one the MKT railroad placed in *Town and Country* magazine emphasized San Antonio's warm climate as opposed to the "chilly North." Sightseers would thrill upon visiting "the old Mission Churches" and Alamo. San Antonio was, "of all America, the oddest blending of modern utility and beauty, with the romance and heroism of the medieval."[107] Additionally, the MKT furnished passengers with picture postcards, including photo reproductions of Mission San José.[108] By 1911, MKT advertising personnel began collaborating with San Antonio officials, such as an ad showing a fashionably dressed couple dining near a balcony as the text touted "eating al fresco in January!" While people in Northern parts of the country were "shivering" and "cooped-up" inside trying to keep warm, folks in San Antonio were enjoying warm-weather activities such as golf and driving open-topped through the country, "where the historic old missions are waiting to be viewed." For additional information, interested readers were directed to J. B. Carrington, secretary of the Publicity League for the San Antonio Chamber of Commerce. Readers were also reminded that "the best way to go is via the Katy."[109] By December 1911, the Publicity League had teamed up with additional lines, including the Iron Mountain Route, to promote the new winter tourist season.[110]

San Antonio city officials and business organizations created their own publications for tourists in addition to working with various railroads. Although ostensibly written for tourists, these publications read more like booster tracts soliciting business and immigration to the city. Hyperbole and superlatives permeated nearly every page: "Beautiful San Antonio: The Commercial and Industrial Center of the Southwest. The Great Health Resort of America. 'The Largest City, in the Wealthiest County, in the Greatest State, in the Grandest Country, in the World.'" The next page quoted the recent 1900 census as it boasted, "The Largest as it is also the Most Beautiful City in the State and the Healthiest City in the United States offering many splendid opportunities for Investments."[111] The text predictably described the missions in a similar fashion: "Those who adore the historic, revel in the quaint old missions and go into ecstasies over the superior artistic skill displayed in the carving and statuary that so emphatically placards the proficiency of the workmen who executed them, notwithstanding that for nearly two centuries the destroying hand of time has been assiduous in efforts to ruin the delicate tracings," named these buildings as favorite attractions.[112]

Other municipally published guidebooks hyped the romantic history of the city. One booklet detailed attractions to "appeal to your patriotic pride" and "picturesque quaintness to delight your sense of the beautiful." Describing San Antonio as "pre-eminently the city of romance," the authors compared the 1836 Alamo massacre to the 1854 "Charge of the Light Brigade" at Balaclava and noted that the missions in addition to San Fernando Cathedral breathed "the spirit of the Spaniard and the Moor in survivals of continental architecture of wonderful beauty."[113] Taking a page from the "See America First" crowd, the authors assured tourists that from wherever they came, "you will find in the historic traditions of old San Antonio that which will quicken your patriotism and make you a more loyal American."[114]

The prosperity of the 1920s encouraged railroads as well as San Antonio's Chamber of Commerce to increase the level and graphic nature of advertising. The primary themes within the ads, romance and adventure, changed little, although patriotism and nativism were also much in evidence. One striking Southern Pacific advertisement from 1921 revealed the confluence of these themes. The illustration featured a figure in buckskins and a raccoon-skin hat taking cover behind the unmistakable gabled parapet topping the modern Alamo facade, shooting at unseen enemies below. The large text nearest his head cried "Remember the Alamo! What Davy Crockett won, for you, today in San Antonio." Additional text claimed that with the loss of the Alamo martyrs, "in the bravest battle against odds that Americans ever fought, the winning of an empire began." Curiously there was no comparison of the Alamo to Thermopylae, which commonly appeared in many other travel narratives. The ad further maintained that Sam Houston rallied his troops, "routed Santa Anna and forever removed the Mexican menace from Texas soil." The text assured readers the Alamo still stood as "a historic shrine which every liberty-loving American delights to visit"[115] (fig. 4.1). Herein lies a thorny question of how "every liberty-loving American" who "delights to visit" the Alamo is defined. Certainly, in the early 1920s, "American" was understood to be white, male, Anglo-Saxon, and Protestant. Any mixed feelings the Tejano population or other Mexican Americans might have toward the Alamo as a symbol of Anglo oppression were ignored.[116]

Stories of the Alamo were familiar to Anglo-Americans during this time, so the graphics and text of this particular advertisement easily tap into collective memories of Crockett and the Alamo. Decades before Fess Parker and John Wayne, Anglo-Americans knew Davy wore a raccoon-skin cap, and many knew what the Alamo looked like (or at least they knew what the Alamo looked like in their time, not when Crockett and his comrades-in-arms actually fought and died there). In the memories of Anglo-Americans, Crockett's martyrdom at the Alamo was essential for Anglo expansion across the continent.

One feature of these various advertising materials that should not be forgotten was the frequent caricature of the Mexican American population. Granted, some images were not as offensive as they might have been; generally,

Fig. 4.1. "Remember the Alamo!" Sunset Route advertisement, Southern Pacific Railroad. *New York Times*, February 7, 1921. JPEG scan from microfilm by author.

men in large sombreros and sarapes, sometimes with guitars serenading their señorita, wrapped in her rebozo with an ornate *peineta* and mantilla. Images of one of the missions (usually Concepción or San José) often appeared as the backdrop for the scene. Romantic, perhaps, but such images nonetheless stereotyped local minorities as exotic Other, especially when contrasted to a fashionably dressed Anglo family.[117] Forays by tourists into San Antonio's "Mexican Quarter" had been described or recommended in travel narratives for decades prior and served to harden stereotypes of Mexican Americans. If the Northern elites found the Anglo population of San Antonio provincial, the unfortunate denizens of the Mexican Quarter (in reality a notorious slum) were considered barely civilized, as one observer seemed to delight in proclaiming: "Many of them have not yet arrived at the dignity of a modern cookstove."[118] Travelogues and travel narratives, as well as advertisements at this time, unfortunately reinforced and exploited racial and ethnic stereotypes to sell products and services and, by virtue of being placed in popular mass media, spread the stereotypes to a larger audience. Finally, Anglos' ventures into San Antonio's Mexican Quarter reinforced their own notions of American identity and superiority; as Shaffer notes, they used the ethnic and socioeconomic Others as "foils against which they could distinguish themselves as cultured and refined Americans."[119]

After the stock market crash of 1929 and onset of the Great Depression, some of the railroads changed their advertising campaigns. Images of San Antonio's missions remained frequent backgrounds, but the text often stressed economy as opposed to the luxury of spending an entire season in the city. The Katy railroad advertised San Antonio as an "inexpensive, different vacation" or "an unusual inexpensive vacation."[120] Despite lower fares, "the lure of Old Spain" with the "Spanish Missions, centuries old," replete with an image of a guitar-strumming vaquero, remained a stock graphic for the Katy.[121] The Southern Pacific meanwhile refocused its ads mostly on its home state of California. A new train from Chicago to El Paso, the Golden State Limited, bypassed San Antonio and reduced travel time and fares.[122]

With these shifts in advertising strategy and particularly to offset potential losses of tourists, the City of San Antonio's Municipal Information Bureau mounted its own ad campaigns. The style and text highlighted similar attractions as those mentioned in guidebooks and railroad ads: congenial weather, the Spanish Missions, the Alamo, outdoor sports, and economic opportunities. The ads appeared in similar venues as those placed by railroads, including the *Chicago Tribune*, *Los Angeles Times*, and *Wall Street*

Journal. Some of the text from selected ads bears further scrutiny for what it says about how San Antonio presented itself to potential tourists. One early ad beckoned tourists to come "south with the sun to San Antonio." Another assured visitors that "an old world charm lingers" on the "Road to Romance" in the city "200 years young!"[123] A curious advertisement appeared in the *Los Angeles Times*: a large outline of the state of Texas showing two rail lines crossing each other at San Antonio. At the same time, a drawing representing a Spanish conquistador with metal cuirass, morion, flag, and sword stood above a figure in tights, cape, plumed chapeau, and rapier (representing the French). The accompanying text proclaimed San Antonio to be "at the Crossroads of Nations"; the city occupied a "spot so lovely that Old World nations warred to possess it two centuries ago!" The French were labeled "intrepid," while the Spanish were "arrogant." The Franciscans solved the crisis by planting missions, thus claiming the region for New Spain.[124]

The idea of Texas as a "crossroads of nations" remains equally valid today for Borderland studies specialists. The missions, as outposts of the Spanish Empire, as sacred spaces, as community centers, and as tourist attractions, have acted as borders for different populations for over three centuries. The romantic and mythological Spanish past sold vacations to the city. Another city-sponsored advertisement used the *espadaña* of Mission Espada as a backdrop to declare San Antonio as the "Most interesting Southern city." Declaring there was "romance in the very name" of the city, the ad stated that "tall palms sigh in the soft breeze . . . venerable missions sit dreaming of past glories" to attract winter tourists.[125] While historian Melita Garza demonstrates how local, San Antonio newspapers "exerted their editorial authority to rescue, preserve, and memorialize Spanish colonial culture as they defined it," they were not the only media guilty of creating or perpetuating these stereotypes.[126] Other mass media across the nation were just as liable.

Historian Richard Garcia describes San Antonio during this time as "at the crossroads of Texan, Mexican, and U.S. myth, memory, and identity."[127] In addition to romantic history, San Antonio's Municipal Information Bureau's advertising campaign accentuated Anglo patriotism. A drawing of the Alamo facade stood over text that claimed, "Every American should see San Antonio." As noted earlier, the bureau's target demographic was "Americans" defined as "Anglo." The advertisement proclaimed that the "missions—outposts of civilization in America—were old when the Declaration of Independence was signed!" However, even by 1776, Mission San José had not yet been completed as the ornate church seen today. Just because the first mission, San Antonio de Valero (the Alamo), was founded in 1718 (only fifty-eight years prior to the founding of the United States), San José in 1720, and the others in the 1730s, does not mean the church buildings as seen today were completed within a few years of the founding date. This is perhaps the most common misconception regarding the missions and was likely the result of ignorance of medieval and baroque styles. It also comes as no surprise that the ad writers were overplaying their hand. San Antonio offered many interesting and beautiful sights, and hyperbole and superlatives were regular tools of the advertising trade, but it is an open question whether some of the ads raised unreasonable expectations. Other attractions mentioned in the ad included the Alamo, "where patriots died for Texas liberty," and a "cosmopolitan capital" that combined the "best traditions of colonial Spain, the old South, and the robust West."[128]

Rena Maverick Green and SACS at Mission San José

As the twentieth century progressed, San Antonio's elite women continued to press for more preservation of the city's built environment, and the missions benefited from their efforts. Mary Rowena (Rena) Maverick Green, like Adina De Zavala, exhibited a love for San Antonio, a high level of independent thinking, and considerable resourcefulness. Despite being widowed at the age of thirty-three with four children, Green added the roles of community activist, suffragette, artist, and historian to her curriculum vitae. With a handful of other like-minded women, she cofounded, with Emily Edwards, the San Antonio Conservation Society (SACS) in March 1924 and during the early 1930s served as its president.[129] One of SACS's earliest and most unusual tactics to raise civic awareness for historic preservation was a puppet show presented to a meeting of San Antonio's city commissioners.[130] The puppets had been made to resemble the sitting commissioners. Green and another SACS member had regularly attended previous meetings and sat quietly in the back sketching each commissioner. The script of the puppet show was based on the ancient fable "The Goose That Laid the Golden Eggs." In the SACS retelling, Mr. San Antonio wanted to eliminate the Goose as an impediment to modern prosperity while Mrs. San Antonio wanted to save the Goose that gave them such golden eggs as "Beauty" and, more important, an egg named "Missions." The Goose represented the city's "peculiarities" that brought forth a bounty in the form of tourists' gold.[131] While the impact this little play had at the time could be debated, it is obvious that SACS viewed the missions as one of the community's "Golden Eggs," an irreplaceable part of the city that added value, attracted additional wealth, and functioned as a site of memory.

In addition to raising community awareness regarding the importance of the missions to San Antonio, SACS reached out to see how other missions in other states had been preserved and incorporated into the economy of those locales. In the fall of 1924, still in its first year and hoping to make a significant and positive impact in the community, SACS contacted the Southwest's greatest living booster, Charles Fletcher Lummis, and the Landmarks Club of California to inquire how their Spanish missions were being preserved and promoted. Lummis responded that he viewed the missions as an expression of the designing artist's vision, as historical relics, as well as "the embodiment of a great spiritual idea."[132] By early 1925, Green had been made chair of SACS's Standing Committee on the Missions and was in more frequent communication with Lummis and others on how best to preserve the mission buildings. Additionally, SACS was in contact with Arthur J. Drossaerts, then bishop of the Roman Catholic Diocese of San Antonio (elevated to archbishop of San Antonio in 1927). Drossaerts initially seemed amenable to SACS's endeavors and promised to contact his clerical counterparts in California regarding their missions. One of the ideas that came from their discourse with the Californians was that the Landmarks Club leased the missions for ten years at a time from the church for a token amount. The lease allowed the club to supervise any architectural repairs and improvements, and the club eschewed modifications that were not authentic or might harm the buildings' role as sacred space. SACS was also able to acquire copies of contracts between the Diocese of the Los Angeles area and the Landmarks Club preliminary to restoration projects at three of the California missions. SACS sent the copies to its lawyers for further study.[133]

Despite suggestions by the lawyers from both SACS and the Diocese of San Antonio that with only minor alterations an arrangement similar to the one the Landmarks Club held with several dioceses in California could be hammered out, Drossaerts stalled. Although the exact nature of the opposition has not yet been found, in 1927 the bishop declined to agree to lease any of the mission properties to SACS. There was precedent for a lease as in 1902; Bishop John A. Forest had given a five-year lease to the De Zavala Chapter of the DRT to make improvements at Mission San Juan.[134] In the late 1920s, Drossaerts was in communication with Franciscan organizations outside the state, trying to recruit some "Sons of St. Francis" to return to "THEIR CITY: the City of the Franciscan Missions of Texas."[135] If Drossaerts had designs on restoring the missions to functional church properties, he may not have wanted SACS to be in the way of his plans. Even as late as March 1931, Drossaerts seemed to be holding on to the idea of bringing a Franciscan community in to set up near San José.[136] However, there were factors that complicated any plans at San José.

At 3:30 in the morning on Friday, March 9, 1928, the bell tower of Mission San José split asunder "as if it had been separated by a giant cleaver" and collapsed. Fortunately, San José's greatest artistic treasures, Rosa's Window in the sacristy and the chapel's ornate facade, were unharmed. Archbishop Drossaerts issued directives to restore the tower "exactly as it was. The same stone which came out of the tower will be put back in, and where replacements are necessary, stone like that formerly used will be used. Even the same ornaments will be used wherever possible."[137] The next day the archbishop reassured parishioners: "Services will be held as usual in Mission San José while repairs are being made."[138] The *Express* correspondent reported that the mission church had been "under constant repair" for eleven years, and just two months prior to the collapse, the tower itself had been "repaired and everything considered necessary was done at the time." Evidently, either the repairs were insufficient or had done more harm than good. Through the *Express*, SACS took the occasion to urge citizens of San Antonio to dedicate themselves, as SACS members had done, to the preservation of the missions. SACS chided those they believed should have taken more tangible steps to "save our historic, romantic, and artistic monuments." In a not-so-subtle jab at Drossaerts for vacillating on the negotiations over the leases, SACS vowed to "re-double efforts to gain the legal position that will enable us to control the permanent preservation work of the community."[139]

According to San Antonio's Spanish-language newspaper, *La Prensa,* in early April 1928, Mrs. Perry J. Lewis, president of SACS, indicated that SACS hoped to be able to preserve all four missions and beautify the grounds with gardens and suggested they were still negotiating with Archbishop Drossaerts. She also stated that while two of the missions had keepers, SACS hoped to provide similar custodians for the other two.[140] Two days later, however, *La Prensa* reported that there was opposition to the idea that SACS should be allowed to care for the missions. Unfortunately, *La Prensa* did not give names or indicate where this opposition came from other than beyond "members of the local Church." Drossaerts told *La Prensa* the church had already allocated $11,000 to repair the collapsed bell tower at San José, and while he did not object to SACS planting gardens around mission properties, he firmly declared that the missions were the property of the Catholic Church, which would look after their own, and any necessary preservation work was best left "in our hands." Lewis replied that SACS was offering a proposal similar to one that allowed a nonsectarian group to care for the "famous missions of California," an agreement that seemed to be working to the satisfaction of both parties.[141]

La Prensa indicated that powers beyond the local church opposed the plan, which would suggest it came from within the archdiocesan hierarchy, but why? Perhaps some of the other priests and bishops within the archdiocese lobbied Drossaerts to keep the missions fully under Catholic control, especially since Drossaerts was trying to recruit Franciscans to return to the San Antonio area and set up ministries at the missions. In this respect, Drossaerts probably valued the missions more as sacred space than tourist attractions. Was it over SACS's secular status? SACS had been very open about its ecumenical membership roster.[142] Did Drossaerts not believe a group of society women could be trusted with a project of this magnitude? Although women led the historic preservation movement early on, by the twentieth century there was a move to put professional architects (overwhelmingly male) in charge.[143] The best answer may be all of the above, as complex historical questions rarely have simple answers. Nonetheless, relations between the church and SACS remained contentious for years following.

Despite opposition from the church, SACS had a backup plan. It simply began purchasing the land surrounding the missions from private owners. This strategy even allowed SACS to purchase land within the original mission compounds and ultimately the granary of Mission San José. Although some parcels were sold back to the church, SACS assured Drossaerts that relinquishing title to these specific properties did nothing to end the organization's work on behalf of the old mission.[144] SACS's unsuccessful attempts to lease the mission properties from the Catholic Church and the subsequent purchase of land surrounding the missions removed the properties from the open market but also effectively commoditized the sacred space. Chidester and Linenthal mention complicating methods such as commodification as one of the ways "American historical experience has shaped the production of sacred space."[145] Just as with De Zavala's attempts to keep the Alamo free from commercial interests, even space formally recognized as sacred also has value as a limited commodity and risks being profaned.

Unfortunately for SACS, raising money to make these purchases in the midst of the Great Depression was not easy to do; but through creative fundraising, calling in debts, yard sales, loans, and government assistance, the women of SACS persevered. A rummage sale in late 1930, before the worst of the Depression reached San Antonio, netted $2,000, while just a few years later in harder economic times, Green expressed some amazement when the DRT managed to pay off a debt of $100 owed for stone.[146] SACS's primary accomplishment during the first half of the 1930s was the reconstruction of the granary at San José. SACS managed this through much lobbying for donations in the form of materials and labor. Additional labor came from Depression-era relief programs. Despite these many travails, SACS managed to restore the granary and its unique flying buttresses at San José. This success led to greater cooperation from Bexar County and the church in getting US federal assistance for rebuilding the rest of San José.[147]

In addition to writing a book hyping the beauty of San Antonio's missions, architect Harvey P. Smith worked to restore San José. As a result, he developed a working relationship with SACS. At the April 1931 meeting, SACS President Taylor introduced Smith to the group as a member of the National Historical Building Committee. He "made an inspiring talk on the Missions and their preservation, how we must safeguard them" and ensure "only that which is true to the Mission Period be featured in their preservation." Similarly, Smith "spoke of San José as the pearl of all Missions, the finest example of Colonial Architecture in New Spain."[148] Smith returned to a SACS meeting in January 1932 to report on his work reconstructing the San José granary. He also showed illustrations of plans for work at San José based on excavations. And he reminded SACS "again of the treasure we have in the Missions," comparing them to California's and highlighting the manner in which Californians promoted their missions. But he remarked that California's missions were separated by some distance, while San Antonio had all five, "more ancient and more beautiful," within a concentrated area. And Smith did not pass up the opportunity to describe San José as "the queen of all missions in the United States" and "the finest piece of Spanish colonial architecture" in the country.[149] Two years later, Smith met with the SACS Board of Directors to give a status update on his work at San José, where he assured them that "only authentic records were being followed" for the restoration work.[150]

The Missions and Centennial '36

On November 6, 1923, advertising consultant Theodore Price delivered an address to a meeting of the Advertising Clubs of the Tenth District at Corsicana, just south of Dallas. He opened his remarks by apologizing for being a New Yorker presuming to tell his audience how best to market Texas to attract business and investment capital. Nonetheless, Price admonished his listeners that besides the state's abundant natural resources, "you have something else whose value and whose appeal I doubt whether you yourselves appreciate. It is your gloriously romantic history." He advocated that a celebration similar to the various world's fairs held in other major cities in honor of the centennial of the first land titles awarded to Stephen F. Austin in 1924 would more effectively show the world what Texas had to offer. "[In] mere bigness it could and should be made to exceed anything else of the kind ever attempted."[151] While 1924 came and went without the proposed celebration, his words had fallen on fertile ground. In 1936, the state commemorated the centennial of its independence from Mexico with a celebration on the scale Price had urged twelve years before with a major exhibition in Dallas and numerous other events around the state. However, Price was mistaken if he truly believed Texans had never leveraged the power of romantic history in marketing the state's advantages for business, investments, and tourism. As we have seen, a heavily romanticized version of Texas history had been standard fodder in advertisements and travel narratives for many years, particularly as the San Antonio publicity department cooperated with railroad advertising departments. By 1935, Texas was well on its way to hosting a centennial celebration in a style that Price surely would have approved. However, in preparing the narrative of Texas history for this oversize celebration, professional, critical history lost out to collective memory (notwithstanding the existing historiography), or as historian Kenneth Ragsdale bluntly stated, "Texans were about to be subjected to the greatest historical brainwashing in the state's history."[152] Modern Texas author Stephen Harrigan agrees: "One of the core goals of the exposition was to 'Texanize Texans,' to acquaint the citizens of the state with the marvels of its industrial might and its unparallelled history."[153]

Contributions and lived experiences of the various minority groups within the state were routinely silenced during the celebration.[154] Literary scholar John Morán González concurs that the narrative of Texas history as told at centennial celebrations marginalized Texans of Mexican descent and justified most any measure of discrimination against them.[155] The marginalization of Tejanos in the centennial narratives of which González speaks blatantly appear in the official guidebook from the Dallas fairgrounds, site of the official exposition and celebration. Hyperbole and superlatives saturated this story of Texas. From this booklet, readers learned that while "the saga of Texas began with the conquistadores," in actuality, "the debt of the free citizens of Texas today is a debt to tall men with long rifles, American frontiersmen." In describing the fair as "An Empire on Parade," the guidebook boasted, "No chapter of American history is richer in romance, dramatic highlights, and stirring events." Readers were also promised that "against a background of history made brilliant by the story of the mission priest and Spanish Don, pioneer and frontiersman, the sharp imprint of Texas will be revealed." The exhibits and shows continually reinforced the collective memory of Texas as a wilderness saved only by the interventions of Anglos. At the Cavalcade of Texas, the triumphalist interpretation continued as an exhibit "written and produced as a living saga of the inexorable advance of civilization, by blood and iron and the enduring will of the white man, in what was once only the wild land of the naked savage." Interestingly, this particular exhibit considered all European explorers (even Spanish) as "white." Finally, at the Old West exhibit, a replica of the Alamo (not quite to full scale) contained numerous documents and relics and reproduced for visitors "the story of the epic battle of the Alamo, one of the most tragic and yet most glorious in all history." This display contained (with apparently no sense of irony) "placards and tablets marking the corresponding spots where various Texas heroes fell in their desperate, hopeless, resistance against fifteen times their number of Mexican troops."[156]

Other centennial advertisements, mementos, pamphlets, posters, and ephemera used similar hagiographic rhetoric. Advertisements suggested interesting vacation spots statewide, such as beaches, dude ranches, "foreign color," mountains, and missions.[157] A brochure titled *All America Is Invited to Visit Texas' Centennial Celebration* oozed similar hyperbole. Texas was divided by cardinal directions, with South Texas (including San Antonio) being the "Cradle of Texas History, Rich in Romance." Only the limited space prevented a more lurid account of the 1836 Alamo battle. Visitors were also directed to the other four missions south of town.[158] Predictably, promotional material was created for Texas schools, including a sourcebook to provide elementary teachers with programs and lesson plans for the centennial year. However, it was the typical romanticized history as elsewhere. Half of the section on "Spanish Texas" was taken up with one of the legends of Rosa's Window at Mission San José, according to which the king of Spain's favorite artist, Pedro Huizar, was sent to decorate the mission. His sweetheart, Rosa, followed a few years later but died before she arrived.[159] Not every example of centennial kitsch included derogatory stereotypes; nonetheless, there is an implication of the Spanish colonial era being "frozen in time" and subsequently safe to be appropriated into Anglos' concept of a mythological Spanish past. Another part of the anti-Mexican racism of the 1930s was a "sin of omission" in that Spanish and Mexican accomplishments were silenced or appropriated into the Anglo progressive historical narrative. Other times, the racism was painfully open and blatant.

As Texas prepared for the various celebrations and events, the Alamo and other missions were not forgotten, as some tried to make them the focal point for some of the celebrations. Fr. Mariano Simon Garriga spearheaded efforts to have US President Franklin D. Roosevelt deliver a nationwide radio address on the anniversary of the 1836 Battle of the Alamo. Garriga served as archdiocese historian for San Antonio and was a member of the Texas Historical Commission.[160] Writing to Congressman Maury Maverick, Garriga expressed deep disappointment that the president could not find the time to make such an address. He reminded Maverick that men from twenty states had fallen at the Alamo, making the battle more of a nationwide attraction. He also played on the Alamo's importance in the Texas creation myth, claiming, "Texas Pride will be . . . deeply hurt" because so many Texans "have their hearts and their patriotic devotion centered in this cherished shrine of Texas Liberty." Calling the 1836 Battle of the Alamo "the turning point in the history of the country," Garriga implored of Maverick what "unpardonable sin" San Antonio had committed that, "now when in the Centennial we actually reach the high spot-we can not get anything better than a letter from the President!"[161] Maverick responded that while Texas was indeed important, the president regularly received huge numbers of similar requests from other groups and states. Maverick also informed Garriga that the president had officially recognized the Texas Centennial as a favor to Maverick, which in and of itself was more than what was usually done. A few days later, Roosevelt stated he would make a trip to Texas sometime during the centennial celebrations.[162] Besides handling Garriga's demands, Maverick spoke to the US House of Representatives on May 14, 1936, recounting Texas's glorious history and inviting his colleagues to visit the centennial celebrations. In addition to the Alamo, Maverick specifically named San Antonio's other four missions and recommended anyone visiting for the centennial should include them on their itinerary.[163] Maverick's and Garriga's passion reveals the level at which they (and certainly many other Texans) held this epic interpretation of the Alamo and Texas's history as part of their identity.

The centennial narratives were the inevitable construction of one hundred years of Anglos' collective memories of a land brimming with natural resources and limitless opportunity but occupied by benighted, exotic Others. According to this narrative, Providence smiled on the Anglos as they audaciously seized the land, thus redeeming it and exploiting it to its fullest potential. While some of the centennial narratives recognized that Texas did have a deep multicultural history, the images and descriptions ultimately contained the exploitive and paternalistic tone of a conqueror, not an equal. Although the primary fair in Dallas did not meet expectations in terms of number of visitors and money taken in, the collateral benefits from increased advertising, increased tourism to other parts of the state, and hotel revenues made a positive economic impact overall.[164] The actual mission buildings in San Antonio received significant attention in terms of money (both state and federal) and resources for the constant maintenance and repairs old buildings require, including $75,000 for restoration work at the Alamo and $20,000 for Mission San José.[165]

Dallas businessman Stanley Marcus once reminisced that the 1936 Texas Centennial celebration was when "the rest of America discovered Texas."[166] But he was wrong; America had already discovered Texas. And one of the reasons America already knew about Texas was San Antonio and its missions, not just through the Alamo, although it certainly received the lion's share of attention, but also through images and descriptions of the other missions frequently appearing in advertisements and literature promoting travel for decades. From numerous formats, including travel advertising, guidebooks, and postcards, America had been informed of the romantic and exotic Spanish missions in San Antonio. Well before the 1936 Texas Centennial, Southern Pacific, the Katy, and other railroads had been promoting Texas tourism in various media. Architects and artists had been copying or inserting decorative features derived from mission architecture into their commissions as well. Perhaps Marcus was too young to recognize the effects, or because his store was based in Dallas, he did not see the tourists flocking to San Antonio. And the tourists were indeed coming, drawn by agreeable weather, pleasurable activities, and interesting sights. The Alamo and the other four missions remained high on the list of interesting sights and were regular features in advertising campaigns. They were all sites of memory, and the events during the first third of the twentieth century confirmed that fact.

5

"Picturesque San Antonio"

From Post-Centennial to the Alamo in Mid-Century Hollywood Epics, 1940s–1960

IN JANUARY 1941, the *San Antonio Light* ran a story highlighting what it claimed was "one of the strangest schools in America," the small Catholic school of about ninety pupils administered by Sister Superior Alma with three other nuns, who conducted their lessons within some of the remaining buildings of the Mission Espada compound. The reporter observed that being off the beaten path, Espada received few tourist visitors, although the nuns might have considered the frequent noise from airplanes taking off and landing at nearby Stinson field just as disruptive. But that only added to the picturesque anachronism of classes being taught in buildings estimated at two hundred years old, while modern flying machines droned overhead. Additional points of interest included the turret that remained standing at one corner of the compound with holes to fire muskets and a small cannon against enemies. The only modern conveniences the journalist noted were electric lights and a refrigerator for the kitchen. Heating and cooking relied on wood-burning stoves, and water had to be trucked in daily, as the well had long since run dry. A priest came four days a week for services, which led the correspondent to observe, "In serving as a school, community center, and place of worship, the mission is still after 200 years performing its original functions" (fig. 5.1).[1] By continuing to serve these original functions within their local neighborhoods now into the twenty-first century, Espada and the other missions epitomize French historian Pierre Nora's definition of "sites of memory" as being vital parts of the "memorial heritage" of their communities.[2] This chapter explores the increased tension and engagement around the various roles the missions

Fig. 5.1. Classroom, Mission Espada. *San Antonio Light*, January 12, 1941. San Antonio Light Photograph Collection. MS 359; CD# 249; L-2637-I.tif. Image courtesy of the University of Texas at San Antonio Libraries, Special Collections and ZUMA Press.

occupied and increasing competition for influence and ownership in restoration efforts by differing parties. This chapter also considers the tensions surrounding the Alamo and how its roles in mid-century Hollywood epic movies by Walt Disney and John Wayne became the primary interpretation within the national collective memory.

During this period, tourism remained an important part of San Antonio's economy, and the missions contributed significantly as primary attractions. However, as the news story demonstrates, these buildings also served different, but equally important roles within the local communities. The role of sacred space is easily lost in discussions of tourist dollars, but it was just as vital for the people who worshipped, went to school, got married, and raised their families at the missions. Examining the interactions and conflicts between different parties who had claims on the missions, including preservationists, local Catholic Church hierarchy, tourists, and parishioners, reveals the missions to be an important nexus, crucial to understanding the cultural complexities within the Borderlands. And historian John F. Sears's observation that nineteenth-century tourist sites combined "the sacred and profane, the spiritual and commercial, the mythic and the trivial, the natural and the artificial, the profound and the superficial, the elite and the popular in a sometimes uneasy combination" can accurately be applied to San Antonio's missions, even well into the twentieth century.[3] These "uneasy combinations" make San Antonio's missions such effective case studies of the multifaceted nature of the Indigenous/Spanish/Mexican/Texan/American Borderlands as epitomized in Gloria Anzaldúa's poem "*Una lucha de fronteras* / A Struggle of Borders," as she continually walked "out of one culture and into another" and was "in all cultures at the same time."[4]

The mid-twentieth century witnessed several significant changes in tourism that, in turn, affected the construction and maintenance of collective memories related to the missions. The austerity of the Great Depression followed by the sacrifices of the Second World War primed the pump for Americans to splurge on themselves once the war ended. At the same time, many businesses extended the benefit of two-week paid vacations to hourly employees, once the exclusive perks of white-collar, salaried employees.[5] The postwar economic boom gave many more Americans opportunities to travel throughout the United States as Europe tried to rebuild after years of self-destruction. In another change, the automobile replaced the railroad as the primary mode of transportation taking travelers from one side of the continent to the other. Family car ownership jumped between 1948 and 1970 from 54 percent to 82 percent. Travel by automobile allowed more flexibility and freedom for many families traveling together.[6]

A key difference between travelers of the nineteenth and early twentieth centuries and the postwar vacationers was motivation. Earlier travelers looked for the picturesque, the exotic, the sublime as part of their own aesthetic edification. Postwar travelers (especially those with children) were on what some scholars have intentionally labeled "pilgrimages," defined as visits to national shrines such as those in Washington, DC, but all the missions of San Antonio equally qualify.[7] Whether visitors came to the missions because they were practicing Roman Catholics, or whether they were looking at places that confirmed their sense of national identity, the missions and the collective memories surrounding them could be both. This second phenomenon of conflating tourism and American national identity is not new and had its origins in ideas extolled by the "See America First" advocates earlier in the twentieth century. However, postwar tourism differed in scale and the degree of nationalism associated with it. Veterans who so recently had fought for democracy and "the American Way" took their families to visit various historic shrines in order to inculcate their values and mores within the next generation of Americans.[8] It is against this backdrop that these pilgrims bring heritage tourism and American identity together at San Antonio's missions.

Maury Maverick and Early Attempts to Create a Missions National Park

Fontaine Maury Maverick was nothing if not a booster for his hometown of San Antonio. He served the city as a representative to Congress during the mid-1930s and afterward as the city's mayor. While in Washington, DC, Maverick was an ardent supporter of President Franklin Roosevelt's New Deal programs and introduced legislation to bring the missions under the protection of the National Park Service (NPS). His efforts, though well intended, were not without controversy. Opposition came from the Archdiocese of San Antonio as well as a local preservation activist who worried that they would somehow lose the missions (and the concomitant ability to control the dominant narratives relating to the missions) to the federal government.

Maverick began voicing concern for the missions and the need for federal protection as early as 1934. In April of that year, he was the guest speaker at a meeting of the Woman's Club. The topic of his address was the necessity to preserve the Alamo and the other Spanish missions, along with Spanish-language street names, from changes wrought by impending highway construction.[9] Once elected to Congress, he very quickly contacted the NPS regarding creating a park around San Antonio's missions. Federal relief money was already paying architect Harvey Smith and labor for restoration work at Mission San José. Within eleven days of his arrival in Washington, Maverick began filing legislation to protect and preserve the missions. Despite Maverick's energy and commitment to this cause, progress bogged down over the question of title to mission properties and ownership of the deeds.[10]

Coinciding with Maverick's efforts in Congress were endeavors in the Texas legislature to facilitate Maverick's federal-level proposals. Pat Jefferson, representative from San Antonio, introduced a bill in the Texas House of Representatives that would allow the State of Texas to proceed with a quitclaim against properties owned by the Catholic Church in order that these properties be given to the United States for use as a national park.[11] The bill, cosponsored by Texas Senator W. K. Hopkins of Gonzales, raised a storm of protest. Fr. Mariano S. Garriga, chancellor for the archdiocese and official custodian of the missions, declared there could be no contesting the church's title to the properties and later predicted so much opposition to the bill that it would not even advance out of committee.[12] Garriga's opposition led to a pithy exchange with Rena Maverick Green of SACS after Garriga referred to the Jefferson-Hopkins bill as "obnoxious." Green, on the contrary, supported her relative Maury Maverick's bid to turn the missions over to the NPS, suggesting, "I don't know but that it might be a good idea to give the Missions to the Federal Government. The Church has neglected them for the past hundred years and surely the government could do no worse."[13] The strained relations between SACS and the Archdiocese of San Antonio had not improved from the late 1920s.

San Antonio historical preservation activist Adina De Zavala also took extreme umbrage at the language of the bills, although by the time her reaction appeared in Texas newspapers, Jefferson had already decided not to push his proposed bill further.[14] De Zavala claimed to have been "stunned" that a congressman elected by Texans could possibly conceive that "asking the Federal Government to establish national parks of the missions in Bexar County" would be beneficial. Worse was that the unnamed congressman "had caused a bill to be introduced in the Legislature of Texas" that authorized the State of Texas, through the General Land Office commissioner, to execute a quitclaim over titles to any mission properties "as the State of Texas may have" in order to create a national park. By De Zavala's interpretation, the only mission in Bexar County that the State of Texas owned was her beloved Alamo. With her self-righteous indignation fired, she called on the people of Texas to "rise in just wrath" and telephone or send telegrams to Texas's US Congress and state representatives alike to demand that both bills be killed. True Texans must appeal to their elected representatives to "vote against any legislation tending to convey title to the United States or to any State or Nation of any of the sacred and historic shrines of Texas, particularly our Alamo—Mission San Antonio de Valero."[15] De Zavala's rhetoric is worthy of note, for despite her humiliating defeat in the Second Battle of the Alamo two decades earlier, she still claimed to speak for the mission-fortress on behalf of all Texans. Similarly, the notion that control of the property would somehow be given away or lost to powers outside of Texas was anathema to her and many others. These fears reappeared in the 1980s as the missions (except the Alamo) did indeed become part of the NPS, and again in the mid-2010s as the bid to have all San Antonio missions recognized as a UNESCO World Heritage Site became reality. To De Zavala and those who shared her views, ownership over the physical properties ensured ownership and control over the narrative about the Alamo and the missions, and this was a loss neither she nor Garriga could accept.

Within a few days, Maverick explained in more detail his goals regarding preserving San Antonio's missions. He recognized De Zavala's concerns but suggested they were misplaced. He clarified that his proposal did not include the Alamo but only the missions of Concepción, San José, San Juan, and Espada. Likewise, one of his bills provided for "the preservation of historic American sites" (including "buildings, objects, and antiquities of national significance"). The second proposal called for the creation of a commission to investigate and report on the "feasibility of establishing a national monument or monuments in the territory occupied by the Spanish colonial missions" within the states of Texas, New Mexico, Arizona, and California. Maverick stated his desire to preserve the history and early architecture of North America, and so long as private individuals maintain these places, "the federal government need not act." Nonetheless, he believed establishing national parks around these sites was a better way of preserving them. Maverick also pointed out that other "civilized" countries protected their heritage more resolutely than the United States did. Furthermore, while some history was indeed being preserved in this nation, "Spanish colonial history, which in many cases is much older," was often being neglected. The missions of the Spanish Borderlands, "the most beautiful examples of architecture in America," also needed to be saved. He connected the missions to the "history of Christianity—with blood and romance, worthy of study by all Americans." He hoped the commission would not only preserve the missions but also construct roads to improve tourists' access and even collect "historical data" about them. Such actions, Maverick explained, were urgently needed, as the buildings and historical records could not withstand the passage of time, and "many historical documents have already been lost, and unless collected and preserved now, many others will be lost forever."[16] The missions, as tangible examples on which memories and identities had been constructed, caught the congressman's imagination and fueled a strong desire to help protect them for future generations.

Besides explaining to members of the press, Maverick had to explain his rationale to his fellow congressmen. Across three days in April 1935, the House Committee on the Public Lands held hearings on Maverick's proposals.

Representative Henry Stubbs of California voiced significant concern that the proposed bills would authorize the federal government to condemn and seize the property of the several Spanish colonial-era missions in his district. Stubbs claimed that his status as a former Protestant minister gave him additional authority to speak on the concern his local Catholic Church officials were having over the bill. He asserted that he was protecting their interests by making certain that the bills did not give the federal government (as represented by the secretary of the interior) the authority to condemn and seize the titles to church properties. Stubbs made the very poignant observation that religious services were still held in each of the mission churches in his district save one, and even though the churches and chapels were 150 years old, "they are sacred spots to those people."[17] San Antonio's mission churches were not the only ones operating as sacred space. Stubbs's comments presciently summarized the importance of the mission churches to their local parishioners, whether in his district in California or for those of San Antonio, as sacred space and sites of memory.

Maverick responded to the property right charge by claiming that because some persons had acted in bad faith in the past, the government's right to use eminent domain needed to be retained in the bills. However, his other comments during this hearing offer interesting insights on this representative, who certainly lived up to his name. Maverick, unlike so many other Anglo-Texans of this time, was considered a friend to San Antonio's Mexican American community and felt their history was integral to American history.[18] Testifying before the House Committee, he bemoaned the "scant attention to the Spanish colonial history and our Mexican history." He emphasized that there was "a great deal of beauty in that civilization; a great deal of piety and sacrifice, and all of our young people should know about this." Preserving the missions from that era, Maverick argued, would be a great step in the right direction.[19] Maverick's characterizations of the Indigenous populations in Texas as "wild beasts" and his hagiographic recounting of how the Franciscans brought the blessings of European civilization to an untamed land reveal that his progressive views went only so far, and his understanding and description of earlier times still reflected an imagined Spanish past. Nonetheless, he defended his proposed bills by reminding his colleagues that preserving the missions was a vital interest for the people of Spanish and Mexican descent in San Antonio. Furthermore, he predicted that people from across the United States would be interested in visiting all the missions of the Southwest as tourist attractions.[20]

Along with making his case before his congressional colleagues, Maverick clarified his rationales to constituents back home. His explanations and inevitable legislative give-and-take, which dropped the perceived threat of using eminent domain, eventually won over some of the members of the Catholic Church in his home district. In August 1935, as part of the general discussions on the proposed bills, Maverick entered into the *Congressional Record* communiqués he had received from San Antonio Catholic Archbishop Arthur Drossaerts and William Menger of the *Southern Messenger* (the English-language Catholic newspaper for Texas). Both men heartily endorsed Maverick's cause. Drossaerts even sent Maverick a second letter praising the congressman's labors: "I think that every American and especially every Texan owes you a vote of gratitude for the intelligent zeal shown for the preservation of our Franciscan missions. . . . More power to you and may full success crown your efforts."[21] Although Maverick was ultimately unsuccessful in establishing national parks around San Antonio's missions in 1935, other parts of his proposals were adopted into public laws that enabled the NPS to better go about preserving American history.[22] His efforts also reveal an interest in creating a unique church-state relationship to better care for these aging but still-valued structures. Such a relationship would not bear fruit for several more years, but the seed was planted during this period.

"Picturesque San Antonio: Where Life Is Different!" and the People Are So Exotic

The late 1930s saw San Antonio embark on a new advertising campaign with the slogan, "Picturesque San Antonio: Where Life Is Different!" In the introductory remarks to his 1939 report, Frank Huntress, chair of the Municipal Advertising Commission, addressed Mayor C. K. Quin and other city commissioners, touting his committee's success in introducing "this country's tourists, investors, developers and homeseekers" to the city's numerous advantages. The campaign was a comprehensive effort to market San Antonio's attractions via ads in nationally circulated newspapers and magazines, "several complete series of motion pictures," as well as "numerous illustrated articles featuring San Antonio . . . published in various newspapers and magazines." Huntress also credited the local advertising firm of Wyatt, Aniol & Auld for "several striking booklets" full of "highly intelligent and forceful copy and illustrations" that effectively publicized the city's charms.[23] The unmistakable message was that San Antonio was *the* place to relax, have fun, and reinforce one's American identity based on the construction of an imagined Spanish past.

According to the report, between April 1938 and May 1939, the publicity campaign distributed weekly stories on San Antonio "to over 500 newspapers throughout the United States." These articles and stories, including photographs, also appeared in both general-interest and trade publications. The results were impressive as the Municipal Advertising Commission received over thirty-four thousand inquiries asking for information on San Antonio. The most requests came from New York and Illinois (over three thousand each), while requests from Pennsylvania were just below three thousand. Over eleven hundred inquiries were received from sixty-seven foreign territories, with Canadians submitting the overwhelming majority (over six hundred; the next highest were fifty-eight requests from England and thirty-eight inquiries from Mexico). Those requesting information were sent a free thirty-two-page booklet that told the "story of the romance and adventure; the unending variety of things to do in sunshine-filled days; the quaintness and old-world atmosphere; [and] the curious blending of the old and new."[24]

This free booklet, titled *Picturesque San Antonio: Where Life Is Different!*, had a colorful cover illustration featuring a smartly dressed Anglo couple taking photographs in front of the Alamo. Just behind this couple appeared a conversation between two Mexican American men wearing large sombreros and bright sarapes draped over their colored shirts and a second fashionable Anglo couple. The photograph on the inside front cover depicted a young man dressed as a vaquero strumming his guitar and serenading his señorita through a window. They re-create and freeze in time a romantic backdrop illustrating a distant past where visiting Anglos looked on contemporary Mexican American artisans and parishioners merely as performers for their amusement. There was the typical glorification of the Alamo martyrs, as well as the description of the city's Mexican American population as benighted Other, where women still "grind their corn and pat out tortillas by hand" (the implied assumption being that a modern, mechanical or electric kitchen appliance could do the job better). The booklet also informed potential tourists about the four Franciscan missions "when priest and soldier together tamed a wilderness. Restoration has left unchanged their scarred and sacred walls. Age has mellowed their intrinsic beauty and made them monuments of a past never to be reclaimed." San José was described as "Queen of the Missions," and the text directed tourists' attention to the ornate facade and Rose Window, as bells still called the faithful to worship.[25] While the booklet's text did not differ widely from commonly available tourist information, over thirty-five thousand copies of this booklet were eventually distributed. Even if only a small number of people then made their vacation to San Antonio, many readers had consumed romantic descriptions of the missions.

The commission's report claimed that just over 51 percent of visitors were coming to San Antonio for the first time. Visitors, whether first time or not, stayed an average of eighteen days, but the report also mentioned that some winter visitors stayed several months. This average holiday length suggests that many visitors were of a privileged class who could afford to take extended vacations. One noteworthy statistic showed that 78 percent of visitors arrived by automobile, while only 18 percent arrived by rail.[26] This marked a significant shift away from rail travel and explains why fewer advertisements from railroads touting passenger service to San Antonio could be found after 1940. Those in charge of publicizing San Antonio's charms naturally put the money where they believed it would be most effective.

The Municipal Advertising Commission reported its budget as just over $96,000. Of that, ad space in newspapers and magazines combined took $51,000. They purchased another $10,000 worth of printed matter, including booklets, posters, and pamphlets. The commission spent $9,800 for ad space in the popular *Saturday Evening Post,* the highest amount for magazine ads. Other ads appeared in *National Geographic, Time, Life,* with *Newsweek* rounding out the top five in terms of dollars spent. Additional titles included *New Yorker, Harper's Bazaar, Vogue,* and *Field and Stream.* The *Chicago Tribune* and *New York Times* claimed the top two spots for money spent on newspaper ads. These ads represented a wide geographic distribution from Boston south to Miami and westward to Omaha; however, there was no advertising west of Denver.[27] The target audience of potential tourists was clearly Eastern and Midwestern rather than west of the Rocky Mountains; and the choice of magazine titles suggests a target demographic solidly in the middle to upper socioeconomic class. Similarly, the city obviously learned from Southern Pacific's earlier advertising successes by using multiple formats of mass media as well as emphasizing the romantic vision of the city's heritage as the ideal spot for a holiday.

Guidebooks Mediating What to See and How to See It in San Antonio

In February 1946, a visitor to Mission San Juan sent a postcard to her daughter in St. Paul, Minnesota. The visitor mentioned that she had seen San Juan (pictured on the front of the card) and intended to visit each of the missions and send a card from each, since she thought it would interest her daughter. The visitor indicated that she was having a wonderful time and intended to stay awhile.[28] Tourists found their way to the missions by various means. Some doubtlessly had seen booklets published by the city's Municipal Information Bureau, commercial guidebooks, and the state-by-state American Guide Series created by the Work Projects Administration (WPA). These materials instructing visitors on what sights were worthy of attention and how to interpret them were often written from the dominant, Anglo-centric point of view. This encouraged readers to construct a particular interpretation of the missions as relics of a romantic Spanish past, long since replaced by more energetic and modern Anglo-Americans.

Multiple Depression-era relief projects touched San Antonio's missions. Some were direct, such as the physical repairs carried out by architect Harvey P. Smith at San José, while other projects, such as the 1940 guide to Texas prepared by WPA writers, were intended for travelers. Each state employed writers using WPA funds to create these guides. The fact that the guides had "official sponsorship of the federal government" gave an impression that the books were authoritative. In actuality, quality and accuracy varied widely. While it is tempting to critique the guide for Texas as perpetuating the myth of Texas exceptionalism, nearly all of the guides were written by local boosters and relied heavily on "Chamber of Commerce clichés," which had the unfortunate effect of hiding unique attractions and making all places sound essentially the same.[29] That caveat aside, the Texas guide was not at all shy about situating the state as "one of the last American frontiers" or playing up the violent "Wild Western" image by bluntly stating that "the six-shooter still arbitrates many a dispute, urban as well as rural" with sympathetic juries if "womenfolk," self-defense, or "certain expletives are spoken unsmilingly" were given as the reason for drawing the gun.[30]

The WPA guide for Texas referenced the potential interests the missions held for visitors. The Alamo defenders received the familiar heroic treatment with questionable historical accuracy. A chapter on religion described that statewide, "nine of the mission establishments remain and are the oldest churches now in use."[31] A chapter on architecture suggested, "For the student of early Spanish architecture in America, the missions of the San Antonio group offer interesting examples" of the "elaborate Churrigueresque style of the late Spanish Renaissance." In the section describing a tour of San Antonio's missions, the book stated that sightseeing buses made the trip twice per day, although detailed driving instructions were also included. The acoustics at Mission Concepción also received a favorable comparison to those at the Mormon Tabernacle of Salt Lake City, Utah. Although the guide correctly credited Pedro Huizar as the artist responsible for the sculpting at Mission San José, it admitted that legends about him "are too numerous for a correct version, but the substance of the stories is that the window was the result of an unhappy romance. . . . Ancestors of the sculptor helped create the beauty of the Alhambra at Granada." Readers were presented the conundrum of whether Huizar was of Spanish-Moorish descent, which invited persistent myths to flourish. And the guide noted that religious services were still being conducted at the missions for local families, still serving as sacred space and site of memory for the parishioners.[32] Historian Christine Bold claims, "In materializing reading, travel guides shift responsibility for the production of myths of national cohesiveness onto the volumes' users: by reading sights within those framing myths—even by reading resistance to those frameworks—the guidebook user is connecting ideologies with place."[33] She is correct, to a point, but her statement goes too far in absolving the authors and publishers who created the guides; we must remember that one of the primary functions of guidebooks has always been to direct the tourists in "what to see and how to see it."[34] The WPA guides, just like many other guidebooks and travel narratives mentioned in this book, were written from (and to project) a particular point of view: elite Anglos looking at exotic Others, situated around remnants of a romanticized Spanish past.

Just a couple of years after the WPA guide was published, Claude Aniol, whose advertising firm had been in charge of the "Picturesque San Antonio" campaign, published his own guidebook to the city. Aniol's book, *San Antonio: City of Missions*, was short (only fifty-seven pages) but profusely illustrated. In some ways, it was very similar to the booklet his firm did for the city just three years earlier, even recycling some of the photographs. The text, on the other hand, was different and concentrated on San Antonio and sights within and just outside the city limits, while the earlier guide booklet emphasized the many opportunities within the entire region for fun in the sun and sightseeing. Aniol was able to use a little more space and describe the missions in more detail with extended photo captions. Unlike *Picturesque San Antonio*, Aniol attributed Rosa's Window to Pedro Huizar, who, according to the text spent five years on the work "after an unhappy romance caused the artist to pour his heart and soul into the design." While Aniol's book mentioned the significant Mexican population of the city, none were illustrated as being socioeconomic equals to the Anglo population to any representative measure. The models appeared to have more Anglo features than not and being dressed in stereotypical Mexican fiesta garb from earlier decades reflected more cultural appropriation.[35]

In 1947, *National Geographic Magazine*, a periodical whose editorial focus did not emphasize selling a particular product or place, published a lengthy article on San Antonio that read much like a booster-written piece for more commercial-oriented publications. Author Mason Sutherland described the city as "the Southwest's capital of carnival," as people from the Deep South, the West, and even Mexico converged to "have fun." Describing the city as "the Venice of the Texas plains," he promised readers visiting the river that "every vista shows a pleasing" scene. Sutherland's guide through the missions was a woman born in Mexico but who had grown up in San Antonio. Starting with San José, he specifically mentioned that Pedro Huizar's masterpiece Rose Window was "copied by hundreds of artists." He also referenced the legends of Huizar's unrequited love and his ancestors assisting with the Alhambra of Grenada, Spain. Sutherland additionally visited missions San Juan and Espada, which he termed "living missions," because descendants of the Indigenous peoples for whom the missions were originally established still lived and attended school there.[36]

Guidebooks have long directed readers where to go for vacations and what to do while there. Few have been quite as blunt as a 1956 title *How to Enjoy Your Western Vacations*. In his introduction, Kent Ruth claimed that seeing interesting sights was only one facet but that "understanding," by developing a greater appreciation for the sights through learning more about the history and cultures being visited, would lead to greater satisfaction in the vacation experience. Ruth acknowledged the rapid growth in the vacation and travel industry since the Second World War. He observed that while forty million workers enjoyed paid vacations, over seventy million Americans took vacations whether paid or not. Additionally, Ruth claimed travel was, at the time of his book, the third-largest industry in the United States, worth over $10 billion. He directed readers to a "GHQ," or a large city with plenty of amenities and tourist interest in its own right that would act as a "general headquarters" for travelers as they made trips out to see additional sights.[37] San Antonio served as one of Ruth's GHQs for visitors to Texas. The city, he noted, was one of the oldest in the state and had "preserved more than any other Texas city the nostalgic flavor of Old Spain." One of the attractions to which Ruth directed tourists was the "depressed, yet far from depressing

Mexican Quarter," which he described as "gaily jammed with small shops, street vendors, open markets, dusty plazas, ornate old churches, and milling crowds."[38] His description somewhat acknowledges the effects of poverty and lack of equal economic opportunities characteristic of the time and place. But the question remains: In directing tourists to visit these exoticized sights, might tourists' dollars help alleviate some of the squalor in which many Mexican Americans lived?

Ruth also recommended visiting San Antonio's missions: "Adding their bit to the city's distinctive charm are the centuries-old missions with their elaborate stonework, lofty bell towers, and crumbling masonry walls." The Alamo melodrama and the cenotaph to Anglo martyrs were, of course, highlighted as "an interesting and (even to non-Texans) impressive tribute to the American spirit of liberty." The Spanish missions in the American Southwest (including Texas) were the "principal architectural heritages of" 150 years of colonial Spanish rule. But the missions of San Antonio offer tourists "the finest masterpieces of Spanish mission architecture," with Mission San José being the most interesting and Concepción the best preserved. Ruth specifically mentions San José's "famed Rose Window (carved by the monk-sculptor Huicar [*sic*], allegedly for a sweetheart who died before she could join him in the New World)" as something that tourists should find appealing.[39]

Like many other guidebook authors, Ruth seemed to believe that his audience was ignorant of the tourist attractions in the American West and needed an expert to spoon-feed them not only which sights were worthy of attention but, even more so, how to truly appreciate those sights. For without the expertise doled out by Ruth, they could not enjoy the whole of the tourist experience. Guidebook authors assumed their traveling readers were capable of being properly educated provided the travelers bought and read *their* books. In this Ruth was no different from so many previous guidebook authors claiming to provide readers a better understanding of how to appreciate the meanings behind the missions and add the romantic nostalgia of colonial Spain to their collective memories.[40]

Ethel Wilson Harris and Archbishop Robert E. Lucey: Saving San José for Tourists

Ethel Wilson Harris and Archbishop Robert E. Lucey are two enigmatic but significant figures in the complex history of San Antonio's missions. Thanks in no small part to their work to preserve and promote tourism to the missions, the buildings survived to be visited by tourists, while still being used by the local population as sacred spaces. Although they each put their indelible stamp on the old missions, there may be room for debate whether the tourists or the parishioners were the greater beneficiaries.

SACS member Ethel Wilson Harris (or "Miz Harrie" as she was sometimes known) lived at Mission San José for over twenty years and developed a deep appreciation for the old buildings, even if she had some eccentric ideas on what mission life may have been like during colonial Spanish times. In his collection of oral histories of people associated with the missions, historian Luis Torres introduces Ethel Wilson Harris as one of those people who "attain mythical proportions during their own lifetimes."[41] Harris was born in Sabinal, Texas, but moved to San Antonio as a young girl. Trips with friends to San Antonio's west side "sparked her lifelong interest in Mexican folklore and handiwork," which later became her career.[42] With encouragement from her husband, a former army officer, she founded and served as president of three important decorative art tile companies in the San Antonio area from 1931 to 1963: Mexican Arts and Crafts, San José Potteries (established next to the mission compound), and Mission Crafts (which operated on the grounds of San José beginning in 1941). In addition to these business ventures, she was "the technical supervisor of the Arts and Crafts Division" of the Works Progress Administration (later renamed the Work Projects Administration) in San Antonio.[43] Examples of tiles and pottery from her companies were exhibited at the Chicago World's Fair of 1933 and the Texas Centennial of 1936. Throughout her long and productive life, she was a tireless promoter of art tile and pottery created using traditional means by Mexican American craftsmen.

Harris's relationship with SACS was complicated, although ultimately symbiotic, with Harris eventually serving as the society's president from 1951 to 1953.[44] After SACS had acquired and rebuilt San José's granary in the 1930s, the organization allowed Harris to open a gift shop within the building to sell art tiles from her Mexican Arts and Crafts company. Having fellow SACS member Harris on-site, who could easily look after the interests of SACS, likely figured heavily into the equation.[45] This close relationship did not, however, prevent SACS and Harris from occasionally clashing over aesthetic interests, such as when Harris wanted to build a large, modern kiln on the grounds of San José. Rena Maverick Green vetoed the idea, arguing, "Can you imagine smoke stacks as a background to the San José?"[46]

Archbishop Robert E. Lucey was born of working-class, Irish Catholic parents in Los Angeles. The tragic death of his father when Robert was a young boy, along with one of his early assignments out of seminary, inculcated a strong sense of social justice and activism. Lucey believed his engagement on behalf of the working class prevented his advancement in Los Angeles, so he was shipped off to be the bishop of Amarillo, Texas, in 1934, where he discovered the ugliness of anti-Hispanic racism. Lucey was a firm believer in social justice, particularly for Mexican Americans, and yet equally committed to exercising his authority within the church hierarchy.[47] Being adamantly pro-union and pro–civil rights did not endear him to many in his flock (even some of his own clergy). In 1941, he moved up the hierarchy and to San Antonio as archbishop.[48] A native of California, his great love for the West Coast missions easily transferred to his new appointment in San Antonio. Upon his arrival, he made restoring the old missions a top priority. He believed the mission enterprise legitimized Catholic historical "claims to having played a fundamental role in making the American nation, especially by blazing the trail of civilization in what Lucey regarded as the wilderness of the savage western lands."[49] Lucey's outspoken nature regarding civil rights would later be recognized by President Harry Truman, who appointed him to a "blue ribbon panel investigating conditions" for both migratory workers and bracero foreign laborers in the United States.[50]

One of the first actions Lucey took in 1941 as the newly installed archbishop of San Antonio was to sign an agreement with Wendell Mayes, chairman of the Texas State Parks Board, and Alvin J. Wirtz of the US Department of the Interior, designating Mission San José as a Texas state park, the first national historic site west of the Mississippi River.[51] A journalist for the *Dallas Morning News* accurately considered the momentous agreement "a precedent-setting measure second to none in the establishment of national historic shrines. Not only is it the first such site created in co-operation with a state park agency but it also is the first national historic site established in co-operation with the Catholic Church; it is also the first to be administered jointly by the church and the national and state park services."[52] Religious historian Thomas Bremer suggests that Lucey had developed a deep interest in the Spanish colonial-era missionary endeavors while growing up in California. Furthermore, Bremer asserts that Lucey's dedication "to preserve the missions for the glorification of the Church's heritage in San Antonio also had a touristic dimension to it. Indeed, the archbishop sought to praise the Church's past by appealing to the needs, tastes, and desires of tourists."[53] The historic precedent set by this church-state agreement prior to the Second World War would be expanded forty years later when three additional

San Antonio missions, Concepción, San Juan, and Espada, were combined into the San Antonio Missions National Historical Park.

Lucey's public rhetoric underscored his admiration for the missions and missionaries, as well as his conviction of the dignity of the Mexican American parishioners who continued to worship in the old structures. In a speech delivered in Austin on April 24, 1952, to the Catholic Conference on the Spanish-Speaking People of Texas, he proclaimed, "Texas is Proud of its Spanish-Mexican Heritage." Lucey observed that Texas was "the meeting place of two cultures, two ways of living.... The two have blended in a new culture enriched by both Anglo and Mexican elements to create the Texan." He also pointed out, "We advertise Texas as a tourist playground to vie with California and Florida" and listed San Antonio's missions, San Fernando Cathedral, and La Villita among the most popular attractions. Lucey then reminded his listeners that without Mexico, the Alamo, "marked as number one tourist spot," would not exist. Lucey called attention to the "Spanish style of architecture" he believed so prevalent in Texas and had "captured the fancy of many who live in the north and east. Texas might argue with California as to which state should have the honors in claiming it for its own and Texas may resent the labeling of it as 'California style' architecture. But the honors go to Mexico and to Spain and it is the heritage of our Mexican-American fellow citizens."[54] Lucey may have made these remarks either as a challenge to the prevailing racism or with a lot of wishful thinking on his part. Nonetheless, his observations emphasized the debt Anglo Texans owe to Tejanos, the importance of San Antonio's missions for tourists, and their appeal beyond state borders.

Lucey was the driving force during 1941–69 in restoring San Antonio's missions and promoting them as tourist attractions. During his term as archbishop, he dedicated nearly $300,000 to the missions by acquisition of surrounding property, repairs, conservation, and renovation. While preservation and reconstruction saved the missions for both parishioners and tourists, it nonetheless remained an open question whether the primary motivation was for visiting tourists or for locals using the buildings as sacred space. Part of ensuring that the missions appealed to tourists was to give Ethel Wilson Harris at Mission San José nearly free rein to impose her own ideas of what she believed the tourists wanted to see, even if it appeared to subordinate the church's role as sacred space.[55]

Ethel Wilson Harris also exemplifies many of the complexities swirling around San José and its multivariate role as tourist attraction, commercial space, sacred space, and performance space for Mexican Americans. Harris cultivated a close relationship with the local Catholic hierarchy, particularly with Lucey, which allowed her to impose her will over individual priests serving the San José community. Through her commercial tile enterprises, she promoted traditional Mexican crafts and provided a paycheck, creative outlet, and a means for her Mexican American employees to express their ethnic identity during a period of great economic hardship. Many of the pottery and tile designs portrayed romanticized Mexican folk scenes or images of San Antonio nightlife, including the legendary "Chili Queens."[56] However, Harris was not of Tejano or Mexican American ethnicity herself. It is difficult, though, to view the relationship she had with her artisans simply as an exploitive one. While there was a definite hierarchy, Harris held a significant amount of respect for the craftspeople who worked for her.[57]

Harris's relationship to the Catholic Church was one of the more curious facets of her time at Mission San José. By 1941, a rebuilt Mission San José was both a Texas state park and a National Historic Site, and Harris was tapped to be the first manager of the site for the State.[58] Harris and Lucey developed a very close working relationship lasting nearly three decades. In an oral history interview from 1976, Harris spoke fondly of Lucey as "a man I love and admire."[59] On the other hand, Harris did little to endear herself to the parishioners who attended church at San José. The archbishop lent valuable assistance to SACS's efforts to close a county road that passed through the old walls and ran just a few yards from the San José chapel. The priest at San José objected to the proposed road closure, as his parishioners were accustomed to parking next to the church. Harris stated that Lucey expressed shock that the priest would push against church hierarchy over parking spaces; she remarked that this priest was reassigned shortly afterward. Similarly, Harris complained to Lucey that some parishioners were on the mission grounds hawking guidebooks and "junk-crosses, and junk this and junk that. Cheap, cheap stuff." Lucey put an end to this practice and assured Harris, "There'll be no more selling of these books. . . . The only person who can sell anything . . . you can sell them, but nobody" else. Little wonder that Harris reminisced that the local parishioners refused to speak to her after Lucey stopped them from marketing their wares. Harris had eliminated the local competition for tourists' dollars so she could engage in her own type of commercialism through sale of her art tiles.[60] In summing up their relationship, Harris bragged that Lucey once assured her that he would "get rid of them [the priests at San José] until I find one that will work with you." As she recalled, it took six priests being replaced.[61]

For Harris, an active parish at San José seemed more an inconvenience than opportunity for educating tourists about Mexican American culture and religious expression. Tourists having a positive experience trumped the role of "mission as sacred space." Harris adamantly believed that "whenever anyone entered that park that they were guests of the State of Texas," and as the park's representative, it was her duty to ensure they left with a positive impression of the park and the State.[62] And this duty she took very seriously. Given her low opinion of the guidebooks sold by locals, not surprisingly she wrote her own. Harris's version was profusely illustrated, including a pretty Mexican American woman in a traditional *china poblana*, sitting in the Rose Window and being serenaded by her guitar-wielding lover with a large sombrero. Although she included one version of the Huizar-Rosa story of star-crossed lovers, she also engaged with some colonial Spanish sources to give it a modicum of historical accuracy.[63] Still, as Harris strove to provide tourists with what she deemed an authentic experience, she hired "strolling minstrels" and dancers demonstrating Mexican folk music; she also moved two of her Mexican American craftsmen onto the grounds so visitors could watch pots being thrown and tiles made; there were women making traditional tortillas; there were decorations (water jugs, an oxcart, etc.) gathered from numerous trips into Mexico; and as her youngest son recalled, there were her peacocks strolling around making raucous sounds.[64]

If meandering guitarists and peacocks strike modern scholars as incongruous with the labor required of eighteenth-century mission life, and if Harris's pulling strings to push out the purveyors of what she considered crass, commercial kitsch in favor of her own enterprise appear hypocritical and imperious, Harris ultimately defies efforts to pigeonhole her and her work. Her son remembered being taken with his siblings on numerous trips into the Mexican Quarter of San Antonio to watch the traditional Christmas pageants. He also recollected his mother producing the performance of the *Los Pastores* play at Mission San José (and insisting that it was performed in its traditional Spanish).[65] Harris used her deep interest in Mexican culture and craftwork to create a romantic and exotic atmosphere at Mission San José for the tourists' pleasure at the expense of authenticity and local parishioners. Nevertheless, she was far from one-dimensional, as she decried on at least one occasion the racism faced by her Mexican employees. In December 1949,

Harris and one of her craftsmen, Angel Rendón, and his nine-year-old son made a trip to West Texas to deliver some art tiles. As they returned, they stopped for dinner at a restaurant in the tiny community of Santa Anna in Coleman County. While waiting for service at a table, they were informed by employees, "We do not serve Spanish people." In her letter to the Texas Good Neighbor Commission complaining of this discriminatory treatment, Harris stated that when the waitress insulted Rendón in front of his child, "I felt insulted along with him." And she demanded the commission keep her informed on what they could and would be doing in this instance.[66] Harris's attempt to document to the proper authority a personalized example of discrimination may be taken by critics to be merely another instance of paternalistic racism. But in sharing her letter with *La Prensa,* she may have been genuinely trying to alleviate the hurt caused by the pernicious anti-Mexican racism that permeated Texan culture.

San Antonio's Spanish missions meet French historian Pierre Nora's definition of "sites of memory" as being "significant entities" that became "symbolic elements of the memorial heritage" of the community.[67] Lucey doubtlessly would have agreed. As Bremer argues, "Lucey's desire to make the missions into aesthetically pleasing and plausibly authentic space coincided with his understanding of them as symbolic monuments to the 'precious heritage' of Texas and the nation. He sought to make the missions not only sacred sites of the Catholic Church but also important tourist attractions where visitors could come to appreciate their heritage."[68] Nora discusses the complexity of sites of memory that are at once "material, symbolic, and functional."[69] Lucey's efforts to restore the missions reflected each of Nora's three facets as he tried to restore the material remains while calling attention to their functions as sacred space and symbolic heritage of the city. In a speech he evidently recycled for multiple occasions, Lucey argued that while the missions belonged "to the Church," they were "invested with a public interest; they are a precious heritage—spiritual, religious, and historic, they are deathless monuments of the early days of this dear and sunny land."[70] Additionally, Bremer asserts that Lucey's efforts on behalf of the San Antonio missions were done "to build a tourist attraction that would rival the missions of his beloved California."[71] In this way, despite his religious authority, Lucey represented more of the tourism aspect of the missions, which itself highlights the complexity that surrounds them. His willingness to allow and even endorse the missions as tourist space over and above their role as sacred space serves as a potent reminder of historian Michel-Rolph Trouillot's prescient observation that "history is messy."[72]

Hollywood's Alamo and Public Memory

Although Mission San Antonio de Valero was the first mission founded in what is now the city of San Antonio, its historical trajectory took a very different path from that of the other missions that followed. The 1836 Battle of the Alamo and its subsequent role of sacred shrine for those martyred in the name of Texas independence wrap an additional layer of complexity on this project and the Gordian knots that bind identity, historical memory, and sacred place. Each of the five missions is a site of memory, but the myths and memories associated with the Alamo threaten to completely overwhelm the other four missions. The numerous attempts to tell the stories of the Alamo, whether on the silver screen or television, have had major impacts on American collective memory. As historian David Lowenthal observes, "Films make history more intense and plausible; figures seen moving and speaking in locales redolent of the past seem more alive than ever."[73] An exploration of the cinematic portrayal of the Alamo and its heroes, the rhetoric from film reviews and editorial reactions, and some of the mid-century controversies regarding their place in the American pantheon of heroes exposes the important place these heroic myths hold in the national imagination.

The Alamo Battle of 1836 has been either the subject or setting for motion pictures almost since the beginning of the medium; the story elements of the "forlorn hope" and sacrifice for a cause on the part of the Anglo heroes and subsequent massacre are undoubtedly the reason for its appeal. The impacts on the collective memory have varied over time due to the quality of production, reputation of those making the movie, age level of the intended audience, and cultural issues of the time (including racism and changing public tastes or tolerances). As of this writing, there have been twenty-eight films, some made for television, others intended for the big screen, where the Alamo is an important part of the story.[74] Of these, only five will be discussed here, and only two will be in depth: two silent films; Walt Disney's 1955 motion picture lifted from his television episodes of the life of Davy Crockett; John Wayne's epic telling of the siege and battle; and a 2004 motion picture that was a major box-office bomb. The mid-century films by Disney and Wayne remain the standard (rightly or wrongly) by which all others are judged.

The earliest Alamo movies were silent films, made in the second decade of the twentieth century. The first of these, *The Immortal Alamo* (1911), was significant for being filmed in San Antonio. Film historian Frank Thompson speculates whether parts of the filming actually took place on the grounds of or within the shrine itself, noting the presence of a cattlemen's convention, adding to what was already an unwieldy throng of curious onlookers.[75] Also, the feud between Adina De Zavala and Clara Driscoll's DRT was winding down, but the Long Barracks would have still been intact if filming did indeed occur. The second Alamo movie was Triangle Film's *Martyrs of the Alamo* from 1915. Racial stereotypes of the era established Anglos be portrayed as noble, chivalrous, and visibly distinct from Mexicans, who were portrayed as debauched and lecherous.[76] This movie could easily be forgotten had stills not appeared in a guide booklet issued by Southern Pacific Railroad. The text of the booklet wallows in maudlin descriptions of patriotism and self-sacrifice as the necessary prelude to Anglo civilization in Texas. Readers were invited to visit San Antonio for its history as well as its opportunities for golf, hunting, and fishing. The other missions were described across several pages: "These interesting, ancient ruins speak in their own way of America's early history. They tell a wonderful story of the efforts and faith of the Spanish monks" to bring Christianity and Spanish civilization to a perceived benighted people. The brief skirmish occurring near Mission Concepción in the War for Texas Independence was elevated to rival the Battle of Gettysburg. Meanwhile, the "beautiful carvings" decorating Mission San José were credited to "the Spanish sculptor Huica [*sic*], who came across the seas for that purpose." The booklet was well illustrated throughout, including the stills from *Martyrs* and other photographs of the missions. A note on the front cover acknowledged Southern Pacific's appreciation to Triangle for being able to use the "historic scenes" from the "classic" film.[77]

If we move forward from the earliest Alamo films to the most recent, 2004 effort, we expect to see considerable differences. If the first movie was actually filmed at the Alamo, the condition of the building, as well as its location in a busy downtown area, demanded all other projects be filmed elsewhere. What may have been lost in authenticity of the setting, a few movie makers tried to make up for by devoting inordinate amounts of resources to the historical accuracy of set design, costumes, extras, and props. Such was the case in the early years of the twenty-first century, when the Disney company tried to take advantage of a surge in patriotism following the terrorist attacks of September 11, 2001.[78] The makers of this movie began with good intentions, assembling a team of respected historians to assist with details from languages, props, and costumes, as well as separating accepted historical facts from the overgrowth of legends. Unfortunately, meticulous attention to details and good-faith efforts to be authentic to the historical record did not result in positive results at the box office. It is tempting to pin the blame on director John Lee Hancock and his scriptwriters for crafting the death of Davy Crockett along the lines of the diary of Enrique de la Peña, the Mexican army officer who claimed Crockett was taken alive and executed on Santa Anna's command immediately following the battle. However, this version of the Alamo story had too many other strikes against it, including subpar acting from well-known stars, audiences' fading interest in history, and a poorly written script that tried to tell too many stories for any to be effective. The net result was a box office take of $22 million, against a budget of $120 million.[79] The final ignominy came when the movie editor for *Newsweek* magazine listed it as number four out of the ten "most disappointing" movies for 2004 because it was such a bore that "nobody went to see it."[80]

But Disney had done better fifty years earlier. In 1954, Disney aired several television broadcasts based on the (highly fictionalized) life of Davy Crockett. In an interview with conservative Hollywood reporter Hedda Hopper, Walt Disney mentioned his desire to bring to life both fictional characters, including Paul Bunyan, John Henry, and Pecos Bill; and real-life persons such as Johnny Appleseed, Jim Bridger, and Davy Crockett. These characters not only had the "sheer entertainment values of our national legendary," but Disney also emphasized that each of these men "earned his keep, riding herd, felling timber, building railroads," and there were "no drones in this great cast of national characters. They were just exaggerated portraits of the normal, busy, toiling man of his day. And they are worth looking at—soberly and in fun—to re-educate our minds and our children's minds, to the lusty, gutty, new world called America."[81] Historians Randy Roberts and James S. Olson situate Disney's interests in American folklore heroes within the context of the Cold War.[82] By this model, there would be no communist "drones" in Disney's pantheon of American heroes, just fiercely independent working men.

Disney's efforts to reintroduce the United States to its folkloric heroes began well, and Crockett became Disney's "first and biggest star, creating overnight a frontier and merchandising craze," based on his new efforts with the medium of television.[83] However, one year after the television debut of Fess Parker as Davy Crockett, Disney spliced together selected episodes into a feature-length motion picture. Shrewd marketing campaigns by multiple companies sparked a "Davy Crockett craze" that brought over two hundred Crockett-themed consumer goods to market. Some estimated that all the Davy Crockett coonskin caps, fringed buckskin jackets and trousers, toy rifles and pistols, Alamo playset replicas, children's pajamas and bedsheets, and more were valued at over $100 million in 1955.[84] Disney himself may have wondered about his latest creation if he saw the observation in *Time* magazine offered by a buyer for retail merchants in Detroit, who gushed, "Why, Davy Crockett is bigger even than Mickey Mouse."[85] As one critic described the phenomenon, "American boys from five to eight were loyal Space Cadets, wholly devoted to blasting each other out of galactic apple trees with their atomic disintegrators. . . . Then, almost overnight, two million clean, patriotic youngsters were seduced into switching allegiance."[86] Instead of defending some Space Command from alien monsters with toy ray guns, these hardy troops now defended their frontier redoubts with flintlock long rifles from attacking Indians and Santa Anna's Mexican soldiery. Through the imaginative play of American youth, the visual images from Disney's movie sets were stored directly into the collective memory.

As Disney's production writers and crews began their work, they found that few scholarly biographies of Crockett existed, and even the popular literature was far from extensive. Nonetheless, this dearth of reliable information freed the writers to take extensive liberties with the subject.[87] As long as Disney's script acknowledged the handful of specific, documented events in Crockett's life (such as his service to Congress and death at the Alamo), he had a nearly blank slate on which to create his latest hero. As a result, Crockett remained something of an enigma for his legions of fans and even scholars for decades. Author John Haverstick, with assistance from two of the children's librarians at New York Public Library, discovered multiple versions of Davy Crockett in a variety of books, ranging from the quasi-historical to the completely legendary.[88] Only two months later, E. J. Kahn, book reviewer for *The New Yorker*, described his frustration in trying to find consistent and reliable information on Crockett through the plethora of books that were newly published or brought back into publication in the wake of Davy's newfound popularity. Kahn admitted to readers that the insatiable curiosity of his eight-year-old son was the driving force behind his quest. Evidently it made a significant difference to some young minds at what age Crockett first killed a bear, the name of his first hunting dog, and even whether he died at the Alamo and the exact manner of his death (foreshadowing future controversies regarding whether Crockett died in the fighting or was captured and executed). Perhaps mid-twentieth-century boys who were around the same age when it was claimed that Crockett made his first kill found it easier to imagine themselves replicating such mighty deeds. Kahn also pointed out that these hero-worshipping youth knew the lyrics to Disney's catchy theme song as well as the Lord's Prayer and with equal amounts of faith and fervor.[89]

Life magazine also looked at the Crockett craze replete with pictures of children playing out their frontier fantasies with the requisite coonskin hats, toy pistols and rifles, and fringed buckskin jackets and taking "turns playing Davy and the wicked Mexicans who did him in."[90] For parents, watching their child's play can be magical, where creating worlds of impossible mashups and anachronisms are part and parcel of the fun. But in the grown-up world, constructing national identities on fallacious myths can result in very real and painful consequences for those excluded or otherwise diminished by the myths and mythmakers. The author astutely observed that "legends stuck to Crockett like sandburs."[91] It also pointed out a near-disastrous mistake Disney made by airing the show depicting Crockett's death at the Alamo before other episodes had been produced: "When Davy died on TV, so many protests poured in that Disney will launch Fess [Parker] in a TV series."[92]

By the spring of 1955, critics and scholars were starting to catch up to Disney's Davy. In a foreshadowing of culture wars over Crockett's image yet to come, a handful of articles that dared to take a critical, or more historically accurate, view of Davy Crockett inspired a stormy backlash. The real storm broke after John Fischer, editor for *Harper's Magazine*, wrote a scathing essay critical of the manner in which so many of America's children had "been bedazzled into worshipping a Crockett who never was—a myth as phony as the Russian legend about Kind Papa Stalin." Crockett, Fischer claimed, was nothing more than a "juvenile delinquent who ran away from home at the age of thirteen to dodge a well-deserved licking by his father." The numerous sins of Fischer's historical Crockett included illiteracy, deserting his wife and children, deserting the army (once a substitute could be hired), sloth, being "a backwoods justice of the peace who boasted of his ignorance of law; an unsuccessful politician; a hack writer" who depended on an anonymous ghost, and apparently worst of all, "hear this, Junior—a violinist."[93] Furthermore, Fischer excoriated his fellow Texans for worshipping the Alamo:

> This is the blood-splashed ruin which every Texan—little or big—venerates as his national shrine. Every year it is drenched with geysers of high-decibel oratory—steamy, impassioned, and gloriously inaccurate. Indeed, inaccuracy has now become a matter of self-defense: for on this subject—and a few others—the Texans have

> brain-washed themselves so thoroughly that any speaker who told the truth would invite a lynching.[94]

Fischer questioned the defenders' understanding of military tactics, but not their bravery, and he plainly stated, "They died well." But he made a very important observation for his own time as well as ours in the present: "Maybe history has two strikes against it. Ever since the fall of Troy, the mythical heroes and comforting legends have always seemed to find a more eager audience than the workaday fact. They still do."[95]

Surprisingly a fortnight passed before an editor for the *Austin Statesman* fired a riposte in the "Yes There Is, Virginia" model. Despite "what that mean old John Fischer tries to tell you in Harper's Magazine," the editor assured his audience that Crockett "was an upstanding man" who "walked tall, shot straight, finished what he started, and first decided what was right" before going ahead. The editorial claimed that Crockett's marksmanship and being a man with "intelligence and rugged virtue" excused his questionable grammar and education. And perhaps there was "some myth about Davy, but he earned it" through his noble sacrifice at the Alamo. Criticizing the iconoclastic "debunkers" and "muckrakers" who sought to disparage American heroes such as George Washington, Ben Franklin, and Thomas Jefferson, the editorialist promised readers these names would "all live on in the admiration and affections of the people." The brief but contemptuous editorial challenged Fischer to "take on some one his own size," such as the Easter Bunny: "A little exploration into the sordid facts and he might come up with something that would bust the country wide open, which he seems to want very much to do."[96] The beleaguered *Harper's* editor claimed the scores of letters received in response were treated seriously but informed the writers that "the facts were right but the times were different. By the measure of his own time, Davy was a good and brave man. . . . After all, we didn't want to kill any Santa Clauses."[97]

By the end of 1955 and early into 1956, the "Davy Crockett Craze" had run its course. As author Peter White offered his postmortem on the fad, he noted that a Washington store had discounted its Davy Crockett T-shirts from $1.29 to $0.30 each, while a "five-and-dime chain" store on New York's swanky Fifth Avenue reduced its counter space from seventy feet dedicated to Crockett paraphernalia by two-thirds. White partly blamed the efforts of "debunkers" such as *Harper's* Fischer. He cautioned, "Just how much Davy's youthful public was affected by these deflations in print is debatable," but a trip to a public school in Manhattan offered some interesting observations. One fifth-grade teacher interviewed stated her students frequently sang and talked about little beyond Crockett, but after reading books with conflicting information, they felt somewhat let down. Some expressed disappointment with the liberties taken by the theme song to Disney's movie (that Davy had not killed a bear at the tender age of three), as well as Hollywood marksmanship where the hero never misses a shot. One student plainly stated a preference for a more authentic hero.[98] On the other hand, the first graders were more forgiving: "Davy is just another old friend now ranking with Gene Autry, Hopalong Cassidy, and Roy Rogers."[99] These children of the 1950s would be the adults of the closing decades of the twentieth century. The seeds of a mythical past based on American folklore were sown thickly during this time, and the country still struggles with the culture wars that continue to bloom.

It is difficult to imagine a heroic movie about such a seminal and romanticized event in Texas history being made by one of the top names in Hollywood of the time not reinforcing the dual images of Texas exceptionalism and unabashed expansionist American manifest destiny. Five years after Disney's interpretation of Crockett inspired one "Crockett Craze," John Wayne upped the ante in 1960. Everything about Wayne's film about the 1836 Alamo battle screamed "EPIC!" In order to make the film as authentically as he envisioned, he literally had to do the heavy lifting himself, so the film was produced by, directed by, and starred Wayne in the leading role. The set itself, instead of using existing Hollywood sets and soundstages, was built from scratch in Brackettville, Texas, approximately one hundred miles from the original battle site. The set featured a life-sized replica of the Alamo chapel and mission compound that took two years to construct. Wayne's art director, Alfred Ybarra, and his contractors conducted painstaking research of the Alamo chapel and the mission compound and employed hundreds of laborers to make the adobe bricks for the chapel. As Roberts and Olson observe, Ybarra's efforts "would have made Adina De Zavala proud."[100] Thousands of extras were hired to accentuate the disparity between Santa Anna's Mexican army and the ragged little band of Texan defenders. Nearly one thousand animals, horses, mules, and Texas Longhorn cattle were brought in and had to be cared for. Wayne invited well-established actors for major parts, including Richard Widmark, Richard Boone, Laurence Harvey, and Chill Wills, as well as up-and-comers such as Frankie Avalon. The price tag for all this "epic" was an eye-popping $12 million.[101] Wayne's interpretation became the dominant version of Crockett and the Alamo within the national collective memory for his alleged historical fidelity, his outsized personality, and patriotic rhetoric prior to the film's release and in response to some of the less-than-stellar reviews received.

Wayne's public rhetoric provided the publicity that helped engrave his interpretation of the Alamo and Crockett myth into American public consciousness. Wayne's off-screen politics matched his on-screen personas; he vigorously opposed communism, the Soviet Union, and excessive government regulations over individual liberties.[102] Based on public comments during this time, his strident anticommunist sentiments and outspoken pro-American feelings are essentially two sides of the same coin. Indeed, anthropologist Richard Flores argues that Wayne's *Alamo* was a bully pulpit from which "to preach his views on patriotism and anticommunism."[103] Conservative syndicated Hollywood columnist Hedda Hopper revealed that Wayne's motivation for *The Alamo* was firmly grounded in American pride. She noted that Wayne's disgust at so many contemporary movies caused him to believe the world needed reminding "that there once were men and women in America who had the guts to stand up and die for things in which they believed. This heroic story is not fiction, it happened only 124 years ago, and it belongs to people everywhere who have an interest in a thing called freedom."[104] For Hopper, Wayne, and others of similar mindset, "freedom" would always be construed within the Cold War lexicon as the only viable alternative to Soviet oppression.[105] And it was this understanding of "freedom" within the national collective memory for which Wayne-as-Crockett fought and died at the Alamo.

As Wayne recollected to Hopper, he first began thinking about making a movie based on the Alamo battle around 1946. The 1836 siege and battle lasted only thirteen days, but it took Wayne fourteen years to research the project, commission a script, secure funding, and make the picture. Due to a perceived lack of support for his grandiose vision, Wayne left Republic Studios and set up his own production company, Batjac.[106] Wayne insisted on historical accuracy and sent Pat Ford (son of legendary film director John Ford) to Texas for initial research. Wayne himself visited the state, claiming to have consulted with renown Texas folklorist J. Frank Dobie about the project. For the script, Wayne turned to James Edward Grant, an experienced, if not accomplished, writer.[107] Wayne finally signed a contract with United Artists in 1956 with the stipulation that he star in a leading role. This stipulation was driven home by Wayne's other financial backers in Texas; if he wanted the Texans' money, Wayne had to be the star, and furthermore, he had to film the movie in Texas.[108]

William Payne, amusements editor of the *Dallas Morning News,* in dissecting Wayne's efforts, started by rejecting the studio's intent to bill the movie as a "western" because this did not capture the "bravery" and "true story of men who died for a cause."[109] Payne continued to watch with keen interest the work being done in Brackettville. And he seemed pleased with how accurately Wayne told the story. He credited Wayne for having "spared no effort for realism" in re-creating the Alamo chapel not as a typical "Hollywood false-front, but good solid adobe brick," even obtaining the "plans sent to Spain by the Catholic fathers who built the mission in 1744." While Wayne was not a native Texan, Payne asserted that "no son of the Lone Star State could have lavished more care in setting the stage for the re-enactment" of the final battle. As he watched the filming of parts of the battle scenes, Payne reflected that the story of the Alamo had "an emotional appeal" that would "send blood racing through the veins of every true Texan." He claimed that "regardless of what brought the 187" defenders to make their stand within the Alamo, true Texans "hold every one in high esteem" for their "supreme sacrifice," which sets Texas "apart from any other state or area in the world." Payne described the breathtaking sight as he stood with other observers, watching several thousand Mexican extras dressed up as Santa Anna's soldiers advance across the Texas plain toward the Alamo set; "the make-believe of movie-making seemed to disappear and we got the feeling we were witnessing the actual battle fought."[110] If his historical interpretations were rather short-sighted, Payne's belief in Texas exceptionalism was certainly plain to see.

In October 1959, while filming was taking place in Brackettville, a letter to the editor appeared in the *Dallas Morning News,* imploring that there was "a moral need for John Wayne's Alamo movie to portray the significant and heroic role Latin-Americans played in helping to gain independence for Texas." The author, Joe Landin, noted how the silences in American media regarding Mexican American contributions to Texan independence had severely disadvantaged these fellow citizens: "They are not called or considered Americans" and suffered multiple discriminatory practices. Landin concluded, "If the true version of the Texas Revolution were given, especially to the new generations, and every red-blooded Texan stood for the truth, these Latin-Texans' pursuit of happiness would be happier."[111] There is no evidence that Wayne saw this letter. However, he defended the historical research done for the film and scripting parts for the opposing Mexicans in an interview with *Esquire* magazine: "See how we treated Santa Anna. He wasn't all bad, although he's always been made out to look that way. We studied him from every angle. You know, he was quite a boy."[112] Nonetheless, Flores reminds us that motion pictures are very much products of the era in which they are made, and even films treating historical topics will reflect the norms contemporary to when the script was written. Thus, Wayne's version of the Alamo reflected mid-twentieth-century racial conventions. Flores maintains that Wayne's *Alamo* cannot be seen as racially neutral regarding Tejanos and Mexicans, notwithstanding a screenplay that was much less overtly racist than earlier motion pictures on the Alamo (especially *Martyrs of the Alamo*), or that Wayne recruited friends from Mexico to portray Santa Anna and other significant Mexican or Tejano roles.[113] The film, as a product of that historical moment, reflected contemporary attitudes regarding race and ethnicity that prevented Mexicans and Tejanos from being considered "American" as Anglos in the 1950s defined the term.[114]

The modus operandi of Wayne's publicist, Russell Birdwell, was to go beyond the primary venues for entertainment news and into the mainstream news outlets. Paying to place advertisements in the trade media was well and good, but additional publicity that came from making headlines in the national news media was even better.[115] In a coup linking the 1960 US presidential campaign, Wayne's hyper-masculine notions of patriotism, and the Alamo movie then in post-production, Birdwell took out a three-page gatefold spread in the July 4 edition of *Life* magazine. The first two pages, illustrated by a publicity painting with the movie's title and tagline, "The Mission That Became a Fortress—The Fortress That Became a Shrine," appeared on the inside front cover of the magazine. The next page was political screed billed as a "Statement of Principle," casting aspersions on any candidate for national office whose tactics included anonymous speechwriters, a carefully crafted and polished image, staged presentations, and otherwise pandering to the masses for votes. Referencing public scandals of the day, Birdwell argued that the populace was disgusted with the "payola, influence peddling, quiz show rigging, the ghost-writing of political speeches—symptoms of a pallid public morality. They are finished with the great deceptions." Instead, the public longed for the mythic American frontier and "a return to the honest, courageous, clear-cut standards of frontier days—the days of America's birth and greatness; the days when the noblest utterances of man came unrehearsed. There were no ghost writers at the Alamo. Only men." Besides his own name, Birdwell attached the names of John Wayne and scriptwriter James Grant.[116] The public relations message became an integral part of the collective memory. With the *Life* magazine ad, Wayne's *Alamo* conflated political manifesto, family entertainment, and American identity, and the message played well with sympathetic audiences.

In the lead-up to the movie's October release date, Wayne's fervent rhetoric became even more newsworthy than the picture itself. Entertainment industry trade magazine *Variety* ran a headline: "John Wayne Admits His 'Alamo' a 'Message' Pic—Americanism."[117] However, all of Wayne's star power and patriotism, Birdwell's publicity campaign, the unprecedented $12 million spent making the movie, the number of extras, and amount of realistic detail in the sets could not change the film from being much more than "a long, preachy melodrama, back-loaded with action."[118] Despite its distribution success, earning $8 million over production costs, the reviews were decidedly mixed. Even Texas newspaper reviewers raised issues with the film. In the *Dallas Morning News,* William Payne overlooked some of screenwriter James Grant's "liberties" with historical facts only because the sum total of camera work, historical details, and soundtrack made up for these deficiencies. Payne criticized the pace of the early part of the film and the omissions of Travis's famed "Victory or Death" letter and the legendary line in the sand. The battle scenes, however, were the most "spectacular" and "realistic" he had ever seen. Payne's bottom line was that the film was "a must for freedom-lovers everywhere—and especially Texans."[119] In his regular column on Texas history and culture, Frank X. Tolbert was more critical. Tolbert's opinion of Wayne's film was "somewhere in between the all-out endorsement" by legendary director John Ford and "the nasty attitude of two national news magazines," leaving a wide gamut of possibilities. While Tolbert praised the beautiful photography and "most exciting" battle scenes, he criticized other sloppy details, including that the herd of cattle used were "obviously" not pure Texas Longhorns. Tolbert concluded that if the film were a third shorter and had employed more competent "technical advisor, 'The Alamo' could have been a truly great film."[120] John Bustin of the *Austin Statesman* damned with faint praise: "It's a long way from being a great motion picture, although at times it's close to being a mediocre one." Bustin believed Wayne's directorial debut fell short in attempting such an epic production, and Grant's script lingered too long over inconsequential details. Finally, he panned Wayne's heavy-handed proselytizing on "freedom, human rights, courage," when the final battle scenes told "more about courage than all the preachy platitudes that passed before it."[121]

No reviewers gave the film an unreserved, resounding endorsement. Philip Scheuer, reviewer for the *Los Angeles Times,* Wayne's hometown newspaper, declared, "The defense of the Alamo in 1836 made a proud and bloodied page in the history of Texas—and the United States of America." Scheuer awarded Wayne an "A for effort" and believed "he has succeeded more than he has failed." Conversely, Scheuer admitted that most of the early parts of the film should have been left on the cutting-room floor "because it is corny."[122] Trade industry standard *Variety* tried to sound encouraging, stating the film had "a good measure of money-making quality" about it and that it was made as "entertainment" rather than "a history lesson." However, the reviewer warned that audiences would have to endure three hours of "happy homilies on American virtues and patriotic platitudes," resembling more the films of an earlier era. Also, the reviewer complained that Grant's script never gave the audience a reason to believe in the three main characters, and the dialogue was too ingratiating, childish, and "crackerbarrel." Camera work, set design, and soundtrack earned commendations, but trying to be producer, director, and lead actor stretched Wayne too far.[123] If Wayne's first directorial effort resembled more the melodramas of earlier times, then considering when he started in the business and how much time he spent learning his craft on just those types of productions, it comes as no great surprise his first effort behind the camera resulted in a continuation of his own work, honed by years in the industry.

The most damning reviews came from New York City newspapers and magazines. *Newsweek* magazine called the film, "'B' for Banal." The reviewer derided it as "the most lavish B-movie ever made" because of a "silly, banal script" and "second-rate supporting cast." The film meandered, while the heroes have difficulty expressing themselves; "a right to the jaw is a gesture of friendship." The reviewer concluded, "The history book was a great deal better."[124] *Time* magazine was more critical, noting that the directorial debut by "Hollywood He-Man John Wayne" was "the biggest Western ever made," but they "have not quite managed to make it the worst." The movie was "flat as Texas" until the final battle. The reviewer admitted a lot happened during those three hours, "a seduction, an orgy, a murder, a battle royal in a barroom," but this was no different than any "other John Wayne western." Worse was the film's "shamelessly inaccurate" treatment of historical fact, with Travis and Bowie being "nastified and sissified almost out of recognition," coupled with the "phony backwoodsiness" and mawkish sentimentality of the dialogue.[125] Bosley Crowther, reviewing for *The New York Times*, panned the storyline as just "another beleaguered blockhouse Western" Wayne had made so many times before in the "same sardonic way." The final climactic battle overwhelmed him and did not make up for enduring two hours of "sticky Western clichés." While Crowther tolerated some rowdy brawling and Chill Wills's homespun witticisms, he complained that these went "too far on the farcical side." In the end, Crowther plainly stated that Fess Parker made a more believable Davy Crockett than did Wayne.[126] Finally, a reviewer for *The New Yorker*, who predicted he might be accused of being "un-American," reproached Wayne (and especially screenwriter Grant) of "having turned a splendid chapter of our past into sentimental and preposterous flapdoodle." The reviewer saluted the memory of the historical Crockett and Bowie and hoped to "live to see the day when somebody in or out of Hollywood" makes a "serious picture on this serious subject." Calling Grant's writing "a model of distortion and vulgarization," the reviewer excoriated his various and sundry "literary inventions" with story and dialogue. The reviewer admitted audiences would be disappointed had Wayne not played Davy Crockett as John Wayne but concluded this version of the Alamo saga was quite forgettable.[127]

Reactions to these negative reviews were swift and reveal to a significant degree how much John Wayne's Battle of the Alamo was interpreted as a battlefront against Soviet communism during the Cold War. Ben Pingneot, of Eagle Pass, Texas, accused the *Time* reviewer of a "hatchet job" and ignoring the "patriotic theme showing diverse and often feuding men banded together with the common purpose of fighting for liberty."[128] Davis Quinn excoriated *The New York Times* for its "lack of enthusiasm for the inspiring kind of courage and toughness that made America" and conforming to "the standard leftist defeatist pattern Hollywood so notoriously propagandizes." Quinn also insinuated that Wayne's known anticommunist sentiments were responsible for the poor reviews. He exclaimed, "Thank God a few Texans and a man like John Wayne are willing to back their traditional American philosophies" with this film. Quinn lamented that such "an important paper like the *New York Times* is so steeped in world liberalism that even its film reviews lack integrity."[129] From San Clemente, Kathleen Huttig believed that communist sympathizers had turned their "big guns" on John Wayne. The nefarious strategy, she alleged, was to circulate reports that his movie was a "box-office flop," thus discouraging others from watching it and creating a financial disaster for Wayne and his backers. Huttig exclaimed, "Let's show Mr. Wayne we still believe in America and respect its heroes . . . by supporting his latest picture, 'The Alamo.'"[130] Some recent immigrants to the United States appreciated Wayne's cinematic and patriotic labors. Sven Wahlroos saw a tribute to his Finnish homeland's valor and "the fight for freedom of all peoples everywhere." Wahlroos also noted that his Hungarian-born wife interpreted *The Alamo* as a proxy for the sieges of Budapest in 1944 and 1956. Wayne's effort moved them to encourage other "patriotic citizens to see this magnificent film."[131] Finally, the DRT could not sit idly by while such an epic treatment of their beloved Alamo was roughly handled in the press. Marry D. Harral, president of the Alamo Mission Chapter of the DRT, admitted to *Variety* some discomfort with the "departures from historical fact"; she nevertheless declared that on the whole, it was an "inspiring" film that "instills into the minds of people today that our wonderful freedom did not come by accident."[132] As Roberts and Olson suggest, Birdwell's publicity campaign "fused the memory of the Alamo with the image and politics of John Wayne." Any criticism of Wayne or the movie was "an attack on" Crockett, Bowie, Travis, and the other martyrs of the 1836 battle. Within some areas, "it even became an assault on the state of Texas." A generation (or more) of Americans would combine Wayne's Crockett with Disney's "to define who Davy Crockett was, what he believed in, and how he died." For historians and others, questioning any of this orthodoxy was to court danger.[133]

The cinematic versions of Crockett and the other Alamo heroes by both Walt Disney and John Wayne firmly resonated with the mid-twentieth-century American public and became the primary interpretation within the national collective memory. Movie historian Don Graham observes, "The Alamo is the oldest Texas story that keeps getting retold for mass audiences in that form of national memory known as the movies." He theorizes that Hollywood's historical epics succeed by both entertaining the audience and resonating with the audiences' collective memory, thus reinforcing "shared values and shared identity." Graham further postulates, "Historical epics like these do not create collective memory so much as they reflect and make use of existing memory."[134] He makes a point that if the movies do not "create" memory, they certainly magnify the intensity and the spread of those memories. Walt Disney and John Wayne did not introduce a new character into the American pantheon of heroes; people knew of Davy Crockett and his death at the Alamo, even if imperfectly. The dearth of definitive historical facts related to Crockett's life and death made it easier to accept the versions presented to the public on the big screen. And on the silver screen these heroes became bigger than life, which embedded them deeper into American collective memories.

The closing decades of the twentieth century will see the missions be caught up in political and cultural battles between competing identities, the dominant majority and minorities no longer willing to accept historical silencing. These late-twentieth-century battles will reprise the beginnings of some of the conflicts discussed in this chapter. There is an old saw that "history does not repeat itself but sometimes it rhymes." The fears expressed by Adina De Zavala and Fr. Mariano Garriga relating to the Alamo and other missions possibly being taken over by the federal government will be replayed by other actors in the 1970s and 1980s as the Catholic Archdiocese and the US National Park Service come together to administer Missions Concepción, San José, San Juan, and Espada. Similar fears will again be voiced in the early twenty-first century by those opposed to including the five San Antonio missions in a proposal to UNESCO for World Heritage Site status. The fears expressed are similar and, in that respect, "rhyme," but they do not play out in exact repetition. Also reprising later in the twentieth century will be the refrain of Alamo hero worship and American patriotism that echoed the rousing chorus played loud and strong by Walt Disney and John Wayne. But battles for the Alamo in myth and memory continue and indeed will never end as each succeeding generation seeks to create its own usable past.

6

The Culmination of San Antonio's Missions as Sites of Memory

Fairs, Parks, and World Heritage Status, 1960–2018

IN A 1964 interview for *Time* magazine, Texas Governor John Connally stated, "New York is 200 years away from its frontier, Texas is only 50 years from it. Fifty years ago, Texans were riding against Pancho Villa. That's history pretty close by."[1] But the contested frontier to which Connally referred had changed dramatically across that half century, and San Antonio would witness even more change over the next fifty years after he made that statement. Myths of a lawless frontier have always loomed large in Texas, retaining significant power into the modern period and feeding into state collective memories. San Antonio's missions have always been, and continue to be, some of the important fields on which contests among varying groups play out. The missions themselves are an integral part of the historical frontier and the contemporary Borderlands. Historians Pekka Hämäläinen and Samuel Truett characterized Borderland histories as "anchored in spatial mobility, situational identity, local contingency, and the ambiguities of power."[2] The importance of the missions to various groups (including parishioners, tourists, descendants of Native Americans, and Texas heritage organizations) explains why, after three hundred years of use, abuse, neglect, and reconstruction, the missions remain such a significant space in the memories of so many. Having multiple claimants on these contested spaces, the missions move beyond simple binary explanations, particularly when examined across three centuries instead of one or two pivotal events. Looking beyond the binary reveals the "continuities and persisting legacies," which we can see in both Borderlands and missions.[3] Even as the missions will continue to evolve and change in response to political, societal, and religious factors, there is a point at which historical study stops and actions become newsworthy current events. This chapter defines that end point as 2015, shortly after the establishment of the missions as a UNESCO World Heritage Site.

The preceding chapters established San Antonio's missions as sites of memory, but what has that status meant for the second half of the twentieth century and as we move into the twenty-first?[4] This chapter continues the interrogation of travel narratives, advertisements, and other representations of travel to reveal how memories, heritage, identities, and historical evidence have interacted at the missions. Tourism continued to be a driving force in the city's economy, and the missions, including the Alamo, continue to be top tourist draws. This period also witnessed the formalized agreement between the NPS and the Archdiocese of San Antonio to work together to preserve and display four of the missions as both sacred space and tourist attraction. This complex church-and-state relationship encountered some opposition but, by and large, has been mutually successful. More intense controversy once again embroiled the Alamo over the actual details associated with the death of Davy Crockett, hero of the Texas creation myth, and emerging historical evidence. Additional controversies erupted over how the DRT, longtime custodians for the Alamo, were maintaining the physical remains as well as controlling the Texas creation-myth narrative within an increasingly racially and ethnically diverse state. Another dimension to the missions' complex history came from a resurgence of people claiming to be descendants of the local Coahuiltecan tribes for whom the missions were initially founded. They argued that as the burial grounds of their ancestors, the missions were sacred space. Finally, San Antonio's missions were recognized collectively by UNESCO as a World Heritage Site. This vaunted status was the culmination of years of hard documentary, preservation, and money-raising efforts. One expected benefit to having this esteemed international recognition is increased tourist traffic to the missions and the city, and the money spent on food, lodging, and souvenirs, all of which are vitally important to the local economy. But even these efforts were not supported by all, so the missions are sites of contention as well as memories.

The identities the tourists found in San Antonio, largely constructed on romance and nostalgia, resembled more a fantasy Spanish heritage than an accurate or authentic reflection of historical reality.[5] However, San Antonio's Spanish and Mexican roots are ever present, ever exposed, whether one is shopping at El Mercado, enjoying a Tex-Mex dinner, or kneeling before an image of Our Lady of Guadalupe at four of the missions. Memory and history have been interacting and informing each other for three centuries, and the missions have been loci, nexus, and border.

Bringing Tourists to San Antonio and the Missions

San Antonio has long recognized the value of tourism and for decades invested considerable expense to draw tourists to the Alamo City. By 1962, San Antonio's tourism industry was such a critical part of the economic health of the State of Texas that gubernatorial candidates established improving tourism as one of their key talking points.[6] Just four years later, the Texas Tourist Development Agency reported to Governor John Connally significant increases in numbers of visitors to state tourist attractions, including a 10 percent increase in visitation to San Antonio's Alamo.[7] Tourists' money in city and state coffers remains a vital part of these economies into the present day.

As previously mentioned, postwar America witnessed an unprecedented travel boom as soldiers returned from active duty to start families and begin new jobs, many of which now included two weeks' paid vacation. This general economic upswing inspired many families to explore the country.[8] Despite the increased travel, in June 1968, the editors for *Changing Times* magazine challenged readers: "Have you really seen the United States of America? Have you visited enough of it to say you truly understand it, have truly experienced it? How intimately do you know this land and its people, its history, its institutions?" They expected a negative answer from most Americans, and the remainder of the article suggested fifteen places that American citizens should visit to improve their national awareness.[9] The editors informed readers that what they offered was not an itinerary to be crammed into a single summer's vacation but ideas for multiple summers, in addition to weekend getaways, because "travel should also be the antithesis of haste." They admonished readers that the "classic quality" of travel was "leisurely learning," as undertaken by travelers of bygone eras making the Grand Tour.[10]

Advertisements and travel narratives appearing in magazines and newspapers remained very influential in advising tourists where to go and what to see and do once there. Travel magazines frequently spoon-fed readers content designed to reinforce preconceived notions about a given place, such as the manner in which *Holiday* magazine used "this collective knowledge to its advantage, building profiles around mythologies of place that flowed through middlebrow culture." Readers of the magazine should envision their vacation to the American West as "their own westward trek, ritually affirming patriotic bonds across time in the process."[11] As the predominantly white, middle-class readers traveled, they could, based on these various representations of travel, reinforce their "American-ness" and sense of manifest destiny and Pax Americana writ large in the postwar era.

The content of the travel narratives regarding San Antonio's missions as presented through advertisements or articles in magazines and newspapers did not change substantially from the early part of the twentieth century. Common themes included imagined romantic scenes of picturesque ruins, saintly friars (often incorrectly identified as "monks") teaching docile Indigenous peoples the mysteries of the holy faith and benefits of European civilization, and mythic heroes sacrificing their precious blood in the name of Texas freedom. However, differences worth noting include the assumption that many travelers would be traveling by automobile rather than railroad. Also, these visitors were not coming to San Antonio for "the season," suggesting that families did not have the means for lengthy stays. This period also saw the emergence of specialized magazines targeting particular groups of readers, whether ethnic, professional, special interest, or regional. Articles highlighting San Antonio's missions could still be found in major metropolitan newspapers, trade journals catering to the travel industry, and important national and regional magazines considered to be contemporary cultural influencers, such as *Changing Times, Travel, Better Homes and Gardens, Travel Holiday, Southern Living, The New York Times,* and the *Chicago Tribune.*

In June 1959, the *Chicago Tribune* published a travelogue of San Antonio that opined, "Perhaps the most romantic era was during the Spanish rule." The "ancient missions, excellently preserved, . . . add an irresistible note of nostalgia. This 'touch of old Spain' permeates the atmosphere and even the casual overnight visitor feels it." A brief description of each mission followed, noting the Alamo's role as "national shrine" and San José's status as "Queen of the missions" due to Huizar's "internationally famous" Rose Window. At both Mission Concepción and San Juan religious services were still conducted, and Espada's aqueduct remained in use. The river wound "its romantic way" through the heart of the city. The *Tribune* journalist concluded that for an inexpensive family vacation "that is really different, more and more Americans are heading south to San Antonio . . . city in the sun."[12] Henry Ferguson, also writing for the *Chicago Tribune,* considered the city a "Venice of the Texas Plains" where the "most romantic path into the skyscraper heart of the city is along the landscaped banks of the San Antonio River." In addition to watching US soldiers wooing local girls along the banks, Ferguson commented on the city's Spanish heritage, beginning with legends related to each of the five missions, such as the women of Spain throwing their gold rings and bracelets as tokens of their affection for absent husbands and sons into the molten metal being cast as a mission bell.[13]

Marguerite Johnson, writing for *The New York Times,* contrasted the peaceful beauty of the four Catholic mission churches to the bloody memories associated with the Alamo. She perceptively noted that the Alamo served as "a symbol of Texas the state and Texas the state of mind." The old chapel served as a museum, but she observed at the other missions that "the bells still ring for services and for the mission classes." Johnson identified the builders as artisans led by monks and priests and Mission San José as "Queen of the Missions." At some point she utilized the diary of Fr. José de Solís to describe life during colonial Spanish times. Photographs, including the ornate facade of San José, accompanied the article. Her description of the Alamo included the text of William Barrett Travis's "Victory or Death" appeal for more troops. And Johnson concluded with General Sam Houston's resounding cry, "Remember the Alamo!," which fixed the old mission in the collective memories of the American public.[14] Just seven months later, another correspondent for *The New York Times,* Charles Layng, visited San Antonio and described plans to connect the four Catholic missions with a fifteen-mile parkway providing tourists "access to nine public parks, the missions and a number of other Spanish landmarks." Part of the impetus for this project came from the planned HemisFair, a world's fair that would open in the city in 1968. The project was intended to facilitate visitors being able to see each of the missions as well as the surviving Espada aqueduct, which, Layng observed, "still carries water from Espada Dam, as it has been doing for 230 years."[15]

When the editors of *Changing Times* magazine compiled their top fifteen places every American should visit, readers were probably not surprised to see Washington, DC; Williamsburg, Virginia; the Grand Canyon; and the Great Smokey Mountains on the list. The inclusion of San Antonio might raise an eyebrow, although the city was well-known as home to the famous Alamo. However, the description only briefly mentioned the 1836 battle and instead emphasized the city's Spanish heritage as represented by the other missions. Reminding readers that the region known as the American Southwest was originally once part of "Spanish Mexico," the essay remarked that its influence could "still be seen and felt in large portions of Texas, New Mexico, Arizona and California, but possibly nowhere with more spirit than in San Antonio."

The editors connected the Alamo to the other four missions as "part of a network of Spanish settlements" to bring European agriculture and lifestyles to the empire's remote frontier. They considered San José to be the "gem of early Spanish architecture and sculpture" and applauded efforts to connect all of the missions through a planned "Mission Road Parkway."[16]

Journalist Rick Timmons suggested that thousands of his fellow Texans have spent "precious vacation time" visiting California's missions "strung in a 600-mile chain" along the coast without realizing that there are missions scattered all across Texas "that are much older" and equally "grand." Timmons mentions Texas missions from El Paso in the west, to the east near the town of Crockett, concentrating on those in San Antonio. Of course, "the most famous mission in the country—Mission San Antonio de Valero, now simply called the Alamo," received its obligatory description, although Timmons admits its eighteenth-century history is usually forgotten in lieu of the 1836 battle, about which all Texas fourth-graders learn. Additionally, readers were reminded that Mission San José, the "queen of the missions," is "preserved as a national historic site" and is best known for "its delicately carved Rose Window." Mission Concepción is described as "somewhat Moorish" and having acoustics comparable to those of "the Mormon Tabernacle," similar to nineteenth-century descriptions. Timmons's article could be brushed off merely as Texan braggadocio were it not for a byline of "Los Angeles Times."[17] Two months after Timmons's piece, *Los Angeles Times* correspondent Richard Joseph complimented the city of San Antonio, claiming a visit should be made a requirement "for every town planner in America." Besides the salubrious climate and picturesque river walk, he noted other attractions, especially "the chain of five old Spanish missions in and near the city." Joseph claimed, "If you're a top-grade mission buff, you can cover all five" as the City has designated connecting streets as the "Mission Trail." For less-robust visitors, he recommended visiting Mission San José, "the biggest and most important." Joseph informed readers of its multiple historical roles: "church, fortress, military post, agricultural community, school, and home for about 350 Indians." The mission was "abandoned shortly after the Civil War and rebuilt and reoccupied in the late 20s and 30s." He also pointed out that it was "officially a state and national historical site as well as an active parish church" and gave visitors "a good understanding of how the Spanish missions helped build up the southwest." Like most every other visitor to San Antonio past and present, Joseph admonished his readers, "One other mission you've got to see," the Alamo. He opined, "As a matter of fact, the good citizens of

San Antonio see to it that you damn well don't forget the Alamo." Amazed at the number of Alamo-branded businesses in the telephone book, Joseph admitted "what the real Alamo will do is get you hooked on Texas history" through the heroic tale of the Alamo martyrs.[18] These promotional pieces appeared in a major newspaper within a state famous for its own collection of Spanish missions and are therefore interesting for spreading information on the Texas missions, which might be seen as competition to their own.

In May 1974, correspondent Robert Deardorff published a description of San Antonio in *Travel* magazine. He opined that while the city "is modern, American, and metropolitan, its major tourist attractions are none of these things." He briefly described the Spanish and subsequent Mexican periods and noted that because of the large Mexican American population, "more than anything else, their architecture, festivals, and culture make San Antonio an entertaining place to explore." Deardorff's primary interest during his visit was the colonial Spanish architecture, but recognizing that he wrote for a general audience, he did not use technical jargon to describe what he found. Thus, he described the Alamo as "a battered, two-story stone building with an arched portal that has two columns on either side of it," having mentioned its 1836 fame earlier. At Mission Concepción, he mentioned the "two-towered, Moorish-looking building decorated with eighteenth-century frescoes." He also described spending the entire afternoon at Mission San José, "Queen of the Missions," for its "magnificent Rose window" and extensive compound with granary, grist mill, and Indian apartments.[19] Finally, he encouraged tourists to visit Missions San Juan and Espada but did not describe them in great detail.

Garrett Sutherland, writing for *Travel/Holiday* magazine, concurred with Deardorff's assessment of San Antonio: "After a wild and bloody past, this ex-frontier town has emerged into one of the most romantic of America's great cities." Sutherland gave his readers a rare (but false) piece of San Antonio lore revealing the acceptance of legend over history: Enchanted by the river, a Franciscan friar named Olivares came to the region. As he reached the place, "he was attacked by two French soldiers and a half-breed Indian, but persuaded his would-be robbers to help him found the mission." Sutherland correctly informed readers that the missions founded along the river were decades older than "their more famous California counterparts," and all but the Alamo were active Catholic parishes. Sutherland also accurately described the missions as more than just the church buildings but included the entire enterprise of education, agriculture, and language in addition to Catholicism.

He added the tale of Pedro Huizar's famous "Rosa's Window." Huizar was identified as a "Spanish stonemason whose ancestors chiseled the tracery at the Alhambra." Sutherland did mention Huizar's legendary lover, Rosa, who never joined Pedro in the New World, but he also informed readers that what the "legend fails to mention is that as Pedro was pining away for his lost love Rosa, he fathered seven children by a local lass before his death at San José," spoiling some of the romance of the legend. Finally, the battle of 1836 got its due as the pivotal event that "immortalized the mission called the Alamo."[20] Romanticized history flowed through these narratives and many others just as the river flows through San Antonio, luring tourists and their money to the city. And while the editors for *Changing Times* encouraged travelers to take advantage of opportunities for "leisurely learning," a significant amount of San Antonio's appeal appeared to be based more on myth and heritage commodity than sound history. In this respect, the substance of the narratives changed little from the nineteenth century into the twentieth.

The Missions, the NPS, and New Adventures in Community Relations

Although San Antonio Congressman Maury Maverick had called for the missions to be put under the administration of the NPS back in the 1930s, such a park was not authorized until 1978 and did not open as an official National Historic Park until 1983.[21] In the 1950s, San Antonio architect Sam Zisman recommended that a national park would allow better "preservation and maintenance of the ancient irrigation system," which was "something the California missions do not have, and is still in use today."[22] Old buildings require a great deal of preservation and maintenance, and securing the necessary resources (funding as well as expertise) has been the driving force for federal involvement at the missions. As religious historian Thomas Bremer argues, the missions' "status as a national park continues to lend the missions a level of national priority that borders on the sacrosanct" as ranking "among the nation's most sacred places," and thus the missions have received "budgetary appropriations that have in fact rescued them from certain extinction brought about by deterioration, encroachment, and abuse."[23] But achieving that status was by no means easy or guaranteed.

The process to become part of the National Park System included a congressional subcommittee hearing held in San Antonio on November 9, 1976, to ascertain community support for creating a national park around the missions. Of the people who testified, support for the park project was overwhelming, which was not surprising since most of the witnesses had some sort of official capacity with municipal or local volunteer organizations that believed the missions belonged in the National Park System. Statements to the subcommittee came from city business, political, and religious leaders, including Abraham Kazen Jr., the congressional representative for the district in which the missions were located (who read into the record a telegraphed endorsement from Lady Bird Johnson, former first lady); Lila Cockrell, mayor of San Antonio; Bexar County Commissioner Albert Bustamante; Fr. Balthasar Janacek, archdiocese representative of the San Antonio Missions Advisory Committee; and Henry Guerra of the Greater San Antonio Chamber of Commerce. Two themes dominated their testimony. First, the missions continued to be active churches and community centers. The buildings may have been crumbling, but the faithful still gathered for Mass, catechism classes, and other parish events. Second, many witnesses remarked that the missions stood as symbols of the Hispanic heritage in Texas, the Southwest, and the United States.[24]

Since 1976 was the Bicentennial Year in the United States, the people coming before the subcommittee accentuated the region's Spanish influence on American history. George Garza of the San Antonio Mexican Chamber of Commerce heartily endorsed the proposed park. He described the missions as "the finest and well-preserved symbols of this [Hispanic] culture and heritage." Henry Guerra similarly emphasized that the "economic, political, cultural, architectural, and engineering heritage symbolized by these missions has proven to have great impact on the Southwest and demonstrates its continuing influence on our Nation." Mayor Cockrell summed up the missions' importance as "active centers of religious, social, and cultural activities. They are a tie to the past, a catalyst for the present, and a hope for the future."[25] Cockrell and the others recognized that the missions continued to play the roles they started back in the eighteenth century. The arguments advanced in this hearing reinforced the missions' status as "sites of memory," being "symbolic element[s]" of the "memorial heritage" for the San Antonio community.[26]

Although support for a national park incorporating the missions was positive at this particular subcommittee hearing, the potential for conflict was acknowledged. In one exchange between Fr. Balthasar Janacek (more commonly known as "Father Balty") and the subcommittee members, the priest recommended that the proposed oversight advisory committee be enlarged from seven to nine members to include one representative named by the archdiocese and one by the parishes. When asked if that was not redundant, he replied that the archdiocese might hold one point of view while parishioners might hold a differing opinion regarding "the missions because they are their homes."[27] Although Fr. Janacek recognized the potential for conflicts, he dismissed the possible differences as insubordination to church hierarchy.

Fr. Janacek's prediction regarding conflict over the proposed park did, in fact, arise. As the process to create a national park at the missions progressed, some local parishioners raised concerns. In late November 1977, San Antonio city officials held a meeting at Stinson Municipal Airport, adjacent to part of the proposed parkland. A local reporter observed that "after three hours . . . none of the 200 citizens present had spoken in favor of the proposed park and several voiced opposition." The key sticking point was the stated need by NPS to acquire extra private property surrounding the mission compounds that linked one compound to the next along a narrow ribbon following the river. The stated rationale was that this would preserve the integrity of the park setting and allow visitors to visually discern the connections that joined the missions in a chain. Unfortunately, some of the properties desired by NPS were homes to several families, some of them multigenerational parishioners of the mission churches. At the community meeting, others held signs stating, "We were here first," and "Let our homes stay." Resident Pauline Sanchez Soto argued that the neighborhood surrounding Mission Espada was more than a mere community, but "a family," and expressed concern about what would become of it should some residents have to move out. The city officials, including Councilwoman Helen Dutmer, acknowledged that they had heard rumors claiming that all residents would be evicted for creating the park, but she emphatically stated, "It simply is not true." The city's representatives also pled that they could not state with any certainty how many or which privately held properties might be lost to the park, since Congress had not approved the park bill.[28] The residents' concerns reflected the importance of the missions as a site of memory to local parishioners and community members as homes.

On November 12, 1978, President Jimmy Carter signed into law the San Antonio Missions National Historical Park bill. Residents of San Antonio's South Side greeted the occasion with both rejoicing and mourning. Ray Yarritu, president of the South San Antonio Chamber of Commerce, was ecstatic: "If San Antonio was a small town, everyone would be driving up and down main street honking their horn because of the news."[29] Others were not as pleased. Magdalena Gonzales, head of the Organized Mission Residents (a group opposed to the park project), and Reverend Manuel Ramon, parish priest at Mission Espada, led a group of a few dozen people in lamenting the potential loss of their community. Gonzales called the occasion the "blackest day in the history of the missions" and claimed, "We want to make sure our missions will remain living entities and not dead monuments to our ancestors." Reverend Ramon was even more critical, claiming that the missions would be turned over to "the money holders, who will prostitute them and turn them into big cash registers." Instead of preserving Mexican culture, "these people constantly want to destroy the people of the missions."[30] In a later interview, Gonzales raised the concern that tourists would have priority over parishioners, citing the example of a funeral at one of the missions that had been interrupted by a tour group. Despite the pastor's explanations, the participation of mariachis in the ceremony encouraged the tourists to begin taking snapshots of the mourners.[31] The disparity in reactions among people living in the same part of the city reveals the folly of looking at the groups (ethnic or otherwise) laying claim to the missions as monolithic in nature. There is a great deal of complexity regarding who was arguing for or against putting the missions under the aegis of the NPS. Even within the Catholic Church unanimity could not be found. On the other hand, such diversity of opinion highlights the usefulness of using San Antonio's missions as case studies for Borderland complexities.

Issues over church-state relations nearly scuttled the project in 1979 when President Carter, after signing the bill establishing the park, then withheld the necessary federal funds for actually running the park.[32] Additional negotiations eventually bore fruit, and in September of that year, Jose Cisneros was formally announced as park superintendent, along with nearly $700,000 for administrative start-up expenses. An additional $250,000 was raised by a private foundation for preservation work on the mission buildings. There was also a recognition that some thorny issues including land acquisition remained, but NPS Director William Whalen promised that local concerns would be heard.[33] Besides the local parishioners' concerns, a clause from the 1941 agreement that brought Mission San José into the NPS fold caused more wrangling among the NPS, the State of Texas, and the archdiocese. This clause stated that should one of the parties decide to terminate its relationship (one example given was if Congress should decide to abolish the NPS), the property would revert back to the original owners, the church and the State of Texas.[34] Finally, on February 20, 1983, the NPS took formal control of the mission footprint and *acequia* (irrigation ditch) properties while the church retained control of the spaces used for worship.[35]

Preserving the missions as their spiritual home, community center, and site of memory remained a vital concern of the parishioners. In 1981, Mission Espada celebrated its 250th anniversary with a parish festival. Despite processions and performances featuring charros, mariachis, and Concheros Indians, what caught reporter Rick Thurmond's eye was a T-shirt worn by a young girl with the message "Our mission is a living entity—not a dead museum." Regular visitor Maria Torres Knox concurred with this sentiment as she "fought back tears" while describing the reverential manner with which the women of the parish cleaned and decorated the church.[36] Fifteen years later tensions still remained. Janie Garza, a resident with deep connections to both the San Juan and Espada communities, was one of the more outspoken opponents of NPS involvement. She believed that the Park Service would impose more bureaucracy and regulations that would outweigh any perceived benefits. Garza expressed disgust at the demise of the mission community around San Juan as the Park Service bought properties and then tore down existing houses. She was equally appalled by the lack of interest in cooperation she perceived between the NPS and the local parishes: "Why does the national park have to 'interpret'? Why can't we interpret? I'm sorry to say this, but why do *gringos* have to interpret our culture?"[37] As chair of the Parish Council at Mission Espada, Garza also expressed serious concerns over certain parish-owned "artifacts and antiques, now that the Missions have become a National Park." Apparently, some pieces of value donated to the parish had disappeared, and the council was demanding to be consulted on the disposal of other parish properties.[38] No reply regarding the donated objects was found.

Garza's concerns over the interpretation of mission culture begs the question of whether an accurate and complete narrative of San Antonio's missions exists for tourists. As we have seen in previous chapters, many of the narratives about the missions tell an overly romantic story that bears little resemblance to historical fact. The NPS narrative is more balanced but essentially covers the mission period and ends with secularization. It does not tell the stories of the local communities that remained and continued to exist in and around the missions.[39] On the other hand, could enough parishioners be recruited to volunteer to act as docents? While some visitors might find these volunteers' lived experiences at the missions fascinating, could they accurately answer questions regarding eighteenth-century religious practices or pre-contact Indigenous lifeways? By the same token, private tour companies that run shuttle buses of tourists from the Alamo to Espada are not held to any standard, and some operators regale tourists with highly romanticized tales, considering a good story to be better than historical fact. Bremer similarly points out these very same disconnects and discomforts among parishioners, volunteer docents, and park rangers in how to best inform tourists of the historical, religious, cultural, and social significance of the mission enterprise. Indeed, he notes that some park rangers will not enter the chapel sanctuaries while in uniform to separate the sacred from the profane but send tourists through and then meet them again when they exit. But as Bremer observes, the rangers have more guidelines than the docents regarding what they tell to tour groups.[40] The lack of oversight or consistency, particularly among non-NPS-affiliated agencies, encourages myth to be accepted in the place of historical fact and exacerbates the gap between academic history and memory. This lack of a consistent and complete narrative also fuels some of the conflicts among the various stakeholders who have claims to the missions.

Davy Crockett Is Dead: Letting Davy Rest in Peace

In May 1955, correspondent Ray Duncan, writing for *Holiday* magazine, observed that in San Antonio, "history is everywhere here, and some of it is debatable."[41] It is an undisputed historical fact that Davy Crockett died on March 6, 1836, at the Battle of the Alamo in San Antonio, Texas. The specifics surrounding his death, however, have been the source of an amazing amount of debate and acrimony. In 1978, former Texas State Historical Association President Dan Kilgore ignited a firestorm that reveals just how contentious the relationship between history and memory can be.[42] It is curious that the "how did Davy die?" debate from the 1970s to the present has been so rancorous; why all this fuss over the exact nature of someone's death 180 years after the fact? Instead of contributing more speculation over whether Crockett died fighting near the Alamo chapel doors or was later captured and executed on Santa Anna's order, this book asks a different question: What did the controversy over his death mean in terms of collective memory? Historian James Crisp bluntly asks a similar question: "Why do we care so much?" For many, to question Crockett's heroic death is to question the reason why he and his doomed compatriots were at the Alamo. It questions the very raison d'être of Anglo Texas, as well as the American concept of manifest destiny. The level of rancor on this topic shows how closely many Texans and Americans hold within their collective memories a heroic Davy Crockett who died in the thick of the fighting for noble and altruistic goals.

Questions over whether the Alamo symbolizes Texas freedom from Mexican tyranny or American territorial conquest to expand chattel slavery are not new. In 1959, James Grant, the scriptwriter for John Wayne's epic film *The Alamo*, speculated with a surprising degree of candor, "This whole 'Alamo' business was nothing much more than a land-grab. Travis was in old San Antonio de Bexar to stir up trouble. And Crockett and Bowie were a couple of malcontents who had come into the territory because things were becoming too civilized for them at home. They were looking for action." However, Grant hastened to add, "But this, of course, does not change the fact that these men died gallantly and heroically."[43] Evidently, a gallant and heroic death is sufficient to cover a myriad of sins.

At the core of this bitter dispute is whether on that fateful morning in 1836 Davy Crockett was killed as a direct result of combat against the overwhelming numbers of Mexican soldiers or whether he was taken prisoner (along with six other survivors), only to be summarily executed on Santa Anna's direct order. For the next 140 years, there were differences of opinion regarding Crockett's final moments, depending on who was telling the tale.[44] The prevailing perspective in Texas was consistent with that of one nineteenth-century Texas historian, R. M. Potter, who claimed that Crockett died surrounded by the bodies of numerous enemies he had killed. But there were dissenting voices. No less a personage than Theodore Roosevelt claimed that Crockett was the last defender to die but offered two possibilities on how that may have happened.[45] In neither case was it intimated that Crockett surrendered. Nor was a craven surrender by Crockett suggested by a Mexican officer, Lieutenant José Enrique de la Peña, who plainly stated that Crockett and half-dozen other Texan survivors had been brought before Santa Anna, only to be executed on his command.[46] De la Peña's diary and disputes over its legitimacy remain at the crux of the modern debates.[47]

Kilgore's book, based on his presidential address at the Texas State Historical Association meeting, was published in 1978 and stirred up a considerable amount of hostility. Coming just three years after the American translation and publication of de la Peña's diary, emotions were still raw.[48] As one Texas journalist observed, "Any Texan worth his ringtail lizard-skin cowboy boots and Willie Nelson albums knows better than to smear the legend of Davy Crockett." The journalist took umbrage that Kilgore claimed that Crockett "had a dismal career in Congress, failed financially, and was motivated to go to the Alamo for less than courageous, liberty-loving reasons."[49] An editorial less than a week later suggested that Kilgore would have a hard time convincing "millions who have seen the 'real' Davy as portrayed by Fess Parker and John Wayne."[50] Indeed, such is the power of motion pictures to create memories through visual effects. Even in distant Boston, people learned of Kilgore's challenge that "Davy Crockett did not die a martyr's death."[51]

Crisp, along with historians Paul Andrew Hutton, David Montejano, and Arnoldo de León, and anthropologists Richard Flores and Holly Beachley Brear, argue that race plays a vital role in understanding the controversy: Davy (Anglo) and his heroic death at the hands of a race seen as inferior (Mexican Others) led to the inspired victory at San Jacinto, which allowed Anglos to take over Texas from those benighted Others.[52] Theirs is the "erudite" and "elitist" scholarly history French sociologist Maurice Halbwachs asserted was divorced from the popular and collective memory.[53] Conversely, amateur historian and retired New York City firefighter William Groneman speaks for the collective memory that believes Davy Crockett fought bravely until the moment of his death.[54] Groneman and his sympathizers contest the scholars mostly by casting aspersions on the veracity and provenance of the sources (namely, de la Peña's diary) used by academics and deriding as "revisionists" those whose arguments are somehow interpreted as besmirching America's pantheon of heroes.[55] Groneman's essential conclusion about the meaning of Crockett's death appears to be little more thought-provoking than America needs heroes and Davy was a worthy and honorable one.[56] Crisp and Groneman have continued their feud at conferences and in print into the twenty-first century.[57]

Flores argues that the legendary and heroic Davy (who died in battle) replaced the more historically accurate Davy (who *might* have been taken captive at the end of the battle and executed afterward) because by the end of the nineteenth century, "valor" had become a "central tenet of patriotism," which was required if Davy was to be installed as an "American hero." He further claims America was in need of such heroes as it struggled to maintain its identity and superiority against the Plains Indians and immigrant masses. In the late twentieth century, Flores asserts that the heroic Crockett was still necessary to inspire Anglos in their xenophobic battles against a rising Mexican American population bent on claiming civil rights previously denied to them.[58]

Although Flores and others have said little regarding the issue of contemporary events, could this racist backlash have contributed to the controversy of Kilgore's questioning the manner of Crockett's death? The English translation of the de la Peña diary was published in 1975, and Kilgore's book followed just three years later. The American public was still stinging from the fall of Saigon in 1975 and the humiliating ending of the Vietnam conflict. Additionally, economic malaise and stagflation undermined confidence in the American way of life in the depths of the Cold War. Despite the 1976 Bicentennial celebrations in the United States, were the population's smiles a bit strained, trying to hide fears for the future? Perhaps Kilgore's perceived questioning of Davy's heroism was just too much for a battered public looking for something to restore their faith in America, particularly those who as children had been a part of the Disney-inspired Crockett hero-worshipping obsession of the 1950s.

Even toward the close of the twentieth century, a heroic death for Crockett and his doomed band made the story of the Alamo all the more romantic and appealing. In February 1994, a *San Antonio Express-News* journalist spoke with visitors from outside Texas about their visit to the Alamo shrine. A lady from Michigan broke down in tears after touring the site. She expressed surprise at her "visceral" reaction but reported feeling "in awe. They [the defenders of 1836] never had a chance, but they never gave up.... I felt this was hallowed ground. I felt enveloped by the ambiance, the atmosphere, I'm just caught up in it somehow." Another woman, a Filipino immigrant by way of New York, claimed to have wanted to see the Alamo firsthand and afterward stated, "This is a symbol of bravery.... They never surrendered." Texas author T. R. Fehrenbach agreed, stating, "The Alamo is a symbol of the human spirit and of courage, which is why it transcends nationality." The visitors "come from all over the world. But I don't think they are coming because it was a parochial story of Texans and Mexicans beating up on each other."[59] So a story of great courage, even in the face of certain death, can be more universally appealing, more tragically romantic, than more recent interpretations of an independence movement to create a new source of cheap land for would-be plantation owners; such is the power of collective memory to select romance over cold, dispassionate historical analysis.

This particular battle for Texans' hearts, minds, and collective memory has ebbed and flowed over the decades. Since the early 1970s, the magazine *Texas Monthly* has been arguably one of the most influential arbiters of Texas culture. Articles about the Alamo and Crockett have been popular enough that the editors seemed interested in printing stories on Texans' favorite icon. Some articles have been written by historians or included interviews with historians who deliberately challenged selected popular myths, including the

Alamo. In November 1986, historian Paul Andrew Hutton wrote an article for the Texas Sesquicentennial and the two-hundredth anniversary of Crockett's birth. Hutton freely admitted that he "wanted to dismantle [Crockett]—to free myself from the shackles of childhood hero worship and prove once and for all my maturity and credibility as a scholar." However, Hutton confessed, "something unexpected began to happen even as the myth began to unravel—I found myself *liking* Davy Crockett." The biography Hutton published wound up being quite friendly to Crockett, but he considered Crockett "a martyr on the altar of Manifest Destiny" and had the temerity to accept and perpetuate the idea of Crockett's surrender and summary execution shortly after the Alamo battle.[60] As a result, of the letters to the editors of *Texas Monthly* that they selected to publish, those critical of Hutton outnumbered those of his supporters. One letter writer self-identified as a Texas history teacher in McAllen, who called Hutton's article "blasphemy," ranted on the importance of maintaining heroes on pedestals: "In this sesquicentennial year Texas heroes should be revered, not destroyed. They should be held in esteem at all times, but especially this year. . . . The world still needs heroes—especially the students. I will never teach my students what he wrote. A real Texan would not." Another detractor identified himself as Jim Dumas, a "fourth-great grandson" of Crockett by his first wife, Polly Finlay, and as "President of the Descendants of David Crockett." Dumas considered Crockett's surrender to be a "myth" based on "hearsay" and alleged that the family had more sources about Davy and the Alamo if Hutton or Dan Kilgore had bothered to ask.[61]

Additional articles in *Texas Monthly* that fed the controversy included Debbie Nathan's 1998 piece, "Forget the Alamo." Nathan offered an interesting assessment that was less on the Alamo itself but introduced to a popular readership some of the new generation of academically trained historians, many of whom did not "romanticize the frontier" or "pay homage to cattle drives" and "don't care how Davy Crockett died. Influenced by the cultural turmoil of the sixties, and study not just heroes but common people, and not just white men, but women, blacks, Mexican Americans, and nonconformists—from abolitionists to labor organizers. As far as they're concerned, the fascination with the Alamo symbolizes all that is wrong with Texas history."[62] Reaction to her article was more negative than positive with one letter writer arguing that all multiculturalism led to was "nihilism," and another berating the "Race, Class, and Gender scholars" for cheating students out of heroic stories that are the "cultural glue that binds us together as one people."[63] Gregory Curtis, editor for *Texas Monthly*, introduced the March 2000 issue with a piece titled "Should We Care?" He explored some of the history and controversy surrounding the de la Peña diary and concluded that a bigger issue was at stake: "The reason for the passionate defense of Davy is that the whole myth of the Alamo, indeed of the whole Texas Revolution, hangs on the way he died. And that myth is that the Battle of the Alamo was a glorious fight by heroes who willingly gave their lives for freedom."[64] Again, while reactions were mixed, the majority were critical of Curtis. For one writer, the exact circumstances of Davy's death were less important: "I have every bit as much respect for Davy if he surrendered" as he did for the other Alamo defenders who died in battle. Another writer lamented, "Pride in one's heritage and history has become politically incorrect," and her children, sixth-generation Texans, "have little pride in their heritage" because they were not taught the "myth" of the Alamo in school.[65] Historian Michael Kammen summarized the acrimony over the precise nature of Crockett's death with the observation, "Myth tends to triumph over historical facts; and in this instance, mass culture and learned culture went their separate ways."[66]

The Return of the Natives; or, Had They Ever Left?

At the main visitor's center at Mission San José, the NPS shows a free video every half hour called "Gente de Razón" (People of Reason). Narrated by local Tejana singer Tish Hinojosa, the film contextualizes the missions and the mission communities as being practically continuous for many hundreds of years. Toward the end of the film, Hinojosa asks her daughter what happened to the Native Americans who came to the missions. Her daughter responds that the Indians "all died." To which Hinojosa admonishes her daughter to "go look in the mirror."[67] Bremer suggests that the "theme of continuity" is important mainly for its tourist appeal to emphasize the "legacy" and "living parishes" of the mission communities.[68] There is one important feature that he fails to mention, the role of collective memory not only for the tourists' sake but also for that of the mission communities.

Bremer posits, "The theme of continuity archaicizes the contemporary worship communities, which in turn lends authoritative relevance to the old buildings while dodging the sticky issue of Church and state separation."[69] He is correct but does not take into consideration the importance of collective memory. When considering how Native Americans, especially those who joined the missions and assimilated into the Spanish culture, may have viewed the missions across the years, Halbwachs's comments on religious communities and memory become particularly incisive. When believers gather in consecrated space, they "re-establish, in addition to their visible community, a common thought and remembrance formed and maintained there through the ages." Furthermore, "the group memory endures much like the buildings presumed to house it," and "a single current of religious thought has uninterruptedly flowed beneath the roofs of such holy places." Even when the church is closed and the group is scattered at times, "it endures and remains what it had been." And "when the group comes together again, there would be no reason to assume it had changed or had even ceased to exist so long as the faithful could pass by the church, view it from afar, or hear the bells," which would encourage them to "hold in mind or readily evoke the image of their congregating together and the ceremonies they have participated in behind these walls."[70] Besides the Catholic parishioners, for whom the missions are sacred space and centers of community, groups of Native Americans, some of whom also grew up in the mission communities, have been experiencing something of a renaissance since the 1990s. In the present day they are reclaiming their collective memories as descendants of those for whom the missions were initially established.

The most significant claims involved the repatriation and reburial of the remains of Native Americans at Mission San Juan under the Native American Graves Protection and Repatriation Act (NAGPRA) of 1990. The groups at San Juan included the American Indians in Texas at the Spanish Colonial Missions; the Native American Church; the Inter-Tribal Council of American Indians; and the Tap Pilam Coahuiltecan Nation. These groups did not always speak with a unified voice and on occasion had differing claims. Fr. Janacek, in his role as the archdiocese liaison to the missions and the NPS, worked with the various Native American groups.[71] However, not all of the claims involved the four Catholic/NPS missions. In January 1994, Gary Gabehart, president of the Inter-Tribal Council of American Indians, argued that the street in front of the Alamo should be closed, claiming it was a burial ground for both Native American and Spanish people, containing upward of one thousand bodies.[72] Although nothing was done at the time, claims that the land immediately in front of the Alamo chapel was a colonial-era cemetery would reappear over two decades later in discussions to renovate Alamo Plaza.

In February 1994 and again in November 1999, two sets of physical remains purported to be Indigenous people were reburied with much more dignity and ritual than when the remains were initially discovered. It was believed the bodies belonged to Indigenous persons who had joined the San Antonio missions during the colonial period and after their deaths were buried on mission property. Their remains were disinterred in the twentieth century as a consequence of repairs and renovations at the missions and had been held for study.[73] In these cases the Inter-Tribal Council of American Indians (in 1994) and the American Indians in Texas at the Spanish Colonial Missions (in 1999) made claims under NAGPRA for the return of Native American remains held at various museums and universities. The 1994 reburial took place in San Antonio's San Fernando Cemetery, No. 2, and a dual ceremony of Native American rituals and a Catholic Mass was held. This addressed the remains of an estimated thirty-seven individuals that had been taken from a mass grave under the post office near Alamo Plaza in the 1930s. Gabehart hoped the ceremonies and interment would bring peace to the ancestors whose afterlife was disturbed but also a measure of respect for local descendants of the Native Americans.[74] The 1999 reburial involved a larger group of remains, perhaps as many as ninety people, discovered at Mission San Juan in the 1960s. Once again, a dual ceremony involving Native American customs and a Catholic Mass were held, and the remains were reburied at San Juan.[75]

With these ceremonial reburials, local descendants of Indigenous people were reasserting their heritage and reestablishing their collective memories in context of the missions, which had been an important part of their communities and their ancestors' lives. In this sense they were reclaiming a degree of continuity regarding the missions' role within the communities that had been supplanted by the Spanish-heritage myths. Contrary to these myths, a significant ethnographic study conducted at the turn of the twenty-first century suggests that within the Mission San Juan community, there are lineal descendants of individuals from the colonial period still living in the local area.[76] And as anthropologist Daniel Gelo observed, "Memories of Indian ancestry persisted in local stories."[77] Rather than simply disappearing through extinction, total assimilation, or flight, the mission Indians are making their presence known in the present.

Not all claims were related to human remains needing reburial. One example was a draft of a letter to Reverend Patrick Flores, archbishop of San Antonio, asking for his signature and return of the document. Flores sent copies to several close advisers, including Fr. Janacek, asking for recommendations. If he signed the document as requested, it would be a blanket acquiescence to demands by a group called Danzante Coahuilteco and would authorize "the use of the missions of San Antonio for the religious use of the Native American community," including "prayer in the original fashion and traditional methods" along with traditional dances, songs, languages, sweat lodges, bonfires, and incense. The basis for the request was that the missions "were originally intended for use by the Native Americans and their descendants" in addition to having been built by the Indigenous peoples.[78]

Flores additionally contacted Félix D. Almaráz Jr., a historian at the University of Texas at San Antonio, for an opinion and canvassed his fellow clergy. In his reply, Almaráz appeared to question this particular Native American group's historical understanding. He opined that the group was making claims based on scant or incorrect historical and archaeological data. Essentially, he noted that "Coahuiltecan" was a broad linguistic term covering a number of groups; it was not lineally traced through families. Also, Almaráz asserted that since the original Coahuiltecans were nomadic hunter-gatherers, they had little historical basis for sweat lodges or similar claimed rituals.[79] Though not mentioned by Almaráz, one of the more glaring historical incongruences regarding the Indians' request is that the Coahuiltecans who originally joined the missions would not have been allowed to use sweat lodges or similar accoutrements but would have been taught to worship and conduct themselves as eighteenth-century Spanish Catholics. However, as stated in an earlier chapter, the exact level of commitment the original mission Indians had for their new faith is an open question, and some friars may have been more open-minded than others. There is no available evidence that Flores approved the request.

As one modern Coahuiltecan, Ray Hernandez, informed a reporter for the *San Antonio Express-News* in 2001, "We always knew we were different. We always knew we were Indian." Hernandez, a council member of the Tap Pilam group of Coahuiltecans, continued, "We were Catholics, but we had our own religion that was very, very closed. The minute we spoke of Indianness and our beliefs, we got knocked down to the lowest level of humanness. But now things are better, and we can talk about this." However, when it came time to rebury the remains turned over to the Tap Pilam group, they "realized that a traditional ceremony did not exist for reburial." Their dilemma was summarized by Patricia Newada of the Native America Center: "You don't jump up to 200 years later and expect to form an American Indian tribe."[80] Anthropologist Alston Thoms concurred, suggesting that through the years, the Coahuiltecans "tended to conceal or camouflage their presence." However, now in a society that tends to be more culturally tolerant, "people with mission Indian heritage once again became readily visible as resurgent Coahuiltecans."[81] As these modern groups of Coahuiltecans walk a fine line between invented traditions and recovered memories, their experience suggests that not all historical silences are forever.[82] Additional reburials have taken place since 2009. Preservation work on the missions in preparation for the bid for World Heritage Site status revealed more human remains, and the archdiocese has worked with Tap Pilam to ensure that a level of dignity and ritual accompanied the reinterments.[83]

Additional cultural elements have been brought back to the missions by the resurgent Native American groups. In 2004, the American Indians at the Spanish Colonial Missions reintroduced the *matachines* at Mission San José. To garner the interests of the next generation, they held instructions in the dances for youths between the ages of six and twelve.[84] Unlike the pre-contact *mitote* dances that were practiced by the various Indigenous groups who joined the missions, the *matachin* was a dance introduced by the Franciscan friars as a means of converting the Coahuiltecans and other native peoples in the Spanish Borderlands to Christianity.[85] As Ramon Juan Vasquez, executive director of the American Indians at the Spanish Colonial Missions stated, "It's part of our culture, it's part of the Southwest culture. Anywhere the Spanish had influence on the indigenous cultures, you will find the *matachines*." Two years earlier, a group of Tarahumara Indians visited San Antonio from their native northern Mexico. They met with members of the Tap Pilam Coahuiltecan Nation and taught some of the Tap Pilam their version of the *matachin*. Vasquez and Isaac Alvarez Cardenas learned the dance and began plans to bring it back to the missions on an annual basis. Cardenas, the dance instructor for the children, summed up their sentiment: "I really believe when the spirits of the missions, the spirits that are still there, see these children, they're going to recognize them when they see all these outfits [costumes the dancers wear]. And I really believe it's going to please them, bring peace to this land."[86]

The End of an Era: The DRT Versus the General Land Office and the Future of the Past

In his book on Americans' collective memory and hallowed battlefields, historian Edward T. Linenthal observes, "The Alamo, like other battlesites, has been the object of veneration and defilement, and its enduring message of patriotic orthodoxy has been subject to redefinition."[87] Since the dawning of the twentieth century, the DRT served as the state-appointed custodians of the Alamo chapel and surrounding property. Internal schism, severe economic depression, and two world wars could not shake their hold over the Alamo and (more important) the narrative passed along to visitors. However, new challenges arose in the 1950s and 1960s with the civil rights and Chicano movements. The DRT's traditionalist narrative of heroic Anglo self-sacrifice for the greater cause of Texas freedom from Mexican tyranny has been challenged as hackneyed and irrelevant to a modern, multicultural society. For several decades, the DRT had been under fire regarding its control and ethno-centric interpretation of the site's history and meaning from multiple groups representing various racial and ethnic interests.[88] Even Fr. Janacek excoriated the DRT's interpretation and religious devotion to the shrine in a sermon delivered at a Mass at the Alamo. He accused the DRT of worshipping dead heroes instead of a living God and for creating a myth that has been used, "in the history of this state, to demean and insult other people, to obscure their history, their role, even in this battlefield and to obscure the hundred plus years of Spaniard and Native American presence upon this hallowed ground."[89]

Persons of Mexican ancestry were some of the "other people" of whom Fr. Janacek spoke. The DRT narrative of the Alamo had been used to "demean and insult" them and to "obscure their history," not to mention their contributions to Texas history, such as Rosie Castro, a self-identified Chicana activist, born in San Antonio in 1947, who remembered the Alamo as "a symbol of bad times." Castro recalled being taken to the Alamo on school field trips and being fed the myths of the "glorious battle." However, as she grew older, she learned a more complete story of the Alamo, and the martyred defenders had feet of clay. Nonetheless, "as a little girl I got the message—we were losers. I can truly say that I hate that place [the Alamo] and everything it stands for."[90] Challenges such as Castro's to the DRT narrative point out the difficulty in negotiating between memory and history. Similarly, anthropologist Richard Flores reminisced about his own negative childhood experience when, during a third-grade field trip to the Alamo, his best friend turned on him, accusing Flores, as a "mes'kin," of killing all the Alamo defenders.[91] Because the DRT controlled the Alamo and its narrative for over a century, in the memories of people such as Castro and Flores, the DRT and Alamo are inextricably (and negatively) linked.

Two years before the 1986 Texas Sesquicentennial the editor for *Texas Monthly* magazine questioned whether the Alamo was being presented at its best. Gregory Curtis posited that the Alamo was "the one landmark in Texas visitors want to see, but once there, most leave after spending just ten or fifteen minutes on the grounds." The minuscule amount of time spent at the shrine, Curtis opined, was due to "so little effort [being] made to explain what the Alamo was" and its significance to Texas history. He argued in favor of displays of artifacts, the addition of explanatory signs, and plainly stated that "it is time to save the Alamo from the way it's preserved today." With the sesquicentennial on the horizon, he could see no better project to tell the story of Texas than by improving the manner in which the Alamo was being presented to visitors.[92] Two months later, in the magazine's letters-to-the-editor section, Wanda Harris Arnold of Lubbock and president general of the DRT haughtily dismissed Curtis's recommendations. However, Bob Bowman of Tyler, who was a member of the Texas Sesquicentennial Commission, lauded Curtis's suggestions, claiming, "The Alamo and Texas are synonymous and we certainly cannot celebrate our 150th birthday without a strong commitment to the monument that, more than anything else in the state, is our historical anchor."[93] In their own way, each of these reactions reflects the power over Texans' collective memories the Alamo holds and why so many Texans wrap their identities so tightly around the crumbling structure. Curtis recognized the foundational role the Alamo has in the Texas creation myth and hoped the importance of that role could be better explained to visitors. Arnold's curt dismissal of the suggestion reflected the DRT's hubris and unwillingness to accept even well-intentioned recommendations. Finally, Bowman also acknowledged the Alamo's importance as "historical anchor" for Texans and believed a better job of preserving the physical plant was in order.

To paraphrase what journalist Jan Jarboe Russell observed in May 1994, what started as a fight to control the street in front of the Alamo "shifted into a fight over the story of the Alamo itself." When a San Antonio city councilman raised concerns about whether the city could close the street to traffic right in front of the Alamo, the DRT "hauled out a 1975 contract in which the city promised never to close the street" and threatened a lawsuit if any move was made in that direction.[94] While a contest over who held jurisdiction over a block or two of city street was the primary spark, additional issues quickly produced a large conflagration that did more public relations harm to the DRT. Gary Gabehart, representing the Inter-Tribal Council of American Indians, requested the street be closed, claiming that nearly one thousand Native Americans had been buried there during the mission era. Others complained about the lack of representation of Tejanos and black people in the

DRT narrative. As Russell opined, "The Daughters resist all such efforts at revisionism, which has left them open to charges of presenting history as they wish it had happened, instead of as it actually happened." The DRT defended itself by claiming that the Alamo "is important for one reason, and that's because of the battle that took place here." They claimed that their mandate from the State of Texas took priority over all other considerations in favor of only one single moment in history.[95] However, by concentrating solely on this single moment in history, the DRT ossified the Alamo, and any considerations of the immense cultural (and architectural) changes that happened before and after 1836 faced nearly impossible challenges to be heard.

By 2009, the overall ambiance of Alamo Plaza immediately in front of the chapel had deteriorated to the point that a group calling itself the Alamo Society began complaining about the touristy and kitschy attractions directly across from the shrine. Bill Chemerka of Barnegat, New Jersey, who founded the group, argued that the City of San Antonio should raze the buildings facing the Alamo and restore the site closer to the 1836 appearance (although this could potentially alter the gabled parapet facade constructed by the US Army in the late 1840s that has since become so familiar). Chemerka called the Alamo Plaza setting a "disgrace. I wouldn't want a McDonald's at Pearl Harbor or a Starbucks on the beaches of Normandy." However, SACS argued that the building storefronts had historical value, even if the businesses within did not, and warned that careful research was needed before anyone began razing buildings.[96] Although these discussions did not immediately involve the DRT, there would need to be negotiations between the City, the DRT, and the US government regarding a federal building on the corner of East Houston and Alamo Plaza over any plans to expand the site's footprint. Also, Chemerka's attitude opposing crass commerce being conducted adjacent to sacred space endorses the DRT's rhetoric of the Alamo as a sacred shrine.

Trouble for the DRT began in earnest in 2010 when cracks in the roof of the chapel became the flashpoint for a larger battle within the heritage organization. Some members believed that the organization was neglecting its sworn duty to protect the chapel, while leaders in the group claimed plans for repair were already in the works. Texas State Senator Leticia Van de Putte expressed concern over the cracks and offered to help.[97] Before long, the disagreements over fixing leaks in the roof escalated into a major public fight over the DRT's management of the shrine. Self-inflicted scandals did not help matters when a state audit in 2009 revealed that a fundraising program based on "Native Texan" car license plates had brought in over $213,000, but less than 20 percent actually was earmarked for preservation and repair of the Alamo.[98] However, in mid-2010, an engineer's report commissioned by the DRT stated that while the cracks were of concern, there were additional problems. While this news was a relief to some, it did not silence some of the sharpest critics from within the DRT itself.[99] Neither did the report prevent the Texas attorney general from beginning an investigation into DRT management practices. Additionally, critical articles appeared in both *Texas Monthly* and *The New York Times*, highlighting the scandals. Jan Jarboe Russell stated, "Feuds among the Daughters are legendary," but noted that this particular fight suggested a measure of weakness in the heretofore invulnerable DRT.[100] Alamo historian and curator Richard Bruce Winders observed in *The New York Times*, "There is a kind of mini civil war going on within the organization. Unfortunately, the Alamo is caught in the middle." One vocal critic claimed, "They honest to God think they own the Alamo."[101] The recalcitrance of the DRT to address its critics in an effective manner raised concerns among outsiders that would continue to weaken the group's effectiveness as managers.

In April 2011, the Texas Senate conducted hearings related to DRT governance and management of the Alamo.[102] Enough unsavory details on DRT finances and failure to allocate sufficient funds for preservation work on the Alamo (one of the DRT's avowed primary functions) were exposed that Senator Van de Putte, whose district included the Alamo, pushed a bill through the Texas legislature that required the DRT and the Texas General Land Office (GLO) to work together to increase transparency regarding DRT financial priorities and preservation. For the editor of the *San Antonio Express-News*, this represented a good start but still did not provide a sufficient level of oversight of the DRT. The editor argued that the GLO should exercise its option of creating a nine-member advisory board (which would include three DRT members, plus the Alamo curator who was hired by the DRT).[103] Only then might the Alamo receive the level of funding needed to carry out the necessary repairs. By December 2011, the DRT and the GLO had hammered out a compromise agreement that after eighteen months could be renewed for five years, but with a limit of four possible renewals. According to the agreement, the GLO was defined as the "custodian" and the DRT relegated to the status of an "independent contractor." According to the agreement, admission to the Alamo would remain free of charge, the DRT "shall explore" various ways to enhance visitors' experiences, the DRT would use GLO processes for visitor complaints and "keep the Alamo in 'good order and repair,'" and the DRT would "address the diverse, rich heritage of the Alamo; maintain the 'dignity and decorum' of the site; and provide educational outreach that emphasizes historical accuracy." In return, the GLO would pay the DRT $10,000 per month for "compliance costs," review the hiring and retention of department heads through the Alamo's administrator, inspect DRT records, and employ "an on-site representative to monitor operations."[104] While these conditions did not satisfy all critics, ultimately the DRT's days as sole guardians of the Alamo were indeed numbered.

The agreement between the GLO and the DRT seemed to be working for a while. In March 2012, Jerry Patterson, Texas Land Commissioner and head of the GLO, noted in an editorial that the Alamo was under attack from both the ravages of time and "a public consciousness that views it as an iconic attraction rather than a shrine to honored dead." He made a point of stating that progress had been made in repairing the roof and having a conservator working on the interior of the chapel. The GLO was helping make funds available for these efforts. However, Patterson opined that a more difficult fight loomed in terms of public awareness of what the Alamo was: a shrine. He considered the Alamo "a symbol of sacrifice for freedom" and compared it to the USS Arizona Memorial at Pearl Harbor and the battlefield of Gettysburg. Rather than the Alamo being just an easily recognizable backdrop for photo-ops, Patterson wanted to "shift public perception of the Alamo back to one of respect and quiet reverence." He promised to work with the DRT "to ensure the Alamo is always portrayed with respect, never diminished in the story of Texas, and remains forever the Shrine of Texas Liberty."[105] Patterson's comments reflect a desire, avowed by many in the DRT, to emphasize the Alamo as a sacred space, not as the first of five Catholic missions in the San Antonio area founded in 1718 but as a shrine to the Alamo martyrs of 1836 and a particular interpretation of the cause for which they fought and died.

In November 2012, the Texas attorney general's office issued a damning report describing the DRT's serious financial mismanagement of the Alamo complex. The report concluded that DRT management "failed to properly maintain the Alamo in good order and repair" as required by code, "mismanaged state funds entrusted to the DRT's control," and "breached the DRT's fiduciary duty to the State of Texas as trustee of the Alamo."[106] According to the *San Antonio Express-News*, this happened when DRT management allowed proceeds from the gift shop ostensibly for repair and maintenance to be mixed with state money, failed to act on engineering reports concerning leaks in the Alamo roof, and failed to "prioritize preservation in the shrine's operating budget," as well as claiming ownership of certain historic relics without adequate provenance and having used state funds to run its private library on the Alamo grounds. However, since the legislature had already replaced the DRT with the GLO as the primary caretaking body, the Texas attorney general decided not to take legal action against the DRT.[107] An *Express-News* editor disagreed and criticized the attorney general's office for not pursuing more punitive action against the DRT.[108]

Additional scandals reported in the local newspaper did not help the DRT's cause. The reported thefts of valuable items (although the definition of "valuable" was disputed), DRT resistance to the GLO requirement that after-hours functions could serve alcohol and continuing disputes over the DRT Library collection exacerbated the friction between the GLO and the DRT.[109] Additionally, this friction occurred as the City was again exploring the feasibility of improving Alamo Plaza. As an *Express-News* reporter observed, "Alamo Plaza is the most complex downtown issue." The journalist complained that the "plaza lacks the visual cues that delineate the Alamo's original footprint," and although the kitschy gift shops brought in a considerable amount of money to city coffers, "they seem blasphemous because, while they might be across the street from the Alamo's current boundaries, they are still on hallowed ground, where men died."[110] This journalist's complaint of commercial activity on "hallowed ground" substantiated historian John F. Sears's astute observation that tourist attractions "combine the sacred and the profane, the religious and the secular, the mythic and the trivial, the spiritual and the commercial."[111] A historic shrine honoring dead heroes less than one hundred yards from a haunted house/indoor roller-coaster adventure complex seems to accentuate Sears's juxtapositions.[112]

People looking for an opportunity to justify the expense of significant improvements to Alamo Plaza got a major boost in 2014. Phil Collins, founding member and lead singer for the popular British musical group Genesis, as well as having a successful solo career has also been a serious collector of Alamo memorabilia and offered to donate his existing collection to the State of Texas. Collins's collection consisted of over two hundred pieces and was valued at over $15 million. According to the agreement, the GLO would take possession of the collection, and a suitable center to house and display the collection would be built.[113] However, at the time of this writing, questions have been raised regarding the authenticity of certain items within the collection.[114] While a building to house the collection was completed in 2023, a larger, more permanent museum is still in progress.

In March 2015, the final blow fell for the DRT. Recently elected Texas Land Commissioner George P. Bush informed the DRT that its contractual agreement to run the Alamo for the GLO was terminated "for cause" effective July 10 of that same year. The GLO listed ten breaches of contract that warranted the termination, including the failure "to prepare and operate under an annual management plan; run the complex 'in a good and prudent manner'; and produce a policy" on resolving visitor complaints. The DRT's Library on the premises, the absence of a succession plan for staff, additional lack of transparency related to personnel issues, and firing of a senior staff member were also mentioned as issues leading to the termination.[115] Two days later, the *Express-News* reported that "the land office and the city each soon will launch a separate master planning process for the Alamo area." Reportedly, Bush also desired to make the Alamo "cash-flow positive."[116] Implied was that the DRT would not implement changes to the physical site that the City and the State wanted to improve tourists' experience, which did not include expecting tourists to continue acting as pilgrims coming to worship at the shrine of martyrs. The DRT remained committed to worshipping dead heroes in a similar fashion as their early twentieth-century ancestors had, in quiet reverence.

There are any number of clichés that could be used to mark the end of a 110-year, intimate history between the Alamo and the DRT. These once-powerful women were responsible for shaping a specific memory that became interwoven into the national narrative. However, as both Texan and American society changed in the late twentieth century to reflect a more diverse population, the DRT's message became less and less relevant. The DRT narrative ossified at a time when the larger state and national narratives were becoming more flexible in recognizing racial, ethnic, and gender groups silenced by earlier versions. The last shot in this latest battle for the Alamo has yet to be fired. For the DRT, the old cliché "gone, but not forgotten" seems apropos. For the GLO, it remains to be seen how it will shape the narrative of the Alamo to appeal to new generations of tourists from within and outside of Texas.

Mission Accomplished: San Antonio's Missions' Achievement of World Heritage Status

"A building built in the 1700s is never finished," Fr. David Garcia astutely observed in March 2010 as the missions were undergoing a $15 million fund-raising campaign and preservation projects. Fr. Garcia was directing the fundraising campaign, named Las Misiones. Part of the impetus for such an ambitious project was economic revitalization of San Antonio's south side of town. But the primary drive reflected the constant need to stabilize and restore the missions. Old buildings require constant upkeep, which is often very expensive, but as Garcia observed, since the missions were central to the community, "the money is used for the betterment of these missions and the betterment of the larger community."[117] The quest for World Heritage status began in 2006, when Virginia Nicholas, president of SACS, appointed a committee to prepare the nomination.[118] SACS did not undertake such an ambitious project alone but brought other stakeholders on board quickly.[119] In early 2007, SACS representative Paula Piper contacted the Catholic Church to assuage concerns that attaining World Heritage status would not place the missions under another layer of bureaucracy: "The Archdiocese will not be encumbered with any new regulations pertaining to the preservation of the mission churches, if they are designated a World Heritage Site. The laws that would apply are being followed by the Archdiocese at this time."[120] The application process took nine years, a great deal of research, hard work by a dedicated group of people across numerous organizations, and a considerable amount of nervous waiting, but on July 5, 2015, UNESCO granted World Heritage Site status to San Antonio's five missions.[121]

One of the themes that appeared in numerous conversations about the missions emphasized "community" and the missions being vital community centers. Fr. Garcia observed, "Weddings, baptisms, funerals, the life of a community as it has been going on for 200 years." Al Remley, chief of interpretation for the NPS agreed, and the effect it had on visitors was seeing "an unbroken cultural community through time."[122] When acclaimed documentary filmmaker Ken Burns made his multipart examination of America's national parks, he made a separate short film on San Antonio's missions and the mission communities. He noted, "Here we have these models of peoples co-existing among different peoples, among different religions, among the church, among citizens of all diverse backgrounds. That's what we celebrate."[123] Seeing the missions as an integral part of their immediate communities and as part of the larger city of San Antonio is key to understanding the missions as sites of memory.

But what is so special about a World Heritage Site designation? What might the missions and San Antonio gain from such status? The criteria for World Heritage status are very strict, and the description carries a considerable amount of prestige; being named a World Heritage Site is an elite designation. UNESCO's World Heritage Convention states that candidates "must be of outstanding universal value" in addition to meeting one of the established ten criteria.[124] The criteria recognize both natural and cultural significance. A proposed site could be a natural wonder of the world such as the Grand Canyon; a representative of a unique culture; an artistic (including architectural) achievement such as the Cathedral of Chartres in France; or a historic urban region such as that surrounding the Grand Mosque of Córdoba, Spain. In addition to prestige, those pushing for the inclusion of the missions anticipate significant benefit to the local economy. For Bexar County, officials predicted achieving World Heritage status would mean over one thousand new jobs, $2 million additional hotel tax revenue, and over "$100 million in additional economic impact."[125] However, gathering community-wide support for the endeavor was also expensive. The missions needed a considerable amount of attention from preservationists in order to look their best for teams of experts UNESCO sent to visit each site as part of the process. Additionally, in September 2011, Bexar County approved a $10,000 payment to assist with securing "international expert opinions" as part of the application process. The money was justified as "an investment in the city's global marketing appeal."[126]

The journey to World Heritage status was not without the occasional political hitch. In 2011, UNESCO admitted a Palestinian delegate, a seemingly harmless action. However, it kicked into play a US law from the 1990s that forbade paying dues to any United Nations agency that allowed a member from Palestine. Without dues money from the United States, UNESCO suddenly lost a significant portion of its funding.[127] And in 2013, when the United States was then considered in arrears on its dues payments, it lost its vote in UNESCO.[128] The hue and cry urging Congress to repay the dues and avoid jeopardizing the missions' opportunity for World Heritage status did not convince everyone. As one budget hawk sarcastically opined in a letter to the editor of the *Express-News*, if achieving World Heritage status was such a great thing and would bring such economic benefit to the city, "then the people of San Antonio should pay the dues. For your information, the U.S. government is broke."[129] Ultimately, the lack of dues did not prevent UNESCO from granting World Heritage status, but the crisis worried a number of supporters.

In January 2014, US Secretary of the Interior Sally Jewell officially nominated the San Antonio missions to be considered by UNESCO for inclusion on the World Heritage Site roster. Secretary Jewell put forward these justifications for inclusion in the materials:

- Criterion (ii): exhibit an important interchange of human values, over a span of time or within a cultural area of the world, on developments in architecture or technology, monumental arts, town-planning or landscape design.
- Criterion (iii): bear a unique or at least exceptional testimony to a cultural tradition or to a civilization which is living or which has disappeared.
- Criterion (iv): be an outstanding example of a type of building, architectural or technological ensemble or landscape which illustrates (a) significant stage(s) in human history.[130]

UNESCO ultimately granted World Heritage Site status based on Criterion (ii). The application materials heavily emphasized the still-functioning *acequias,* which allowed for significant cultural interchange between the colonizing Spanish and the colonized Indigenous people, as together they carved agricultural fields that would provide food for the missions. The application noted, "The creation and ongoing maintenance of these systems brought together in common cause the indigenous mission inhabitants and the missionaries, leading to an exceptional interchange of cultures. The most dramatic was the change in lifestyle adopted by the formerly nomadic Coahuiltecans to become settled agriculturalists."[131] The application painted an extremely positive overall picture of the missionary enterprise. However, given the millions of dollars the city hoped to recoup with increased tourism, smoothing over history's rough edges should not be surprising. Debates may continue on whether this intense change in lifestyle was good or bad for the Coahuiltecans, or how much choice they may have had at the time, or how much agency they retained after joining the missions. Many of those who joined the missions and survived the epidemics assimilated into the local Spanish population. In doing so, they survived to pass along their culture *and memories* to the next generation, and the generation after that, and so forth as part of the cultural interchange that the UNESCO Criterion described. Due to the significant level of Spanish (and later Mexican) cultural influence, it is little wonder that cultural geographer Daniel Arreola considers San Antonio the cultural capital of the national Mexican American community.[132]

Opposition came from people circulating rumors that World Heritage Site status would somehow give the UN governing power over the missions (including the Alamo). In September 2013, an emailed article by George Rodriguez, former president of San Antonio's Tea Party, hinted that the

Alamo "may fall under U.N. influence." He blamed Mayor Julián Castro of having "no problem with the U.N. influencing or even managing the Alamo." Tea Party supporter and historical reenactor William Grisham agreed with the sentiment, claiming, "The Alamo is a Texas thing, San Antonio in particular." Texas Land Commissioner Patterson dismissed these accusations as "horse hockey."[133] Nonetheless, in early 2015, Texas State Senator Donna Campbell of New Braunfels filed Senate Bill 191, which sought to bar any foreign entity from "owning, controlling, or managing" the Alamo. She claimed her legislation was prompted by the nomination of the San Antonio missions (including the Alamo) to UNESCO for World Heritage designation. Campbell asserted, "The Alamo is the story of Texas. It should always be maintained and cared for by Texans."[134] At a hearing on her proposed bill, Campbell claimed being a World Heritage Site was "not necessarily an honor," and "anything that starts with U.N. gives me cause for concern."[135] Campbell believed that her concerns were justified, since during the previous session the Texas legislature had changed the DRT's historic role as caretakers of the Alamo. As John Oliver, Campbell's senior policy adviser, explained, "Her overriding concern regarding the UNESCO designation [was] that Texans could lose control of the narrative regarding the sacred history of our state."[136] Preserving "the sacred history of our state" is revealing about the senator's motives and desire to maintain the long-standing "heroic Anglo" narrative of Texas history in general, and the Alamo in particular, within Texan collective memories. However, her bill died in committee.[137] After World Heritage status was awarded in July, Oliver expressed the senator's disapproval, accusing the UN of ignoring "the heroic acts of the brave men who died fighting for Texas independence. Because the U.N. is not recognizing the Alamo based on the blood shed there by Texans for freedom and independence, it's not something that she's overly enthusiastic about."[138] Campbell, like others before her, stood for the narrow traditionalist interpretation of the Alamo based solely on two weeks in 1836.

When UNESCO formally granted World Heritage status on July 5, 2015, there were many more people celebrating than complaining. Crystal Nix-Hines, US ambassador to UNESCO, thanked the committee but also acknowledged the eighteenth-century Indigenous peoples of Texas who "put these stones in place and dug these aqueducts." City Councilwoman Rebecca Viagran considered the award "a monumental moment for all our families who have lived around the missions." Two members of the UNESCO committee in charge of making the decisions, representatives from Japan and Lebanon, recognized the 1836 Battle of the Alamo in Texas's struggle for independence. Despite the anticipated economic benefits, Paul Ringenbach, the lead author on the nomination, stated, "What's important for me is the source of pride it's going to bring to the people of San Antonio, especially descendants of the mission Indians."[139] Fr. Rommel Perez, pastor at Mission Espada, was grateful for the news after the lengthy and arduous process. The designation, he said, "was an opportunity for all of us to know that we are part of history and we have received a gift from our ancestors, the Friars, the first missionaries, and Franciscans who spiritually and physically built missions that are parishes and centers of worship." Armando Cuevas sat in a pew at Mission San José to say a prayer of gratitude for family and the World Heritage designation. He told a reporter he lived in the area and first came to San José as a little boy. The announcement that World Heritage status had been granted prompted him to come and celebrate. Another visitor thought the city should have better signage to the missions but was otherwise very excited about the designation: "It's second only to LaMarcus Aldridge getting signed to the Spurs."[140] A week after the UNESCO announcement, Fr. Garcia presided over a special celebratory Mass at Mission Concepción.[141]

Legacy and Impact

In his synthesis on the Spanish Borderlands, historian David Weber gives scant attention to the legacies of the Texas missions. Yet without the missions the colonial frontier of Tejas, as well as our modern maps, would look very different. It all started over three hundred years ago with Mission San Antonio de Valero. The mission came first, followed closely by the presidio of San Fernando, and despite the friction between the missionaries and soldiers, they depended on each other and, together with the Native American neophytes, eked out a precarious existence at the edge of the Spanish Empire. More Spanish colonists followed and, despite difficulties, eventually found their niche, and the little frontier villa began evolving slowly into one of the ten largest cities in the United States. Weber poignantly observes, "When Spain's hegemony over the southern rim of North America ended in 1821, its long tenure left an enduring legacy that extended beyond the tangible transformation of people and places." Additionally, "Spain's legacy also lingered in American historical memory, where it took on a life of its own." San Antonio's missions are a vital part of this legacy and over the course of three hundred years became sites of memory, both locally, and nationally.

History and memory are related but remain quite different, and as Weber suggests, "The quest for a usable past has produced multiple interpretations of the Spanish experience on North American frontiers—constructions that have contended with one another over time to transform our understanding and to become in themselves powerful legacies of Spain's centuries in North America."[142] Romantic myths of mission ruins, saintly friars, and the stoic martyrdom of the Alamo heroes have been contested by archaeological and historical research and, despite being found wanting, have nonetheless endured in collective memories, just as the missions themselves have persisted in memory and in stone across three centuries.

How the missions will be remembered as they move into the next century depends on many variables, but the strength of the local communities and commitment of resources lead one to be hopeful that the missions will persist in many memories for decades to come. Historians are well placed to make effective and positive contributions, but everyone must be willing to have a civil discourse in search of understanding higher truths rather than resorting to the combative polemics that are all too common. Whether these memories will be based on a more accurate reflection of nuanced, factual perspectives or continue with the romanticized fictional accounts, only time will tell. Regardless, so long as the physical presence of the missions remains, they will continue to be visited by tourists, used as active churches, discussed by politicians, and serve as sites of memory for the region and beyond. Their multiple identities relating to their status as sites of memory will continue to inform and shape the collective memories of San Antonians, Texans, and Americans in ways that, like their Borderland setting, are sometimes peaceful and sometimes contentious for generations to come.

Notes

Introduction

1. "San Antonio's 300th Anniversary Celebration," accessed January 30, 2018, http://www.sanantonio300.org/.
2. Jane Kellogg Murray, "Viva San Antonio," *Texas Highways*, January 2018, 44. *Texas Highways* magazine is published by the Travel Information Division of the Texas Department of Transportation to market travel and tourism within the state.
3. United States Census Bureau, "Census Bureau Reveals Fastest-Growing Large Cities," Press Release, CB18-78, May 24, 2018, https://www.census.gov/newsroom/press-releases/2018/estimates-cities.html?intcmp=s1-subcounty.
4. Jan Jarboe Russell, "San Antonio Is the Mother of Texas," *Texas Monthly*, May 2018, 82.
5. Daniel D. Arreola, *Tejano South Texas: A Mexican American Cultural Province* (Austin: University of Texas Press, 2002), 131–49.
6. Michel-Rolph Trouillot, *Silencing the Past: Power and the Production of History* (Boston: Beacon Press, 1995), 116.
7. See, for example, Frederick Jackson Turner, "The Significance of the Frontier in American History," in *Rereading Frederick Jackson Turner*, with commentary by John Mack Faragher (New Haven, CT: Yale University Press, 1998), 31–60; Walter Prescott Webb, *The Great Plains* (Boston: Houghton Mifflin, 1931); and Walter Prescott Webb, *The Great Frontier* (Boston: Houghton Mifflin, 1952).
8. See, for example, David J. Weber, *The Spanish Frontier in North America* (New Haven, CT: Yale University Press, 1992); Patricia Nelson Limerick, *The Legacy of Conquest: The Unbroken Past of the American West* (New York: Norton, 1987); and Robert V. Hine and John Mack Faragher, *The American West: A New Interpretive History* (New Haven, CT: Yale University Press, 2000).

9. Jesús F. de la Teja, "The Spanish Borderlands: An Overview," in *Bridging Cultures: Reflections on the Heritage Identity of the Texas-Mexico Borderlands*, ed. Harriett D. Romo and William A. Dupont (College Station: Texas A&M University Press, 2021), 14.
10. For one of the earliest works on Spain's missionizing attempts in what is now the American Southwest, see Herbert E. Bolton, "The Mission as Frontier Institution in the Spanish-American Colonies," *American Historical Review* 23, no. 1 (1917): 42–61, http://www.jstor.org/stable/1837685.
11. Kenneth Hafertepe, "Experiencing the Complex Character of San Antonio and South Central Texas Through Their Vernacular Buildings and Cultural Landscapes," in *A Field Guide to the Vernacular Buildings of the San Antonio Area*, ed. Brent R. Fortenberry (College Station: Texas A&M University Press, 2021), 1.
12. Fernand Braudel, *On History*, trans. Sarah Mathews (Chicago: University of Chicago Press, 1980), 27, 45–46.
13. Carl Becker, "Everyman His Own Historian," *American Historical Review* 37, no. 2 (1932): 223.
14. George Santayana, *The Life of Reason: Or, The Phases of Progress*, 2nd ed., vol. 1, *Reason in Common Sense* (New York: Charles Scribner's Sons, 1922), 284.
15. George Santayana, *The Life of Reason: Or, The Phases of Progress*, 2nd ed., vol. 5, *Reason in Science* (New York: Charles Scribner's Sons, 1922), 40, 41 (emphasis added).
16. Maurice Halbwachs, *The Collective Memory*, trans. Francis J. Ditter Jr. and Vida Yazdi Ditter (1950; repr., New York: Harper Colophon Books, 1980), 50–52.
17. Halbwachs, *The Collective Memory*, 79–80.
18. Maurice Halbwachs, *On Collective Memory*, ed., trans., and with an introduction by Lewis A. Coser (Chicago: University of Chicago Press, 1992), 49–51.
19. John Bodnar, *Remaking America: Public Memory, Commemoration, and Patriotism in the Twentieth Century* (Princeton, NJ: Princeton University Press, 1992), 15.
20. Michael Kammen, *Mystic Chords of Memory: The Transformation of Tradition in American Culture* (New York: Vintage Books, 1993; first published New York: Knopf, 1991; page references are to 1993 Vintage ed.), 626.
21. Frans F. J. Schouton, "Heritage as Historical Reality," in *Heritage, Tourism and Society*, ed. David T. Herbert (New York: Pinter, 1997), 21.
22. David Lowenthal, *The Heritage Crusade and the Spoils of History* (New York: Cambridge University Press, 1998), x, 248.
23. Pierre Nora, *Realms of Memory: Rethinking the French Past*, trans. Arthur Goldhammer, English-language edition ed. and foreword by Lawrence D. Kritzman, 3 vols. (New York: Columbia University Press, 1996), 1: xvii, 14.

Chapter 1

1. Marion A. Habig, *The Alamo Chain of Missions: A History of San Antonio's Five Old Spanish Missions* (Chicago: Franciscan Herald Press, 1968; repr., Livingston, TX: Pioneer Enterprises, 1997; page references to 1997 ed.), 29; Fray Francisco Celiz,

Diary of the Alarcón Expedition into Texas, 1718–1719, trans. Fritz Leo Hoffman (1935; repr., New York: Arno Press, 1967), 49; and Jesús F. de la Teja, *San Antonio de Béxar: A Community on New Spain's Northern Frontier* (Albuquerque: University of New Mexico Press, 1995), 8. I will refer to Mission San Antonio de Valero as "Valero" for the duration of the Spanish period in Texas. During the Mexican period and especially after the 1836 battle, the former mission becomes more commonly known as "the Alamo," and this book will reflect that change.

2. Habig, *Alamo Chain of Missions*, 83; Fr. Antonio Margil de Jesús, *Nothingness Itself: Selected Writings of Ven. Fr. Antonio Margil, 1690–1724*, ed. Marion A. Habig, trans. Benedict Leutenegger (Chicago: Franciscan Herald Press, 1976), 266–71.
3. *The San José Papers: The Primary Sources for the History of Missions San José y San Miguel de Aguayo from Its Founding in 1720 to the Present*, trans. Fr. Benedict Leutenegger et al., comp. and annotated by Fr. Marion A. Habig, 3 vols. (San Antonio: Old Spanish Missions Historical Research Library at San José Mission, 1978), 1:27–34.
4. John Francis Bannon, *The Spanish Borderlands Frontier, 1513–1821* (Albuquerque: University of New Mexico Press, 1974); Donald E. Chipman, *Spanish Texas, 1519–1821* (Austin: University of Texas Press, 1992); and William C. Foster, *Spanish Expeditions into Texas, 1689–1768* (Austin: University of Texas Press, 1995).
5. Francis X. Galán, *Los Adaes: The First Capital of Spanish Texas* (College Station: Texas A&M University Press, 2020), 18, 21; and David J. Weber, *The Spanish Frontier in North America* (New Haven, CT: Yale University Press, 1992), 162–65.
6. Foster, *Spanish Expeditions into Texas*, 51–57.
7. Domingo Terán de los Ríos, "The Expedition of Don Domingo Terán de los Ríos into Texas," trans. Mattie Austin Hatcher, in *Wilderness Missions*, ed. Jesús F. de la Teja (Austin: Texas Catholic Historical Society, 1999), 13. Fr. Massanet's description was very similar to Terán's. He added that the Native American name for the place was "Yanaguana" (54).
8. Juliana Barr, *Peace Came in the Form of a Woman: Indians and Spaniards in the Texas Borderlands* (Chapel Hill: University of North Carolina Press, 2007), 5. See also F. Todd Smith, *From Dominance to Disappearance: The Indians of Texas and the Near Southwest, 1786–1859* (Lincoln: University of Nebraska Press, 2005), 1–32.
9. *Los Adaes*, 21–22; Weber, *Spanish Frontier in North America*, 154–55; and Maria F. Wade, *Missions, Missionaries, and Native Americans: Long-Term Processes and Daily Practices* (Gainesville: University Press of Florida, 2008), 110–13.
10. Chipman, *Spanish Texas, 1519–1821*, 77–83, 116–19; Foster, *Spanish Expeditions into Texas*, 17–33.
11. Paul J. Foik, "Captain Don Domingo Ramón's Diary of His Expedition into Texas in 1716," in *Wilderness Missions*, ed. Jesús F. de la Teja (Austin: Texas Catholic Historical Society, 1999), 138.
12. Margil, *Nothingness Itself*, 220–27 (quote on 225).
13. Foster, *Spanish Expeditions into Texas*, 127–43; and de la Teja, *San Antonio de Béxar*, 1–8.

14. Herbert E. Bolton, "The Mission as Frontier Institution in the Spanish-American Colonies," *American Historical Review* 23, no. 1 (1917): 42–61, http://www.jstor.org/stable/1837685; Habig, *Alamo Chain of Missions*, 17–23; Mardith K. Schuetz, "The Indians of the San Antonio Missions, 1718–1821" (PhD diss., University of Texas at Austin, 1980), 15–20; and Félix D. Almaráz Jr., *The San Antonio Missions and Their System of Land Tenure* (Austin: University of Texas Press, 1989), 2. See also Wade, *Missions, Missionaries, and Native Americans.*
15. Schuetz, "Indians of the San Antonio Missions," 2–20.
16. Elizabeth A. H. John, *Storms Brewed in Other Men's Worlds: The Confrontation of Indians, Spanish, and French in the Southwest, 1540–1795* (College Station: Texas A&M University Press, 1975), 171–72; and Schuetz, "Indians of the San Antonio Missions," 2–20.
17. Schuetz, "Indians of the San Antonio Missions," 2–20.
18. Schuetz, "Indians of the San Antonio Missions," 19.
19. Robert H. Jackson, *The Missions and the Frontiers of Spanish America: A Comparative Study of the Impact of Environmental, Economic, Political, and Socio-cultural Variations on the Missions in the Rio de la Plata Region and on the Northern Frontier of New Spain* (Scottsdale, AZ: Pentacle Press, 2005), 321; and Robert H. Jackson, "Congregation and Depopulation: Demographic Patterns in the Texas Missions," *Journal of South Texas* 17, no. 2 (2004): 6–38. Critics of the missions in other parts of the Borderlands include Ramón A. Gutiérrez, *When Jesus Came, the Corn Mothers Went Away: Marriage, Sexuality, and Power in New Mexico, 1500–1846* (Stanford, CA: Stanford University Press, 1991); H. Henrietta Stockel, *On the Bloody Road to Jesus: Christianity and the Chiricahua Apaches* (Albuquerque: University of New Mexico Press, 2004); and Jesús F. de la Teja and Ross Frank, eds., *Choice, Persuasion, and Coercion: Social Control on Spain's North American Frontiers* (Albuquerque: University of New Mexico Press, 2005).
20. Schuetz, "Indians of the San Antonio Missions," 222–23.
21. Tsim D. Schneider and Lee M. Panich, "Native Agency at the Margins of Empire: Indigenous Landscapes, Spanish Missions, and Contested Histories," in *Indigenous Landscapes and Spanish Missions: New Perspectives from Archaeology and Ethnohistory*, ed. Lee M. Panich and Tsim D. Schneider (Tucson: University of Arizona Press, 2014), 5–22.
22. Weber, *Spanish Frontier in North America*, 94. See also Delno C. West, "Medieval Ideas of Apocalyptic Mission and the Early Franciscans in Mexico," *The Americas* 45, no. 3 (1989): 293–313, http://www.jstor.org/stable/1007224/.
23. Gutiérrez, *When Jesus Came*, 128–30; and David Rex Galindo, *To Sin No More: Franciscans and Conversion in the Hispanic World, 1683–1830* (Stanford, CA: Stanford University Press and the Academy of American Franciscan History, 2017), 103–6.
24. Weber, *Spanish Frontier in North America*, 112–13, 124–25, 307; and Bolton, "The Mission as Frontier Institution," 44–49.
25. Louise M. Burkhart, *The Slippery Earth: Nahua-Christian Moral Dialog in Sixteenth-Century Mexico* (Tucson: University of Arizona Press, 1989); James Lockhart, *The Nahuas After the Conquest: A Social and Cultural History of the Indians of Central*

Mexico, Sixteenth Through Eighteenth Centuries (Stanford, CA: Stanford University Press, 1992); Viviana Díaz Balsera, *The Pyramid Under the Cross: Franciscan Discourses of Evangelization and the Nahua Christian Subject in Sixteenth-Century Mexico* (Tucson: University of Arizona Press, 2005); and Patricia Lopes Don, *Bonfires of Culture: Franciscans, Indigenous Leaders, and the Inquisition in Early Mexico, 1524–1540* (Norman: University of Oklahoma Press, 2010). See also Fr. Benedict Leutenegger, *Fr. Gerónimo de Mendieta's History: An Introduction to the Antecedents of the Spanish Missions in Texas*, with introduction by Fr. Marion A. Habig (San Antonio: Old Spanish Missions Historical Research Library, 1978), 17–18; and Colin G. Calloway, *New Worlds for All: Indians, Europeans, and the Remaking of Early America* (Baltimore: Johns Hopkins University Press, 1997), 68–91.

26. Weber, *Spanish Frontier in North America*, 98, 113, 119; Wade, *Missions, Missionaries, and Native Americans*, 214–15; and Galindo, *To Sin No More*, 274.
27. Weber, *Spanish Frontier in North America*, 118; and Calloway, *New Worlds for All*, 71, 91.
28. Galindo, *To Sin No More*, 139–40.
29. James E. Ivey, *Of Various Magnificence: The Architectural History of the Missions of San Antonio, Texas in the Colonial Period and the Nineteenth Century*, with contributions by Marlys Bush Thurber and Santiago Escobedo (Santa Fe, NM: National Park Service, ca. 2006), 67 (unpublished manuscript in the author's possession; hereafter cited as *OVM*). This manuscript began as *Historical Structures Report* and grew into a detailed architectural history of all the mission churches in San Antonio. The author is grateful for his copy through the generosity of one of the volunteer docents working at Mission Concepción.
30. Gilberto M. Hinojosa, "Friars and Indians: Towards a Perspective of Cultural Interaction in the San Antonio Missions," *US Catholic Historian* 9, no. 1/2 (1990): 25–26; Weber, *Spanish Frontier in North America*, 107–8, 110–11; and David J. Weber, *Bárbaros: Spaniards and Their Savages in the Age of Enlightenment* (New Haven, CT: Yale University Press, 2005), 102.
31. Jay T. Harrison, "Franciscan Concepts of the Congregated Mission and the Apostolic Ministry in Eighteenth-Century Texas," in *From La Florida to La California: Franciscan Evangelization in the Spanish Borderlands*, ed. Timothy J. Johnson and Gert Melville (Berkeley, CA: Academy of American Franciscan History, 2013), 324–25.
32. De la Teja, *San Antonio de Béxar*, 17–18, 76–80, 120–21.
33. Don Thomás Phelipe de Winthuysen, "Winthuysen Reporting Condition of Presidios and Missions in Texas and Recommending Removal of Capital from Los Adaes to Béxar. Includes Brief Description of Topography, Climate, Construction, Crops and Reduction of Indians, August 19, 1744," Bexar Archives Online, 1717–1895, Briscoe Center for American History, University of Texas at Austin, accessed July 25, 2018, https://briscoecenter.org/. Winthuysen (sometimes spelled "Tomás Felipe Winthuisen") was a governor of Texas, 1741–43.
34. Harrison, "Franciscan Concepts of the Congregated Mission," 338.

35. Gerald E. Poyo, "The Canary Island Immigrants of San Antonio: From Ethnic Exclusivity to Community in Eighteenth-Century Béxar," in *Tejano Origins in Eighteenth-Century San Antonio*, ed. Gerald E. Poyo and Gilberto M. Hinojosa (Austin: University of Texas Press, 1991), 41–58; and de la Teja, *San Antonio de Béxar*, 90, 120. See also Benedict Leutenegger and Benito Fernández, "Memorial of Father Benito Fernández Concerning the Canary Islanders, 1741," *Southwestern Historical Quarterly* 82, no. 3 (1979): 265–96, http://www.jstor.org/stable/30238589; and de la Teja, *San Antonio de Béxar*, 158–60.
36. Pekka Hämäläinen, *The Comanche Empire* (New Haven, CT: Yale University Press, 2008), 2.
37. Margil, *Nothingness Itself*, 251. Margil is referring to the missions then being reestablished in East Texas, three of which would be transferred to the San Antonio region in 1731.
38. Herbert Eugene Bolton, *Texas in the Middle Eighteenth Century: Studies in Spanish Colonial History and Administration* (1915; repr., Austin: University of Texas Press and Texas State Historical Association, 1970), 12.
39. Gilberto M. Hinojosa, "The Religious-Indian Communities: The Goals of the Friars," in *Tejano Origins in Eighteenth-Century San Antonio*, ed. Gerald E. Poyo and Gilberto M. Hinojosa (Austin: University of Texas Press, 1991), 61–83; Wade, *Missions, Missionaries, and Native Americans*, 114–15; Weber, *Spanish Frontier*, 115, 123, 193–94; and Weber, *Bárbaros*, 92.
40. Adán Benavides, "Sacred Space, Profane Reality: The Politics of Building a Church in Eighteenth-Century Texas," *Southwestern Historical Quarterly* 107, no. 1 (2003): 1, http://www.jstor.org/stable/30239423.
41. Maurice Halbwachs, *The Collective Memory*, trans. Francis J. Ditter Jr. and Vida Yazdi Ditter (1950; repr., New York: Harper Colophon Books, 1980), 151.
42. De la Teja, *San Antonio de Béxar*, 150–56.
43. Fray Mariano de los Dolores y Viana, *Letters and Memorials of Fray Mariano de los Dolores y Viana, 1737–1762: Documents on the Missions of Texas from the Archives of the College of Querétaro*, trans. Fr. Benedict Leutenegger (San Antonio: Old Spanish Missions Historical Research Library at Our Lady of the Lake University, 1985), 331–32, 335, 337, 339. See also Jacinto Quirarte, *The Art and Architecture of the Texas Missions* (Austin: University of Texas Press, 2002), chaps. 3, 4, 5, 6, 7, for descriptions of art and the vestments at Valero, San José, Concepción, San Juan, and Espada, respectively.
44. James A. Sandos, *Converting California: Indians and Franciscans in the Missions* (New Haven, CT: Yale University Press, 2004), 128–53; and Kristin Dutcher Mann, *The Power of Song: Music and Dance in the Mission Communities of Northern New Spain, 1590–1810* (Stanford, CA: Stanford University Press and Academy of American Franciscan History, 2010), 24–41.
45. Rev. Peter P. Forrestal, "The Solis Diary of 1767," *Preliminary Studies of the Texas Catholic Historical Society* 1, no. 6 (1931): 21. See also Margaret Kenney Kress, "Diary of a Visit of Inspection of the Texas Missions Made by Fray Gaspar José de Solís in

the Year 1767–68," *Southwestern Historical Quarterly* 35, no. 1 (1931): 51–52, http://www.jstor.org/stable/30235387.

46. David Chidester and Edward T. Linenthal, eds., *American Sacred Space* (Bloomington: Indiana University Press, 1995), 15; and Jeanette Rodriguez and Ted Fortier, *Cultural Memory: Resistance, Faith, and Identity* (Austin: University of Texas Press, 2007), 1.
47. Joel W. Martin, "Introduction," in *Native Americans, Christianity, and the Reshaping of the American Religious Landscape*, by Joel W. Martin and Mark A. Nicholas (Chapel Hill: University of North Carolina Press, 2010), 3–15.
48. Fray Benito Fernandez de Santa Ana, *Letters and Memorials of the Father Presidente Fray Benito Fernandez de Santa Ana, 1736–1754: Documents on the Missions of Texas from the Archives of the College of Querétaro*, trans. Fr. Benedict Leutenegger (San Antonio: Old Spanish Missions Historical Research Library at Our Lady of the Lake University, 1981), 21, 25, 39–40, 82; and Dolores y Viana, *Letters and Memorials of Fray Mariano de los Dolores y Viana*, 29, 340.
49. Fernandez de Santa Ana, *Letters and Memorials of the Father Presidente Fray Benito Fernandez de Santa Ana*, 40.
50. Mann, *The Power of Song*, 35; and Schuetz, "Indians of the San Antonio Missions," 93–99.
51. Fr. Bartholomé García, *Manual para administrar los santos sacramentos de penitencia, eucharistia, extrema uncion, y matrimonio: Dar gracias despues de comulgar y ayudar, a bien morir a los Indios de los naciones: Pajalates, Orejones, Pacaos, Pacóas, Tiliijayas, Alasapas, Pausanes, y otras muchas diferentes, que se hallan en los missiones del Rio de San Antonio y Rio Grande, Pertenencientes à el Colegio de la Santissima Cruz de la Ciudad de Queretaro, como son: los Pacuâches, Mescâles, Pampôpas, Tâcames, Chayopînes, Venados, Pamâques, y toda la juventud de Pihuiques, Borrados, Sanipaos, y Manos de Perro* (Mexico City, 1760), 15, Gale, *Sabin Americana* database.
52. Mann, *Power of Song*, 146.
53. *Guidelines for a Texas Mission: Instructions for the Missionary of Mission Concepción in San Antonio*, vol. 1, *Documents Relating to the Old Spanish Missions of Texas*, ed. Howard Benoist and María Eva Flores, trans. Benedict Leutenegger, 4th ed. (San Antonio: Old Spanish Missions Historical Research Library 1994), 37.
54. Silvio Zavala, "The Frontier of Hispanic America," in *The Frontier in Perspective*, ed. Walker D. Wyman and Clifton B. Kroeber (Madison: University of Wisconsin Press, 1957), 47. Zavala was a history professor in Mexico and the director of the Museo Nacional de Historia.
55. Benavides, "Sacred Space, Profane Reality," 1 (emphasis in original).
56. Louis P. Nelson, ed., *American Sanctuary: Understanding Sacred Spaces* (Bloomington: Indiana University Press, 2006), 8.
57. For some of the better, relatively recent works, see Anna Nau, "Cultural Confluence: The Architecture of Eighteenth-Century San Antonio Missions," *The Classicist* 19, "Texas" (2022): 38–45; Ivey, *OVM*; Thomas S. Bremer, *Blessed with Tourists: The Borderlands of Religion and Tourism in San Antonio* (Chapel Hill: University of North Carolina Press, 2004); and Quirarte, *Art and Architecture of the Texas Missions*.

58. Juan Agustín Morfi, *History of Texas, 1673–1779*, trans. Carlos Eduardo Castañeda (1935; repr., New York: Arno Press, 1967), 96.
59. Ivey, *OVM*, 40; Mardith K. Schuetz, "Professional Artisans in the Hispanic Southwest: The Churches of San Antonio, Texas," *The Americas* 40, no. 1 (1983): 18–19, http://www.jstor.org/stable/981099.
60. Benavides, "Sacred Space, Profane Reality," 8.
61. Schuetz, "Professional Artisans," 17–18; and John McAndrew, *The Open-Air Churches of Sixteenth-Century Mexico: Atrios, Posas, Open Chapels, and Other Studies* (Cambridge, MA: Harvard University Press, 1965), 169.
62. Ivey, *OVM*, 14. This is from Ivey's introduction, in which the pages are numbered separately from the main text. See also Manuel Toussaint, *Colonial Art in Mexico*, ed. and trans. Elizabeth Wilder Weismann (Austin: University of Texas Press, 1967), 5, 125–28, 277; George Kubler and Martin Soria, *Art and Architecture in Spain and Portugal and Their American Dominions, 1500–1800* (Baltimore: Penguin Books, 1959), 124–25; Schuetz, "Professional Artisans," 17–18, 24; and McAndrew, *Open-Air Churches of Sixteenth-Century Mexico*, 169.
63. Valerie Fraser, *The Architecture of Conquest: Building in the Viceroyalty of Peru, 1535–1635* (Cambridge: Cambridge University Press, 1990), 153.
64. Ivey, *OVM*, 411.
65. Ivey, *OVM*, 40–44, 72–75.
66. Toussaint, *Colonial Art in Mexico*, 277–78.
67. Ivey, *OVM*, 70.
68. Schuetz, "Professional Artisans," 35–36. There may have been additional "master" craftsmen among those listed whose race/ethnicity was unknown at the time.
69. Morfi, *History of Texas*, 96; Schuetz, "Professional Artisans," 19; and Ivey, *OVM*, 73.
70. Ivey, *OVM*, 78. Though no contract or other documentation between Tello and the Franciscans has yet been found, it is doubtful he would have come to the frontier without one.
71. Ivey, *OVM*, 78–80 (quote on 80). Ivey claimed that working on multiple projects simultaneously was not unheard of for architects during this time. Our Lady of Candelaria is now known as San Fernando Cathedral in downtown San Antonio.
72. Ivey, *OVM*, 78.
73. *Criminal Proceedings Against Antonio Tello, Charged with Killing Matías Treviso. August 21, 1744*, 71–80, trans. from the Bexar Archives, Dolph Briscoe Center for American History, University of Texas at Austin, accessed August 1, 2013, https://briscoecenter.org/. The original Spanish is also available through this website. See also Mardith K. Schuetz-Miller, "The Scandal Involving San Antonio de Valero's First Master Builder," *Journal of the Southwest* 58, no. 4 (2016): 743–49, https://doi.org/10.1353/jsw.2016.0019.
74. *Criminal Proceedings Against Antonio Tello*, 81–102; see also Schuetz-Miller, "Scandal Involving," 747; and Ivey, *OVM*, 81–82. Guerra appeared to have married twice more and continued to live in the San Antonio community.

75. Ivey, *OVM*, 82–86. See also Jack D. Eaton, *Excavations at the Alamo Shrine: Mission San Antonio de Valero*, Special Report No. 10 (San Antonio: Center for Archaeological Research, University of Texas at San Antonio, 1980), 13.
76. Fr. Mariano Francisco de los Dolores y Biana, *1759 Report of Fr. Mariano Francisco de los Dolores y Biana*, trans. Rosalind Z. Rock from Archivo Franciscano—Convento de Queretaro/Celaya, Our Lady of the Lake University (San Antonio: San Antonio Missions National Historical Park, 2007), 21, http://www.nps.gov/saan/learn/historyculture/stories.htm.
77. Dolores y Viana, *Letters and Memorials of Fray Mariano de los Dolores y Viana*, 331. See also Schuetz-Miller, "Scandal Involving," 747–48.
78. Ivey, *OVM*, 82–86.
79. Ivey, *OVM*, 89–90. Palafox's wife arrived in San Antonio the next year as part of his compensation.
80. Forrestal, "The Solis Diary of 1767," 18; Kress, "Diary of a Visit of Inspection of the Texas Missions Made by Fray Gaspar José de Solís," 48; and Ivey, *OVM*, 89–90.
81. Eugene George, "Espada Doorway: A Lesson in Harmony," *Perspective* 9, no. 1 (1980): 13.
82. George, "Espada Doorway," 14. These horseshoe arches are sometimes known as "Moorish arches" for the resemblance to those at the Great Mosque of Córdoba, Spain.
83. Ivey, *OVM*, 283.
84. "Provincia de Texas: Estado general de tropa de el presidio y vecindario de la Villa de San Fernando, empadronado y revisado por mi, el coronel de los reales ejercitos, do Domingo Cabello, gobernador de dicha provincial, en los dias 1, 2, y 3 del mes de julio de 1779," Archivo General de Indias: Audencia de Guadalajara, legajo 283, microfilm located in UTSA Libraries Special Collections (currently at the Institute of Texan Cultures, San Antonio; hereafter cited as "Cabello roster, 1779"). See also *Census by Families of San José Mission, 1792*, Bexar Archives, Dolph Briscoe Center for American History, University of Texas at Austin, accessed April 7, 2015, https://briscoecenter.org/.
85. Schuetz, "Professional Artisans," 31.
86. Ivey, *OVM*, 94, 169.
87. Schuetz, "Professional Artisans," 31–32.
88. Ivey, *OVM*, 94, 93–95.
89. Fr. Juan Agustín de Morfi, *Diario y Derrotero (1777–1781) por Fray Juan Agustín de Morfi*, Edición de Eugenio de Hoyo y Malcolm D. McLean (Monterrey, Nuevo León, Mexico: Instituto Technológico y de Estudios Superiores, 1967), 102–4 (translation by the author).
90. Morfi, *History of Texas, 1673–1779*, 95–96.
91. Mardith K. Schuetz, trans., *Architectural Practice in Mexico City: A Manual for Journeyman Architects of the Eighteenth Century* (Tucson: University of Arizona Press, 1987), 4.
92. Morfi, *History of Texas, 1673–1779*, 95–96.

93. Ivey, *OVM*, 96–97. Ivey credited Edward King, a journalist who traveled in Texas in the early 1870s, with first publishing the version with Huizar as the Spanish monarch's favorite sculptor, although the story was probably well-known locally before then. See Edward King, *The Great South* (Hartford: American Publishing, 1875). King also published his dispatch on San Antonio and the missions in the popular magazine *Scribner's Monthly* (January 1874). For more of the legends of Huizar, see Luis Torres, *Voices from the San Antonio Missions* (Lubbock: Texas Tech University Press, 1997), 289–92; Marion A. Habig, *San Antonio's Mission San José: State and National Historic Site, 1720–1968* (San Antonio: Naylor, 1968), 211–13, 237–38; James B. Cunningham, *A Legend of Mission San* José (San Antonio: Nic Tengg, ca. 1930?); Robert Sturmberg, *History of San Antonio and of the Early Days in Texas* (San Antonio: Press of the Standard Printing Co., 1920), 125. There is a great deal of speculation about whether the window is properly known as "Rosa's Window" or simply "a rose window." Technically, the window is less a circular, stained-glass rose window often associated with European Gothic cathedrals; or an oculus, often oval-shaped in Baroque and Rococo times; but is clear glass window. Another tradition posits that the name originated with Saint Rose of Lima, Peru (canonized 1671), one of the earliest New World saints.
94. For questions on the fluidity of ethnic identities and social status in the Borderlands, see Jesús F. de la Teja, "Why Urbano and María Trinidad Can't Get Married: Social Relations in Late Colonial San Antonio," *Southwestern Historical Quarterly* 112, no. 2 (2008): 121–46, http://www.jstor.org/stable/30239620.
95. Huizar appears as "Pedro Guizar." See "Cabello roster, 1779."
96. Schuetz, "Professional Artisans," 32; "Cabello roster, 1779"; Ivey, *OVM*, 96–98; *Census by Families of Mission Concepción, 1792*, Bexar Archives, Dolph Briscoe Center for American History, University of Texas at Austin, accessed April 7, 2015, https://briscoecenter.org/; and Schuetz, "Indians of the San Antonio Missions," 303–8.
97. Ivey, *OVM*, 96–97.
98. Timothy Matovina, *Guadalupe and Her Faithful: Latino Catholics in San Antonio, from Colonial Origins to the Present* (Baltimore: Johns Hopkins University Press, 2005), 10–17, 64.
99. Schuetz, "Professional Artisans," 29; and Quirarte, *Art and Architecture of the Texas Missions*, 86–92.
100. Ivey, *OVM*, 305.
101. Weber, *Spanish Frontier in North America*, 242–43; and Habig, *Alamo Chain of Missions*, 26.
102. Hämäläinen, *The Comanche Empire*, 5, 6.
103. Chipman, *Spanish Texas*, 203–4.
104. Fr. José Francisco López, "The Texas Missions in 1785," trans. J. Autrey Dabbs, *Preliminary Studies of the Texas Catholic Historical Society* 3, no. 6 (1940): 5–9, 12–13.
105. Ivey, *OVM*, 10. This is from his "Introduction," which is numbered separately from the rest of the manuscript.
106. Chipman, *Spanish Texas*, 202.

107. Benedict Leutenegger, "Report on the San Antonio Missions in 1792," *Southwestern Historical Quarterly* 77, no. 4 (1974): 490, http://www.jstor.org/stable/30241978.
108. Leutenegger, "Report on the San Antonio Missions," 490–91.
109. Leutenegger, "Report on the San Antonio Missions," 493.
110. John O. Leal, *Mission Nuestra Señora de la Purisima Concepción de Acuña Records, 1796–1818* (San Antonio: Privately published by John O. Leal, 1993), n.p. Copy at the Daughters of the Republic of Texas Library at the Alamo, San Antonio, Texas (hereafter cited as DRT Library). Leal cited Bexar County Microfilm Roll 32, #959, 1805.
111. De la Teja, "Why Urbano and María Trinidad Can't Get Married," 121–46; Raúl Ramos, *Beyond the Alamo: Forging Mexican Ethnicity in San Antonio, 1821–1861* (Chapel Hill: University of North Carolina Press, 2008), 66.
112. Leal, *Mission Nuestra Señora de la Purisima Concepción*. Leal cited Bexar County Microfilm Roll 41, #0732, 1809.
113. *Census of Espada Mission, Feb. 27, 1815*, Folder O. S. M. Espada-Census 1815, 1819, Box 1, Old Spanish Missions Collections, Catholic Archives of San Antonio (hereafter cited as CASA). These data were reproduced and translated from Bexar County Microfilm Roll 54, #0732, 1815.
114. *Census of Espada Mission and San Juan Capistrano, 1819*, Folder O. S. M. Espada-Census 1815, 1819, Box 1, Old Spanish Missions Collections, CASA. These data were reproduced and translated from Bexar County Microfilm Roll 63, #655, 1818–19.
115. Ivey, *OVM*, 19–22, 387–402.
116. Almaráz, *San Antonio Missions*, 18.
117. Zebulon Montgomery Pike, *The Journals of Zebulon Montgomery Pike: With Letters and Related Documents*, ed. Donald Jackson, 2 vols. (Norman: University of Oklahoma Press, 1966), 2:78. See also Zebulon Montgomery Pike, *An Account of Expeditions to the Sources of the Mississippi and Through the Western Parts of Louisiana to the Sources of the Arkansaw, Kans, La Platte, and Pierre Jaun Rivers: Performed by Order of the Government of the United States During the years 1805, 1806, and 1807: and Tour Through the Interior Parts of New Spain, when Conducted Through These Provinces by Order of the Captain-General in the Year 1807* (Philadelphia: C & A Conrad, 1810), Gale Cengage Learning Sabin Americana database.
118. Pike, *Journals*, 78–79. Marion Habig asserted that the priest was Fr. Bernardino Vallejo at Mission San José. See Habig, *Alamo Chain of Missions*, 105.
119. Josiah Conder, *The Modern Traveller: A Popular Description, Geographical, Historical and Topographical of the Various Countries of the Globe*, 10 vols. (Boston: Wells and Lilly, 1830), 7:28, Gale Cengage Learning Sabin Americana database.
120. M. Pierre Marie François Pagès, *Travels Round the World: In the Years 1767, 1768, 1769, 1770, 1771*, 2 vols. (London: J. Murray, 1791), 1:99–102, Gale Cengage Learning Eighteenth Century Collection Online.
121. Alexander von Humboldt, *Political Essay on the Kingdom of New Spain: Containing Researches Relative to the Geography of Mexico . . . the Physical Aspect of the Country, the Population, the State of Agriculture and Manufacturing and Commercial Industry . . . and the Military Defence of New Spain*, 2 vols. (New York: I. Riley, 1811), Gale Cengage Learning Sabin Americana database.

122. Habig, *Alamo Chain of Missions*, 70–71.
123. James E. Ivey, "The Completion of the Church Roof of San Antonio de Valero," *Anales del Instituto de Investigaciones Estéticas* 29, no. 91 (2007): 133–41, http://www.analesiie.unam.mx/index.php/analesiie/article/view/2246. In this article Ivey asserted that in his "Sacred Space, Profane Reality" essay, Adán Benevides had attributed a drawing to the wrong church. Benevides claimed that a particular architectural drawing from the Bexar Archives was a plan for the roof of San Fernando in the mid-1700s. Ivey claimed that the drawing was executed in 1810 for a proposal to convert the old Valero mission chapel into a more usable military storehouse.
124. Ivey, "Roof of San Antonio de Valero," 150–51.
125. Almaráz, "Material Decline and Secular Avarice," 22.
126. Jean Louis Berlandier, *Journey to Mexico During the Years 1826 to 1834*, 7 vols. in 2, trans. Sheila M. Ohlendorf, Josette M. Bigelow, and Mary M. Standifer (Austin: Texas State Historical Association, 1980), 292, 293.

Chapter 2

1. Mary A. Maverick, *Memoirs of Mary A. Maverick, Arranged by Mary A. Maverick and Her Son Geo. Madison Maverick*, ed. Rena Maverick Green (San Antonio: Alamo Printing, 1921), 25–26; and Pekka Hämäläinen, *The Comanche Empire* (New Haven, CT: Yale University Press, 2008).
2. Raúl A. Ramos, *Beyond the Alamo: Forging Mexican Ethnicity in San Antonio, 1821–1861* (Chapel Hill: University of North Carolina Press, 2008), 69.
3. Carlos E. Castañeda, *Our Catholic Heritage in Texas, 1519–1936*, vol. 6, *Transition Period: The Fight for Freedom, 1810–1836* (1951; repr., New York: Arno Press, 1976), 307.
4. Félix D. Almaráz Jr., *The San Antonio Missions and Their System of Land Tenure* (Austin: University of Texas Press, 1989), 17.
5. Robert E. Wright, "Father Refugio de la Garza: Controverted Religious Leader," in *Tejano Leadership in Mexican and Revolutionary Texas*, ed. Jesús F. de la Teja (College Station: Texas A&M University Press, 2010), 77–101 (quote on 80).
6. Félix D. Almaráz Jr., "San Antonio's Old Franciscan Missions: Material Decline and Secular Avarice in the Transition from Hispanic to Mexican Control," *The Americas* 44, no. 1 (1987): 6, http://www.jstor.org/stable/1006846; and Almaráz, *San Antonio Missions*.
7. Jean Louis Berlandier, *Journey to Mexico During the Years 1826 to 1834*, 7 vols. in 2, trans. Sheila M. Ohlendorf, Josette M. Bigelow, and Mary M. Standifer (Austin: Texas State Historical Association, 1980), 292.
8. Castañeda, *Our Catholic Heritage*, 6:97–98; and Marion A. Habig, *The Alamo Chain of Missions: A History of San Antonio's Five Old Spanish Missions* (Chicago: Franciscan Herald Press, 1968; repr., Livingston, TX: Pioneer Enterprises, 1997; page references to 1997 ed.), 144.
9. Habig, *Alamo Chain of Missions*, 148; Randy Roberts and James S. Olson, *A Line in the Sand: The Alamo in Blood and Memory* (New York: Touchstone, published by Simon and Schuster, 2002), 45–46, 56–60.

10. Roberts and Olson, *Line in the Sand*, 109, 112.
11. Roberts and Olson, *Line in the Sand*, 112–20.
12. Roberts and Olson, *Line in the Sand*, 121–68.
13. José Enrique de la Peña, *With Santa Anna in Texas: A Personal Narrative of the Revolution*, ed. and trans. Carmen Perry (College Station: Texas A&M University Press, 1975), 54.
14. Roberts and Olson, *Line in the Sand*, 187–89. See also H. W. Brands, *Lone Star Nation: How a Ragged Army of Volunteers Won the Battle for Texas Independence—and Changed America* (New York: Doubleday, 2004).
15. Pierre Nora, *Realms of Memory: Rethinking the French Past*, trans. Arthur Goldhammer, English-language edition ed. and foreword by Lawrence D. Kritzman, 3 vols. (New York: Columbia University Press, 1996), 1:xvii.
16. Michael Kammen, *Mystic Chords of Memory: The Transformation of Tradition in American Culture* (New York: Vintage Books, 1993; first published New York: Knopf, 1991; page references are to 1993 Vintage ed.), 53.
17. *The Southern Patriot* (Charleston, SC), August 17, 1841, Readex America's Historical Newspapers.
18. Ramos, *Beyond the Alamo*, 81. See also Timothy Matovina and Jesús F. de la Teja, eds., *Recollections of a Tejano Life: Antonio Menchaca in Texas History* (Austin: University of Texas Press, 2013).
19. David Montejano, *Anglos and Mexicans in the Making of Texas, 1836–1986* (Austin: University of Texas Press, 1987), 34–35.
20. Arnoldo De León, *The Tejano Community, 1836–1900*, with a new foreword by Richard Griswold del Castillo and new afterword by the author (Dallas: Southern Methodist University Press, 1997; originally published Albuquerque: University of New Mexico Press, 1987; page references are to the 1997 ed.), 23.
21. Andrés Reséndez, *Changing National Identities at the Frontier: Texas and New Mexico, 1800–1850* (Cambridge: Cambridge University Press, 2004), 3 (emphasis in the original).
22. Maverick, *Memoirs of Mary A. Maverick*, 53–54.
23. Timothy M. Matovina, *Tejano Religion and Ethnicity: San Antonio, 1821–1860* (Austin: University of Texas Press, 1995), 4.
24. Maverick, *Memoirs of Mary A. Maverick*, 54; Matovina, *Tejano Religion and Ethnicity*, 38, 44–45 (quote).
25. Jeanette Rodriguez and Ted Fortier, *Cultural Memory: Resistance, Faith, and Identity* (Austin: University of Texas Press, 2007), 1.
26. Michel-Rolph Trouillot, *Silencing the Past: Power and the Production of History* (Boston: Beacon Press, 1995), 1–2, 9–11, 26–29; and Matovina and de la Teja, *Recollections of a Tejano Life*, 2–4, 11–12.
27. Holly Beachley Brear, *Inherit the Alamo: Myth and Ritual at an American Shrine* (Austin: University of Texas Press, 1995); and Richard R. Flores, *Remembering the Alamo: Memory, Modernity, & the Master Symbol* (Austin: University of Texas Press, 2002).
28. Brear, *Inherit the Alamo*, 38–43.

29. Paul Andrew Hutton, "The Alamo as Icon," in *The Texas Military Experience: From the Texas Revolution Through World War II*, ed. Joseph G. Dawson III (College Station: Texas A&M University Press, 1995), 17. See also Roberts and Olson, *Line in the Sand*, 172.
30. Brear, *Inherit the Alamo*, 38; Roberts and Olson, *Line in the Sand*, 166–76; Dora Elizondo Guerra, "Two Silver Pesos and a Blanket: The Texas Revolution and the Non-combatant Women Who Survived the Battle of the Alamo," in *Women and the Texas Revolution*, ed. Mary L. Scheer (Denton: University of North Texas Press, 2012), 123–24; Ron J. Jackson Jr. and Lee Spencer White, *Joe: The Slave Who Became an Alamo Legend* (Norman: University of Oklahoma Press, 2015); and Bill Groneman, "Alamo Noncombatants," *Handbook of Texas Online*, accessed August 15, 2015, http://www.tshaonline.org/handbook/online/articles/qsa01.
31. Roberts and Olson, *Line in the Sand*, 172. See also Jimmy L. Bryan Jr., *The American Elsewhere: Adventures and Manliness in the Age of Expansion* (Lawrence: University Press of Kansas, 2017).
32. Arthur Ikin, *Texas: Its History, Topography, Agriculture, Commerce, and General Statistics*, reprint with introduction by James M. Day (1841; repr., Austin: Texian Press, 1964), 11–12.
33. "Monument of the Alamo," *Telegraph and Texas Register* (Houston), July 26, 1843, Readex America's Historical Newspapers. This monument was eventually moved into the State Capitol Building, where it was heavily damaged in the 1881 fire. See Amelia W. Williams, "Alamo Monuments," *Handbook of Texas Online*, accessed July 20, 2019, http://www.tshaonline.org/handbook/online/articles/gga01.
34. Hutton, "The Alamo as Icon," 14.
35. Hutton, "The Alamo as Icon," 14; and Roberts and Olson, *Line in the Sand*, 172. See also Murray Pittock, *Culloden: (Cùill Lodair)* (Oxford: Oxford University Press, 2016), for a prescient description of this lopsided battle, ignored for years afterward, being aggrandized into the pivotal event that made Great Britain into a "united" kingdom; and Georges Duby, *The Legend of Bouvines: War, Religion, and Culture in the Middle Ages*, trans. Catherine Tihanyi (Berkeley: University of California Press, 1990), for his convincing discussion of a single battle in 1214 that became a defining moment in the French national narrative.
36. Castañeda, *Our Catholic Heritage*, 7:46–48; and Patrick Foley, *Missionary Bishop: Jean-Marie Odin in Galveston and New Orleans* (College Station: Texas A&M University Press, 2013), 60–61, 75–79.
37. Castañeda, *Our Catholic Heritage*, 7:49–51.
38. Jean Marie Odin, "Mission of Texas," *United States Catholic Magazine and Monthly Review* 3, no. 11 (1844): 726, ProQuest American Periodicals Series.
39. Joseph William Schmitz, *The Society of Mary in Texas* (San Antonio: Naylor, 1951), 44–47.
40. "The Missions," *San Antonio Ledger and Texan*, September 22, 1860, Readex America's Historical Newspapers; see also Castañeda, *Our Catholic Heritage*, 7:216–22.

41. Fr. Hoermann later wrote a maudlin romance based on San José during the Spanish period. P. Alto S. Hoermann, *The Daughter of Tehuan: Or, Texas of the Past Century*, trans. Alois Braun (San Antonio: Standard Printing, 1932). See also James E. Ivey, *Of Various Magnificence: The Architectural History of the Missions of San Antonio, Texas in the Colonial Period and the Nineteenth Century*, with contributions by Marlys Bush Thurber and Santiago Escobedo (Santa Fe, NM: National Park Service, ca. 2006), 363–66 (unpublished manuscript in the author's possession; hereafter cited as *OVM*).
42. Stephen Stagner, "Epics, Science, and the Lost Frontier: Texas Historical Writing, 1836–1936," *Western Historical Quarterly* 12, no. 2 (1981): 166, https://www.jstor.org/stable/968122.
43. Daniel J. Boorstin, *Americans: The National Experience* (New York: Random House, 1965), 123, 162.
44. "Miscellaneous," *Enquirer* (Richmond, VA), November 13, 1832, Readex America's Historical Newspapers.
45. Joseph Emerson Field, *Three Years in Texas: Including a View of the Texan Revolution and an Account of the Principal Battles: Together with Descriptions of the Soil, Commercial and Agricultural Advantages, &c.* (Boston: Abel Tompkins, 1836), 1 (image number 7), Gale Cengage Learning Sabin Americana.
46. William Kennedy, *Texas: The Rise, Progress, and Prospects of the Republic of Texas, Two Volumes in One* (1841; repr., Clifton, NJ: Augustus M. Kelly, 1974), 218–23, and 246 for a few statements on the Texas missionaries.
47. Kennedy, *Texas*, 223. For more on the "Black Legend" of Spanish cruelties toward Indigenous peoples, see David J. Weber, *The Spanish Frontier in North America* (New Haven, CT: Yale University Press, 1992), 336–41.
48. Richard S. Hunt and Jesse F. Randel, *A New Guide to Texas: Consisting of a Brief Outline of the History of Its Settlement, and the Colonization and Land Laws; a General View of the Surface of the Country; Its Climate, Soil, Productions, &c. with a Particular Description of the Counties, Cities, and Towns* (1845; repr., Austin: Jenkins Publishing and Pemberton Press, 1970), 60.
49. Ferdinand Roemer, *Texas: With Particular Reference to German Immigration and the Physical Appearance of the Country*, trans. Oswald Mueller (1935; repr., San Marcos, TX: German-Texan Heritage Society and the Texian Press, 1983), 26–32. Roemer originally published his book in 1849 in Bonn, Prussia.
50. Roemer, *Texas*, 125–28; Astrid Haas, *Lone Star Vistas: Travel Writing on Texas, 1821–1861* (Austin: University of Texas Press, 2021), 94–103; and Maurice Halbwachs, *The Collective Memory*, trans. Francis J. Ditter Jr. and Vida Yazdi Ditter (1950; New York: Harper Colophon Books, 1980), 151. Halbwachs notes the relationship between the sacred space of a church building and fellow believers (not limited only to parishioners) who enter. Perhaps Roemer was feeling this sensation.
51. Roemer, *Texas*, 128–30.
52. John F. Sears, *Sacred Places: American Tourist Attractions in the Nineteenth Century* (New York: Oxford University Press, 1989), 4.

53. Sears, *Sacred Places*, 10. See also Eric G. E. Zuelow, *A History of Modern Tourism* (London: Palgrave Macmillan, 2016), 39–40, for the Romantic era's influence on European tourism.
54. Will B. MacKintosh, *Selling the Sights: The Invention of the Tourist in American Culture* (New York: New York University Press, 2019), 95.
55. MacKintosh, *Selling the Sights*, 4, 14, 85–86.
56. George Wilkins Kendall, *Narrative of the Texan Santa Fé Expedition* (1844; repr., Austin: Steck, 1935), 48 (emphasis in the original), 49–50, 50–51.
57. William Bollaert, *William Bollaert's Texas*, ed. W. Eugene Hollon and Ruth Lapham Butler (Norman: University of Oklahoma Press, 1956), xv–xvi, 222–24.
58. Bollaert, *William Bollaert's Texas*, 225–26, 231–34. Evidently sufficient quantities of wine dulled the odor of the guano.
59. [William Bollaert], "Hunting in Western Texas, and Visit to San Antonio de Bejar in 1843," *A New Sporting Magazine*, December 1848, 435, 432, ProQuest British Periodicals. The only author attribution is "By A Traveller." The portion of this article that described the hunting trip was later edited into what became chapter 11 of *William Bollaert's Texas*.
60. Josiah Gregg, *Diary & Letters of Josiah Gregg: Southwestern Enterprises, 1840–1847*, ed. Maurice Garland Fulton (Norman: University of Oklahoma Press, 1941), 236–37, 232–33, 234–35. During this period, many primary sources referred to the non-Anglo population of San Antonio as "Mexican," simply assuming miscegenation with Native Americans, African Americans, and Spaniards. See also Arnoldo de León, *They Called Them Greasers: Anglo Attitudes Toward Mexicans in Texas, 1821–1900* (Austin: University of Texas Press, 1995), 14–23, 40.
61. "Volunteers," *Niles National Register*, October 24, 1846, 118–19, ProQuest American Periodicals Series. The portion of this report that described San Antonio and the missions also appeared in the magazine *Catholic Telegraph* (which reprinted the article from *The St. Louis Republican*) less than one week later, again further distributing information about the missions and encouraging travel to San Antonio among a national audience. See "Mexico and the Invasion," *Catholic Telegraph*, October 29, 1846, 348, ProQuest American Periodicals Series.
62. "The Defence of the Alamo in 1836," *Littell's Living Age*, October 24, 1846, 175–77, ProQuest American Periodicals Series.
63. "War News," *New Hampshire Sentinel* (Keene, NH), November 11, 1846, Readex America's Historical Newspapers.
64. "Song of the Texan Ranger," *Georgia Telegraph* (Macon), December 1, 1846, Readex America's Historical Newspapers.
65. Edward Everett, "A Narrative of Military Experience in Several Capacities," *Transactions of the Illinois State Historical Society for the Year 1905* (Springfield: Illinois State Historical Library, 1905), 179–236; Richard Eighme Ahlborn, *The San Antonio Missions: Edward Everett and the American Occupation, 1847* (Fort Worth: Amon Carter Museum, 1985), 1–4; and Thomas Smith, "The U.S. Army and the Alamo,1846–1877," *Southwestern Historical Quarterly* 118, no. 3 (2015): 263–64.
66. Everett, "Narrative of Military Experience," 203–4.

67. Edward Everett to Mr. S. W. Everett, "Dear Brother," August 14, 1846, Edward Everett Papers, Cushing Memorial Library, Texas A&M University (hereafter cited as Everett Collection).
68. Everett, "Narrative of Military Experience," 204–5.
69. Edward Everett to Mr. S. W. Everett, "Dear Sam," September 14, 1846, Everett Collection; Everett, "Narrative of Military Experience," 206–7.
70. Smith, "The Army and the Alamo," 265–69; Everett, "Narrative of Military Experience," 214–15.
71. Kevin R. Young, "Major Babbitt and the Alamo 'Hump,'" *Military Images* 6, no. 1 (1984): 17; and Smith, "The Army and the Alamo," 269–71.
72. Smith, "The Army and the Alamo," 272–73.
73. Young, "Babbitt and the Alamo," 16; and Smith, "The Army and the Alamo," 273.
74. Young, "Babbitt and the Alamo," 16–17.
75. Smith, "The Army and the Alamo," 273–74; and Susan Prendergast Schoelwer and Tom W. Gläser, *Alamo Images: Changing Perceptions of a Texas Experience* (Dallas: Southern Methodist University Press, 1985), 35–36.
76. Schoelwer and Gläser, *Alamo Images*, 35–36; and Smith, "The Army and the Alamo," 273–74. See also Jack D. Eaton, *Excavations at the Alamo Shrine, Mission San Antonio de Valero*, Special Report No. 10 (San Antonio: Center for Archaeological Research, University of Texas at San Antonio, 1980), 15–16, 54.
77. Marshall S. McLennan, "The Baroque Parapet: Cultural Diffusion and the Sense of Place in the American Southwest," *PAST: Pioneer America Society Transactions* 33 (October 2010): 40–53.
78. Eaton, *Excavations at the Alamo Shrine*, 16.
79. Everett, "Journals and Memoirs, 1846–1899," Everett Collection.
80. Ahlborn, *The San Antonio Missions*, 42–45; and *Report of the Secretary of War, Communicating, in Compliance with a Resolution of the Senate, a Map Showing the Operations of the Army of the United States in Texas and the Adjacent Mexican States on the Rio Grande; Accompanied by Astronomical Observations, and Descriptive and Military Memoirs of the Country*, Sen. Rep. No. 31-S, exdoc32 (1849), ProQuest Congressional.
81. Ahlborn, *The San Antonio Missions*, 57–58. Seth Eastman was a minor painter in the Hudson River school who visited San Antonio in the late 1840s. Theodore Gentilz was a French immigrant who settled in San Antonio sometime in the 1850s and painted scenes of everyday San Antonio life. Everett's watercolors are in the Amon Carter Museum of American Art in Fort Worth.
82. Ahlborn, *The San Antonio Missions*, 58; "Bexar and Its Antiquities," *Gleason's Pictorial Drawing-Room Companion*, February 18, 1854, 103–5, EBSCO American Antiquarian Society Historical Periodicals Collection.
83. Schoelwer and Gläser, *Alamo Images*, 38.
84. John D. Cox, *Traveling South: Travel Narratives and the Construction of American Identity* (Athens: University of Georgia Press, 2005), 4.
85. Entry dated "Monday, February 26, 1849," in Rutherford B. Hayes, *Diary and Letters of Rutherford Birchard Hayes: Nineteenth President of the United States*, ed. Charles

Richard Williams (Columbus: Ohio State Archaeological and Historical Society and F. J. Heer Printing, 1922), 1:261–62.

86. "Miscellaneous. Life in Texas," *Pittsfield Sun* (Pittsfield, MA), July 6, 1848, Readex America's Historical Newspapers.
87. Patricia Nelson Limerick, *The Legacy of Conquest: The Unbroken Past of the American West* (New York: W. W. Norton, 1987), 233–34.
88. John Russell Bartlett, *Personal Narrative of Explorations and Incidents in Texas, New Mexico, California, Sonora, and Chihuahua, Connected with the United States and Mexican Boundary Commission During the Years 1850, '51, '52, and '53* (1854; repr., Chicago: Rio Grande Press, 1965), 1:38–39.
89. Bartlett, *Personal Narrative*, 1:40. See also Frederick Law Olmsted, *A Journey Through Texas: Or, A Saddle-Trip on the Southwestern Frontier* (1857, repr., Austin: University of Texas Press, 1978), 149.
90. Bartlett, *Personal Narrative*, 1:41.
91. Bartlett, *Personal Narrative*, 1:41–43, 44–45.
92. Cox, *Traveling South*, 2, 8.
93. Olmsted, *Journey Through Texas*, 117, 143–47.
94. Cox, *Traveling South*, 163–64.
95. Olmsted, *Journey Through Texas*, 150–51.
96. Sears, *Sacred Places*, 10; and Limerick, *The Legacy of Conquest*, 27.
97. Olmsted, *Journey Through Texas*, 149–52.
98. Olmsted, *Journey Through Texas*, 154, 154–56.
99. Cox, *Traveling South*, 142.
100. Frederick Law Olmsted, *The Papers of Frederick Law Olmsted*, vol. 2, *Slavery and the South, 1852–1857*, ed. Charles E. Beveridge and Charles Capin McLaughlin (Baltimore: Johns Hopkins University Press, 1981), 460–61.
101. Frederick Law Olmsted, "San Antonio, Texas," *Friends' Review*, May 2, 1857, 540–42.
102. W. W. P., "Travel," *Yale Literary Magazine*, March 1860, 203–9, EBSCO American Antiquarian Society Historical Periodicals Collection.
103. "A Hotel Wanted in San Antonio," *San Antonio Ledger and Texan*, June 23, 1853, Readex America's Historical Newspapers.
104. Joshua Brown, *Beyond the Lines: Pictorial Reporting, Everyday Life, and the Crisis of Gilded Age America* (Berkeley: University of California Press, 2002), 7–59. See also Richard Everett, "Things in and About San Antonio," *Frank Leslie's Illustrated Newspaper* (New York), January 15, 1859, Portal to Texas History, http://texashistory.unt.edu/ark:/67531/metapth30324/.
105. "Scenes in Texas," *Graham's American Monthly Magazine of Literature, Art, and Fashion*, January 1851, 37–40, ProQuest American Periodicals Series online.
106. *New York Times*, March 5, 1866.
107. Sidney Lanier, *The Centennial Edition of the Works of Sidney Lanier*, vol. 6, *Florida and Miscellaneous Prose*, ed. Philip Graham (Baltimore: Johns Hopkins University Press, 1945), 190. San Antonio had a reputation in the latter half of the nineteenth century as a haven for people suffering from tuberculosis. See Char Miller, "Tourist Trap: Visitors and the Modern San Antonio Economy," in *The Culture of Tourism,*

the Tourism of Culture: Selling the Past to the Present in the American Southwest, ed. Hal K. Rothman (Albuquerque: University of New Mexico Press, 2003), 212–17.

108. Lanier, *Florida and Miscellaneous Prose*, 6:202. See also *Southern Magazine*, July 1873, 83–99, and August 1873, 138–52. An edited version of this essay was used for a guidebook on the city in 1890 and will be discussed in a later chapter.
109. Lanier, *Florida and Miscellaneous Prose*, 2:233–34, 241–42, 242–43.
110. Edward King, "Glimpses of Texas I: A Visit to San Antonio," *Scribner's Monthly*, January 1874, 302–30; and Edward King, *The Great South* (1875; repr., New York: Arno Press, 1969). For a thought-provoking critique of King's work as an example of colonialist literature, see Jennifer Rae Greeson, "Expropriating *The Great South* and Exporting 'Local Color': Global and Hemispheric Imaginaries of the First Reconstruction," *American Literary History* 18, no. 3 (2006): 496–505, EBSCO America: History & Life, doi:10.1093/alh/aj1010.
111. King, "Glimpses of Texas," 302–3, 309.
112. King, "Glimpses of Texas," 314–15.
113. King, "Glimpses of Texas," 317.
114. Ivey, *OVM*, 96. Ivey may well be correct that this was the earliest account published outside San Antonio, but as an oral tradition it was probably decades older.
115. King, "Glimpses of Texas," 322–24.
116. Ivey, *OVM*, 366. Ivey cites a secondary source, Marion Habig's *The Alamo Chain of Missions*, for this information. Unfortunately, numerous attempts to track down a primary source, an official Catholic document, or even local newspaper accounts have been unsuccessful.
117. Ivey, *OVM*, 352.
118. Ivey, *OVM*, 352.

Chapter 3

1. *San Antonio Daily Express*, February 6, 1877. See also Donald E. Everett, "San Antonio Welcomes the 'Sunset'-1877," *Southwestern Historical Quarterly* 65, no. 1 (1961): 47–60.
2. *San Antonio Daily Express*, February 6, 1877.
3. *San Antonio Daily Express*, February 20, 1877.
4. *San Antonio Daily Express*, February 22, 1877.
5. Eric G. E. Zuelow, *A History of Modern Tourism* (New York: Palgrave Macmillan, 2016), 89; and Marguerite S. Shaffer, *See America First: Tourism and National Identity, 1880–1940* (Washington, DC: Smithsonian Books, 2001), 3.
6. Shaffer, *See America First*, 280–81; and Zuelow, *History of Modern Tourism*, 97.
7. David Montejano, *Anglos and Mexicans in the Making of Texas, 1836–1986* (Austin: University of Texas Press, 1987), 92.
8. *New York Times*, November 17, 1874, ProQuest Historical New York Times.
9. Montejano, *Anglos and Mexicans in the Making of Texas*, 92.
10. *New York Times*, November 17, 1874. For much of the late nineteenth century, San Antonio had a reputation as a haven for people suffering from tuberculosis.

See Char Miller, "Tourist Trap: Visitors and the Modern San Antonio Economy," in *The Culture of Tourism, the Tourism of Culture: Selling the Past to the Present in the American Southwest*, ed. Hal K. Rothman (Albuquerque: University of New Mexico Press, 2003), 206–28.

11. Pierre Nora, *Realms of Memory: Rethinking the French Past*, trans. Arthur Goldhammer, English-language edition ed. and foreword by Lawrence D. Kritzman, 3 vols. (New York: Columbia University Press, 1996), 1:xvii.
12. Carey McWilliams, *North from Mexico: The Spanish-Speaking People of the United States*, rev. ed. with added material by Matt S. Meier (Westport, CT: Praeger, 1990), 43–53.
13. Martin Padget, *Indian Country: Travels in the American Southwest, 1840–1935* (Albuquerque: University of New Mexico Press, 2004), 12.
14. Herbert Gottfried, *Landscape in American Guides and View Books: Visual History of Touring and Travel* (Lanham, MD: Lexington Books, 2013), 2, 52–53. Gottfried differentiates between "guidebooks" and "view books," but for the purposes of this book they can both be considered types of travel narratives.
15. Zuelow, *History of Modern Tourism*, 77.
16. Shaffer, *See America First*, 4–5. See also M. Christine Boyer, *The City of Collective Memory: Its Historical Imagery and Architectural Entertainment* (Cambridge, MA: MIT Press, 1994), 247, 305; and Jamie Winders, "Imperfectly Imperial: Northern Travel Writers in the Postbellum U.S. South, 1865–1880," *Annals of the Association of American Geographers* 95, no. 2 (2005): 394–95, http://www.jstor.org/stable/3694125.
17. Boyer, *City of Collective Memory*, 247. See also Kristin L. Hoganson, *Consumers' Imperium: The Global Production of American Domesticity, 1865–1920* (Chapel Hill: University of North Carolina Press, 2007), 153–208.
18. Joshua Brown, *Beyond the Lines: Pictorial Reporting, Everyday Life, and the Crisis of Gilded Age America* (Berkeley: University of California Press, 2002), 32–40.
19. Mark J. Noonan, *Reading the* Century Illustrated Monthly Magazine*: American Literature and Culture, 1870–1893* (Kent, OH: Kent State University Press, 2010), xi, 21, 23, 27, x.
20. Matthew Schneirov, *The Dream of a New Social Order: Popular Magazines in America, 1893–1914* (New York: Columbia University Press, 1994), 2–5, 27. Titles including *Scribner's/Century, Harper's Monthly*, and *Atlantic Monthly* tripled their circulation numbers between 1890 and 1905. By 1900, monthly magazines circulated sixty-five million copies total, while newspapers had no more than fifty-seven million. The 1900 census recorded 70.8 million people in the United States, suggesting over 90 percent of the population could be potentially influenced by the magazines' editors. For census data, see US Census Bureau, "Statistics of Population," *Report on Population of the Twelfth Census, 1900 Census*, V.1, Population, Pt.1, accessed December 15, 2020, https://www2.census.gov/library/publications/decennial/1900/volume-1/volume-1-p2.pdf.
21. Alan Trachtenberg, *The Incorporation of America: Culture and Society in the Gilded Age* (New York: Hill and Wang, 2007), 8.

22. Padget, *Indian Country*, 12.
23. John D. Cox, *Traveling South: Travel Narratives and the Construction of American Identity* (Athens: University of Georgia Press, 2005), 5–6, 157.
24. Shaffer, *See America First*, 4.
25. Shaffer, *See American First*, 5.
26. Schneirov, *Dream of a New Social Order*, 28.
27. Shaffer, *See American First*, 280.
28. Trachtenberg, *Incorporation of America*, 24.
29. John F. Sears, *Sacred Places: American Tourist Attractions in the Nineteenth Century* (New York: Oxford University Press, 1989), 157.
30. R. M. Potter, "The Fall of the Alamo," *Magazine of American History*, January 1878, 1.
31. "San Antonio de Bexar," *Harper's New Monthly Magazine*, October 1877, 838–39. The unsigned essay was later credited to Harriet P. Spofford. A "vara" is an old Spanish unit roughly equivalent to one yard.
32. "San Antonio de Bexar," 839, 841, 840.
33. "San Antonio de Bexar," 840–41, 842–43, 844–46.
34. "San Antonio de Bexar," 839–40.
35. Southern Pacific Company, *"Eden": An Excursion from New Orleans to the Pacific by Rail, Through Texas & Mexico via the "Star and Crescent" and "Sunset" Route* (Houston: T. W. Peirce Jr., 1882), 28–40.
36. Richard J. Orsi, *Sunset Limited: The Southern Pacific Railroad and the Development of the American West, 1850–1950* (Berkeley: University of California Press, 2005), 498–99.
37. *Daily Picayune* (New Orleans), June 25, 1882, Readex America's Historical Newspapers. See also Dorothy McLeod MacInerney, William Warren Rogers, and Robert David Ward, "Oscar Wilde Lectures in Texas, 1882," *Southwestern Historical Quarterly* 106, no. 4 (2003): 550–73, http://www.jstor.org/stable/30239392.
38. *Daily Picayune* (New Orleans), June 25, 1882, Readex America's Historical Newspapers.
39. MacInerney et al., "Oscar Wilde Lectures," 572.
40. Mrs. V. T. Polk, "San Antonio and Its Old Missions," *Frank Leslie's Popular Monthly*, July 1883, 40, 41, 41–42, ProQuest American Periodical Series Online. Her claim is unsubstantiated as most other sources suggest the stone came from local quarries. Curiously, the name "Huizar" is conspicuously absent from her descriptions of the decor of San José.
41. Polk, "San Antonio and Its Old Missions," 42.
42. *Telegraph and Messenger* (Macon, GA), June 10, 1883, Readex America's Historical Newspapers. This quote is lifted nearly verbatim from Harriet Spofford's 1877 *Harper's New Monthly* article (838), which was also reprinted with permission by Southern Pacific for its tourist booklet, *"Eden"* (32).
43. *Telegraph and Messenger* (Macon, GA), June 10, 1883, Readex America's Historical Newspapers.
44. *New York Times*, June 12, 1887, ProQuest Historical Newspapers. Most likely these red bricks date to renovation work begun in 1860 by the Diocese of San Antonio

to house a group of Benedictine friars and restore a greater degree of functionality. National Park Service archaeologist James Ivey suggests the Gothic arches in which the bricks were placed are not original but late nineteenth century. See James E. Ivey, *Of Various Magnificence: The Architectural History of the Missions of San Antonio, Texas in the Colonial Period and the Nineteenth Century*, with contributions by Marlys Bush Thurber and Santiago Escobedo (Santa Fe, NM: National Park Service, ca. 2006), 363–66, unpublished manuscript in the author's possession (hereafter cited as *OVM*).

45. *New York Times*, June 12, 1887. This correspondent additionally captured the nightlife on Alamo Plaza by emphasizing its exotic and foreign looks, smells, and tastes. He relegated most local Tejanos to the lowest and dangerous caste, with the men stereotyped as dark and threatening violence while the women were beguiling and sultry. Each stereotype "in equal measure is due the strong flavor of antique romance that lingers about in San Antonio and maintains its quaintness." Additional "strong flavor" came from the fiery and mysterious chili con carne sold at impromptu stands on the plaza in the evenings. Readers were reminded that "San Antonio is a frontier city" and the economic hub for the region. Additionally, as a "frontier city," it was a very "cosmopolitan" community made of Anglo-Americans, Mexicans, Germans, African Americans, and "Bohemians," to name a few. The correspondent admitted that a trip to the "poorer Mexican quarter" did not have any specific attractions other than it was "quaint and curious to American eyes."
46. Phoebe S. Kropp, *California Vieja: Culture and Memory in a Modern American Place* (Berkeley: University of California Press, 2006), 76; and Ivey, *OVM*, 352.
47. *Atlanta Constitution*, July 12, 1891, ProQuest Historical Newspapers.
48. "Quaint Old Santone," *Atlanta Constitution*, August 13, 1893, ProQuest Historical Newspapers.
49. *Philadelphia Inquirer*, March 20, 1892, Readex America's Historical Newspapers.
50. Margaret Kennedy, "Picturesque San Antonio," *Peterson's Magazine*, December 1889, 544, 544, 544, 546, 547, ProQuest American Periodicals Series online.
51. Kennedy, "Picturesque San Antonio," 547. The source from which Kennedy lifted her quote has yet to be found.
52. Kennedy, "Picturesque San Antonio," 548, 549. The identity of this French architect and date of his visit to San Antonio remains a mystery, but Kennedy was not the only source consulted to make this declaration.
53. Kennedy, "Picturesque San Antonio," 549. However, there is no mention of "Rosa" as inspiration for the elaborate carvings.
54. Kennedy, "Picturesque San Antonio," 549. This particular image of Mary is as Our Lady of Guadalupe, patron saint of Mexico.
55. T. J. Jackson Lears, *No Place of Grace: Antimodernism and the Transformation of American Culture, 1880–1920* (New York: Pantheon Books, 1981), xiii–xvii, 143, 161, 185–86.
56. Herbert Durand, *The City of Missions: San Antonio, Texas. Its Romantic History. Its Delightful Climate and Healthful Surroundings. Its Enterprise and Wonderful Prosperity* (St. Louis: Woodward and Tiernan Printing, 1894), 4–5.

57. Durand, *City of Missions*, 6–8. See also James E. Crisp, "Memory, Truth, and Pain: Myth and Censorship in the Celebration of Texas History," in *Lone Star Pasts: Memory and History in Texas*, ed. Gregg Cantrell and Elizabeth Hayes Turner (College Station: Texas A&M University Press, 2007), 87–91.
58. Dydia DeLyser, *Ramona Memories: Tourism and the Shaping of Southern California* (Minneapolis: University of Minnesota Press, 2005), 31–63. See also Kropp, *California Vieja*, 35–41; and Errol Wayne Stevens, "Helen Hunt Jackson's 'Ramona': Social Problem Novel as Tourist Guide," *California History* 77, no. 3 (1998): 158–67, https://www.jstor.org/stable/25462491.
59. Ben C. Truman, *From the Crescent City to the Golden Gate via the Sunset Route of the Southern Pacific Company* (New York: Liberty Printing, 1886), 24.
60. Truman, *From the Crescent City to the Golden Gate*, 24–28. See also Southern Pacific Company, *"Eden."*
61. H. S. Kneedler, *Through Storyland to Sunset Seas: What Four People Saw on a Journey Through the Southwest to the Pacific Coast* (N.p.: Passenger Department Southern Pacific, 1895).
62. Kneedler, *Through Storyland to Sunset Seas*, 61, 64–65, 67.
63. *Chicago Daily Tribune*, October 19, 1895, ProQuest Historical Chicago Tribune.
64. *Austin Daily Statesman*, November 19, 1895, ProQuest Historical Austin American Statesman; and *Atlanta Constitution*, January 26, 1896, ProQuest Historical Atlanta Constitution.
65. DeLyser, *Ramona Memories*, 31–32.
66. Stephen Gould, *The Alamo City Guide* (New York: Macgowan and Slipper, Printers, 1882), 88, HathiTrust; and William Corner, *San Antonio de Bexar: A Guide and History* (1890; repr., San Antonio: Graphic Arts, 1977).
67. Corner, *San Antonio de Bexar*, 68–94.
68. Gould, *Alamo City Guide*, 3, 21, 138–40.
69. Gould, *Alamo City Guide*, 31, 32, 33, 34.
70. Corner, *San Antonio de Bexar*, 7.
71. Corner, *San Antonio de Bexar*, 8, 8–12.
72. Corner, *San Antonio de Bexar*, 13, 13–19.
73. Ivey, *OVM*, 363–66.
74. Corner, *San Antonio de Bexar*, 20.
75. Corner, *San Antonio de Bexar*, page of photographs between pages 20 and 21, 15, 21–22.
76. Ivey, "*OVM*, 271–72, 300.
77. Corner, *San Antonio de Bexar*, 22.
78. "Death of Father Bouchu," *Southern Messenger*, August 22, 1907, Priest File—Bouchu, Francis, Catholic Archives of San Antonio, Texas (hereafter cited as CASA). See also "Rev. Francis Bouchu, Pioneer Priest," in *Archdiocese of San Antonio, 1874–1949: An Illustrated Record of the Foundation and Growth of Parishes, Missions, and Religious Institutions in That Part of Texas Under the Spiritual Jurisdiction of the See of San Antonio*, ed. M. J. Gilbert (San Antonio: Schneider Printing, 1949), 126–27.

79. Francis Bouchu, "Dear Uncle," letter dated March 21, 1868, trans. Sally E. Patterson, Bouchu, Francis Papers, Catholic Archives of Texas, Austin.
80. Thomas S. Bremer, *Blessed with Tourists: The Borderlands of Religion and Tourism in San Antonio* (Chapel Hill: University of North Carolina Press, 2004), 66.
81. "Last Will and Testament," Estate of Francis Bouchu, deceased, No. 4702, #41/587–89. Scanned copy obtained from the Special Collections and Texana Collection, Sisters of Charity of the Incarnate Word archives, J. E. and L. E. Mabee Library, University of the Incarnate Word, San Antonio.
82. Ivey, *OVM*, 383–85.
83. Maurice Halbwachs, *The Collective Memory*, trans. Francis J. Ditter Jr. and Vida Yazdi Ditter (1950; repr., New York: Harper Colophon Books, 1980), 151–52.
84. Corner, *San Antonio de Bexar*, 117.
85. Corner, *San Antonio de Bexar*, 117–19, 124. See also George O. Coalson, "Villanueva, Andrea Castañón," *Handbook of Texas Online*, accessed August 8, 2016, http://www.tshaonline.org/handbook/online/articles/fvi20. Coalson gives her dates as 1785–1899. Attempts to find Castañón in the census records were inconclusive. An "Andrea Gastanon" was listed on the 1860 census as being forty-one years old, but it gave her birth year as 1785 (a thirty-four-year discrepancy). See *1860 United States Federal Census*, San Antonio Ward 1, Bexar, Texas, Roll: M653_1288, Page: 361, Image: 249, accessed August 8, 2016, Ancestry.com.
86. *Austin American-Statesman*, March 1, 1891, ProQuest Historical Newspapers.
87. Corner, *San Antonio de Bexar*, 117–19; *St. Louis Republic*, October 1, 1892, Readex America's Historical Newspapers; Mena Kemp Ogan, "The Heroine of the Alamo," *National Magazine*, May/June 1893, 23–28, ProQuest American Periodical Series Online; Henry G. Tinsley, "Remember the Alamo," *Current Literature*, May 1898, 422–25, ProQuest American Periodical Series Online; *Chicago Daily Tribune*, February 19, 1899, ProQuest Historical Newspapers; *Idaho Daily Statesman*, February 11, 1899, Readex America's Historical Newspapers; *Las Novedades* (New York), February 16, 1899, Readex America's Historical Newspapers; *Savannah Tribune*, February 18, 1899; *Baltimore Sun*, February 14, 1899, ProQuest Historical Newspapers; *Chicago Daily Tribune*, March 13, 1899, ProQuest Historical Newspapers; *San Antonio Daily Express*, February 11, 1899, Readex America's Historical Newspapers. See also Walter B. Stevens, *Through Texas: A Series of Interesting Letters* (St. Louis: General Passenger Department of the Missouri Pacific Railway, 1892), 72–78. Stevens's letters had been written for and published in the *St. Louis Globe-Democrat* in the fall of 1892.
88. Richard R. Flores, *Remembering the Alamo: Memory, Modernity, & the Master Symbol* (Austin: University of Texas Press, 2002); and Holly Beachley Brear, *Inherit the Alamo: Myth and Ritual at an American Shrine* (Austin: University of Texas Press, 1995).
89. Randy Roberts and James S. Olson, *A Line in the Sand: The Alamo in Blood and Memory* (New York: Simon and Schuster, 2001), 154–55.
90. Orsi, *Sunset Limited*, 156–57.
91. Orsi, *Sunset Limited*, 157.

92. Orsi, *Sunset Limited*, 158.
93. Southern Pacific Company, Passenger Department, *Wayside Notes on the Sunset Route* (San Francisco: Southern Pacific Company, 1908), 92–93, 93–94 Internet Archive, http://www.archive.org/details/sunsetwaysidenotoosoutrich.
94. Passenger Department, *The Missions of Texas on the Sunset Route* (Houston: Cumming & Sons, [between 1900 and 1909]), 1, 4, 12. Title page marked "Compliments of Passenger Department, Houston, Texas."
95. Frederick Jackson Turner, "The Significance of the Frontier in American History," in *Rereading Frederick Jackson Turner: "The Significance of the Frontier in American History" and Other Essays*, ed. and with commentary by John Mack Faragher (New Haven, CT: Yale University Press, 1998), 31–60.
96. Gottfried, *Landscape in American Guides and View Books*, 44.
97. Char Miller, "Proving Ground: Richard Harding Davis in the American West," *Southwest Review* 90, no. 1 (2005): 13–28, http://www.jstor.org/stable/43472407.
98. Richard Harding Davis, "The West from a Car Window," *Harper's Weekly*, March 5, 1892, 221, HarpWeek. See also Miller, "Proving Ground," 14–15.
99. Davis, "The West from a Car Window," 222. Davis referenced Corner's guidebook and Sidney Lanier's history as being especially informative for visitors.
100. Stevens. *Through Texas*, 79–80, 80. For more on Orientalism, see Edward W. Said, *Orientalism*, 25th anniversary ed. with a new preface by the author (New York: Vintage Books, 1994).
101. Stevens, *Through Texas*, 80, 82.
102. Stevens, *Through Texas*, 82. See also Kropp, *California Vieja*, 76.
103. Stevens, *Through Texas*, 79.
104. Kirk Munroe, "San Antonio de Bexar," *Harper's Weekly*, September 25, 1897, 957–58, 957, HarpWeek.
105. Munroe, "San Antonio de Bexar," 957. However, there was no mention of "Rosa" or any other woman who might have served as inspiration.
106. Munroe, "San Antonio de Bexar," 958.
107. Stephen Crane, "Stephen Crane in Texas," in *The University of Virginia Edition of the Works of Stephen Crane*, vol. 8, *Tales, Sketches, and Reports*, ed. Fredson Bowers, with introduction by Edwin H. Cady (Charlottesville: University of Virginia Press, 1973), 468, 468–69.
108. Crane, "Stephen Crane in Texas," 469, 469–70.
109. Munroe, "San Antonio de Bexar," 469–71, 471, 471.
110. Munroe, "San Antonio de Bexar," 1131. The newspapers cited in this collection of Crane's works were *Pittsburgh Leader*, January 8, 1899; *Savannah Morning News*, January 8, 1899; *Omaha Daily Bee*, January 8, 1899; *Louisville Courier-Journal*, January 8, 1899; and *St. Louis Globe-Democrat*, January 8, 1899. A search of the Library of Congress's digital newspaper project, "Chronicling America: Historic American Newspapers," revealed two additional sources: *Evening Star* (Washington, DC), January 7, 1899, and *Salt Lake City Herald*, January 8, 1899, http://chroniclingamerica.loc.gov/.
111. Zuelow, *History of Modern Tourism*, 89.

Chapter 4

1. *Chicago Daily Tribune*, February 5, 1911, ProQuest Historical Chicago Tribune.
2. Daniel D. Arreola, *Tejano South Texas: A Mexican American Cultural Province* (Austin: University of Texas Press, 2002), 7, 131–49. Arreola argues that San Antonio is the cultural capital for Tejanos living in the southern part of the state.
3. Parts of this chapter have appeared in Joel D. Kitchens, "Making Historical Memory: Women's Leadership in the Preservation of San Antonio's Missions," *Southwestern Historical Quarterly* 121, no. 2 (2017): 171–96.
4. David Montejano, *Anglos and Mexicans in the Making of Texas, 1836–1986* (Austin: University of Texas Press, 1987), 253–54.
5. Richard A. Garcia, *Rise of the Mexican American Middle Class: San Antonio, 1929–1941* (College Station: Texas A&M University Press, 1991), 29.
6. Edward Hungerford, "The City of Little Squares: The Charm of San Antonio, Texas, Where Revolution Breeds," *Harper's Weekly*, November 9, 1912, 11–12, HarpWeek database.
7. *San Antonio Daily Light*, April 5, 1886, Portal to Texas History, http://texashistory.unt.edu/ark:/67531/metatapth144811/.
8. Lewis F. Fisher, *Saving San Antonio: The Precarious Preservation of a Heritage* (Lubbock: Texas Tech University Press, 1996), 40–43.
9. Barbara J. Howe, "Women in the Nineteenth-Century Preservation Movement," in *Restoring Women's History Through Historic Preservation*, ed. Gail Lee Dubrow and Jennifer B. Goodman (Baltimore: Johns Hopkins University Press, 2003), 17.
10. James M. Lindgren, "'A New Departure in Historic, Patriotic Work': Personalism, Professionalism, and Conflicting Concepts of Material Culture in the Late Nineteenth and Early Twentieth Centuries," *Public Historian* 18, no. 2 (1996): 46, http://www.jstor.org/stable/3377912/. See also James M. Lindgren, "'A Spirit That Fires the Imagination': Historic Preservation and Cultural Regeneration in Virginia and New England, 1850–1950," in *Giving Preservation a History: Histories of Historic Preservation in the United States*, ed. Max Page and Randall Mason (New York: Routledge, 2004), 108–9.
11. Barbara J. Howe, "Women in Historic Preservation: The Legacy of Ann Pamela Cunningham," *Public Historian* 12, no. 1 (1990): 35–38, http://www.jstor.org/stable/3378321.
12. Max Page and Randall Mason, "Rethinking the Roots of the Historic Preservation Movement," in *Giving Preservation a History: Histories of Historic Preservation in the United States*, ed. Max Page and Randall Mason (New York: Routledge, 2004), 10.
13. Judy Mattivi Morley, *Historic Preservation & the Imagined West: Albuquerque, Denver, & Seattle* (Lawrence: University Press of Kansas, 2006), 2.
14. W. Fitzhugh Brundage, "No Deed but Memory," in *Where These Memories Grow: History, Memory, and Southern Identity*, ed. W. Fitzhugh Brundage (Chapel Hill: University of North Carolina Press, 2000), 14.
15. Gregg Cantrell and Elizabeth Hayes Turner, "Introduction: A Study of History, Memory, and Collective Memory in Texas," in *Lone Star Pasts: Memory and History in Texas*, ed. Gregg Cantrell and Elizabeth Hayes Turner (College Station:

Texas A&M University Press, 2007), 6. See also Maurice Halbwachs, *On Collective Memory*, ed., trans., and introduction by Lewis A. Coser (Chicago: University of Chicago Press, 1992), 49, 51; and Yi-Fu Tuan, *Space and Place: The Perspective of Experience* (Minneapolis: University of Minnesota Press, 1977), 195.

16. *San Antonio Express*, August 20, 1900, Readex America's Historical Newspapers.
17. "Preserve the Missions," *San Antonio Express*, February 3, 1902, Readex America's Historical Newspapers.
18. *St. Louis Post-Dispatch*, February 9, 1902; October 26, 1902; and November 30, 1902, ProQuest Historical Newspapers.
19. "Our Duty to the Old Missions," *Dallas Morning News*, December 8, 1902, Readex America's Historical Newspapers. Hemenway's timely and generous donation was credited with saving Boston's old South Church, and Cunningham led the efforts to save George Washington's Mount Vernon home.
20. "Our Duty to the Old Missions," *Dallas Morning News*, December 8, 1902, Readex America's Historical Newspapers. See also Laura Lyons McLemore, *Adele Briscoe Looscan: Daughter of the Republic* (Fort Worth: Texas Christian University Press, 2016), 210–13. In this chapter there are a number of misspellings of the name "Pedro Huizar," the artist credited with the elaborate decorations and sculpting at Mission San José, including "Hincar" and "Huicar."
21. *San Antonio Express*, October 25, 1903, Readex America's Historical Newspapers.
22. L. Richard Ables, "The Second Battle for the Alamo," *Southwestern Historical Quarterly* 70, no. 3 (1967): 372–413, http://www.jstor.org/stable/30237905; Fisher, *Saving San Antonio*, 53–60; Richard R. Flores, *Remembering the Alamo: Memory, Modernity, & the Master Symbol* (Austin: University of Texas Press, 2002), 61–92; Scott Zesch, "Adina De Zavala and the Second Siege of the Alamo," *CRM Journal* 5, no. 1 (2008): 31–44; and Kitchens, "Making Historical Memory," 176–85.
23. Holly Beachley Brear, "We Run the Alamo and You Don't: Alamo Battles of Ethnicity and Gender," in *Where These Memories Grow: History, Memory, and Southern Identity*, ed. W. Fitzhugh Brundage (Chapel Hill: University of North Carolina Press, 2000), 301.
24. Ables, "Second Battle," 372–75. Although Clara Driscoll had married H. H. Sevier in 1906, when the marriage broke up three decades later, she went back to using her maiden name. This book will use "Driscoll" for the sake of clarity.
25. Fisher, *Saving San Antonio*, 56–57.
26. "History of the Title to the Alamo Mission," *San Antonio Daily Express*, January 29, 1905, Readex America's Historical Newspapers.
27. Ables, "Second Battle," 377–78.
28. Cantrell and Turner, "Introduction," 6.
29. Ables, "Second Battle," 378, 381–82.
30. Adelaide E. Byrd, "Historic Alamo: Texas Ladies Save It from Destruction," *Morning Olympian* (Olympia, WA), September 2, 1904, Readex America's Historical Newspapers.
31. *St. Louis Post-Dispatch*, November 26, 1905, ProQuest Historical Newspapers; and Ables, "Second Battle," 385–88.

32. Ables, "Second Battle," 394–96.
33. *St. Louis Post-Dispatch*, February 24, 1907, ProQuest Historical Newspapers; and Ables, "Second Battle," 397–98.
34. *St. Louis Post-Dispatch*, February 24, 1907, ProQuest Historical Newspapers.
35. *Dallas Morning News*, February 16, 1907, Readex America's Historical Newspapers.
36. *Dallas Morning News*, February 25, 1907, Readex America's Historical Newspapers.
37. Lindgren, "A New Departure," 46.
38. *Dallas Morning News*, March 26, 1907, Readex America's Historical Newspapers.
39. George Wharton James to Adina De Zavala, April 22, 1907, Adina Emilia De Zavala Papers, 1766 (1831–1955), Dolph Briscoe Center for American History, University of Texas at Austin (hereafter cited as De Zavala Papers); and "Comments upon the Alamo Improvements," *Austin American-Statesman*, May 2, 1907, ProQuest Historical Newspapers.
40. David Chidester and Edward T. Linenthal, eds., *American Sacred Space* (Bloomington: Indiana University Press, 1995), 15.
41. Cantrell and Turner, "Introduction," 6.
42. Chidester and Linenthal, *American Sacred Space*, 16; see also Flores, *Remembering the Alamo*, 145.
43. *St. Louis Post-Dispatch*, April 28, 1907, ProQuest Historical Newspapers. A brief description of the conflict appeared in the *Indianapolis Morning Star*, May 28, 1907, ProQuest Historical Newspapers. See also Ables, "Second Battle," 400–402. For the DRT relinquishing control over the Alamo, see Scott Huddleston, "DRT's Days at Alamo Numbered: Group's Management of Shrine Ends July 10," *San Antonio Express-News*, March 13, 2015, NewsBank Access World News.
44. Ables, "Second Battle," 402–3.
45. *Atlanta Constitution*, February 12, 1908, ProQuest Historical Newspapers; *St. Louis Post-Dispatch*, February 12, 1908, ProQuest Historical Newspapers; *Louisville Courier-Journal*, February 12, 1908, ProQuest Historical Newspapers; and *New York Times*, February 12, 1908, ProQuest Historical Newspapers.
46. Ables, "Second Battle," 403–4; and *New York Times*, February 13, 1908, ProQuest Historical Newspapers.
47. *St. Louis Post-Dispatch*, February 13, 1908, ProQuest Historical Newspapers.
48. *Atlanta Constitution*, February 14, 1908, ProQuest Historical Newspapers.
49. *New York Times*, February 14, 1908, ProQuest Historical Newspapers.
50. Tuan, *Space and Place*, 197.
51. *San Antonio Express*, December 29–30, 1911 (microfilm); and *Dallas Morning News*, December 25 and December 31, 1911, Readex America's Historical Newspapers; Ables, "Second Battle," 410; and Gregg Cantrell, "The Bones of Stephen F. Austin: History and Memory in Progressive-Era Texas," in *Lone Star Pasts: Memory and History in Texas*, foreword by W. Fitzhugh Brundage, ed. Gregg Cantrell and Elizabeth Hayes Turner (College Station: Texas A&M University Press, 2007), 59–61.
52. *Dallas Morning News*, January 15, 1913, Readex America's Historical Newspapers.

53. Ables, "Second Battle," 404–13. See also Michael Kammen, *Mystic Chords of Memory: The Transformation of Tradition in American Culture* (New York: Vintage Books, 1993; first published New York: Knopf, 1991; page references are to 1993 Vintage ed.), 240–42.
54. Ables, "Second Battle," 411–12; and Cantrell, "Bones," 63.
55. Charles Hueurmann to Governor O. B. Colquitt, March 6, 1912, Charles Hueurmann Collection, San Antonio Conservation Society (hereafter cited as Hueurmann Collection).
56. Julius Real to Charles Hueurmann, January 25, 1913, Hueurmann Collection.
57. Adina De Zavala to Charles Hueurmann, February 18, 1913, Hueurmann Collection.
58. Julius H. Erkner to Mrs. A. B. Looscan, August 22, 1913, Hueurmann Collection. Hueurmann received a copy of this letter for recommending that Erkner contact Looscan. In April 1914, Clara Driscoll announced she would not permit the DRT to charge an admission fee to Alamo grounds even had the organization been forced to pay any court settlement to Governor Colquitt. See "Funds for the Alamo," *Austin American-Statesman*, April 27, 1914, ProQuest Historical Newspapers.
59. *New York World*, December 7, 1913.
60. Gregg Cantrell, "Bones," 61–62; and Lindgren, "A New Departure," 53.
61. George W. Tyler to Adina De Zavala, October 15, 1908, De Zavala Papers. Tyler was writing from Belton, Texas, and predicted that the missions could be used as museums.
62. Kenneth Hafertepe, "Restoration, Reconstruction, or Romance? The Case of the Spanish Governor's Palace in Hispanic-Era San Antonio, Texas," *Journal of the Society of Architectural Historians* 67, no. 3 (2008): 412, https://www.jstor.org/stable/10.1525/jsah.2008.67.3.412.
63. Herbert Gottfried, *Landscape in American Guides and View Books: Visual History of Touring and Travel* (Lanham, MD: Lexington Books, 2013), 52–53.
64. Pierre Nora, *Realms of Memory: Rethinking the French Past*, trans. Arthur Goldhammer, English-language edition ed. and foreword by Lawrence D. Kritzman, 3 vols. (New York: Columbia University Press, 1996), 1:xvii.
65. Richard R. Flores, "Adina de Zavala and the Politics of Restoration: Introduction," in *History and Legends of the Alamo and Other Missions in and Around San Antonio*, by Adina de Zavala, ed. Richard R. Flores (Houston: Arte Público Press, 1996), xxviii–lii.
66. Flores, "Adina De Zavala," xxxiii–xlix. For more on the suppression of inconvenient historical truths by elites, see Michel-Rolph Trouillot, *Silencing the Past: Power and the Production of History* (Boston: Beacon Press, 1995).
67. Kenneth Hafertepe, "The Romantic Rhetoric of the Spanish Governor's Palace, San Antonio, Texas," *Southwestern Historical Quarterly* 107, no. 2 (2003): 241–42, https://www.jstor.org/stable/30242173.
68. Adina De Zavala, *History and Legends of the Alamo and Other Missions in and Around San Antonio*, ed. Richard Flores (Houston: Arte Público Press, 1996), 16–17.
69. *San Antonio Express*, December 21, 1917, Portal to Texas History, http://texashistory.unt.edu/ark:/67531/metapth433837/.

70. *San Antonio Express*, December 24, 1917, Portal to Texas History, http://texashistory.unt.edu/ark:/67531/metapth434331/.
71. Gottfried, *Landscape in American Guides*, 52–53.
72. William B. May, "Chronicles of a Highway: El Nuevo Camino Real," *Sunset*, December 1898, 21–25, HathiTrust Digital Library, http://www.hathitrust.org/; and C. A. Scott, "San Antonio Texas in 1867," *Sunset*, December 1900, 59–66, HathiTrust Digital Library, http://www.hathitrust.org/.
73. H. M. Mayo, "Travelers Pen Sketches of Cities in the South and West: El Paso to New Orleans—Marfa, San Antonio, and Houston," *Sunset*, December 1899, 59, HathiTrust Digital Library, http://www.hathitrust.org/.
74. G. C. Collingwood, "The City of the Alamo: How the Romance of San Antonio's Past Blends with Its Present Marvelous Development," *Sunset*, April 1906, 532–33, 546–47.
75. Alice M. Keatinge, "Texas Missions Today," *Sunset*, April 1905, 591, 592, 594–95.
76. Agnes C. Laut, "Why Go Abroad? The Mission in the Arizona Desert," *Sunset*, January 1913, 27–32.
77. Laut, "Why Go Abroad?," 397.
78. Laut, "Why Go Abroad?," 400.
79. T. J. Jackson Lears, *No Place of Grace: Antimodernism and the Transformation of American Culture, 1880–1920* (New York: Pantheon Books, 1981), xiii, 142.
80. Paul A. Ewing, "The Borderland Missions," *Sunset*, October 1927, 24–26, 24, 25.
81. Richard J. Orsi, *Sunset Limited: The Southern Pacific Railroad and the Development of the American West, 1850–1950* (Berkeley: University of California Press, 2005), 158–59.
82. Jay C. Henry, *Architecture in Texas, 1895–1945* (Austin: University of Texas Press, 1993), 144–45.
83. Arthur Howard Noll, "The Texas 'Missions,'" *American Architect and Building News*, August 28, 1897, 71, ProQuest American Periodicals Series Online.
84. For more on Orientalism, see Edward W. Said, *Orientalism*, with a new preface by the author (New York: Vintage Books, 1994).
85. Olaf Z. Cervin, "The Spanish-Mexican Missions of the United States," *Architectural Record*, September 1903, 191. For more information on how the long Moorish occupation of the Iberian Peninsula informed art and architecture in the Americas, see Manuel Toussaint, *Colonial Art in Mexico*, ed. and trans. Elizabeth Wilder Weismann (Austin: University of Texas Press, 1967), 5, 125–28; and George Kubler and Martin Soria, *Art and Architecture of Spain and Portugal and Their American Dominions, 1500–1800* (Baltimore: Penguin Books, 1959), 124–25.
86. Cervin, "The Spanish-Mexican Missions," 189.
87. William S. Rice, "The Texas Mission Buildings," *Builder*, March 1, 1904, 19, ProQuest American Periodicals Series Online.
88. Untitled and undated newspaper clipping, Vertical File-Biography—Smith, Harvey P., Sr., DRT Library.
89. Harvey P. Smith, *Romantic San Antonio* (San Antonio: Jackson Printing, 1918). The book went through multiple editions.

90. Smith, *Romantic San Antonio* (1918), 5; and Harvey P. Smith, *Romantic San Antonio: A Descriptive Journey to the Many Picturesque and Romantic Places in and Around Old San Antonio*, rev. ed. (San Antonio: Naylor, 1936), 15–16.
91. Smith, *Romantic San Antonio* (1918), 10; and Smith, *Romantic San Antonio* (1936), 21.
92. Smith, *Romantic San Antonio* (1936), 21. Smith was the lead architect for the Depression-era relief efforts to rebuild San José.
93. On January 30, 2020, the author conducted a search of the OCLC WorldCat database for books with the title phrase "Queen of the Missions" in reference to San José. Wilma Madlem published *San Jose Mission, Its Legends, Lore, and History; Story of "the Queen of Missions"* (San Antonio: Naylor, 1934), and Reverend John Ilg wrote *San Jose: Queen of the Missions* (San Antonio: Franciscan Fathers, 1936). Although locals may have referred to San José as "Queen of the Missions" for many years earlier, the phrase did not appear in popular printed works until this time period, probably in the effort to gain publicity for the mission as it was being restored by Depression-era relief organizations.
94. Rexford Newcomb, "A Remnant of Spanish Renaissance Architecture in Texas," *Western Architect*, January 1919, 3, 4. Newcomb wrote several books on Spanish architecture in the United States.
95. Atlee B. Ayers, "The Earliest Mission Buildings of San Antonio, Texas," *American Architect and The Architectural Review*, August 27, 1924, 171–78, 171, 172–74. Harvey Smith worked for Ayers from 1915 to 1916.
96. F. S. Laurence, "The Old Spanish Missions in and About San Antonio," *American Architect and the Architectural Review*, November 21, 1923, 445, 448, 446, 450. Laurence was the executive secretary of the National Terra Cotta Society.
97. Kristin L. Hoganson, *Consumers' Imperium: The Global Production of American Domesticity, 1865–1920* (Chapel Hill: University of North Carolina Press, 2007), 43.
98. "The Spanish Tradition of the South," *Architectural Forum*, November 1931, 586. This short article had more photographs than text, but all were of the Alamo and San José. For more on the historiographic debate over issues of racism and post-colonialism in Mission Revival (also known as Spanish Colonial Revival) architecture, see David Gebhard, "The Spanish Colonial Revival in Southern California, 1895–1930," *Journal of the Society of Architectural Historians* 26, no. 2 (1967): 131–47, http://www.jstor.org/stable/988417; Abigail A. Van Slyck, "Mañana, Mañana: Racial Stereotypes and the Anglo Rediscovery of the Southwest's Vernacular Architecture, 1890–1920," *Perspectives in Vernacular Architecture* 5 (1995): 95–108, http://www.jstor.org/stable/3514248; and Hoganson, *Consumers' Imperium*, 41.
99. Helen Delpar, *The Enormous Vogue of Things Mexican: Cultural Relations Between the United States and Mexico, 1920–1935* (Tuscaloosa: University of Alabama Press, 1992).
100. Martin Padget, *Indian Country: Travels in the American Southwest, 1840–1935* (Albuquerque: University of New Mexico Press, 2004): 2–4, 11–12, 171–72. See also Gottfried, *Landscape in American Guides*, 2.
101. Marguerite S. Shaffer, *See America First: Tourism and National Identity, 1880–1940* (Washington, DC: Smithsonian Books, 2001), 26, 4–6.

102. Michael E. Zega, "Advertising the Southwest," *Journal of the Southwest* 43, no. 3 (2001): 281, 283, 282.
103. Charles S. Fee, "How the Southern Pacific Advertises," *Graphic Arts: A Magazine for Printers and the Use of Printing*, December 1911, 420. See also Southern Pacific Company, *Louisiana and Texas for the Winter Tourist* (New Orleans: Southern Pacific Company, 1911), as an example of this type of advertising.
104. Orsi, *Sunset Limited*, 157–63.
105. Hoganson, *Consumers' Imperium*, 153–208. See also Erika Marie Bsumek, "Exchanging Places: Virtual Tourism, Vicarious Travel, and the Consumption of Southwestern Indian Artifacts," in *The Culture of Tourism, the Tourism of Culture: Selling the Past to the Present in the American Southwest*, ed. Hal K. Rothman (Albuquerque: University of New Mexico Press, 2003), 118–39.
106. *Chicago Daily Tribune*, February 5, 1911, ProQuest Historical Chicago Tribune.
107. Missouri, Kansas, and Texas advertisement, *Town and Country*, January 20, 1906, 29, ProQuest American Periodicals Series Online. Although frequently referred to as "medieval" in advertisements and travel narratives, San Antonio's missions were founded and constructed in a much later epoch, but this anachronism is part and parcel of the romance.
108. "Compliments, the MKT," postcard dated January 10, 1906 to Mrs. A. B. Clark, Caratunk, Maine. In the author's possession.
109. *Chicago Daily Tribune*, January 22, 1911, ProQuest Historical Chicago Tribune.
110. *Chicago Daily Tribune*, December 10, 1911, ProQuest Historical Chicago Tribune.
111. *Beautiful San Antonio: The Commercial and Industrial Center of the Southwest* (San Antonio: Business Men's Club, 1906), cover, 2, San Antonio Guidebook Collection, 1890–ca. 1979, DRT6, DRT Library (hereafter cited as San Antonio Guidebook Collection). However, for a contravening viewpoint, see Char Miller, "Tourist Trap: Visitors and the Modern San Antonio Economy," in *The Culture of Tourism, the Tourism of Culture: Selling the Past to the Present in the American Southwest*, ed. Hal. K. Rothman (Albuquerque: University of New Mexico Press, 2003), 212–17, for the mercenary ways San Antonio made money off people suffering from tuberculosis.
112. *Beautiful San Antonio*, 6.
113. L. F. Kelly and S. Williamson, *Beautiful San Antonio* (San Antonio: Bureau of Advertising, ca. 1910), 2, San Antonio Guidebook Collection.
114. Kelly and Williamson, *Beautiful San Antonio*, 22. See also *San Antonio* (San Antonio: Chamber of Commerce of San Antonio, ca. 1920), San Antonio Guidebook Collection.
115. *Wall Street Journal*, February 1, 1921, ProQuest Historical Wall Street Journal. It also appeared in the *New York Times*, February 7, 1921.
116. See Holly Beachley Brear, *Inherit the Alamo: Myth and Ritual at an American Shrine* (Austin: University of Texas Press, 1995), 24–44, 106–20, 138–39; and Flores, *Remembering the Alamo*, 15–34, 157–61, on the mixed emotions that many Mexican Americans hold about the Alamo.

117. *New York Times*, January 18 and December 8, 1924, ProQuest Historical New York Times; and *Wall Street Journal*, March 31, 1927, ProQuest Historical Wall Street Journal.
118. *Christian Science Monitor*, November 9, 1912, ProQuest Historical Christian Science Monitor.
119. Shaffer, *See America First*, 280–81.
120. *Chicago Daily Tribune*, January 4, 1931, and December 18, 1932, ProQuest Historical Chicago Tribune.
121. *Chicago Daily Tribune*, December 29, 1935, ProQuest Historical Chicago Tribune.
122. *New York Times*, May 15 and December 5, 1933, ProQuest Historical New York Times.
123. *Chicago Daily Tribune*, February 5 and February 19, 1930, ProQuest Historical Chicago Tribune.
124. *Los Angeles Times*, March 20, 1930, ProQuest Historical Los Angeles Times.
125. *Chicago Daily Tribune*, October 26, 1930, ProQuest Historical Chicago Tribune.
126. Melita M. Garza, *They Came to Toil: Newspaper Representations of Mexicans and Immigrants in the Great Depression* (Austin: University of Texas Press, 2018), 11.
127. Garcia, *Rise of the Mexican American Middle Class*, 3.
128. *Chicago Daily Tribune*, October 12, 1930, ProQuest Historical Chicago Tribune.
129. Fisher, *Saving San Antonio: The Precarious Preservation*, 93; and Anne Leslie Fenstermaker, "Green, Mary Rowena [Rena] Maverick," *Handbook of Texas Online*, accessed April 13, 2016, http://www.tshaonline.org/handbook/online/articles/fgr36.
130. Fisher, *Saving San Antonio: The Precarious Preservation*, 2–9.
131. SACS (San Antonio Conservation Society) "Minutes" folder, August 2, 1924, Rena Maverick Green Papers, 1924–59, Dolph Briscoe Center for American History, University of Texas at Austin (hereafter cited as Rena Maverick Green Papers); and Fisher, *Saving San Antonio: The Precarious Preservation*, 3–8.
132. SACS "Minutes" folder, October 4, 1924, Rena Maverick Green Papers.
133. SACS "Minutes" folder, January 10, February 7, May 2, and October 3, 1925, Rena Maverick Green Papers; and Fisher, *Saving San Antonio: The Precarious Preservation*, 148–51.
134. Fisher, *Saving San Antonio: The Precarious Preservation*, 151.
135. A. Drossaerts to Fr. Vincent Schremp, O.F.M., January 19, 1928, Arthur Drossaerts Papers, Catholic Archives of San Antonio (hereafter cited as CASA; emphasis in the original).
136. Meeting Minutes for March 7, 1931, Rena Maverick Green Papers. Participants included Bishop Drossaerts; Fr. Garriga of San Fernando Cathedral; Fr. Emery, a Franciscan friar; and Rena M. Green and "Mrs. Taylor" representing SACS. The meeting reported that the Franciscans were looking to build a "monastery" near San José "entirely in keeping with the atmosphere of the Mission." In this meeting the SACS members tried to strike a deal to sell some of their property to the church and use the proceeds to purchase the San José granary for preservation.
137. *San Antonio Express*, March 10, 1928.
138. *San Antonio Express*, March 11, 1928.

139. *San Antonio Express*, March 10, 1928.
140. *La Prensa*, April 4, 1928, Readex America's Historical Newspapers. Translation by the author.
141. *La Prensa*, April 6, 1928, Readex America's Historical Newspapers. Translation by the author.
142. Fisher, *Saving San Antonio: The Precarious Preservation*, 148–51.
143. Lindgren, "A New Departure," 53.
144. Archbishop Drossaerts to SACS, March 26, 1931, Rena Maverick Green Papers.
145. Chidester and Linenthal, *American Sacred Space*, 28.
146. Fisher, *Saving San Antonio: The Precarious Preservation*, 151–60. See Meeting Minutes, December 19, 1930, Book 1, which report that a recent rummage sale netted $2,000 for land purchases around Mission San José, Duplicate Minutes of All SACS Meetings, March 22, 1924–May 1, 1941, SACS Library (hereafter cited as Duplicate Minutes); and Rena Maverick Green to Mrs. Taylor, February 23, 1934, Rena Maverick Green Papers. This letter was probably sent to Amanda Taylor, SACS president, and mentioned receiving $100 from the DRT. See also Amanda C. Taylor to Mrs. Robert McGarraugh, June 10, 1935, "Dear Mary," Rena Maverick Green Papers.
147. Fisher, *Saving San Antonio: The Precarious Preservation*, 151–60.
148. Meeting Minutes, April 30, 1931, Book 1, Duplicate Minutes, SACS Library. During this same meeting, concern was raised about the planned Franciscan construction at San José.
149. Meeting Minutes, January 27, 1932, Book 1, Duplicate Minutes, SACS Library.
150. Meeting Minutes, Board of Directors meeting, April 25, 1934, Book 1, Duplicate Minutes, SACS Library. At the next board meeting on May 9, 1934, there was concern that CWA (Civil Works Administration) resources were being used only on the SACS-owned property at Mission San José while the chapel was neglected. The board voted unanimously to contact federal authorities and request that all money for workers and materials be used for restoring the church building, with the granary and other SACS properties being lower priorities.
151. Theo H. Price, "What Texas Has to Advertise and How to Advertise It," *Commerce and Finance*, November 14, 1923, 2107–9.
152. Kenneth B. Ragsdale, *Centennial '36: The Year America Discovered Texas* (College Station: Texas A&M University Press, 1987), 3–5, 19, 39.
153. Stephen Harrigan, *Big Wonderful Thing: A History of Texas* (Austin: University of Texas Press, 2019), 3.
154. Trouillot, *Silencing the Past*.
155. John Morán González, *Border Renaissance: The Texas Centennial and the Emergence of Mexican American Literature* (Austin: University of Texas Press, 2009), 6–11.
156. *The Official Guide Book, Texas Centennial Exposition, June 6–Nov. 29, 1936* (Dallas: Texas Centennial Central Exposition, ca. 1936), 9, 15, 63, 97.
157. *Chicago Daily Tribune*, April 5, 1936, ProQuest Historical Chicago Tribune; and *New York Times*, April 5, April 19, and May 31, 1936, ProQuest Historical New York Times.

158. *All America Is Invited to Visit Texas' Centennial Celebration* (Dallas: State Headquarters, Texas Centennial Celebrations, 1935), n.p., DeGolyer Library, Southern Methodist University, Dallas (hereafter cited as DeGolyer, SMU).
159. Wylie A. Parker, *Here Is Texas: A Sourcebook of Centennial Program Material* (San Antonio: Naylor, 1936), 55.
160. Rita Crabbe, "Garriga, Mariano Simon," *Handbook of Texas Online*, accessed February 10, 2020, http://www.tshaonline.org/handbook/online/articles/fga31.
161. M. S. Garriga to Honorable Maury Maverick, Washington, DC, February 29, 1936, M. S. Garriga Papers (unprocessed as of June 19, 2019), Catholic Archives of Texas, Texas Catholic Conference of Bishops, Austin (hereafter cited as Garriga Papers).
162. Maury Maverick to Fr. Garriga, March 3, 1936 (printed on US Congress letterhead), Garriga Papers. See also Western Union Telegram from Morris Sheppard to Fr. Garriga, March 6, 1936, Garriga Papers.
163. 80 Cong. Rec. H7351–7354 (statement of Rep. Maverick), bound ed., accessed June 25, 2019, ProQuest Congressional.
164. Ragsdale, *Centennial '36*, 294–96, 299–301.
165. *Dallas Morning News*, April 18, 1936, Readex America's Historical Newspapers; and Ragsdale, *Centennial '36*, 171–72.
166. Quoted in Ragsdale, *Centennial '36*, 302.

Chapter 5

1. *San Antonio Light*, January 12, 1941, Newspaper Archive. See also Luis Torres, *Voices from the San Antonio Missions* (Lubbock: Texas Tech University Press, 1997), 50–51, 63.
2. Pierre Nora, *Realms of Memory: Rethinking the French Past*, trans. Arthur Goldhammer, English-language edition ed. and foreword by Lawrence D. Kritzman, 3 vols. (New York: Columbia University Press, 1996), 1:xvii.
3. John F. Sears, *Sacred Places: American Tourist Attractions in the Nineteenth Century* (New York: Oxford University Press, 1989), 10.
4. Gloria Anzaldúa, *Borderlands/La Frontera: The New Mestiza*, 2nd ed. (San Francisco: Aunt Lute Books, 1999), 99–102. Anzaldúa takes the idea of *la raza cosmica* (the cosmic race) from Mexican philosopher José Vasconcelos and expands it as her "new *mestiza*" concept to describe the multifaceted, multicultural hybrid blend of life in the Borderlands. Because she is a poet, Anzaldúa's depiction contains more metaphor, but nonetheless touches on some of the contradictions and ambiguities listed by Sears. I contend that San Antonio's missions should also be considered "borders," as they are the loci where the hybrid blend of Spanish, Indigenous, Mexican, and Anglo cultural admixture percolates into a new synecdoche for the Borderlands.
5. Richard K. Popp, *The Holiday Makers: Magazines, Advertising, and Mass Tourism in Postwar America* (Baton Rouge: Louisiana State University Press, 2012), 13–30; see also Susan Sessions Rugh, *Are We There Yet? The Golden Age of American Family Vacations* (Lawrence: University Press of Kansas, 2008). 17.
6. Rugh, *Are We There Yet?*, 12; and Popp, *Holiday Makers*, 59.

7. Rugh, *Are We There Yet?*, 41–42; and Thomas S. Bremer, *Blessed with Tourists: The Borderlands of Religion and Tourism in San Antonio* (Chapel Hill: University of North Carolina Press, 2004), 6–9.
8. Rugh, *Are We There Yet?*, 41–42. For more on the origins of the "See America First" movement, see Marguerite S. Shaffer, *See America First: Tourism and National Identity, 1880–1940* (Washington, DC: Smithsonian Books, 2001).
9. *San Antonio Express*, April 12, 1934, Newspaper Archive Database.
10. Charles B. Hosmer Jr., *Preservation Comes of Age: From Williamsburg to the National Trust, 1926–1949* (Charlottesville: University of Virginia Press, for the National Trust for Historic Preservation in the United States, 1981), 1:280–81.
11. *San Antonio Express*, March 8, 1935.
12. *San Antonio Express*, March 6 and March 8, 1935.
13. Undated memo, M. S. Garriga Papers (unprocessed as of June 19, 2019), Catholic Archives of Texas, Texas Catholic Conference of Bishops, Austin (hereafter cited as Garriga Papers).
14. *San Antonio Express*, March 9, 1935.
15. *Dallas Morning News*, March 11, 1935, and *Houston Post*, March 12, 1935, Readex America's Historical Newspapers.
16. *Houston Post*, March 17, 1935, Readex America's Historical Newspapers.
17. Preservation of Historic American Sites, Buildings, Objects, and Antiquities of National Significance: Hearings on H. R. 6670 and H. R. 6734, April 1, 2, and 5, 1935, Before the Committee on the Public Lands, 74th Cong., 7, 12 (1935), ProQuest Congressional database.
18. Richard B. Henderson, *Maury Maverick: A Political Biography* (Austin: University of Texas Press, 1970), 199.
19. *Preservation of Historic American Sites*, Statement of Maury Maverick, 10.
20. *Preservation of Historic American Sites*, Statement of Maury Maverick, 10–11.
21. 74 Cong. Rec. 12737 (1935), accessed June 25, 2019, ProQuest Congressional database.
22. Hosmer, *Preservation Comes of Age*, 1:280–81; Lewis F. Fisher, *Saving San Antonio: The Precarious Preservation of a Heritage* (Lubbock: Texas Tech University Press, 1996), 164–66.
23. Municipal Advertising Commission of San Antonio, Texas, *Building Greater San Antonio by Advertising: A Report of the Activities of the Municipal Advertising Commission of San Antonio, Texas for Period January, 1938 thru May, 1939*, San Antonio Guidebook Collection, Daughters of the Republic of Texas Research Library, San Antonio (hereafter cited as San Antonio Guidebook Collection).
24. Municipal Advertising Commission of San Antonio, Texas, *Building Greater San Antonio by Advertising*, San Antonio Guidebook Collection.
25. *Picturesque San Antonio: Where Life Is Different* (San Antonio: Municipal Information Bureau, ca. 1939), n.p., estimated 1, 10, 11–12, San Antonio Guidebook Collection.
26. Municipal Advertising Commission of San Antonio, Texas, *Building Greater San Antonio by Advertising*, San Antonio Guidebook Collection.

27. Municipal Advertising Commission of San Antonio, Texas, *Building Greater San Antonio by Advertising,* San Antonio Guidebook Collection.
28. "Dear Frieda," Postcard to Mrs. Richard A. Wood from her mother, February 8, 1946. In author's possession.
29. Christine Bold, *The WPA Guides: Mapping America* (Jackson: University Press of Mississippi, 1999), 3–4, 29–30, EBSCO.
30. *Texas: A Guide to the Lone Star State, Compiled by Workers of the Writers' Program of the Work Projects Administration in the State of Texas* (New York: Hastings House, 1940, by the Texas State Highway Commission), 4–5. The issue of violence begs the question of whether it would induce people to travel the state's highways or keep them away out of fear if offenses might have such dire consequences.
31. *Texas: A Guide to the Lone Star State,* 43–45, 106. This would include the San Antonio missions, as well as those in El Paso and near Goliad.
32. *Texas: A Guide to the Lone Star State,* 150–51, 349–53, 351, 349–53.
33. Bold, *WPA Guides,* 5.
34. Eric G. E. Zuelow, *A History of Modern Tourism* (New York: Palgrave Macmillan, 2016), 77.
35. Claude B. Aniol, *San Antonio: City of Missions* (New York: Hastings House, 1942), 7–23, 15, 31, 34. These same models were used in several photographs from *Picturesque San Antonio* (n.p., but estimated title page, 12, 14).
36. Mason Sutherland, "Carnival in San Antonio," *National Geographic Magazine,* December 1947, 813, 815–16.
37. Kent Ruth, *How to Enjoy Your Western Vacations* (Norman: University of Oklahoma Press, 1956), vii–viii, viii, ix.
38. Ruth, *How to Enjoy Your Western Vacations,* 35, 44.
39. Ruth, *How to Enjoy Your Western Vacations,* 44, 47–48, 49.
40. See Carey McWilliams, *North from Mexico: The Spanish-Speaking People of the United States,* rev. ed., with added material by Matt S. Meier (Westport, CT: Praeger, 1990), 43–53, for more on Anglos' propensity to create a fantasy Spanish heritage in the Southwest.
41. Torres, *Voices from the San Antonio Missions,* 194.
42. *San Antonio Express-News,* September 22, 1984.
43. Susan Toomey Frost, *Colors on Clay: The San José Tile Workshops of San Antonio* (San Antonio: Trinity University Press, 2009), 3–4.
44. Frost, *Colors on Clay,* 48; and *San Antonio Light,* September 22, 1984.
45. Frost, *Colors on Clay,* 148–49.
46. Rena Maverick Green to Harvey P. Smith, December 3, 1937, Rena Maverick Green Papers, 1924–59, Dolph Briscoe Center for American History, University of Texas at Austin (hereafter cited as Rena Maverick Green Papers). See also Frost, *Colors on Clay,* 48–49.
47. Saul E. Bronder, *Social Justice and Church Authority: The Public Life of Archbishop Robert E. Lucey* (Philadelphia: Temple University Press, 1982), 6–9, 21–30, 4–5. Bronder specifically credits the anticapitalist encyclicals from Popes Leo XIII

and Pius XI that emphasize the inherent dignity of laboring classes for inspiring Lucey's interest in social justice issues.

48. Stephen A. Privett, *The U.S. Catholic Church and Its Hispanic Members: The Pastoral Vision of Archbishop Robert E. Lucey* (San Antonio: Trinity University Press, 1988), 3–13.
49. Bremer, *Blessed with Tourists*, 84, 93.
50. Bronder, *Social Justice and Church Authority*, 76–80 (quote on 80); see also Carlos Kevin Blanton, *George I. Sánchez: The Long Fight for Mexican American Immigration* (New Haven, CT: Yale University Press, 2014), 145–49.
51. *Dallas Morning News*, May 7, 1941, Readex America's Historical Newspapers; and Bremer, *Blessed with Tourists*, 84.
52. *Dallas Morning News*, May 7, 1941, Readex America's Historical Newspapers.
53. Bremer, *Blessed with Tourists*, 86.
54. Robert E. Lucey, "Speech, Catholic Conference on the Spanish-Speaking People of Texas, Austin, Texas, April 24, 1952," Addresses, 1952, Robert E. Lucey Papers, Catholic Archives of San Antonio (underline in the original; hereafter cited as Lucey Papers).
55. Bremer, *Blessed with Tourists*, 86.
56. Frost, *Colors on Clay*. Frost's book is richly illustrated with several decades' worth of examples of the tiles that came from Harris's kilns. This was a time when traditional Mexican art and designs enjoyed a period of keen interest in American culture. See also Helen Delpar, *The Enormous Vogue of Things Mexican: Cultural Relations Between the United States and Mexico, 1920–1935* (Tuscaloosa: University of Alabama Press, 1992). Between the mid-1800s and the early 1900s, San Antonio's "Chili Queens" sold chili con carne from makeshift tables on the city's main plazas. While most of these women were of Mexican descent, there were a few Anglos who also had tables. Their customers were both locals and tourists who were on their way to or from the theaters or casinos or just out to partake in the city's nightlife. Over time, the Chili Queens became minor celebrities in their own right through articles in local and national newspapers.
57. Frost, *Colors on Clay*, 10–21, 165–71; and "Ethel Wilson Harris," Interview with Ethel Wilson Harris by Esther MacMillan, September 17, 1976, Bexar County Historical Commission, Oral History Program, Daughters of the Republic of Texas Library at the Alamo, Folder "Biography—Harris, Ethel Wilson," 4001102, 43 (hereafter cited as EWH Oral History, DRT Library).
58. James Wright Steely, *Parks for Texas: Enduring Landscapes of the New Deal* (Austin: University of Texas Press, 1999), 165–66; Frost, *Colors on Clay*, 4–5; and Torres, *Voices from the San Antonio Missions*, 194–213.
59. EWH Oral History, DRT Library, 29.
60. EWH Oral History, DRT Library, 31–32. See also Bremer, *Blessed with Tourists*, 79.
61. EWH Oral History, DRT Library, 31.
62. EWH Oral History, DRT Library, 39.
63. Ethel Wilson Harris, *San José Mission: Queen of the Missions* (San Antonio: Accurate Litho, 1942), 27, 29. On the last page, outlining activities at the mission,

Harris stated, "Pottery and tiles are made and sold within the Mission walls by the Mission Crafts, using native clays and craftsmen" (33).

64. Bremer, *Blessed with Tourists*, 78–80, 93; and Torres, *Voices from the San Antonio Missions*, 207–8.
65. Torres, *Voices from the San Antonio Missions*, 201–8. *Los Pastores* is a traditional Mexican play that recounts the story of the shepherds' journey to visit the newborn Christ Child in Bethlehem.
66. "Arquitectos de nuestros propios destinos: ¿La discriminacion contra los Mexicanos en Texas no es ya serio problema?," *La Prensa*, December 18, 1949, Readex America's Historical Newspapers. Translation by the author.
67. Nora, *Realms of Memory*, xvii.
68. Bremer, *Blessed with Tourists*, 92.
69. Nora, *Realms of Memory*, 14.
70. "Sermon in Honor of the Restoration of La Bahia Presidio, Goliad, Texas, Sunday, October 8, 1967," Addresses, 1967 Lucey Papers, CASA. Bremer quotes this phrase nearly verbatim but cites a different speech from 1973. See Bremer, *Blessed with Tourists*, 92, 176n122.
71. Bremer, *Blessed with Tourists*, 92.
72. Michel-Rolph Trouillot, *Silencing the Past: Power and the Production of History* (Boston: Beacon Press, 1995), 110.
73. David Lowenthal, *The Past Is a Foreign Country* (New York: Cambridge University Press, 1985), 258.
74. Frank Thompson, *The Alamo: A Cultural History* (Dallas: Taylor Trade Publishing, 2001), 243. See also Frank Thompson, *Alamo Movies* (East Berlin, PA: Old Mill Books, 1991); and Frank Thompson, *The Alamo: The Illustrated Story of the Epic Film* (New York: New Market Press, 2004), for the latest cinematic version.
75. Thompson, *Alamo: A Cultural History*, 174–88. This is considered a "lost" film as only a few stills are known to exist.
76. Flores, *Remembering the Alamo*, 98–108.
77. *San Antonio* (Houston: Southern Pacific Lines, ca. 1916), 2–3, 20–21, 28, 29–30, cover.
78. Don Graham, "Mission Statement: The Alamo and the Fallacy of Historical Accuracy in Epic Filmmaking," in *Lone Star Pasts: Memory and History in Texas*, ed. Gregg Cantrell and Elizabeth Hayes Turner (College Station: Texas A&M University Press, 2007), 244.
79. Graham, "Mission Statement," 250–59.
80. "10 Most Disappointing Movies of 2004," *Newsweek*, December 30, 2004, 63, EBSCO.
81. Hedda Hopper, "Disney Brings Native American Folklore Characters to Public as Film Heroes," *Los Angeles Times*, May 9, 1948, ProQuest Historical Los Angeles Times.
82. Randy Roberts and James S. Olson, *A Line in the Sand: The Alamo in Blood and Memory* (New York: Simon and Schuster, 2001), 235–43.
83. Roberts and Olson, *Line in the Sand*, 239. This would be Disney's first live star.

84. "U.S. Again Is Subdued by Davy," *Life*, April 35, 1955, 27, EBSCO; Peter T. White, "Ex-King of the Wild Frontier," *New York Times Magazine*, December 11, 1955, 27; and Roberts and Olson, *Line in the Sand*, 243–44.
85. "Wild Frontier," *Time* 65 (January 3, 1955): 90, EBSCO.
86. John Fischer, "Personal and Otherwise: The Embarrassing Truth About Davy Crockett, the Alamo, Yoknapatawpha County, and Other Dear Myths," *Harper's Magazine*, July 1, 1955, 16, ProQuest Periodicals Archive Online.
87. Roberts and Olson, *Line in the Sand*, 239–40.
88. John Haverstick, "The Two Davy Crocketts," *Saturday Review*, July 1955, 19, 30. The librarians gave Haverstick a bibliography of ten titles about Crockett, plus two not yet published, and an additional five titles (including a coloring book) based on Disney's production.
89. E. J. Kahn, "Books: Be Sure You're Right, Then Go Ahead," *New Yorker*, September 1955, 71, 71–77, 72.
90. "U.S. Again Is Subdued by Davy," 33.
91. "U.S. Again Is Subdued by Davy," 28. It is interesting to observe in the accompanying photographs that the coonskin caps were not limited to boys, but at least two young girls are seen emulating their older brothers' hero worship (see 30–31).
92. "U.S. Again Is Subdued by Davy," 29.
93. Fischer, "The Embarrassing Truth About Davy Crockett," 16; see also Roberts and Olson, *Line in the Sand*, 250–53.
94. Fischer, "The Embarrassing Truth About Davy Crockett," 16.
95. Fischer, "The Embarrassing Truth About Davy Crockett," 16–17.
96. "Yes There Is, Virginia," *Austin Statesman*, July 15, 1955, ProQuest Historical Austin American Statesman.
97. "Crockett and Circulation," *Newsweek*, July 18, 1955, 60–62.
98. White, "Ex-King," 27.
99. White, "Ex-King," 27.
100. Roberts and Olson, *Line in the Sand*, 264, 270; and Donald Clark and Christopher Andersen, *John Wayne's* The Alamo*: The Making of an Epic Film: In TODD-AO* (Hillside, IL: Midwest Publishing, 1994).
101. Roberts and Olson, *Line in the Sand*, 254–76; and Clark and Andersen, *John Wayne's* The Alamo, 24–43.
102. Roberts and Olson, *Line in the Sand*, 271.
103. Flores, *Remembering the Alamo*, 119.
104. Hedda Hopper, "Wayne Has Mission: Arouse Patriotism," *Los Angeles Times*, October 23, 1960, accessed April 29, 2016, ProQuest Historical Los Angeles Times.
105. Flores, *Remembering the Alamo*, 149.
106. Hopper, "Wayne Has Mission"; Clark and Andersen, *John Wayne's* The Alamo, 6–13; and Roberts and Olson, *Line in the Sand*, 261–62.
107. Roberts and Olson, *Line in the Sand*, 261; and Nina McCain, "John Wayne Talks of Men at Alamo," *Dallas Morning News*, January 31, 1960, Readex Historical Dallas Morning News. See also Thomas B. Morgan, "God and Man in Hollywood," *Esquire*,

May 1, 1963, 125, EBSCO Esquire Magazine Archive, where Wayne claimed that Dobie "and other Texas historians had cooperated" in researching the Alamo story.

108. Clark and Andersen, *John Wayne's* The Alamo, 15–22; and Roberts and Olson, *Line in the Sand*, 262–64.
109. William A. Payne, "Mr. Henaghan, 'Alamo' Is No Western, It's Drama of Heroes," *Dallas Morning News*, July 31, 1959, Readex Historical Dallas Morning News; and Richard Nason, "Biggest Western to Cost $8,000,000," *New York Times*, July 29, 1959, ProQuest Historical New York Times.
110. William A. Payne, "Adopted Son Taking Care of History," *Dallas Morning News*, December 13, 1959, Readex Historical Dallas Morning News.
111. Joe R. Landin, "Latins Contributed to Texas Progress," *Dallas Morning News*, October 21, 1959, Readex Historical Dallas Morning News. For more on historical silencing, see Trouillot, *Silencing the Past.*
112. Morgan, "God and Man in Hollywood," 125.
113. Flores, *Remembering the Alamo*, 114, 118–29; and Clark and Andersen, *John Wayne's* The Alamo, 45–59.
114. Flores, *Remembering the Alamo*, 152–55.
115. Roberts and Olson, *Line in the Sand*, 271–72.
116. Russell Birdwell, "There Were No Ghost Writers at the Alamo," *Life*, July 4, 1960, inside front cover, 1, EBSCO Life Magazine Archive. Modern scholars will recognize that Santa Anna's Mexican forces were merely defending territory that at the time of the battle still belonged to Mexico. Texian representatives were still meeting and crafting the Texas Declaration of Independence and Constitution when the Alamo fell on March 6, 1836.
117. "John Wayne Admits His 'Alamo' A 'Message' Pic—Americanism," *Variety*, October 26, 1960, 5, accessed December 16, 2020, ProQuest Entertainment Industry Magazine Archives.
118. Roberts and Olson, *Line in the Sand*, 273.
119. William A. Payne, "Wayne Motion Picture Makes Alamo Siege Live," *Dallas Morning News*, October 26, 1960, Readex Historical Dallas Morning News.
120. Frank X. Tolbert, "Tolbert's Texas: 'Alamo' Exciting but Too Lengthy," *Dallas Morning News*, November 3, 1960, Readex Historical Dallas Morning News.
121. John Bustin, "Show World," *Austin Statesman*, March 2, 1961, ProQuest Historical Austin American Statesman.
122. Philip K. Scheuer, "'Alamo' Wayne Dream Realized," *Los Angeles Times*, October 27, 1960, ProQuest Historical Los Angeles Times.
123. "The Alamo," *Variety*, October 26, 1960, 6, ProQuest Entertainment Industry Magazine Archives.
124. "'B' for Banal," *Newsweek*, October 31, 1960, 90.
125. "Alamo," *Time*, November 7, 1960, 76.
126. Bosley Crowther, "Screen: John Wayne's 3-Hour Remembrance of 'The Alamo,'" *New York Times*, October 27, 1960, ProQuest Historic New York Times.
127. "The Current Cinema," *New Yorker*, November 5, 1960, 187–88.

128. Ben E. Pingenot, "The Alamo," *Time*, November 28, 1960, 5–6, EBSCO Time Magazine Archive.
129. Davis Quinn, "Readers Go on Record," *New York Times*, November 6, 1960, ProQuest Historical New York Times.
130. Kathleen Huttig, "Ticket Ralley," *Los Angeles Times*, November 24, 1960, ProQuest Historical Los Angeles Times.
131. Sven Wahlroos, "Moving Movie," *Los Angeles Times*, March 8, 1961, ProQuest Historical Los Angeles Times.
132. "Daughters of Texas: Fie on N. Y. Critics," *Variety*, November 16, 1960, 2, ProQuest Entertainment Industry Magazine Archives.
133. Roberts and Olson, *Line in the Sand*, 276. For additional information on Wayne's efforts to make his epic film, see Randy Roberts and James S. Olson, *John Wayne: American* (Lincoln: University of Nebraska Press, 1995), 456–79, for additional information on Wayne's efforts to make his epic film.
134. Graham. "Mission Statement," 242, 244.

Chapter 6

1. "Texas: Close to the Land," *Time*, January 17, 1964, 19.
2. Pekka Hämäläinen and Samuel Truett, "On Borderlands," *Journal of American History* 98, no. 2 (2011): 338, http://www.jstor.org/stable/41509959.
3. Hämäläinen and Truett, "On Borderlands," 359. For a discussion on the merits of using the *longue durée* as a means of historical methodology, see Fernand Braudel, "History and the Social Sciences: The *Longue Durée*," in *On History*, by Fernand Braudel, trans. Sarah Matthews (Chicago: University of Chicago Press, 1980), 25–54.
4. Pierre Nora, *Realms of Memory: Rethinking the French Past*, trans. Arthur Goldhammer, English-language edition ed. and foreword by Lawrence D. Kritzman, 3 vols. (New York: Columbia University Press, 1996), 1:xvii.
5. Carey McWilliams, *North from Mexico: The Spanish-Speaking People of the United States*, rev. ed., with added material by Matt S. Meier (Westport, CT: Praeger, 1990), 43–53.
6. "They Talk of Tourists at Alamo,!" *Austin Statesman*, May 4, 1962, ProQuest Historical Austin American Statesman.
7. "Texas Tourism Showed 3.4 Million Gain in '65," *Austin Statesman*, February 19, 1966, ProQuest Historical Austin American Statesman.
8. Richard K. Popp, *The Holiday Makers: Magazines, Advertising, and Mass Tourism in Postwar America* (Baton Rouge: Louisiana State University Press, 2012), 11–18.
9. "How to Discover the Real America: The 15 Places That Everyone Should Visit," *Changing Times*, June 1968, 17, ProQuest ABI/Inform.
10. "How to Discover the Real America," 18. See Eric G. E. Zuelow, *A History of Modern Tourism* (New York: Palgrave Macmillan, 2016), for an informative discussion of the distinctions between "tourists" and "travelers" and the expectations that travel would bring edification and self-improvement.

11. Popp, *The Holiday Makers*, 4, 91–92, 109.
12. "San Antonio Mirrors Its Past," *Chicago Tribune*, June 14, 1959, ProQuest Historical Chicago Tribune. This article also appeared in a shortened form on June 21, 1959, in the *Baltimore Sun*, ProQuest Historical Baltimore Sun. Although no wire service was credited, sharing the reports increased San Antonio's visibility to more potential tourists.
13. Henry N. Ferguson, "San Antonio Is Venice of the Texas Plains," *Chicago Tribune*, December 1, 1963, ProQuest Historical Chicago Tribune.
14. Marguerite Johnson, "Texas Treasures: Missions Along San Antonio River Are a Page out of a Colorful Past," *New York Times*, February 27, 1966, ProQuest Historical New York Times.
15. Charles Layng, "San Antonio Plans a 15-Mile Mission Parkway," *New York Times*, October 16, 1966, ProQuest Historical New York Times.
16. "How to Discover the Real America," 21–22.
17. Rick Timmons, "Missions in Texas Beat California's," *Austin Statesman*, October 16, 1970, ProQuest Historical Austin American Statesman. A search for a related article in the digital ProQuest Historic Los Angeles Times was unsuccessful. As the digital copy is made from the existing microfilm, Timmons's story may have appeared in an edition that was not preserved.
18. Richard Joseph, "San Antonio—Texas Town a Rose by Any Other Name," *Los Angeles Times*, December 13, 1970, ProQuest Historical Los Angeles Times.
19. Robert Deardorff, "Step by Step Through San Antonio," *Travel*, May 1974, 26–28, 30–31.
20. Garrett Sutherland, "San Antonio," *Travel/Holiday*, November 1979, 64.
21. See *San Antonio Light*, September 18, 1935, NewsBank Access World News; and Thomas S. Bremer, *Blessed with Tourists: The Borderlands of Religion and Tourism in San Antonio* (Chapel Hill: University of North Carolina Press, 2004), 111.
22. *Dallas Morning News*, June 24, 1958, Readex America's Historical Newspapers.
23. Bremer, *Blessed with Tourists*, 113–14.
24. US Congress, House, Hearing Before the Subcommittee on National Parks and Recreation of the Committee on Interior and Insular Affairs: To Authorize the Establishment of the San Antonio Missions National Historical Park in the State of Texas, and for Other Purposes, H.R. 14064, 94th Cong., 2d sess., November 9, 1976, 11–88.
25. US Congress, House, Hearing, H.R. 14064, 44–45, 31–32, 15.
26. Nora, *Realms of Memory*, xvii.
27. US Congress, House, Hearing, H.R. 14064, 29.
28. Tom Nelson, "Citizens Still Upset by Plans for Park," *San Antonio Express*, November 30, 1977, NewsBank Access World News.
29. Ralph Winningham, "Mission Parks Bill Met with Praise, Mourning," *San Antonio Express*, November 12, 1978, NewsBank Access World News.
30. Winningham, "Mission Parks Bill"; see also Lamont Wood, "Mission Pastor Mourns Bill," *San Antonio Light*, November 12, 1978, NewsBank Access World News.

31. Linda Jones, "Parishioners Voice Fears: 'Way of Life Threatened,'" *San Antonio Light*, November 26, 1978, NewsBank Access World News.
32. *Washington Post*, February 18, 1979, ProQuest Historic Washington Post.
33. "Mission Park Gets $694,000," *San Antonio Light*, September 21, 1979, NewsBank Access World News.
34. "Priests, Parishioners to Air Proposals on Missions' Land," *San Antonio Express*, August 20, 1980; and Don Politico, "Battle of San Jose Is over Control," *San Antonio Light*, February 28, 1982, NewsBank Access World News.
35. Bremer, *Blessed with Tourists*, 112–13.
36. Rick Thurmond, "Mission Espada a 'Living Entity,'" *San Antonio Light*, October 5, 1981, NewsBank Access World News.
37. Torres, *Voices from the San Antonio Missions*, 79 (emphasis in the original). The interview was conducted in 1995, over a decade after the NPS moved in.
38. Resolution by the Parish Council, San Francisco de la Espada, July 11, 1983, Old Spanish Missions Collection, Catholic Archives of the Archdiocese of San Antonio (hereafter cited as CASA).
39. Since July 2023, the NPS website for the San Antonio Missions National Historical Park has had a link containing stories of descendants of the missions called "We're Still Here: San Antonio Mission Descendant Stories," updated June 12, 2024, https://www.nps.gov/saan/learn/historyculture/we-re-still-here-san-antonio-mission-descendant-stories.htm.
40. Bremer, *Blessed with Tourists*, 121–31.
41. Ray Duncan, "Heart of Texas," *Holiday* May 1955, 140–41.
42. Dan Kilgore and James E. Crisp, *How Did Davy Die? And Why Do We Care So Much?* (College Station: Texas A&M University Press, 2010), 57–60.
43. Fred Hift, "John Wayne Is Manning Three Posts," *Christian Science Monitor*, October 27, 1959, ProQuest Historical Christian Science Monitor.
44. Kilgore and Crisp, *How Did Davy Die?*, 9–48.
45. R. M. Potter, "The Fall of the Alamo," *Magazine of American History*, January 1878, 13; and Theodore Roosevelt, "Remember the Alamo: Hero-Tales from American History," *St. Nicholas: An Illustrated Magazine for Young Folks*, September 1895, 926–28, ProQuest American Periodicals Series Online. Roosevelt's text suggests a wounded and weakened Crockett was shot by a group of musketeers, as no single Mexican soldier could finish him with a bayonet. However, Roosevelt also acknowledges that other writers had claimed Crockett was felled by his wounds but taken still alive to Santa Anna, who then ordered his execution. The illustration accompanying Roosevelt's article shows a defeated man in buckskins and coonskin cap with his back against a wall and pistol dangling from one hand being shot by a rank of enemy soldiers drawn up as a firing squad (928).
46. José Enrique de la Peña, *With Santa Anna in Texas: A Personal Narrative of the Revolution*, trans. Carmen Perry (College Station: Texas A&M University Press, 1975), 53.
47. James E. Crisp, *Sleuthing the Alamo: Davy Crockett's Last Stand and Other Mysteries of the Texas Revolution* (London: Oxford University Press, 2005), 61–138; and

Bill Groneman, *Death of a Legend: The Myth and Mystery Surrounding the Death of Davy Crockett* (Plano: Republic of Texas Press, 1999), 113–58. See also David B. Gracy II, "'Just as I Have Written It': A Study of the Authenticity of the Manuscript of José Enrique de la Peña's Account of the Texas Campaign," *Southwestern Historical Quarterly* 105, no. 2 (2001): 254–91.

48. John Lumpkin, "Davy Crockett Captured? Alamo Legend Disputed," *Dallas Morning News*, September 10, 1975, Readex America's Historical Newspapers; and Jack Maguire, "Historical Account Says Crockett Was Executed," *Austin American-Statesman*, June 6, 1976, ProQuest Historical Newspapers. Kilgore also noted that Carmen Perry, the translator, was awarded the ignominious "Bum Steer" award by *Texas Monthly* magazine. Kilgore and Crisp, *How Did Davy Die?*, 14.
49. "History Buff Massacres Crockett Legend," *Austin American-Statesman*, April 21, 1978, ProQuest Historical Newspapers. The article was slightly edited and reprinted the next day.
50. "Down on Davy," *Austin American-Statesman*, April 25, 1978, ProQuest Historical Newspapers.
51. "Davy Crockett in Trouble with Texas Historian," *Christian Science Monitor*, May 8, 1978, ProQuest Historical Newspapers. However, the writer's choice of words requires a bit more inquiry. How does a person's execution not qualify as a "martyr's death" when the same person's death in battle would? Certainly, the early Christians executed by the Romans are considered martyrs by many modern believers.
52. Kilgore and Crisp, *How Did Davy Die?*, 89–95; Paul Andrew Hutton, "The Alamo as Icon," in *The Texas Military Experience: From the Texas Revolution Through World War II*, ed. Joseph G. Dawson III (College Station: Texas A&M University Press, 1995), 14; Richard R. Flores, *Remembering the Alamo: Memory, Modernity, and the Master Symbol* (Austin: University of Texas Press, 2002), 147–52; David Montejano, *Anglos and Mexicans in the Making of Texas, 1836–1986* (Austin: University of Texas Press, 1987), 223–25; Arnoldo de León, *They Called Them Greasers: Anglo Attitudes Toward Mexicans in Texas, 1821–1900* (Austin: University of Texas Press, 1983), 66; and Holly Beachley Brear, *Inherit the Alamo: Myth and Ritual at an American Shrine* (Austin: University of Texas Press, 1995).
53. Maurice Halbwachs, *The Collective Memory*, trans. Francis J. Ditter Jr. and Vida Yazdi Ditter (New York: Harper and Row, 1980), 78–80.
54. William Groneman III, *David Crocket: Hero of the Common Man* (New York: Forge, 2005), 162–75. Groneman has also published under the name "Bill Groneman."
55. Groneman, *David Crockett*, 179–83; and Crisp, *Sleuthing the Alamo*, 65–102.
56. Groneman, *David Crockett*, 189–90.
57. Jan Reid, "Davy Crock?," *Texas Monthly*, May 1995, 74, EBSCO; and Kilgore and Crisp, *How Did Davy Die?*, 96–103.
58. Flores, *Remembering the Alamo*, 146, 145–47, 149–52.
59. Robert Rivard, "Remember the Alamo: The Growing Debate over the Shrine of Texas Liberty," *San Antonio Express-News*, February 27, 1994, NewsBank Access World News. Texas historians such as Walter Buenger and Ty Cashion

have criticized Fehrenbach's Texas history books as obsolete and unsuitable for a modern, multicultural Texas. But Cashion admits that in the popular mind, Fehrenbach casts a very long shadow. See Walter L. Buenger, "Three Truths in Texas," in *Beyond Texas Through Time: Breaking away from Past Interpretations*, ed. Walter L. Buenger and Arnoldo De León (College Station: Texas A&M University Press, 2011), 7; and Ty Cashion, *Lone Star Mind* (Norman: University of Oklahoma Press, 2018), 8–9.

60. Paul Andrew Hutton, "Davy Crockett, Still King of the Wild Frontier: And a Hell of a Nice Guy Besides," *Texas Monthly*, November 1986, 122, 246 (emphasis in the original).
61. "Roar of the Crowd," *Texas Monthly*, January 1987, 10.
62. Debbie Nathan, "Forget the Alamo," *Texas Monthly*, April 1998, ProQuest ABI/Inform.
63. "Roar of the Crowd," *Texas Monthly*, June 1998, ProQuest ABI/Inform.
64. Gregory Curtis, "Should We Care?," *Texas Monthly*, March 2000, 9–12, EBSCO.
65. "Roar of the Crowd," *Texas Monthly*, May 2000, 14. Bill Groneman also wrote in to offer corrections to Curtis's editorial.
66. Michael Kammen, *Mystic Chords of Memory: The Transformation of Tradition in American Culture* (New York: Vintage Books, 1993; first published New York: Knopf, 1991; page references are to 1993 Vintage ed.), 647.
67. Bremer, *Blessed with Tourists*, 121; and *Gente de Razón: People of the Missions*, dir. John Grabowska (Tucson, AZ: Western National Parks Association, 1998), DVD.
68. Bremer, *Blessed with Tourists*, 121.
69. Bremer, *Blessed with Tourists*, 121–22.
70. Halbwachs, *Collective Memory*, 151–52.
71. Monsignor Balthasar J. Janacek Archival Papers, CASA (hereafter cited as Janacek Papers, CASA).
72. "Indians Want Road Closed in Front of Alamo," *Houston Chronicle*, January 26, 1994, NewsBank America's News.
73. *San Antonio Express-News*, February 20, 1994, and November 26, 1999, NewsBank Access World News.
74. *San Antonio Express-News*, February 20, 1994, NewsBank Access World News.
75. *San Antonio Express-News*, November 26 and November 27, 1999, NewsBank Access World News.
76. Alston V. Thoms, ed., *Reassessing Cultural Extinction: Change and Survival at Mission San Juan Capistrano, Texas* (College Station and San Antonio: Center for Ecological Archaeology, Texas A&M University, and San Antonio Missions National Historic Park, 2001), iii, 50–53.
77. Daniel J. Gelo, "The Indigenous Borderlands: Cultures Without Borders," in *Bridging Cultures: Reflections on the Heritage Identity of the Texas-Mexico Borderlands*, by Harriett D. Romo and William A. Dupont (College Station: Texas A&M University Press, 2021), 34.

78. Memo, March 22, 1995, from Archbishop Patrick F. Flores to Bishops Bernard Popp and John Yanta, and Monsignors Patrick J. Murry, Larry Stuebben, and Balty Janacek, Re: Native American Letter, with attachments, Janacek Papers, CASA.
79. Memo, May 6, 1995, Dr. Félix D. Almaráz Jr. to Archbishop Patrick Flores, Janacek Papers, CASA.
80. John Davidson, "Coahuiltecans," *San Antonio Express-News*, April 1, 2001, NewsBank Access World News.
81. Thoms, *Reassessing Cultural Extinction*, 44.
82. For invented traditions, see Eric Hobsbawm and Terence Ranger, eds., *The Invention of Tradition* (Cambridge: Cambridge University Press, 1992); and on historical silences, see Michel Rolph Trouillot, *Silencing the Past: Power and the Production of History* (Boston: Beacon Press, 1995).
83. *San Antonio Express-News*, November 26, 2009, November 19, 2012; January 25, 2013; February 22, 2013; July 21, 2016; August 29, 2016; September 4, 2017; March 25, 2018; and May 1, 2018, NewsBank America's News.
84. "Native Dance of Missions Reintroduced," *San Antonio Express-News*, May 28, 2004, NewsBank America's News.
85. Howard Benoist and María Eva Flores, eds., *Documents Relating to the Old Spanish Missions of Texas: Guidelines for a Texas Mission: Instructions for the Missionary of Mission Concepción in San Antonio* (San Antonio: Old Spanish Missions Historical Research Library, Our Lady of the Lake University, 1994), 1:35; and Kristin Dutcher Mann, *The Power of Song: Music and Dance in the Mission Communities of Northern New Spain, 1590–1810* (Stanford, CA: Stanford University Press and the Academy of American Franciscan History in Berkeley, 2010), 146–51.
86. "Native Dance of Missions Reintroduced," *San Antonio Express-News*, May 28, 2004.
87. Edward Tabor Linenthal, *Sacred Ground: Americans and Their Battlefields*, 2nd ed. (Urbana: University of Illinois Press, 1993), 55.
88. Holly Beachley Brear, "We Run the Alamo and You Don't: Alamo Battles of Ethnicity and Gender," in *Where These Memories Grow: History, Memory, and Southern Identity*, ed. W. Fitzhugh Brundage (Chapel Hill: University of North Carolina Press, 2000), 302; and Brear, *Inherit the Alamo*, 95–131.
89. "Talk Given at 'Music at the Missions' Mass, June 19, 1988, at Mission San Antonio de Valero–The Alamo," Janacek Papers, CASA.
90. Zev Chafets, "The Post-Hispanic Hispanic Politician: Will Julián Castro, the 35-Year-Old Mayor of San Antonio be the Next Great Latino Hope on the National Stage?," *New York Times*, May 9, 2010, ProQuest Historical New York Times. Rosie Castro was the mother of then–San Antonio Mayor Julián Castro.
91. Flores, *Remembering the Alamo*, xiii.
92. Gregory Curtis, "Behind the Lines," *Texas Monthly*, February 1984, 5, 8.
93. "Roar of the Crowd," *Texas Monthly*, April 1984, 16–18.
94. Jan Jarboe Russell, "We Will Never Surrender, or Retreat," *Texas Monthly*, May 1994, EBSCO.
95. Russell, "We Will Never Surrender."
96. *San Antonio Express-News*, March 6, 2009, NewsBank Access World News.

97. Scott Huddleston, "Problem Hangs over Alamo," *San Antonio Express-News*, March 6, 2010, NewsBank Access World News. This article also appeared the same day under a different title in the *Houston Chronicle*, NewsBank Access World News.
98. Scott Huddleston, "Alamo Keepers' Spending Criticized, 17.5% of License Plate Proceeds Spent on Shrine," *Houston Chronicle*, September 29, 2009, NewsBank Access World News.
99. Josh Baugh, "Cracks in Roof of Alamo OK Says Report, but Other Fixes Are Suggested to Prevent Seepage," *Houston Chronicle*, August 1, 2010, NewsBank Access World News.
100. Jan Jarboe Russell, "No Retreat! No Surrender!," *Texas Monthly*, October 2010, EBSCO.
101. James McKinley, "Critics Accuse Group of a Serious Texas Sin: Forgetting the Alamo," *New York Times*, December 5, 2010, ProQuest Historical New York Times.
102. *San Antonio Express-News*, April 12, 2011, NewsBank Access World News.
103. "Our Turn: Improvement in Alamo Oversight," *San Antonio Express-News*, June 5, 2011, NewsBank Access World News.
104. *San Antonio Express-News*, December 16, 2011, NewsBank Access World News.
105. Jerry Patterson, "Guest Voices: Alamo's Place as a Shrine Lost," *San Antonio Express*, March 7, 2012, NewsBank America's News.
106. Office of the Attorney General of Texas, *Report to the Texas Legislature Investigation of the Daughters of the Republic of Texas*, November 2012, 13. The author would like to thank Mark Lambert, director of the Texas General Land Office Archives, for sending a copy of this report as well as other research materials and suggestions.
107. *San Antonio Express-News*, November 22, 2012, NewsBank Access World News.
108. *San Antonio Express-News*, November 29, 2012, NewsBank Access World News.
109. *San Antonio Express-News*, January 6, 2013, NewsBank Access World News.
110. *San Antonio Express-News*, August 11, 2013, NewsBank Access World News.
111. John F. Sears, *Sacred Places: American Tourist Attractions in the Nineteenth Century* (New York: Oxford University Press, 1989), 211.
112. The tourist attraction located in the historic Woolworth building combined a haunted house, indoor roller-coaster-style ride, with a museum dedicated to Guinness World Records. However, according to SACS and Lewis Fisher, this Woolworth building is "a civil rights landmark" for having the first lunch counter to serve African Americans in the South. See Lewis F. Fisher, *Saving San Antonio: The Preservation of a Heritage*, 2nd ed. (San Antonio: Maverick Books, an Imprint of Trinity University Press, 2016), 511.
113. *San Antonio Express-News*, June 25 and June 27, 2014, NewsBank Access World News.
114. Chris Tomlinson, Jason Stanford, and Bryan Burrough, "The Battle of the Alamo!" *Texas Monthly*, June 2021, 86–142, EBSCO.
115. *San Antonio Express-News*, March 13, 2015, NewsBank Access World News.
116. *San Antonio Express-News*, March 15, 2015, NewsBank Access World News.
117. *San Antonio Express-News*, March 18, 2010, NewsBank Access World News.
118. Fisher, *Saving San Antonio: The Preservation of a Heritage*, 552–53.

119. Civic and private commercial organizations other than SACS and the Archdiocese of San Antonio contributed personnel and other resources, including the City of San Antonio, Bexar County, the DRT, the Texas GLO, the US NPS (including San Antonio Missions National Historical Park), the San Antonio River Authority, Los Compadres de San Antonio Missions National Historical Park, the National Parks Conservation Association, and Ford, Powell & Carson, Architects and Planners. See US Department of the Interior, *San Antonio Missions: Nomination for Inscription on the World Heritage List*, prepared by Paul Ringenbach, 2015, 326–30, "Nomination File," https://whc.unesco.org/en/list/1466/documents/.
120. Paula D. Piper to Fr. Martin Leopold, Moderator of the Curia, Archdiocese of San Antonio, January 24, 2007, copy to Father Balty, Janacek Papers, CASA.
121. "Society in Action: Society Made World Heritage Nomination Its 'Mission,'" June 25, 2015, SACS, https://www.saconservation.org/Advocacy/SocietyinAction/tabid/119/ArticleID/563/ArtMID/508/Society-Made-World-Heritage-Nomination-its-Mission.aspx; see also Scott Huddleston, "Missions Gain World Honor," *San Antonio Express-News*, July 6, 2015, NewsBank America's News.
122. Colin McDonald, "Union of Church and State," *San Antonio Express-News*, August 17, 2008, NewsBank America's News.
123. Vianna Davila, "Missions Catch Filmmaker's Attention," *San Antonio Express-News*, September 27, 2009, NewsBank America's News.
124. UNESCO, "The Criteria for Selection," UNESCO World Heritage Convention, accessed August 18, 2016, http://whc.unesco.org/en/criteria.
125. *San Antonio Express-News*, July 7, 2013, NewsBank Access World News.
126. *San Antonio Express-News*, September 28, 2011, NewsBank Access World News.
127. "Another View: Pay UNESCO Dues, Get Missions' Status," *San Antonio Express-News*, June 6, 2013, NewsBank Access World News; *San Antonio Express-News*, July 7, 2013, NewsBank Access World News.
128. *San Antonio Express-News*, December 1 and December 13, 2013, NewsBank Access World News.
129. *San Antonio Express-News*, January 10, 2014, NewsBank Access World News.
130. Missions of San Antonio, *San Antonio Missions, Texas, United States of America: Nomination to the World Heritage List by the United States of America*, January 2014, 159–62, http://www.missionsofsanantonio.org/publications.html. See also UNESCO, "Criteria for Selection."
131. Missions of San Antonio, *San Antonio Missions*, 159.
132. Daniel D. Arreola, *Tejano South Texas: A Mexican American Cultural Province* (Austin: University of Texas Press, 2002), 131–49, 189–205.
133. Scott Huddleston, "Officials Bash Rumors That Alamo, Other Missions Will Be Run by U.N.," *San Antonio Express-News*, October 31, 2013, NewsBank America's News.
134. *San Antonio Express-News*, February 9, 2015, NewsBank Access World News.
135. *San Antonio Express-News*, February 25, 2015, NewsBank Access World News.
136. *San Antonio Express-News*, April 22, 2015, NewsBank Access World News.
137. "SB 191," Texas Legislature Online, accessed August 8, 2022, https://capitol.texas.gov/BillLookup/History.aspx?LegSess=84R&Bill=SB191.

138. Gilbert Garcia, "Puro San Antonio: Sen. Campbell's Alamo Paranoia Fuels World Heritage Truthers," *San Antonio Express-News*, July 12, 2015, NewsBank America's News.
139. Scott Huddleston, "Missions Gain World Honor: UNESCO Committee Grants Heritage Site Recognition," *San Antonio Express-News*, July 6, 2015, NewsBank America's News.
140. Vincent T. Davis, "Heritage Status Draws Visitors to Missions," *San Antonio Express-News*, July 7, 2015, NewsBank America's News.
141. "Mass to Celebrate World Heritage Site Designation," *San Antonio Express-News*, July 12, 2015, NewsBank America's News.
142. David J. Weber, *The Spanish Frontier in North America* (New Haven, CT: Yale University Press, 1992), 335.

Bibliography

Primary Sources, Manuscripts

Bexar County Historical Commission, Oral History Program. Interview with Ethel Wilson Harris by Esther MacMillan, September 17, 1976. Daughters of the Republic of Texas Research Library, San Antonio, Texas.

Bouchu, Francis. Papers. Catholic Archives of Texas, Texas Catholic Conference of Bishops, Austin, Texas.

Bouchu, Francis. Priest File. Catholic Archives of San Antonio (CASA), San Antonio, Texas.

De Zavala, Adina Emilia. Papers, 1766 (1831–1855). Dolph Briscoe Center for American History, University of Texas at Austin.

Drossaerts, Arthur. Papers. Catholic Archives of Texas, Texas Catholic Conference of Bishops, Austin, Texas.

Everett, Edward. Papers. Cushing Memorial Library, Texas A&M University, College Station, Texas.

Garriga, M. S. Papers (unprocessed as of June 19, 2019). Catholic Archives of Texas, Texas Catholic Conference of Bishops, Austin, Texas.

Green, Rena Maverick. Papers, 1924–1959. Dolph Briscoe Center for American History, University of Texas at Austin.

Hueurmann, Charles. Collection. San Antonio Conservation Society Library, San Antonio, Texas.

Janacek, Monsignor Balthasar J. Archival Papers. Catholic Archives of San Antonio (CASA), San Antonio, Texas.

Lucey, Robert E. Papers. Catholic Archives of San Antonio (CASA), San Antonio, Texas.

Meeting Minutes. San Antonio Conservation Society Library, San Antonio, Texas.

Old Spanish Missions. Collection. Catholic Archives of San Antonio (CASA), San Antonio, Texas.

San Antonio Guidebook Collection. Daughters of the Republic of Texas Research Library, San Antonio, Texas.

Smith, Harvey P., Sr. Vertical File-Biography. Daughters of the Republic of Texas Research Library, San Antonio, Texas.

Special Collections and Texana Collection. Sisters of Charity of the Incarnate Word Archives, J. E. and L. E. Mabee Library, University of the Incarnate Word, San Antonio, Texas.

Primary Sources, Newspapers (in Microfilm and/or Electronic Format)

Atlanta Constitution

Austin American-Statesman (including *Austin Statesman* and *Daily Statesman*)

Baltimore Patriot & Mercantile Advertiser

Baltimore Sun

Chicago Tribune (and *Daily Tribune*)

Christian Science Monitor (Boston)

Daily Picayune (New Orleans)

Dallas Morning News

Enquirer (Richmond, VA)

Evening Star (Washington, DC)

Georgia Telegraph (Macon, GA)

Houston Chronicle

Houston Post

Idaho Daily Statesman (Boise)

Indianapolis Morning Star

La Prensa (San Antonio)

Las Novedades (New York City)

Los Angeles Times

Louisville Courier-Journal

Morning Olympian (Olympia, WA)

New Hampshire Sentinel (Keene)

New York Times

New York World

Omaha Daily Bee

Philadelphia Inquirer

Pittsburgh Leader

Pittsfield Sun (Pittsfield, MA)

Salt Lake City Herald

San Antonio Express (including *Daily Express* and *Express-News*)

San Antonio Ledger and Texan

San Antonio Light (and *San Antonio Daily Light*)

Savannah Morning News

Savannah Tribune

Southern Magazine
Southern Patriot (Charleston, SC)
St. Louis Globe-Democrat
St. Louis Post-Dispatch
St. Louis Republic
Telegraph and Messenger (Macon, GA)
Telegraph and Texas Register (Houston)
Wall Street Journal
Washington Post

Primary Sources, Published Materials, Databases, and Websites

1860 United States Federal Census. Accessed August 8, 2016. Ancestry Library Edition.
74 Cong. Rec. 12737 (1935). Accessed June 25, 2019. ProQuest Congressional.
80 Cong. Rec. H7351–7354 (statement of Rep. Maverick). Bound edition. Accessed June 25, 2019. ProQuest Congressional.
"Alamo." *Time*, November 7, 1960.
"The Alamo." *Variety*, October 26, 1960. ProQuest Entertainment Industry Magazine Archives.
All America Is Invited to Visit Texas' Centennial Celebration. Dallas: State Headquarters, Texas Centennial Celebrations, 1935.
Aniol, Claude B. *San Antonio: City of Missions*. New York: Hastings House, 1942.
Ayers, Atlee B. "The Earliest Mission Buildings of San Antonio, Texas." *American Architect and the Architectural Review*, August 27, 1924.
"'B' for Banal." *Newsweek*, October 31, 1960.
Bartlett, John Russell. *Personal Narrative of Explorations and Incidents in Texas, New Mexico, California, Sonora, and Chihuahua, Connected with the United States and Mexican Boundary Commission During the Years 1850, '51, '52, and '53*. New York: Appleton, 1854. Reprint, Chicago: Rio Grande Press, 1965.
Beautiful San Antonio: The Commercial and Industrial Center of the Southwest. San Antonio: Business Men's Club, 1906.
Benjamin, Robert S. "HemisFair '68: And a Glimpse of the City Where It Is to Be Held." *Mexican-American Review*, March 1967.
Benoist, Howard, and María Eva Flores, eds. *Documents Relating to the Old Spanish Missions of Texas: Guidelines for a Texas Mission: Instructions for the Missionary of Mission Concepción in San Antonio*. Vol. 1. San Antonio: Old Spanish Missions Historical Research Library, Our Lady of the Lake University, 1994.
Berlandier, Jean Louis. *Journey to Mexico During the Years 1826 to 1834*. 7 vols. in 2. Translated by Sheila M. Ohlendorf, Josette M. Bigelow, and Mary M. Standifer. Austin: Texas State Historical Association, 1980.
"Bexar and Its Antiquities." *Gleason's Pictorial Drawing-Room Companion*, February 18, 1854. EBSCO American Antiquarian Society Historical Periodicals Collection.
Birdwell, Russell. "There Were No Ghost Writers at the Alamo." *Life*, July 4, 1960. EBSCO Life Magazine Archive.

[Bollaert, William]. "Hunting in Western Texas, and Visit to San Antonio de Bejar in 1843." *A New Sporting Magazine*, December 1848. ProQuest British Periodicals.

Bollaert, William. *William Bollaert's Texas*. Edited by W. Eugene Hollon and Ruth Lapham Butler. Norman: University of Oklahoma Press, 1956.

Celiz, Fray Francisco. *Diary of the Alarcón Expedition into Texas, 1718–1719*. Translated by Fritz Leo Hoffman. Los Angeles: Quivira Society, 1935. Reprint, New York: Arno Press, 1967.

Census by Families of Mission Concepción, 1792. Translated from Bexar Archives, Dolph Briscoe Center for American History, University of Texas at Austin. Accessed May 12, 2025. Bexar Archives Online, https://briscoecenter.org/.

Census by Families of San José Mission, 1792. Translated from Bexar Archives, Dolph Briscoe Center for American History, University of Texas at Austin. Accessed May 12, 2025. Bexar Archives Online, https://briscoecenter.org/.

Census of Espada Mission, Feb. 27, 1815. Folder O. S. M. Espada-Census 1815, 1819, Box 1, Old Spanish Missions Collections, Catholic Archives of San Antonio (CASA), San Antonio, Texas.

Census of Espada Mission and San Juan Capistrano, 1819. Folder O. S. M. Espada-Census 1815, 1819, Box 1, Old Spanish Missions Collections, Catholic Archives of San Antonio (CASA), San Antonio, Texas.

Cervin, Olaf Z. "The Spanish-Mexican Missions of the United States." *Architectural Record*, September 1903.

[Chamber of Commerce]. *San Antonio*. San Antonio: Chamber of Commerce of San Antonio, ca. 1920.

Collingwood, G. C. "The City of the Alamo: How the Romance of San Antonio's Past Blends with Its Present Marvelous Development." *Sunset*, April 1906.

Conder, Josiah. *The Modern Traveller: A Popular Description, Geographical, Historical and Topographical of the Various Countries of the Globe*. 10 vols. Boston: Wells and Lilly, 1830. Gale Cengage Learning Sabin Americana database.

Corner, William. *San Antonio de Bexar: A Guide and History*. San Antonio: Bainbridge and Corner, 1890. Reprint, San Antonio: Graphic Arts, 1977.

Crane, Stephen. *The University of Virginia Edition of the Works of Stephen Crane*. Edited by Fredson Bowers. 11 vols. Charlottesville: University of Virginia Press, 1973.

Criminal Proceedings Against Antonio Tello, Charged with Killing Matías Treviso. August 21, 1744. Translated by Helen Mar Hunnicutt from the Bexar Archives, 71–102. Dolph Briscoe Center for American History, University of Texas at Austin. Accessed May 12, 2025. Bexar Archives Online, https://briscoecenter.org/.

"Crockett and Circulation." *Newsweek*, July 18, 1955.

Cunningham, James B. *A Legend of Mission San José*. San Antonio: Nic Tengg, ca. 1930.

"The Current Cinema." *New Yorker*, November 5, 1960.

Curtis, Gregory. "Behind the Lines." *Texas Monthly*, February 1984.

Curtis, Gregory. "Should We Care?" *Texas Monthly*, March 2000. EBSCO.

"Daughters of Texas: Fie on N.Y. Critics." *Variety*, November 16, 1960. ProQuest Entertainment Industry Magazine Archives.

Davis, Kenneth S. "Coonskin Superman." *New York Times Magazine*, April 24, 1955.

Davis, Richard Harding. "The West from a Car Window." *Harper's Weekly*, March 5, 1892. HarpWeek.

"Davy Crockett—King of the Wild Frontier." *Variety*, May 18, 1955. ProQuest Entertainment Industry Magazine Archive.

"Davy: Row and a Riddle." *Newsweek*, July 4, 1955.

de la Peña, José Enrique. *With Santa Anna in Texas: A Personal Narrative of the Revolution*. Translated and edited by Carmen Perry. College Station: Texas A&M University Press, 1975.

de la Teja, Jesús F., ed. *Wilderness Missions: Preliminary Studies of the Texas Catholic Historical Society II*. Austin: Texas Catholic Historical Society, 1999.

De Zavala, Adina. *History and Legends of the Alamo and Other Missions in and Around San Antonio*. Edited by Richard Flores. San Antonio: Adina De Zavala, 1917. Reprint, Houston: Arte Público Press, 1996.

Deardorff, Robert. "Step by Step Through San Antonio." *Travel*, May 1974.

"Death of Father Bouchu." *Southern Messenger*, August 22, 1907.

"Decline of a Hero." *Collier's*, November 1955.

"The Defence of the Alamo in 1836." *Littell's Living Age*, October 24, 1846. ProQuest American Periodicals Series.

Didion, Joan. "Wayne at the Alamo." *National Review*, December 31, 1960. EBSCO National Review Archive.

Dolores y Biana, Fr. Mariano Francisco de los. *1759 Report of Fr. Mariano Francisco de los Dolores y Biana*. Translated by Rosalind Z. Rock from Archivo Franciscano—Convento de Querétaro/Celaya, Our Lady of the Lake University. San Antonio: San Antonio Missions National Historical Park, 2007. Printed copy in possession of the author.

Dolores y Viana, Fray Mariano de los. *Letters and Memorials of Fray Mariano de los Dolores y Viana, 1737–1762: Documents on the Missions of Texas from the Archives of the College of Querétaro*. Translated by Fr. Benedict Leutenegger. San Antonio: Old Spanish Missions Historical Research Library at Our Lady of the Lake University, 1985.

Duncan, Ray. "Heart of Texas." *Holiday*, May 1955.

Durand, Herbert. *The City of Missions: San Antonio, Texas. Its Romantic and Patriotic History. Its Delightful Climate and Healthful Surroundings. Its Enterprise and Wonderful Prosperity*. St. Louis: Woodward and Tiernan Printing, 1894.

Everett, Edward. "A Narrative of Military Experience in Several Capacities." *Transactions of the Illinois State Historical Society for the Year 1905*. Springfield: Illinois State Historical Library, 1905.

Everett, Richard. "Things in and About San Antonio." *Frank Leslie's Illustrated Newspaper*, January 15, 1859. Portal to Texas History, http://texashistory.unt.edu/ark:/67531/metapth30324/.

Ewing, Paul A. "The Borderland Missions." *Sunset*, October 1927.

Farbar, Jerome. "Investment in the Greatest State: What Texas Needs and What She Offers." *Sunset*, November 1912.

Fee, Charles S. "How the Southern Pacific Advertises." *Graphic Arts: A Magazine for Printers and the Use of Printing*, December 1911.

Fernandez de Santa Ana, Fray Benito. *Letters and Memorials of the Father Presidente Fray Benito Fernandez de Santa Ana, 1736–1754: Documents on the Missions of Texas from the Archives of the College of Querétaro*. Translated by Fr. Benedict Leutenegger. San Antonio: Old Spanish Missions Historical Research Library at Our Lady of the Lake University, 1981.

Field, Joseph Emerson. *Three Years in Texas: Including a View of the Texan Revolution and an Account of the Principal Battles: Together with Descriptions of the Soil, Commercial and Agricultural Advantages, &c.* Boston: Abel Tompkins, 1836. Gale Cengage Learning Sabin Americana database.

Fischer, John. "Personal and Otherwise: The Embarrassing Truth About Davy Crockett, the Alamo, Yoknapatawpha County, and Other Dear Myths." *Harper's Magazine*, July 1, 1955. ProQuest Periodicals Archive Online.

Forrestal, Rev. Peter P. "The Solis Diary of 1767." *Preliminary Studies of the Texas Catholic Historical Society* 1, no. 6 (1931): 1–42.

García, Fr. Bartholomé. *Manual para administrar los santos sacramentos de penitencia, eucharistia, extrema uncion, y matrimonio: Dar gracias despues de comulgar y ayudar, a bien morir a los Indios de los naciones: Pajalates, Orejones, Pacaos, Pacóas, Tiliijayas, Alasapas, Pausanes, y otras muchas diferentes, que se hallan en los missiones del Rio de San Antonio y Rio Grande, pertenencientes à el Colegio de la Santissima Cruz de la Ciudad de Queretaro, como son: Los Pacuâches, Mescâles, Pampôpas, Tâcames, Chayopînes, Venados, Pamâques, y toda la juventud de Pihuiques, Borrados, Sanipaos, y Manos de Perro*. Mexico City, 1760. Gale, Sabin Americana database.

Gente de Razón: People of the Missions. Directed by John Grabowska. Tucson, AZ: Western National Parks Association, 1998. DVD.

Gould, Stephen. *The Alamo City Guide, San Antonio, Texas*. New York: Macgowan and Slipper, 1882. HathiTrust database.

Gregg, Josiah. *Diary & Letters of Josiah Gregg: Southwestern Enterprises, 1840–1847*. Edited by Maurice Garland Fulton. Norman: University of Oklahoma Press, 1941.

Guidelines for a Texas Mission: Instructions for the Missionary of Mission Concepción in San Antonio. Vol. 1, *Documents Relating to the Old Spanish Missions of Texas*. Edited by Howard Benoist and María Eva Flores. Translated by Benedict Leutenegger. 4th ed. San Antonio: Old Spanish Missions Historical Research Library, 1994.

Harris, Ethel Wilson. *San José Mission: Queen of the Missions*. San Antonio: Accurate Litho, 1942.

Haverstick, John. "The Two Davy Crocketts." *Saturday Review*, July 1955.

Hayes, Rutherford B. *Diary and Letters of Rutherford Birchard Hayes: Nineteenth President of the United States*. Edited by Charles Richard Williams. Columbus: Ohio State Archaeological and Historical Society and F. J. Heer Printing, 1922.

"How to Discover the Real America: The 15 Places That Everyone Should Visit." *Changing Times*, June 1968. ProQuest ABI/Inform.

Humboldt, Alexander von. *Political Essay on the Kingdom of New Spain: Containing Researches Relative to the Geography of Mexico . . . the Physical Aspect of the Country, the Population, the State of Agriculture and Manufacturing and Commercial Industry . . . and the Military Defence of New Spain.* 2 vols. New York: I Riley, 1811. Gale Cengage Learning Sabin Americana database.

Hungerford, Edward. "The City of Little Squares: The Charm of San Antonio, Texas, Where Revolution Breeds." *Harper's Weekly,* November 9, 1912. HarpWeek database.

Hunt, Richard S., and Jesse F. Randel. *A New Guide to Texas: Consisting of a Brief Outline of the History of Its Settlement, and the Colonization and Land Laws; a General View of the Surface of the Country; Its Climate, Soil, Productions, &c. with a Particular Description of the Counties, Cities, and Towns.* New York: Sherman and Smith, 1845. Reprint, Jenkins Publishing and Pemberton Press, 1970.

Hutton, Paul Andrew. "Davy Crockett, Still King of the Wild Frontier: And a Hell of a Nice Guy Besides." *Texas Monthly,* November 1986.

Ikin, Arthur. *Texas: Its History, Topography, Agriculture, Commerce, and General Statistics.* London: Sherwood, Gilbert, and Piper, 1841. Reprint with introduction by James M. Day. Austin: Texian Press, 1964.

Ilg, Rev. John. *San Jose: Queen of the Missions.* San Antonio: Franciscan Fathers, 1936.

Inside the Gates. Daughters of the Republic of Texas Research Library, Library blog. Accessed May 20, 2025. https://drtlibrary.wordpress.com/.

Jesús, Fr. Antonio Margil de. *Nothingness Itself: Selected Writings of Ven. Fr. Antonio Margil, 1690–1724.* Edited by Marion A. Habig. Translated by Benedict Leutenegger. Chicago: Franciscan Herald Press, 1976.

"John Wayne Admits His 'Alamo' a 'Message' Pic—Americanism." *Variety,* October 26, 1960. ProQuest Entertainment Industry Magazine Archives.

Johnson, Alvin S. "Mexico in San Antonio." *New Republic,* June 24, 1916. EBSCO New Republic Archive.

Kahn, E. J. "Books: Be Sure You're Right, Then Go Ahead." *New Yorker,* September 1955.

Kalb, Bernard. "Dan'l, Dan'l Boone." *New York Times Magazine,* October 9, 1955.

Keatinge, Alice M. "Texas Missions Today." *Sunset,* April 1905.

Kelly, L. F., and S. Williamson. *Beautiful San Antonio.* San Antonio: Bureau of Advertising, ca. 1910.

Kendall, George Wilkins. *Narrative of the Texan Santa Fé Expedition.* London: Wiley and Putnam, 1844. Reprint, Austin: Steck, 1935.

Kennedy, Margaret. "Picturesque San Antonio." *Peterson's Magazine,* December 1889. ProQuest American Periodicals Series.

Kennedy, William. *Texas: The Rise, Progress, and Prospects of the Republic of Texas.* London: R. Hastings, 1841. Reprint, Clifton, NJ: Augustus M. Kelly, 1974.

King, Edward. "Glimpses of Texas I: A Visit to San Antonio." *Scribner's Monthly,* January 1874.

King, Edward. *The Great South.* Hartford: American Publishing, 1875. Reprint, New York: Arno Press, 1969.

Kneedler, H. S. *Through Storyland to Sunset Seas: What Four People Saw on a Journey Through the Southwest to the Pacific Coast.* N.p.: Passenger Department Southern Pacific, 1895.

Kress, Margaret Kenney. "Diary of a Visit of Inspection of the Texas Missions Made by Fray Gaspar José de Solís in the Year 1767–68." *Southwestern Historical Quarterly* 35, no. 1 (1931): 28–76. http://www.jstor.org/stable/30235387.

Lanier, Sidney. *The Centennial Edition of the Works of Sidney Lanier*. 10 vols. Edited by Philip Graham. Baltimore: Johns Hopkins University Press, 1945.

Laurence, F. S. "The Old Spanish Missions in and About San Antonio." *American Architect and the Architectural Review*, November 21, 1923.

Laut, Agnes C. "Why Go Abroad? Historic San Antonio." *Sunset*, April 1913.

Laut, Agnes C. "Why Go Abroad? The Mission in the Arizona Desert." *Sunset*, January 1913.

Leal, John O. *Mission Nuestra Señora de la Purisima Concepción de Acuña Records, 1796–1818*. San Antonio: Privately published by John O. Leal, 1993.

Leutenegger, Benedict. "Report on the San Antonio Missions in 1792." *Southwestern Historical Quarterly* 77, no. 4 (1974): 487–498. http://www.jstor.org/stable/30241978.

Leutenegger, Benedict, and Benito Fernández. "Memorial of Father Benito Fernández Concerning the Canary Islanders, 1741." *Southwestern Historical Quarterly* 82, no. 3 (1979): 265–96. http://www.jstor.org/stable/30238589.

López, Fr. José Francisco. "The Texas Missions in 1785." Translated by J. Autrey Dabbs. *Preliminary Studies of the Texas Catholic Historical Society* 3, no. 6 (1940): 5–24.

Madlem, Wilma. *San Jose Mission, Its Legends, Lore, and History: Story of "the Queen of Missions."* San Antonio: Naylor, 1934.

Maverick, Mary A. *Memoirs of Mary A. Maverick, Arranged by Mary A. Maverick and Her Son Geo. Madison Maverick*. Edited by Rena Maverick Green. San Antonio: Alamo Printing, 1921.

May, William B. "Chronicles of a Highway: El Nuevo Camino Real." *Sunset*, December 1898. HathiTrust Digital Library.

Mayo, H. M. "Travelers Pen Sketches of Cities in the South and West: El Paso to New Orleans—Marfa, San Antonio, and Houston." *Sunset*, December 1899. HathiTrust Digital Library.

"Mexico and the Invasion." *Catholic Telegraph*, October 29, 1846. ProQuest American Periodicals Series.

Missions of San Antonio. *San Antonio Missions, Texas, United States of America: Nomination to the World Heritage List by the United States of America*. January 2014. http://www.missionsofsanantonio.org/publications.html.

Missouri, Kansas, and Texas advertisement. *Town and Country*, January 20, 1906, 29. ProQuest American Periodicals Series.

Morfi, Juan Agustín. *Diario y Derrotero (1777–1781) por Fray Juan Agustín de Morfi*. Edited by Eugenio de Hoyo and Malcolm D. McLean. Monterrey, Nuevo León, Mexico: Instituto Technológico y de Estudios Superiores, 1967.

Morfi, Juan Agustín. *History of Texas, 1673–1779*. 2 vols. Translated by Carlos Eduardo Castañeda. Albuquerque, NM: Quivira Society, 1935. Reprint, New York: Arno Press, 1967.

Morgan, Thomas B. "God and Man in Hollywood." *Esquire*, May 1, 1963. EBSCO Esquire Magazine Archive.

Municipal Information Bureau, San Antonio, Texas. *Picturesque San Antonio: Where Life Is Different*. San Antonio: Municipal Information Bureau, ca. 1939.

Munroe, Kirk. "San Antonio de Bexar." *Harper's Weekly*, September 25, 1897. HarpWeek.

Nathan, Debbie. "Forget the Alamo." *Texas Monthly*, April 1998. ProQuest ABI/Inform.

Newcomb, Rexford. "A Remnant of Spanish Renaissance Architecture in Texas." *Western Architect*, January 1919.

Noll, Arthur Howard. "The Texas 'Missions.'" *American Architect and Building News*, August 28, 1897. ProQuest American Periodicals Series.

Odin, Jean Marie. "Mission of Texas." *United States Catholic Magazine and Monthly Review* 3, no. 11 (1844): 724–30. ProQuest American Periodicals Series.

The Official Guide Book, Texas Centennial Exposition, June 6–Nov. 29, 1936. Dallas: Texas Centennial Central Exposition, ca. 1936.

Ogan, Mena Kemp. "The Heroine of the Alamo." *National Magazine*, May/June, 1893. ProQuest American Periodical Series.

Olmsted, Frederick Law. *A Journey Through Texas: Or, A Saddle-Trip on the Southwestern Frontier*. New York: Dix, Edwards, 1857. Reprint, Austin: University of Texas Press, 1978.

Olmsted, Frederick Law. *The Papers of Frederick Law Olmsted*. Edited by Charles E. Beveridge and Charles Capin McLaughlin. Baltimore: Johns Hopkins University Press, 1981.

Olmsted, Frederick Law. "San Antonio, Texas." *Friends' Review*, May 2, 1857.

O'Sullivan, John L. "Annexation." *United States Magazine, and Democratic Review*. July/August 1845. ProQuest American Periodicals Series.

Pagès, M. Pierre Marie François. *Travels Round the World: In the Years 1767, 1768, 1769, 1770, 1771*. 2 vols. London: J. Murray, 1791. Gale Cengage Learning Eighteenth Century Collection Online.

Parker, Wylie A. *Here Is Texas: A Sourcebook of Centennial Program Material*. San Antonio: Naylor, 1936.

Pike, Zebulon Montgomery. *An Account of Expeditions to the Sources of the Mississippi and Through the Western Parts of Louisiana to the Sources of the Arkansaw, Kans, La Platte, and Pierre Jaun Rivers: Performed by Order of the Government of the United States During the years 1805, 1806, and 1807: And Tour Through the Interior Parts of New Spain, When Conducted Through These Provinces by Order of the Captain-General in the Year 1807*. Philadelphia: C & A Conrad, 1810. Gale Cengage Learning Sabin Americana database.

Pike, Zebulon Montgomery. *The Journals of Zebulon Montgomery Pike: With Letters and Related Documents*. Edited by Donald Jackson. 2 vols. Norman: University of Oklahoma Press, 1966.

Pingenot, Ben E. "The Alamo." *Time*, November 28, 1960. EBSCO Time Magazine Archive.

Polk, Mrs. V. T. "San Antonio and Its Old Missions." *Frank Leslie's Popular Monthly*, July 1883. ProQuest American Periodical Series.

Potter, R. M. "The Fall of the Alamo." *Magazine of American History*, January 1878.

Price, Theo H. "What Texas Has to Advertise and How to Advertise It." *Commerce and Finance*, November 14, 1923.

"*Provincia de Texas: Estado general de tropa de el presidio y vecindario de la Villa de San Fernando, empadronado y revisado por mi, el coronel de los reales ejercitos, do Domingo Cabello, gobernador de dicha provincial, en los dias 1, 2, y 3 del mes de julio de 1779*." Archivo General de Indias: Audencia de Guadalajara, legajo 283. Microfilm in UTSA Libraries Special Collections.

Ramón, Domingo. "Captain Don Domingo Ramón's Diary of His Expedition into Texas in 1716." Translated by Paul J. Foik. In *Wilderness Missions: Preliminary Studies of the Texas Catholic Historical Society, II*, edited by Jesús F. de la Teja, 129–48. Austin: Texas Catholic Historical Society, 1999.

Reid, Jan. "Davy Crock?" *Texas Monthly*, May 1995.

Rice, William S. "The Texas Mission Buildings." *Builder*, March 1, 1904. ProQuest American Periodicals Series.

"Roar of the Crowd." *Texas Monthly*, April 1984.

"Roar of the Crowd." *Texas Monthly*, January 1987.

"Roar of the Crowd." *Texas Monthly*, June 1998. ProQuest ABI/Inform.

"Roar of the Crowd." *Texas Monthly*, May 2000.

Roemer, Ferdinand. *Texas: With Particular Reference to German Immigration and the Physical Appearance of the Country*. Translated by Oswald Mueller. San Antonio: Standard Printing, 1935. Reprint, San Marcos: German-Texan Heritage Society and the Texian Press, 1983.

Roosevelt, Theodore. "Remember the Alamo: Hero-Tales from American History." *St. Nicholas: An Illustrated Magazine for Young Folks*, September 1895.

Russell, Jan Jarboe. "No Retreat! No Surrender!" *Texas Monthly*, October 2010. EBSCO.

Russell, Jan Jarboe. "San Antonio Is the Mother of Texas." *Texas Monthly*, May 2018. EBSCO.

Russell, Jan Jarboe. "We Will Never Surrender, or Retreat." *Texas Monthly*, May 1994. EBSCO.

Ruth, Kent. *How to Enjoy Your Western Vacations*. Norman: University of Oklahoma Press, 1956.

San Antonio. Houston: Southern Pacific Lines, ca. 1916.

San Antonio Conservation Society (SACS). "Society in Action: Society Made World Heritage Nomination Its 'Mission.'" SACS, June 25, 2015. https://www.saconservation.org/announcements/society-made-world-heritage-nomination-mission/.

San Antonio Missions, Texas, United States of America: Nomination to the World Heritage List by the United States of America. January 2014. https://whc.unesco.org/uploads/nominations/1466.pdf.

"San Antonio, Texas." *North American Review*, October 1903. ProQuest American Periodicals Series.

"San Antonio's 300th Anniversary Celebration." Accessed January 30, 2018. http://www.sanantonio300.org/.

The San José Papers: The Primary Sources for the History of Missions San José y San Miguel de Aguayo from Its Founding in 1720 to the Present. Translated by Fr. Benedict Leutenegger et al. Compiled and annotated by Fr. Marion A. Habig. 3 vols. San Antonio: Old Spanish Missions Historical Research Library at San José Mission, 1978.

"SB 191." Texas Legislature Online. Accessed August 8, 2022. https://capitol.texas.gov/BillLookup/History.aspx?LegSess=84R&Bill=SB191.

"Scenes in Texas." *Graham's American Monthly Magazine of Literature, Art, and Fashion,* January 1851. ProQuest American Periodicals Series.

Schreiner, George A. "San Antonio, Texas: A Progressive Commercial Center." *Bankers' Magazine,* October 1910. ProQuest American Periodical Series.

Scott, C. A. "San Antonio Texas in 1867." *Sunset,* December 1900. HathiTrust Digital Library.

"The Siege of the Alamo: John Wayne's New Picture Re-creates a Great Chapter in American History." *Good Housekeeping,* October 1960.

Smith, Harvey P. *Romantic San Antonio.* San Antonio: Jackson Printing, 1918.

Smith, Harvey P. *Romantic San Antonio: A Descriptive Journey to the Many Picturesque and Romantic Places in and Around Old San Antonio.* Rev. ed. San Antonio: Naylor, 1936.

Southern Pacific Company. *"Eden": An Excursion from New Orleans to the Pacific by Rail, Through Texas & Mexico via the "Star and Crescent" and "Sunset" Route.* Houston: T. W. Peirce Jr., 1882.

Southern Pacific Company. *Louisiana and Texas for the Winter Tourist.* New Orleans: Southern Pacific Company, 1911.

[Southern Pacific Company], Passenger Department. *The Missions of Texas on the Sunset Route.* Houston: Cumming and Sons, [1900–1909?].

Southern Pacific Company, Passenger Department. *Wayside Notes on the Sunset Route.* Southern Pacific Company, 1908. http://www.archive.org/details/sunsetwaysidenotoosoutrich.

"The Spanish Tradition of the South." *Architectural Forum,* November 1931.

[Spofford, Harriet P.] "San Antonio de Bexar." *Harper's New Monthly Magazine,* October 1877.

Stevens, Walter B. *Through Texas: A Series of Interesting Letters.* St. Louis: General Passenger Department of the Missouri Pacific Railway, 1892.

Sturmberg, Robert. *History of San Antonio and of the Early Days in Texas.* San Antonio: Press of the Standard Printing Co., 1920.

Sutherland, Garrett. "San Antonio." *Travel/Holiday,* November 1979.

Sutherland, Mason. "Carnival in San Antonio." *National Geographic Magazine,* December 1947.

Terán de los Ríos, Domingo. "The Expedition of Don Domingo Terán de los Ríos into Texas." Translated by Mattie Austin Hatcher. In *Wilderness Missions: Preliminary Studies of the Texas Catholic Historical Society, II,* edited by Jesús F. de la Teja, 1–66. Austin: Texas Catholic Historical Society, 1999.

Texas State Highway Commission. *Texas: A Guide to the Lone Star State, Compiled by Workers of the Writers' Program of the Work Projects Administration in the State of Texas*. New York: Hastings House, 1940.

"This World's Fair Has a Long Future." *Business Week*, March 30, 1968.

Tinsley, Henry G. "Remember the Alamo." *Current Literature*, May 1898. ProQuest American Periodical Series.

Tomlinson, Chris, Jason Stanford, and Bryan Burrough. "The Battle of the Alamo!" *Texas Monthly*, June 2021. EBSCO.

Torres, Luis. *Voices from the San Antonio Missions*. Lubbock: Texas Tech University Press, 1997.

Truman, Ben C. *From the Crescent City to the Golden Gate via the Sunset Route of the Southern Pacific Company*. New York: Liberty Printing, 1886.

UNESCO. "The Criteria for Selection." World Heritage Convention. Accessed August 18, 2016. http://whc.unesco.org/en/criteria.

UNESCO. "World Heritage List." World Heritage Convention. Accessed September 9, 2015. http://whc.unesco.org/en/list/.

"U.S. Again Is Subdued by Davy." *Life*, April 25, 1955. EBSCO.

US Census Bureau. *1860 U.S. Census, Population Schedule*. Accessed May 20, 2025. Ancestry Library Edition.

US Census Bureau. "Statistics of Population." *Report on Population of the Twelfth Census, 1900 Census*. V.1, Population, Pt. 1. Accessed May 20, 2025. https://www2.census.gov/library/publications/decennial/1900/volume-1/volume-1-p2.pdf.

US Congress. House. Hearing before the Subcommittee on National Parks and Recreation of the Committee on Interior and Insular Affairs: To Authorize the Establishment of the San Antonio Missions National Historical Park in the State of Texas, and for Other Purposes. 94th Cong., 2d sess., November 9, 1976. ProQuest Congressional.

US Congress. House. Preservation of Historic American Sites, Buildings, Objects, and Antiquities of National Significance: Hearings on H.R. 6670 and H.R. 6734 Before the Committee on the Public Lands, 74th Cong., 1st sess., April 1, 2, and 5, 1935. ProQuest Congressional database.

US Congress. Senate. Report of the Secretary of War, Communicating in Compliance with a Resolution of the Senate, a Map Showing the Operations of the Army of the United States in Texas and the Adjacent Mexican States on the Rio Grande; Accompanied by Astronomical Observations, and Descriptive and Military Memoirs of the Country. 31st Cong., 1st sess., 1849. S. exdoc 32. ProQuest Congressional.

United States Department of the Interior. *San Antonio Missions: Nomination for Inscription on the World Heritage List*. 2015. "Nomination File." https://whc.unesco.org/en/list/1466/documents/.

"Volunteers." *Niles National Register*, October 24, 1846. ProQuest American Periodicals Series.

White, Peter T. "Ex-King of the Wild Frontier." *New York Times Magazine*, December 11, 1955.

"Wild Frontier." *Time*, January 3, 1955. EBSCO.

Winthuysen, Don Thomás Phelipe de. "Winthuysen Reporting Condition of Presidios and Missions in Texas and Recommending Removal of Capital from Los Adaes to Béxar. Includes Brief Description of Topography, Climate, Construction, Crops and Reduction of Indians, August 19, 1744." Briscoe Center for American History, University of Texas at Austin. Accessed May 20, 2025. Bexar Archives Online, 1717–1895, https://briscoecenter.org/.

W. W. P. "Travel." *Yale Literary Magazine*, March, 1860, 203–9. EBSCO American Antiquarian Society Historical Periodicals Collection.

Primary Sources, Unpublished and Miscellaneous Materials

Municipal Advertising Commission of San Antonio, Texas. *Building Greater San Antonio by Advertising: A Report of the Activities of the Municipal Advertising Commission of San Antonio, Texas for Period January 1938 thru May 1939*. San Antonio Guidebook Collection, Daughters of the Republic of Texas Research Library, San Antonio, Texas.

State of Texas, Office of the Attorney General. *Report to the Texas Legislature Investigation of the Daughters of the Republic of Texas*. November 2012.

Secondary Sources, Published

Ables, L. Richard. "The Second Battle for the Alamo." *Southwestern Historical Quarterly* 70, no. 3 (1967): 372–413. http://www.jstor.org/stable/30237905.

Ahlborn, Richard Eighme. *The San Antonio Missions: Edward Everett and the American Occupation, 1847*. Fort Worth: Amon Carter Museum, 1985.

Almaráz, Félix D., Jr. *The San Antonio Missions and Their System of Land Tenure*. Austin: University of Texas Press, 1989.

Almaráz, Félix D., Jr. "San Antonio's Old Franciscan Missions: Material Decline and Secular Avarice in the Transition from Hispanic to Mexican Control." *The Americas* 44, no. 1 (1987): 1–22. http://www.jstor.org/stable/1006846.

Alonzo, Armando. *Tejano Legacy: Rancheros and Settlers in South Texas, 1734–1900*. Albuquerque: University of New Mexico Press, 1998.

Anderson, Benedict. *Imagined Communities: Reflections on the Origins and Spread of Nationalism*. Rev. ed. London: Verso, 2006.

Anzaldúa, Gloria. *Borderlands/La Frontera: The New Mestiza*. 2nd ed. San Francisco: Aunt Lute Books, 1999.

Arreola, Daniel D. *Tejano South Texas: A Mexican American Cultural Province*. Austin: University of Texas Press, 2002.

Balsera, Viviana Díaz. *The Pyramid Under the Cross: Franciscan Discourses of Evangelization and the Nahua Christian Subject in Sixteenth-Century Mexico*. Tucson: University of Arizona Press, 2005.

Bannon, John Francis. *The Spanish Borderlands Frontier, 1513–1821*. Albuquerque: University of New Mexico Press, 1974.

Barr, Juliana. *Peace Came in the Form of a Woman: Indians and Spaniards in the Texas Borderlands*. Chapel Hill: University of North Carolina Press, 2007.

Bayard, Ralph, C. M. *Lone-Star Vanguard: The Catholic Re-occupation of Texas (1838–1848)*. St. Louis: Vincentian Press, 1945.

Becker, Carl. "Everyman His Own Historian." *American Historical Review* 37, no. 2 (1932): 221–36. http://www.jstor.org/stable/1838208.

Benavides, Adán. "Sacred Space, Profane Reality: The Politics of Building a Church in Eighteenth-Century Texas." *Southwestern Historical Quarterly* 107, no. 1 (2003): 1–33. http://www.jstor.org/stable/30239423.

Blanton, Carlos Kevin. *George I. Sánchez: The Long Fight for Mexican American Integration*. New Haven, CT: Yale University Press, 2014.

Bodnar, John. *Remaking America: Public Memory, Commemoration, and Patriotism in the Twentieth Century*. Princeton, NJ: Princeton University Press, 1992.

Bold, Christine. *The WPA Guides: Mapping America*. Jackson: University Press of Mississippi, 1999. Accessed in e-book format via EBSCO.

Bolton, Herbert E. "The Mission as Frontier Institution in the Spanish-American Colonies." *American Historical Review* 23, no. 1 (1917): 42–61. http://www.jstor.org/stable/1837685.

Bolton, Herbert E. *Texas in the Middle Eighteenth Century: Studies in Spanish Colonial History and Administration*. Berkeley: University of California Press, 1915. Reprint, Austin: University of Texas Press and the Texas State Historical Association, 1970.

Boorstin, Daniel J. *The Americans: The National Experience*. New York: Random House, 1965.

Boyer, M. Christine. *The City of Collective Memory: Its Historical Imagery and Architectural Entertainments*. Cambridge, MA: MIT Press, 1994.

Brands, H. W. *Lone Star Nation: How a Ragged Army of Volunteers Won the Battle for Texas Independence and Changed America*. New York: Doubleday, 2004.

Braudel, Fernand. *On History*. Translated by Sarah Matthews. Chicago: University of Chicago Press, 1980.

Brear, Holly Beachley. *Inherit the Alamo: Myth and Ritual at an American Shrine*. Austin: University of Texas Press, 1995.

Brear, Holly Beachley. "We Run the Alamo and You Don't: Alamo Battles of Ethnicity and Gender." In *Where These Memories Grow: History, Memory, and Southern History*, edited by W. Fitzhugh Brundage, 299–318. Chapel Hill: University of North Carolina Press, 2000.

Bremer, Thomas S. *Blessed with Tourists: The Borderlands of Religion and Tourism in San Antonio*. Chapel Hill: University of North Carolina Press, 2004.

Bronder, Saul E. *Social Justice & Church Authority: The Public Life of Archbishop Robert E. Lucey*. Philadelphia: Temple University Press, 1982.

Brooks, Charles Mattoon, Jr. *Texas Missions: Their Romance and Architecture*. Dallas: Dealey and Lowe, 1936.

Brown, Joshua. *Beyond the Lines: Pictorial Reporting, Everyday Life, and the Crisis of Gilded Age America*. Berkeley: University of California Press, 2002.

Brundage, W. Fitzhugh. "No Deed but Memory." In *Where These Memories Grow: History, Memory, and Southern Identity*, edited by W. Fitzhugh Brundage, 1–28. Chapel Hill: University of North Carolina Press, 2000.

Bryan, Jimmy L., Jr. *The American Elsewhere: Adventures and Manliness in the Age of Expansion*. Lawrence: University Press of Kansas, 2017.

Bsumek, Erika Marie. "Exchanging Places: Virtual Tourism, Vicarious Travel, and the Consumption of Southwestern Indian Artifacts." In *The Culture of Tourism, the Tourism of Culture: Selling the Past to the Present in the American Southwest*, edited by Hal K. Rothman, 118–39. Albuquerque: University of New Mexico Press, 2003.

Buenger, Walter L. "Three Truths in Texas." In *Beyond Texas Through Time: Breaking Away from Past Interpretations*, edited by Walter L. Buenger and Arnoldo De León, 1–49. College Station: Texas A&M University Press, 2011.

Burkhart, Louise M. *The Slippery Earth: Nahua-Christian Moral Dialog in Sixteenth-Century Mexico*. Tucson: University of Arizona Press, 1989.

Calloway, Colin G. *New Worlds for All: Indians, Europeans, and the Remaking of Early America*. Baltimore: Johns Hopkins University Press, 1997.

Campbell, Randolph B. *An Empire for Slavery: The Peculiar Institution in Texas, 1821–1865*. Baton Rouge: Louisiana State University Press, 1989.

Campbell, Randolph B. *Gone to Texas: A History of the Lone Star State*. New York: Oxford University Press, 2003.

Cantrell, Gregg. "The Bones of Stephen F. Austin: History and Memory in Progressive-Era Texas." In *Lone Star Pasts: Memory and History in Texas*, edited by Gregg Cantrell and Elizabeth Hayes Turner, 39–74. College Station: Texas A&M University Press, 2007.

Cantrell, Gregg, and Elizabeth Hayes Turner. "Introduction: A Study of History, Memory, and Collective Memory in Texas." In *Lone Star Pasts: Memory and History in Texas*, edited by Gregg Cantrell and Elizabeth Hayes Turner, 1–14. College Station: Texas A&M University Press, 2007.

Cantrell, Gregg, and Elizabeth Hayes Turner, eds. *Lone Star Pasts: Memory and History in Texas*. Foreword by W. Fitzhugh Brundage. College Station: Texas A&M University Press, 2007.

Cashion, Ty. *Lone Star Mind*. Norman: University of Oklahoma Press, 2018.

Castañeda, Carlos E. *Our Catholic Heritage in Texas, 1519–1936*. Edited by Paul J. Foik. 7 vols. Austin: Von Beckmann-Jones, 1936–58.

Chidester, David, and Edward T. Linenthal, eds. *American Sacred Space*. Bloomington: Indiana University Press, 1995.

Chipman, Donald E. *Spanish Texas, 1519–1821*. Austin: University of Texas Press, 1992.

Christensen, Bonnie. *Red Lodge and the Mythic West: Coal Miners to Cowboys*. Lawrence: University Press of Kansas, 2002.

Clark, Donald, and Christopher Andersen. *John Wayne's* The Alamo: *The Making of an Epic Film: In TODD-AO*. Hillside, IL: Midwest Publishing, 1994.

Clemmons, Leigh. *Branding Texas: Performing Culture in the Lone Star State*. Austin: University of Texas Press, 2008.

Coalson, George O. "Villanueva, Andrea Castañón." *Handbook of Texas Online*. Accessed August 8, 2016. http://www.tshaonline.org/handbook/online/articles/fvi20.

Cocks, Catherine. *Doing the Town: The Rise of Urban Tourism in the United States, 1850–1915*. Berkeley: University of California Press, 2001.

Confino, Alon. "Collective Memory and Cultural History: Problems of Method." *American Historical Review* 102, no. 5 (1997): 1386–1403. http://www.jstor.org/stable/2171069.

Cox, John D. *Traveling South: Travel Narratives and the Construction of American Identity*. Athens: University of Georgia Press, 2005.

Crabbe, Rita. "Garriga, Mariano Simon." *Handbook of Texas Online*. Accessed February 10, 2020. http://www.tshaonline.org/handbook/online/articles/fga31.

Crisp, James E. *Sleuthing the Alamo: Davy Crockett's Last Stand and Other Mysteries of the Texas Revolution*. New York: Oxford University Press, 2005.

Davis, Natalie Zemon, and Randolph Starn. "Introduction." Special Issue, *Memory and Counter-Memory* 26 (Spring 1989): 1–6. http://www.jstor.org/stable/2928519.

de la Teja, Jesús F. *San Antonio de Béxar: A Community on New Spain's Northern Frontier*. Albuquerque: University of New Mexico Press, 1995.

de la Teja, Jesús. "The Spanish Borderlands: An Overview." In *Bridging Cultures: Reflections on the Heritage Identity of the Texas-Mexico Borderlands*, edited by Harriett D. Romo and William A. Dupont, 5–25. College Station: Texas A&M University Press, 2021.

de la Teja, Jesús F., ed. *Tejano Leadership in Mexican and Revolutionary Texas*. College Station: Texas A&M University Press, 2010.

de la Teja, Jesús F. "Why Urbano and María Trinidad Can't Get Married: Social Relations in Late Colonial San Antonio." *Southwestern Historical Quarterly* 112, no. 2 (2008): 121–46. http://www.jstor.org/stable/30239620.

de la Teja, Jesús F., and Ross Frank, eds. *Choice, Persuasion, and Coercion: Social Control on Spain's North American Frontiers*. Albuquerque: University of New Mexico Press, 2005.

Delpar, Helen. *The Enormous Vogue of Things Mexican: Cultural Relations Between the United States and Mexico, 1920–1935*. Tuscaloosa: University of Alabama Press, 1992.

DeLyser, Dydia. *Ramona Memories: Tourism and the Shaping of Southern California*. Minneapolis: University of Minnesota Press, 2005.

Don, Patricia Lopes. *Bonfires of Culture: Franciscans, Indigenous Leaders, and the Inquisition in Early Mexico, 1524–1540*. Norman: University of Oklahoma Press, 2010.

Duby, Georges. *The Legend of Bouvines: War, Religion, and Culture in the Middle Ages*. Translated by Catherine Tihanyi. Berkeley: University of California Press, 1990.

Early, James. *Presidio, Mission, and Pueblo: Spanish Architecture and Urbanism in the United States*. Dallas: Southern Methodist University Press, 2004.

Eaton, Jack D. *Excavations at the Alamo Shrine: Mission San Antonio de Valero*. Special Report No. 10. San Antonio: Center for Archaeological Research, University of Texas at San Antonio, 1980.

Everett, Donald E. "San Antonio Welcomes the 'Sunset'-1877." *Southwestern Historical Quarterly* 65, no. 1 (1961): 47–60. http://www.jstor.org/stable/30236190.

Fenstermaker, Anne Leslie. "Green, Mary Rowena [Rena] Maverick." *Handbook of Texas Online*. Accessed April 13, 2016. http://www.tshaonline.org/handbook/online/articles/fgr36.

Fisher, Lewis F. *Saving San Antonio: The Precarious Preservation of a Heritage*. Lubbock: Texas Tech University Press, 1996.

Fisher, Lewis F. *Saving San Antonio: The Preservation of a Heritage*. 2nd ed. San Antonio: Maverick Books, an Imprint of Trinity University Press, 2016.

Flores, Richard R. "Adina De Zavala and the Politics of Restoration: Introduction." In *History and Legends of the Alamo and Other Missions in and Around San Antonio*, edited by Richard R. Flores, v–lviii. Houston: Arte Público Press, 1996.

Flores, Richard R. *Remembering the Alamo: Memory, Modernity, and the Master Symbol*. Austin: University of Texas Press, 2002.

Foley, Patrick. *Missionary Bishop: Jean-Marie Odin in Galveston and New Orleans*. College Station: Texas A&M University Press, 2013.

Fortenberry, Brent R., ed. *A Field Guide to the Vernacular Buildings of the San Antonio Area*. College Station: Texas A&M University Press, 2021.

Foster, William C. *Spanish Expeditions into Texas, 1689–1768*. Austin: University of Texas Press, 1995.

Fraser, Valerie. *The Architecture of Conquest: Building in the Viceroyalty of Peru, 1535–1635*. Cambridge: Cambridge University Press, 1990.

Frost, Susan Toomey. *Colors on Clay: The San José Tile Workshops of San Antonio*. San Antonio: Trinity University Press, 2009.

Galán, Francis X. *Los Adaes: The First Capital of Spanish Texas*. College Station: Texas A&M University Press, 2020.

Galindo, David Rex. *To Sin No More: Franciscans and Conversion in the Hispanic World, 1683–1830*. Stanford, CA: Stanford University Press and the Academy of American Franciscan History, 2017.

Garcia, Richard A. *Rise of the Mexican American Middle Class: San Antonio, 1929–1941*. College Station: Texas A&M University Press, 1991.

Garza, Melita M. *They Came to Toil: Newspaper Representations of Mexicans and Immigrants in the Great Depression*. Austin: University of Texas Press, 2017.

Gebhard, David. "The Spanish Colonial Revival in Southern California, 1895–1930." *Journal of the Society of Architectural Historians* 26, no. 2 (1967): 131–47. http://www.jstor.org/stable/988417.

Gelo, Daniel J. "The Indigenous Borderlands: Cultures Without Borders." In *Bridging Cultures: Reflections on the Heritage Identity of the Texas-Mexico Borderlands*, edited by Harriett D. Romo and William A. Dupont, 26–50. College Station: Texas A&M University Press, 2021.

George, Eugene. "Espada Doorway: A Lesson in Harmony." *Perspective* 9, no. 1 (1980): 13–14.

Gilbert, M. J., ed. *Archdiocese of San Antonio, 1874–1949: An Illustrated Record of the Foundation and Growth of Parishes, Missions, and Religious Institutions in That Part of Texas Under the Spiritual Jurisdiction of the See of San Antonio*. San Antonio: Schneider Printing, 1949.

González, John Morán. *Border Renaissance: The Texas Centennial and the Emergence of Mexican American Literature*. Austin: University of Texas Press, 2009.

Gottfried, Herbert. *Landscape in American Guides and View Books: Visual History of Touring and Travel*. Lanham, MD: Lexington Books, 2013.

Gracy, David B. II, "'Just as I Have Written It': A Study of the Authenticity of the Manuscript of Jose Enrique de la Peña's Account of the Texas Campaign." *Southwestern Historical Quarterly* 105, no. 2 (2001): 254–91.

Graham, Don. "Mission Statement: The Alamo and the Fallacy of Historical Accuracy in Epic Filmmaking." In *Lone Star Pasts: Memory and History in Texas*, edited by Gregg Cantrell and Elizabeth Hayes Turner, 242–69. College Station: Texas A&M University Press, 2007.

Greeson, Jennifer Rae. "Expropriating *The Great South* and Exporting 'Local Color': Global and Hemispheric Imaginaries of the First Reconstruction." *American Literary History* 18, no. 3 (2006): 496–505. EBSCO America: History & Life, doi:10.1093/alh/aj1010.

Grider, Silvia Ann. "How Texans Remember the Alamo." In *Usable Pasts: Traditions and Group Expressions in North America*, edited by Tad Tuleja, 274–90. Logan: Utah State University Press, 1997.

Groneman, Bill. "Alamo Noncombatants." *Handbook of Texas Online*. Accessed August 15, 2015. http://www.tshaonline.org/handbook/online/articles/qsa01.

Groneman, Bill. *David Crockett: Hero of the Common Man*. New York: Forge, 2005.

Groneman, Bill. *Death of a Legend: The Myth and Mystery Surrounding the Death of Davy Crockett*. Plano: Republic of Texas Press, 1999.

Gruen, J. Philip. *Manifest Destinations: Cities and Tourists in the Nineteenth-Century American West*. Norman: University of Oklahoma Press, 2014.

Guerra, Dora Elizondo. "Two Silver Pesos and a Blanket: The Texas Revolution and the Non-combatant Women Who Survived the Battle of the Alamo." In *Women and the Texas Revolution*, edited by Mary L. Scheer, 123–52. Denton: University of North Texas Press, 2012.

Gutiérrez, Ramón A. *When Jesus Came, the Corn Mothers Went Away: Marriage, Sexuality, and Power in New Mexico, 1500–1846*. Stanford, CA: Stanford University Press, 1991.

Haas, Astrid. *Lone Star Vistas: Travel Writing on Texas, 1821–1861*. Austin: University of Texas Press, 2021.

Haas, Lisbeth. *Conquests and Historical Identities in California, 1796–1936*. Berkeley: University of California Press, 1995.

Habig, Marion A. *The Alamo Chain of Missions: A History of San Antonio's Five Old Missions*. Chicago: Franciscan Herald Press, 1968. Reprint, Livingston, TX: Pioneer Enterprises, 1997. Page references to 1997 reprint.

Habig, Marion A. *San Antonio's Mission San Jose: State and National Historic Site, 1720–1968*. San Antonio: Naylor, 1968.

Hafertepe, Kenneth. "Experiencing the Complex Character of San Antonio and South Central Texas Through Their Vernacular Buildings and Cultural Landscapes."

In *A Field Guide to the Vernacular Buildings of the San Antonio Area*, edited by Brent R. Fortenberry, 1–23. College Station: Texas A&M University Press, 2021.

Hafertepe, Kenneth. "Restoration, Reconstruction, or Romance? The Case of the Spanish Governor's Palace in Hispanic-Era San Antonio, Texas." *Journal of the Society of Architectural Historians* 67, no. 3 (2008): 412–33. https://www.jstor.org/stable/10.1525/jsah.2008.67.3.412.

Hafertepe, Kenneth. "The Romantic Rhetoric of the Spanish Governor's Palace, San Antonio, Texas." *Southwestern Historical Quarterly* 107, no. 2 (2003): 238–77. https://www.jstor.org/stable/30242173.

Halbwachs, Maurice. *The Collective Memory*. Translated by Francis J. Ditter and Vida Yazdi Ditter. Paris: Presses Universitaires de France, 1950. Reprint, New York: Harper Colophon, 1980.

Halbwachs, Maurice. *On Collective Memory*. Edited, translated, and with an introduction by Lewis A. Coser. Chicago: University of Chicago Press, 1992.

Hämäläinen, Pekka. *The Comanche Empire*. New Haven, CT: Yale University Press, 2008.

Hämäläinen, Pekka, and Samuel Truett. "On Borderlands." *Journal of American History* 98, no. 2 (2011): 338–61. http://www.jstor.org/stable/41509959.

Harrigan, Stephen. *Big Wonderful Thing: A History of Texas*. Austin: University of Texas Press, 2019.

Harrison, Jay T. "Franciscan Concepts of the Congregated Mission and the Apostolic Ministry in Eighteenth-Century Texas." In *From La Florida to La California: Franciscan Evangelization in the Spanish Borderlands*, edited by Timothy J. Johnson and Gert Melville, 323–39. Berkeley: Academy of American Franciscan History, 2013.

Henderson, Richard B. *Maury Maverick: A Political Biography*. Austin: University of Texas Press, 1970.

Henry, Jay C. *Architecture in Texas, 1895–1945*. Austin: University of Texas Press, 1993.

Hine, Robert V., and John Mack Faragher. *The American West: A New Interpretive History*. New Haven, CT: Yale University Press, 2000.

Hinojosa, Gilberto M. "Friars and Indians: Towards a Perspective of Cultural Interaction in the San Antonio Missions." *US Catholic Historian* 9, no. 1/2 (1990): 7–26.

Hobsbawm, Eric, and Terence Ranger, eds. *The Invention of Tradition*. Cambridge: Cambridge University Press, 1992.

Hoermann, P. Alto S. *The Daughter of Tehuan: Or, Texas of the Past Century*. Translated by Alois Braun. San Antonio: Standard Printing, 1932.

Hoganson, Kristin L. *Consumers' Imperium: The Global Production of American Domesticity, 1865–1920*. Chapel Hill: University of North Carolina Press, 2007.

Holmesley, Sterlin, *HemisFair '68 and the Transformation of San Antonio*. San Antonio: Maverick Publishing, 2003.

Horsman, Reginald. *Race and Manifest Destiny: The Origins of American Racial Anglo-Saxonism*. Cambridge, MA: Harvard University Press, 1981.

Hosmer, Charles B., Jr. *Preservation Comes of Age: From Williamsburg to the National Trust, 1926–1949*. Charlottesville: University of Virginia Press, for the National Trust for Historic Preservation in the United States, 1981.

Howe, Barbara J. "Women in Historic Preservation: The Legacy of Ann Pamela Cunningham." *Public Historian* 12, no. 1 (1990): 31–61. http://www.jstor.org/stable/3378321.

Howe, Barbara. "Women in the Nineteenth-Century Preservation Movement." In *Restoring Women's History Through Historic Preservation*, edited by Gail Lee Dubrow and Jennifer B. Goodman, 17–36. Baltimore: Johns Hopkins University Press, 2003.

Hutton, Paul Andrew. "The Alamo as Icon." In *The Texas Military Experience: From the Texas Revolution Through World War II*, edited by Joseph G. Dawson III, 14–31. College Station: Texas A&M University Press, 1995.

Ivey, James E. "The Completion of the Church Roof of San Antonio de Valero." *Anales del Instituto de Investigaciones Estéticas* 29, no. 91 (2007): 133–41. http://www.analesiie.unam.mx/index.php/analesiie/article/view/2246.

Jackson, Jack. *Los Mesteños: Spanish Ranching in Texas, 1721–1821*. College Station: Texas A&M University Press, 1986.

Jackson, Robert H. "Congregation and Depopulation: Demographic Patterns in the Texas Missions." *Journal of South Texas* 17, no. 2 (2004): 6–38.

Jackson, Robert H. *From Savages to Subjects: Missions in the History of the American Southwest*. Armonk, NY: M. E. Sharpe, 2000.

Jackson, Robert. *Missions and the Frontiers of Spanish America: A Comparative Study of the Impact of Environmental, Economic, Political, and Socio-cultural Variations on the Missions in the Rio de la Plata Region and on the Northern Frontier of New Spain*. Prescott, AZ: Pentacle Press, 2005.

Jackson, Ron J., Jr., and Lee Spencer White. *Joe: The Slave Who Became an Alamo Legend*. Norman: University of Oklahoma Press, 2015.

John, Elizabeth A. H. *Storms Brewed in Other Men's Worlds: The Confrontation of Indians, Spanish, and French in the Southwest, 1540–1795*. College Station: Texas A&M University Press, 1975.

Johnson, David R. *In the Loop: A Political and Economic History of San Antonio*. San Antonio: Maverick Books of Trinity University Press, 2020.

Johnson, Timothy J., and Gert Melville, eds. *From La Florida to La California: Franciscan Evangelization in the Spanish Borderlands*. Berkeley, CA: Academy of American Franciscan History, 2013.

Kagan, Richard L. "From Noah to Moses: The Genesis of Historical Scholarship on Spain in the United States." In *Spain in America: The Origins of Hispanism in the United States*, edited by Richard L. Kagan, 21–48. Urbana: University of Illinois Press, 2002.

Kagan, Richard L. "Prescott's Paradigm: American Historical Scholarship and the Decline of Spain." *American Historical Review* 101, no. 2 (1996): 423–46. http://www.jstor.org/stable/2170397.

Kammen, Michael. *Mystic Chords of Memory: The Transformation of Tradition in American Culture*. New York: Vintage Books, 1993. First published in New York: Knopf, 1991. Page references are to 1993 Vintage ed.

Kilgore, Dan, and James E. Crisp. *How Did Davy Die? And Why Do We Care So Much?* College Station: Texas A&M University Press, 2010.

Kitchens, Joel D. "Making Historical Memory: Women's Leadership in the Preservation of San Antonio's Missions." *Southwestern Historical Quarterly* 121, no. 2 (2017): 170–96. doi:10.1353/swh.2017.0053.

Kropp, Phoebe S. *California Vieja: Culture and Memory in a Modern American Place*. Berkeley: University of California Press, 2006.

Kubler, George. *The Religious Architecture of New Mexico in the Colonial Period and Since the American Occupation*. 5th ed. Albuquerque: University of New Mexico Press, 1990.

Kubler, George, and Martin Soria. *Art and Architecture of Spain and Portugal and Their American Dominions, 1500–1800*. Baltimore: Penguin Books, 1959.

Lane, Belden C. *Landscapes of the Sacred: Geography and Narrative in American Spirituality*. Baltimore: Johns Hopkins University Press, 2001.

Lanier, Sidney. *The Centennial Edition of the Works of Sidney Lanier*. Vol. 6, *Florida and Miscellaneous Prose*, edited by Philip Graham. Baltimore: Johns Hopkins University Press, 1945.

Lawson, Russell M. *Frontier Naturalist: Jean Louis Berlandier and the Exploration of Northern Mexico and Texas*. Albuquerque: University of New Mexico Press, 2012.

Lears, T. J. Jackson. *No Place of Grace: Antimodernism and the Transformation of American Culture, 1880–1920*. New York: Pantheon Books, 1981.

León, Arnoldo de. *The Tejano Community, 1836–1900*. New foreword by Richard Griswold del Castillo. New afterword by the author. Dallas: Southern Methodist University Press, 1997.

León, Arnoldo de. *They Called Them Greasers: Anglo Attitudes Toward Mexicans in Texas, 1821–1900*. Austin: University of Texas Press, 1995.

Leutenegger, Fr. Benedict. *Fr. Gerónimo de Mendieta's History: An Introduction to the Antecedents of the Spanish Missions in Texas*. Introduction by Fr. Marion A. Habig. San Antonio: Old Spanish Missions Historical Research Library, 1978.

Limerick, Patricia Nelson. *The Legacy of Conquest: The Unbroken Past of the American West*. New York: W. W. Norton, 1987.

Lindgren, James M. "'A New Departure in Historic, Patriotic Work': Personalism, Professionalism, and Conflicting Concepts of Material Culture in the Late Nineteenth and Early Twentieth Centuries." *Public Historian* 18, no. 2 (1996): 41–60. https://doi.org/10.2307/3377912.

Lindgren, James M. "'A Spirit That Fires the Imagination': Historic Preservation and Cultural Regeneration in Virginia and New England, 1850–1950." In *Giving Preservation a History: Histories of Historic Preservation in the United States*, edited by Max Page and Randall Mason, 107–30. New York: Routledge, 2004.

Linenthal, Edward Tabor. *Sacred Ground: Americans and Their Battlefields*. 2nd ed. Urbana: University of Illinois Press, 1993.

Lockhart, James. *The Nahuas After the Conquest: A Social and Cultural History of the Indians of Central Mexico, Sixteenth Through Eighteenth Centuries*. Stanford, CA: Stanford University Press, 1992.

Loughran, Trish. *The Republic in Print: Print Culture in the Age of U.S. Nation Building, 1770–1870*. New York: Columbia University Press, 2007.

Lowenthal, David. *The Heritage Crusade and the Spoils of History*. New York: Cambridge University Press, 1998.

Lowenthal, David. *The Past Is a Foreign Country*. New York: Cambridge University Press, 1985.

MacInerney, Dorothy McLeod, William Warren Rogers, and Robert David Ward. "Oscar Wilde Lectures in Texas, 1882." *Southwestern Historical Quarterly* 106, no. 4 (2003): 550–73. http://www.jstor.org/stable/30239392.

MacKintosh, Will B. *Selling the Sights: The Invention of the Tourist in American Culture*. New York: York University Press, 2019.

Mann, Kristin Dutcher. *The Power of Song: Music and Dance in the Mission Communities of Northern New Spain, 1590–1810*. Stanford, CA: Stanford University Press and Academy of American Franciscan History, 2010.

Martin, Joel W. "Introduction." In *Native Americans, Christianity, and the Reshaping of the American Religious Landscape*, edited by Joel W. Martin and Mark A. Nicholas, 1–20. Chapel Hill: University of North Carolina Press, 2010.

Martin, Joel W., and Mark A. Nicholas. *Native Americans, Christianity, and the Reshaping of the American Religious Landscape*. Chapel Hill: University of North Carolina Press, 2010.

Matovina, Timothy. *The Alamo Remembered: Tejano Accounts and Perspectives*. Austin: University of Texas Press, 1995.

Matovina, Timothy. *Guadalupe and Her Faithful: Latino Catholics in San Antonio, from Colonial Origins to the Present*. Baltimore: Johns Hopkins University Press, 2005.

Matovina, Timothy. *Tejano Religion and Ethnicity: San Antonio, 1821–1860*. Austin: University of Texas Press, 1995.

Matovina, Timothy, and Jesús F. de la Teja, eds. *Recollections of a Tejano Life: Antonio Menchaca in Texas History*. Austin: University of Texas Press, 2013.

McAndrew, John. *The Open-Air Churches of Sixteenth-Century Mexico: Atrios, Posas, Open Chapels, and Other Studies*. Cambridge, MA: Harvard University Press, 1965.

McComb, David G. *Spare Time in Texas: Recreation and History in the Lone Star State*. Austin: University of Texas Press, 2008.

McLemore, Laura Lyons. *Adele Briscoe Looscan: Daughter of the Republic*. Fort Worth: Texas Christian University Press, 2016.

McLennan, Marshall S. "The Baroque Parapet: Cultural Diffusion and the Sense of Place in the American Southwest." *PAST: Pioneer America Society Transactions* 33 (October 2010): 40–53.

McWilliams, Carey. *North from Mexico: The Spanish-Speaking People of the United States*. Rev. ed. with added material by Matt S. Meier. Westport, CT: Praeger, 1990.

Miller, Char. "Proving Ground: Richard Harding Davis in the American West." *Southwest Review* 90, no. 1 (2005): 13–28. http://www.jstor.org/stable/43472407.

Miller, Char. "Tourist Trap: Visitors and the Modern San Antonio Economy." In *The Culture of Tourism, the Tourism of Culture: Selling the Past to the Present in the American Southwest*, edited by Hal K. Rothman, 206–28. Albuquerque: University of New Mexico Press, 2003.

Montejano, David. *Anglos and Mexicans in the Making of Texas, 1836–1986*. Austin: University of Texas Press, 1987.

Montejano, David. *Quixote's Soldiers: A Local History of the Chicano Movement, 1966–1981*. Austin: University of Texas Press, 2010.

Morley, Judy Mattivi. *Historic Preservation & the Imagined West: Albuquerque, Denver, & Seattle*. Lawrence: University Press of Kansas, 2006.

Mullen, Robert J. *Architecture and Its Sculpture in Viceregal Mexico*. Austin: University of Texas Press, 1997.

Murray, Jane Kellogg. "Viva San Antonio." *Texas Highways*, January 2018.

Nau, Anna. "Cultural Confluence: The Architecture of Eighteenth-Century San Antonio Missions." *The Classicist* 19 (2022): 38–45.

Nau, Anna. "Heritage and Identity in the Early Twentieth-Century Preservation of the San Antonio Missions." *Arris: Journal of the Southeast Chapter of the Society of Architectural Historians* 28 (January 2017): 30–45.

Nelson, Louis P., ed. *American Sanctuary: Understanding Sacred Spaces*. Bloomington: Indiana University Press, 2006.

Noonan, Mark J. *Reading the* Century Illustrated Monthly Magazine*: American Literature and Culture, 1870–1893*. Kent, OH: Kent State University Press, 2010.

Nora, Pierre. *Realms of Memory: Rethinking the French Past*. Translated by Arthur Goldhammer. English-language ed. edited and foreword by Lawrence D. Kritzman. 3 vols. New York: Columbia University Press, 1996.

Orsi, Richard J. *Sunset Limited: The Southern Pacific Railroad and the Development of the American West, 1850–1930*. Berkeley: University of California Press, 2000.

Padget, Martin. *Indian Country: Travels in the American Southwest, 1840–1935*. Albuquerque: University of New Mexico Press, 2004.

Page, Max, and Randall Mason. "Rethinking the Roots of the Historic Preservation Movement." In *Giving Preservation a History: Histories of Historic Preservation in the United States*, edited by Max Page and Randall Mason, 3–16. New York: Routledge, 2004.

Persons, Billie. "Secular Life in the San Antonio Missions." *Southwestern Historical Quarterly* 62, no. 1 (1958): 45–62.

Pittock, Murray. *Culloden: (Cùill Lodair)*. Oxford: Oxford University Press, 2016.

Popp, Richard K. *The Holiday Makers: Magazines, Advertising, and Mass Tourism in Postwar America*. Baton Rouge: Louisiana State University Press, 2012.

Poyo, Gerald E. "The Canary Island Immigrants of San Antonio: From Ethnic Exclusivity to Community in Eighteenth-Century Béxar." In *Tejano Origins in Eighteenth-Century San Antonio*, edited by Gerald E. Poyo and Gilberto M. Hinojosa, 41–58. Austin: University of Texas Press, 1991.

Poyo, Gerald E., ed. *Tejano Journey, 1770–1850*. Austin: University of Texas Press, 1996.

Poyo, Gerald E., and Gilberto M. Hinojosa. "Spanish Texas and Borderlands Historiography in Transition: Implications for United States History." *Journal of American History* 75, no. 2 (1988): 394–96. http://www.jstor.org/stable/1887864.

Poyo, Gerald E., and Gilberto M. Hinojosa, eds. *Tejano Origins in Eighteenth-Century San Antonio*. Austin: University of Texas Press, 1991.

Privett, Stephen A. *The U.S. Catholic Church and Its Hispanic Members: The Pastoral Vision of Archbishop Robert E. Lucey*. San Antonio: Trinity University Press, 1988.

Quirarte, Jacinto. *The Art and Architecture of the Texas Missions*. Austin: University of Texas Press, 2002.

Ragsdale, Kenneth B. *Centennial '36: The Year America Discovered Texas*. College Station: Texas A&M University Press, 1987.

Ramos, Raúl A. *Beyond the Alamo: Forging Mexican Ethnicity in San Antonio, 1821–1861*. Chapel Hill: University of North Carolina Press, 2008.

Reps, John W. *Cities of the American West: A History of Frontier Urban Planning*. Princeton, NJ: Princeton University Press, 1979.

Reséndez, Andrés. *Changing National Identities at the Frontier: Texas and New Mexico, 1800–1850*. Cambridge: Cambridge University Press, 2004.

Roberts, Randy, and James S. Olson. *John Wayne: American*. Lincoln: University of Nebraska Press, 1995.

Roberts, Randy, and James S. Olson. *A Line in the Sand: The Alamo in Blood and Memory*. New York: Touchstone, published by Simon and Schuster, 2002.

Rodríguez, Jeanette, and Ted Fortier. *Cultural Memory: Resistance, Faith, and Identity*. Austin: University of Texas Press, 2007.

Romo, Harriett D., and William A. Dupont, eds. *Bridging Cultures: Reflections on the Heritage Identity of the Texas-Mexico Borderlands*. College Station: Texas A&M University Press, 2021.

Rosaldo, Renato. *Culture and Truth: The Remaking of Social Analysis*. Boston: Beacon Press, 1989.

Rugh, Susan Sessions. *Are We There Yet? The Golden Age of American Family Vacations*. Lawrence: University Press of Kansas, 2008.

Sahlins, Peter. *Boundaries: The Making of France and Spain in the Pyrenees*. Berkeley: University of California Press, 1989.

Said, Edward W. *Orientalism*. With a new preface by the author. New York: Vintage Books, 1994.

Saldívar, Ramón. *The Borderlands of Culture: Américo Paredes and the Transnational Imaginary*. Durham, NC: Duke University Press, 2006.

Sandos, James A. *Converting California: Indians and Franciscans in the Missions*. New Haven, CT: Yale University Press, 2004.

Santayana, George. *The Life of Reason: Or, The Phases of Progress*. 2nd ed.. Vol. 1., *Reason in Common Sense*. New York: Charles Scribner's Sons, 1922.

Santayana, George. *The Life of Reason: Or, The Phases of Progress*. 2nd ed. Vol. 5, *Reason in Science*. New York: Charles Scribner's Sons, 1922.

Schmitz, Joseph William. *The Society of Mary in Texas*. San Antonio: Naylor, 1951.

Schneider, Tsim D., and Lee M. Panich. "Native Agency at the Margins of Empire: Indigenous Landscapes, Spanish Missions, and Contested Histories." In *Indigenous Landscapes and Spanish Missions: New Perspectives from Archaeology and Ethnohistory*, edited by Lee M. Panich and Tsim D. Schneider, 5–22. Tucson: University of Arizona Press, 2014.

Schneirov, Matthew. *The Dream of a New Social Order: Popular Magazines in America, 1893–1914*. New York: Columbia University Press, 1994.

Schoelwer, Susan Prendergast, and Tom W. Gläser. *Alamo Images: Changing Perceptions of a Texas Experience*. Dallas: Southern Methodist University Press, 1985.

Schouton, Frans F. J. "Heritage as Historical Reality." In *Heritage, Tourism and Society*, edited by David T. Herbert, 21–31. New York: Pinter, 1997.

Schuetz, Mardith K., trans. *Architectural Practice in Mexico City: A Manual for Journeyman Architects of the Eighteenth Century*. Tucson: University of Arizona Press, 1987.

Schuetz, Mardith K. "Professional Artisans in the Hispanic Southwest: The Churches of San Antonio, Texas." *The Americas* 40, no. 1 (1983): 17–70. http://www.jstor.org/stable/981099.

Schuetz-Miller, Mardith. "Pre-Euclidian Geometry in the Design of Mission Churches of the Spanish Borderlands." *Journal of the Southwest* 48, no. 4 (2006): 331–619.

Schuetz-Miller, Mardith. "The Scandal Involving San Antonio de Valero's First Master Builder." *Journal of the Southwest* 58, no. 4 (2016): 743–49. https://doi.org/10.1353/jsw.2016.0019.

Sears, John F. *Sacred Places: American Tourist Attractions in the Nineteenth Century*. New York: Oxford University Press, 1989.

Shaffer, Marguerite S. *See America First: Tourism and National Identity, 1880–1940*. Washington, DC: Smithsonian Books, 2001.

Silbey, Joel H. *Storm over Texas: The Annexation Controversy and the Road to Civil War*. New York: Oxford University Press, 2005

Smith, F. Todd. *From Dominance to Disappearance: The Indians of Texas and the Near Southwest, 1786–1859*. Lincoln: University of Nebraska Press, 2005.

Smith, Thomas. "The U.S. Army and the Alamo, 1846–1877." *Southwestern Historical Quarterly* 118, no. 3 (2015): 263–86.

Stagner, Stephen. "Epics, Science, and the Lost Frontier: Texas Historical Writing, 1836–1936." *Western Historical Quarterly* 12, no. 2 (1981): 165–81. https://www.jstor.org/stable/968122.

Steely, James Wright. *Parks for Texas: Enduring Landscapes of the New Deal*. Austin: University of Texas Press, 1999.

Stevens, Errol Wayne. "Helen Hunt Jackson's *Ramona*: Social Problem Novel as Tourist Guide." *California History* 77, no. 3 (1998): 158–67. https://www.jstor.org/stable/25462491.

Stipe, Robert E., ed. *A Richer Heritage: Historic Preservation in the Twenty-First Century*. Chapel Hill: University of North Carolina Press, 2003.

Stockel, H. Henrietta. *On the Bloody Road to Jesus: Christianity and the Chiricahua Apaches*. Albuquerque: University of New Mexico Press, 2004.

Streeby, Shelley. *American Sensations: Class, Empire, and the Production of Popular Culture*. Berkeley: University of California Press, 2002.

Thompson, Frank. *Alamo Movies*. East Berlin, PA: Old Mill Books, 1991.

Thompson, Frank. *The Alamo: A Cultural History*. Dallas: Taylor Trade Publishing, 2001.

Thompson, Frank. *The Alamo: The Illustrated Story of the Epic Film*. New York: Newmarket Press, 2004.

Thoms, Alston V., ed. *Reassessing Cultural Extinction: Change and Survival at Mission San Juan Capistrano, Texas*. College Station and San Antonio: Center for Ecological Archaeology, Texas A&M University, and San Antonio Missions National Historic Park, 2001.

Torget, Andrew J. *Seeds of Empire: Cotton, Slavery, and the Transformation of the Texas Borderlands, 1800–1850*. Chapel Hill: University of North Carolina Press, 2015.

Toussaint, Manuel. *Colonial Art in Mexico*. Edited and translated by Elizabeth Wilder Weismann. Austin: University of Texas Press, 1967.

Trachtenberg, Alan. *The Incorporation of America: Culture and Society in the Gilded Age*. New York: Hill and Wang, 2007.

Trouillot, Michel-Rolph. *Silencing the Past: Power and the Production of History*. Boston: Beacon Press, 1995.

Tuan, Yi-Fu. *Space and Place: The Perspective of Experience*. Minneapolis: University of Minnesota Press, 1977.

Turner, Frederick Jackson. "The Significance of the Frontier in American History." In *Rereading Frederick Jackson Turner: "The Significance of the Frontier in American History" and Other Essays*, edited and with commentary by John Mack Faragher, 31–60. New Haven, CT: Yale University Press, 1998.

Van Slyck, Abigail A. "Mañana, Mañana: Racial Stereotypes and the Anglo Rediscovery of the Southwest's Vernacular Architecture, 1890–1920." *Perspectives in Vernacular Architecture* 5 (1995): 95–108. http://www.jstor.org/stable/3514248.

Wade, Maria F. *Missions, Missionaries, and Native Americans: Long-Term Processes and Daily Practices*. Gainesville: University Press of Florida, 2008.

Webb, Walter Prescott. *The Great Frontier*. Boston: Houghton Mifflin, 1952.

Webb, Walter Prescott. *The Great Plains*. Boston: Houghton Mifflin, 1931.

Weber, David J. *Bárbaros: Spaniards and Their Savages in the Age of Enlightenment*. New Haven, CT: Yale University Press, 2005.

Weber, David J. *The Spanish Frontier in North America*. New Haven, CT: Yale University Press, 1992.

West, Delno C. "Medieval Ideas of Apocalyptic Mission and the Early Franciscans in Mexico." *The Americas* 45, no. 3 (1989): 293–313. http://www.jstor.org/stable/1007224.

White, Hayden. *Tropics of Discourse: Essays on Cultural Criticism*. Baltimore: Johns Hopkins University Press, 1985.

White, Richard. *The Middle Ground: Indians, Empires, and Republics in the Great Lakes Region, 1650–1815*. Cambridge: Cambridge University Press, 1991.

Wiebe, Robert H. *The Search for Order, 1877–1920*. New York: Hill and Wang, 1967.

Williams, Amelia W. "Alamo Monuments." *Handbook of Texas Online*. Accessed July 20, 2019. http://www.tshaonline.org/handbook/online/articles/gga01.

Wilson, Chris. *The Myth of Santa Fe: Creating a Modern Regional Tradition*. Albuquerque: University of New Mexico Press, 1997.

Winders, Jamie. "Imperfectly Imperial: Northern Travel Writers in the Postbellum U.S. South, 1865–1880." *Annals of the Association of American Geographers* 95, no. 2 (2005): 391–410. http://www.jstor.org/stable/3694125.

Wright, Robert E. "Father Refugio de la Garza: Controverted Religious Leader." In *Tejano Leadership in Mexican and Revolutionary Texas*, edited by Jesús F. de la Teja, 76–101. College Station: Texas A&M University Press, 2010.

Wrobel, David M. *Promised Lands: Promotion, Memory, and the Creation of the American West*. Lawrence: University Press of Kansas, 2002.

Wyman, Walker D., and Clifton B. Kroeber, eds. *The Frontier in Perspective*. Madison: University of Wisconsin Press, 1957.

Young, Kevin R. "Major Babbitt and the Alamo 'Hump.'" *Military Images* 6, no. 1 (1984): 16–17.

Zavala, Silvio. "The Frontier of Hispanic America." In *The Frontier in Perspective*, edited by Walker D. Wyman and Clifton B. Kroeber, 35–58. Madison: University of Wisconsin Press, 1957.

Zega, Michael E. "Advertising the Southwest." *Journal of the Southwest* 43, no. 3 (2001): 281–315.

Zesch, Scott. "Adina De Zavala and the Second Siege of the Alamo." *CRM Journal* 5, no. 1 (2008): 31–44.

Zuelow, Eric G. E. *A History of Modern Tourism*. London: Palgrave Macmillan, 2016.

Secondary Sources, Unpublished

Crowley, Nancy E. "The Influence of Local and Imported Factors on the Design and Construction of the Spanish Missions in San Antonio, Texas." Master's thesis, Texas A&M University, 2006.

Ivey, James E. *Of Various Magnificence: The Architectural History of the Missions of San Antonio, Texas in the Colonial Period and the Nineteenth Century*. With contributions by Marlys Bush Thurber and Santiago Escobedo. Santa Fe, NM: National Park Service, ca. 2006.

Kitchens, Joel D. "San Antonio's Spanish Missions and the Persistence of Memory, 1718–2015." PhD diss., Texas A&M University, 2016.

Schuetz, Mardith Keithly. "The Indians of the San Antonio Missions, 1718–1821." PhD diss., University of Texas at Austin, 1980.

Index